The Sociology of Freedom

KAIROS

In ancient Greek philosophy, *kairos* signifies the right time or the "moment of transition." We believe that we live in such a transitional period. The most important task of social science in time of transformation is to transform itself into a force of liberation. Kairos, an editorial imprint of the Anthropology and Social Change department housed in the California Institute of Integral Studies, publishes groundbreaking works in critical social sciences, including anthropology, sociology, geography, theory of education, political ecology, political theory, and history.

Series editor: Andrej Grubačić

Recent and featured Kairos books:

Building Free Life: Dialogues with Öcalan edited by International Initiative

Practical Utopia: Strategies for a Desirable Society by Michael Albert

In, Against, and Beyond Capitalism: The San Francisco Lectures by John Holloway

Anthropocene or Capitalocene? Nature, History, and the Crisis of Capitalism edited by Jason W. Moore

We Are the Crisis of Capital: A John Holloway Reader by John Holloway

Archive That, Comrade! Left Legacies and the Counter Culture of Remembrance by Phil Cohen

Re-enchanting the World: Feminism and the Politics of the Commons by Silvia Federici

Autonomy Is in Our Hearts: Zapatista Autonomous Government through the Lens of the Tsotsil Language by Dylan Eldredge Fitzwater

The Battle for the Mountain of the Kurds: Self-Determination and Ethnic Cleansing in the Afrin Region of Rojava by Thomas Schmidinger

Beyond the Periphery of the Skin: Rethinking, Remaking, and Reclaiming the Body in Contemporary Capitalism by Silvia Federici

For more information visit www.pmpress.org/blog/kairos/

The Sociology of Freedom

Manifesto of the Democratic Civilization
Volume III

Abdullah Öcalan

International Initiative Edition

KAIROS

The Sociology of Freedom: Manifesto of the Democratic Civilization, Volume III
Abdullah Öcalan
© 2020 PM Press.

ISBN: 978-1-62963-710-5 (paperback)
ISBN: 978-1-62963-765-5 (hardback)
ISBN: 978-1-62963-773-0 (ebook)
Library of Congress Control Number: 2019933020

Cover Image: "Perperik" by Ercan Altuntaş, oil and natural colors on canvas, 60 × 80 cm
Cover by John Yates / www.stealworks.com
Interior design by briandesign

10 9 8 7 6 5 4 3 2 1

PM Press
PO Box 23912
Oakland, CA 94623
www.pmpress.org

Printed in the USA.

Published with International Initiative Edition
International Initiative
"Freedom for Abdullah Öcalan – Peace in Kurdistan"
P.O. Box 100 511
D-50445 Cologne
Germany
www.freeocalan.org

Original title: Özgürlük Sosyolojisi
First published in 2009 by Mezopotamien Verlag, Neuss
Translation by Havin Guneser

Contents

Foreword

John Holloway

It is a great honor to be asked to write this foreword.[1] I do it with pride, for who the author is and for the movement he represents. I do it to express my support for him in his struggle against a terrible imprisonment and my support for the struggles of the people of Kurdistan in their attempt to create a different world, a different way of living, in the midst of the most terrible violence. I do it to protest against the brutality of the Turkish state and of all the other complicit states.

The book was written by Abdullah Öcalan in prison. Arrested illegally in Kenya by NATO forces in 1999, he has been incarcerated since then on the prison island of İmralı. For much of that time he has been held in total isolation and frequently punished by having his books and pen and paper removed, in breach of basic rights stipulated in the Geneva Convention. In spite of this, he has succeeded in writing five volumes explaining his political ideas, volumes to be presented in his defense at the European Court of Human Rights (ECtHR). The present book is the third volume, written in prison in 2008 and published here in English for the first time. Through all these years of imprisonment, Öcalan's ideas have been a major source of inspiration for the Kurdish movement in its struggles, centered on the province of Rojava in northeastern Syria, to create a different way of living, a form of social organization that they call "democratic modernity."

The danger in writing a foreword to a book written by such a towering figure is that one sanctifies him, saying simply "how wonderful!" thus contributing to the formation of a personality cult that is undoubtedly present in the movement itself. This is very clearly not what Öcalan wants. At several points in the text he makes clear that for him this is part of a dialogue, and that he is looking for reactions to his ideas.

When I started reading the book, I was clear that I wanted to express my support but not at all sure that I would be convinced by the book itself. This initial attitude then gradually fell away and turned into a very different reading, one in which I was absorbed by the force of the argument. I say "gradually," because, coming from Europe and Latin America, it took me a while to adjust to a different frame of reference and become engaged in an argument that is not about a world "over there" but critically and crucially about my world, our world—about our world and the possibility that we can still pull the emergency brake on the train of destruction and create something different.

Öcalan's book is an important contribution to the dialogue of hope, a dialogue that is being conducted all over the world, sometimes by voices that are articulate and well-organized, like the Zapatistas in southeast Mexico, often by groups resisting the depredations of mining companies or urban planners, or women fighting against male violence; sometimes, it's just students who look up from their books and think, "There has to be a way out, there has to be the possibility of creating a different world." As the dark around us grows, as authoritarianism and militarism push us closer to the precipice, millions and millions and millions of voices join in the dialogue of "desperation and hope": there has to be a way out; there has to be a way forward.

For Öcalan, hope lies in restoring the "free functioning of moral and political society" (ch. 7, 152). This is the revolutionary task: "The task of revolutionaries cannot be defined as creating any social model of their making but more correctly as playing a role in contributing to the development of moral and political society" (ch 7, 138). This moral and political society exists as a repressed substratum in all societies: "the democratic civilization system—essentially the moral and political totality of social nature—has always existed and sustained itself as the flip side of the official history of civilization. Despite all the oppression and exploitation at the hands of the official world-system, the other face of society could not be destroyed. In fact, it is impossible to destroy it. "Just as capitalism cannot sustain itself without noncapitalist society, civilization—the official world system—also cannot sustain itself without the democratic civilization system" (ch, 7, 143).

Moral and political society, as I understand it, is the gel of everyday life: the normally unspectacular comings and goings of people: the trust, the mutual support, the friendships, the loves, the sharing of food, the preparing of food, the washing of dishes and of clothes, the gossiping, the sharing and shaping of moral ideas—all those activities that are common to all of us, those activities that hold our lives together and constitute and reconstitute communities. But for the last five thousand years, ever since the Sumerian empire, moral and political society has been repressed and blocked by official civilization, the civilization based on power, on monopoly, on patriarchy, on capital, on cities. But this civilization of power has never succeeded in freeing itself from the moral and political substratum, however much it may claim to have done so. "Without the capital and power monopoly, moral and political society is the natural state of society. All human societies must have these qualities from their birth to their decay. Slave-owning, feudal, capitalist, and socialist society molds are like clothes they hope to put on social nature; they do not express the truth. In spite of what they claim, there are no such societies. These societies, whose original state was moral and political, were unable to fully develop, because they were continuously oppressed, exploited, and colonized by the capital and power monopolies" (ch. 7, 151–52). The civilization of power, then, is like a suit of armor thrown over moral and political society that hides and constricts and blocks its development and that is now increasingly societycidal, threatening to destroy society completely. The history of moral and political society (or democratic civilization) is a history of resistance, rebellion and struggle for life: "The history of democratic civilization, to a great extent, is the history of resistance, rebellion, and insistence on the life of the moral and political society of the tribes and aşirets in their struggle for freedom, democracy, and equality in the face of the attacks by the civilization" (ch. 7, 182).

There is a beauty in this conception. Revolution becomes "of course." Of course, we need a revolution, and, of course, we must do it. But, of course, there is nothing more normal, nothing more obvious! Revolution is woven into the experience and creativity of our daily lives. It is we who create and re-create, day in, day out, the moral and political society that is the substance of our everyday intercourse. It is we who confront the obstacles to that creativity every day: the fact that we have to go to work or prepare for exams or are barred from access to the means necessary to realize our creativity. We are all aware of the power-civilization (capitalism, patriarchy, whatever we want to call it) that blocks our way, but, at the same time, we are rooted in a different sociality that gives meaning and direction to our lives: a moral and political sociality that resists and rebels, that pushes and pushes against its repression by official civilization.

The resistance and rebellion are constantly changing pattern, refusing here, refusing there, pushing here, pushing there against the attacks that come constantly from the civilization of power. The of-course-ness of resistance and rebellion shifts as the attacks against us move and our own sensibilities drive in different directions. Öcalan displays an extraordinary sensitivity to the shifting patterns of struggle. This is important, for, despite being locked up in isolation, his argument resonates strongly with current debates in all sorts of ways. Far from being a book relevant only to the Kurdish struggle, *The Sociology of Freedom* is an important contribution to current debates about capitalism, patriarchy, ecology, and the state. For Öcalan, the civilization of power is (and has been since the time of the Sumerian empire) built on the enslavement of women and the subjugation of nature, and its organizational form has been the state. Hence and of course, women's struggles against patriarchy and the many struggles to transform the relationship between humans and other forms of life (and indeed the understanding of life itself) are and must be at the center of any revolution aimed at redeeming moral and political society. Hence and of course, the struggle is an anti-state struggle in its organization and aim: its organization is based on the assembly and its aim is not (emphatically not) the creation of a Kurdish state but the liberation of Kurdistan and the world from the state, from the state as an oppressive form of organization. The implications of Öcalan's work are profound and exciting. It has an enormous influence on the Kurdish movement, reflected in the forms of organization and the leading role played by women in the struggle. And, beyond that, the resonance of his work with current struggles and debates throughout the world is truly extraordinary.

To feel this resonance is to be pulled into debate with the author. As we read the text, we move through phases of agreement, enthusiasm, doubt, disagreement, perhaps even annoyance—as we would with any good, provocative author, as we would with Bookchin (by whom Öcalan is strongly influenced and whose *Ecology of Freedom* is the model for the title of the present work)[2] or Graeber or Negri or Wallerstein or Federici or many others. To respect an author is to criticize her. To read Öcalan uncritically just because he is the symbol of a great movement would be to put another lock on his prison door, to embalm him before he died. Even if we know that this foreword and other texts may never get through his prison door, we have to engage with what he is saying. Precisely because of the enormous admiration that I feel for someone who has dedicated his life to trying to change the world and has had such an influence on an amazing movement of change taking place in the most awful conditions, precisely because of that, I feel drawn into debate, into saying "wonderful, but perhaps. . ."

My own doubts center on the questions of historicity-negativity, money and market, working class, nation. The constant references in the book to Sumerian civilization, to Babylon and Assyria, to the Zoroastrian tradition, certainly extend my thinking into unexplored areas but at the same time make me feel that there is a danger of losing sight of the urgency of our situation. Perhaps there is a wider tendency (one thinks of Bookchin or of David Graeber's *Debt: The First 5000 Years*)[3] to shift from the analysis of capitalism to a much longer perspective, to see capitalism as just the latest phase in the development of patriarchy, for example. Certainly, Öcalan is right to draw our attention to the continuities of domination, but perhaps our immediate concern needs to be with the specific form of domination that is driving us toward our destruction. Perhaps we have to say yes, but the official power-civilization that dominates in the world today has a name: capitalism. Capitalism has its own dynamic and its own fragilities and vulnerabilities that are quite distinct from—and infinitely more destructive than—those of the Sumerian civilization. By capitalism, I understand not an economic system but a totalizing system of "domination and resistance" that includes, crucially, the subordination of women and the exploitation of nature but has its own fragility based on its dependence on us, i.e., on the conversion of our activity into abstract, value-producing labor. This specific dependence-fragility has to be central to any development of a sociology of freedom.

The long-historical approach can lead us paradoxically into an ahistorical idealization of the resistance, of our resistance. Moral and political society, which Öcalan sees to be the center of our resistance and our hope, cannot stand outside the system of domination: it is inevitably penetrated by the power-civilization (capital) that dominates it. Again, Öcalan stands in the center of international debate, for here in Latin America too there is a tendency to idealize the community, especially the indigenous community, as a source of hope standing outside the system. This can easily lead to a romanticism but also to a dangerous dichotomy between inside and outside, reminiscent in some ways of Marcuse's *One-Dimensional Man*,[4] a very different book. Hope is then projected onto the outside: the moral and political society, the indigenous community, the socially marginalized, and this *outside* is then contrasted with an *inside* that is seen as totally integrated into the system. This is very strong in Öcalan's treatment of the working class: "Just as the slave and serf were the extensions of their masters and lords, the concessionist [i.e., wage—JH] worker is always an extension of the boss" (ch. 7, 186). The same inside-outside dichotomy can also be seen when justified attacks on Eurocentrism slide into a dismissal of Europe (and indeed the northern part of North America) as possible locations of rebellion. Inversely, and at its worse, the same dichotomy leads to an exoticization of hope: for people of the "North," hope lies in the "Global South," in Kurdistan or Latin America, exciting places that are comfortably far away.

A different approach is to say that all domination tears us apart, both collectively and individually. There is no clear distinction between the integrated and the excluded. We are all subjugated, but there is always an excess, an overflowing, an inconformity, a rebellion, a dignity. Ordinariness lies in that excess. Hence, the depth of the Zapatista quote: "We are quite ordinary women and men, children and old people, that is, rebels, non-conformists, misfits, dreamers." This daily overflowing, this daily excess is central to the of-course-ness of revolution. This rebel dignity, this push toward a world of dignity, is always present, more or less latent, more or less forceful. In general, the more forceful the repression, the more forceful the rebellion, at least potentially: this is the way that Marx introduces his idea of the revolutionary nature of the working class. As workers, we are exploited and, therefore, in revolt against our exploitation. As slaves, we are subjugated and, therefore, in revolt against our enslavement, whether that revolt is latent or patent, potential or actual. We are never just an extension of the boss. It is not that some people have dignity and others do not: rather, it is that dignity is the struggle against its own negation, stronger in some than in others, latent in all.

If domination tears us apart, that must be true too of the moral and political society. Öcalan's conception of a moral and political society that is present as a substratum or social cohesion in any social order, however "civilized," is a thing of beauty, but the history of moral and political society is a history of resistance, as he points out. It is not innocent, it does not stand outside the dominating civilization that is its enemy but is inevitably penetrated by it. Money is the most obvious and most potent form of penetration of capital into our daily lives. Moral and political society exists as a powerful, wonderful force, but it does not exist positively: it exists negatively, in the mode of being denied and, therefore, as struggle against its own negation.

The same is true of freedom. We are not there yet, we do not know what freedom would be like. Freedom exists as resistance, as struggle against and beyond its own denial, as longing, as flapping our wings and wanting to fly, but we cannot do it yet. To try to convert Öcalan's great book into the basis of a positive sociology of freedom would be to go in the wrong direction. It is, rather, a provocation to be picked up and pushed further.

The idea that domination tears us apart, individually and collectively, is also relevant to Öcalan's discussion of the nation, an important part of his argument. He distinguishes very carefully two concepts of nation—the state-nationalism that tends toward fascism and the "second way of becoming a nation is to transform the same or similar language and cultural groups—which are part of moral and political society—into a democratic society on the basis of democratic politics. All tribes, aşirets, peoples, and even families play their part as units of moral and political society in forming such a nation" (ch. 7, 183). This sort of nation, he says, is "the antidote to capital and power monopolies" (ch. 7, 184). The nationalism advocated by Öcalan is very different from the state-nationalism that is growing all over the world; it is a nationalism that promotes the struggle of all peoples against the state-capital-power, without in any way claiming a superiority for the Kurdish people. Yet I feel uncomfortable with the notion of a people or nation as a grouping with historical continuity or identity. I may or may not have been born in the same region as my ancestors of three hundred years ago, I may or may not speak the same language, but I am fairly sure that my daily experience is very different from theirs and likely to be much closer to the experience of someone living on the other side of the earth today. The idea of a distinctive prolonged and intergenerational flow of social experience that underlies any concept of nation may have some limited validity in peasant societies but is surely much less relevant for the majority of the world's population that lives in cities. And yet the idea of the nation remains as a powerful fiction that kills millions. The danger of thinking of nation as a unit is that it glosses over divisions within the "nation," such as class divisions between exploiters and exploited. Also, however different the two ideas of nation analyzed by Öcalan, there is a danger of a glide between one and the other. The struggle of the states that are fighting against the Kurdish movement (principally the Turkish, Syrian, Russian, Iraqi, and US states) is probably not so much to destroy Kurdish nationalism as to statify it, to convert the push for autonomy into a demand for recognition as an "autonomous" state or province, akin to or an extension of the existing Kurdistan Region of Iraq. Perhaps it is better to think of the struggles for another world as being necessarily not only anti-state but also anti-national.

I have a similar worry in relation to Öcalan's concept of the market. Quite unlike Marx, who sees the source of capitalist destruction as lying in the fact that human wealth is produced as commodities to be sold on the market, with the relations between people mediated by money, Öcalan argues that "democratic civilization does not oppose the market. On the contrary, because it offers a truly free environment, it has the only genuine free market economy. It does not deny the market's creative competitive role. What it opposes are techniques for amassing speculative revenue" (ch. 7, 186). It is important to point out that the sort of market that Öcalan has in mind is certainly not the financial markets of Wall Street, it is something closer to a bazaar, a place controlled by the community where products are exchanged to cover basic needs. In this sense, it is a concept close to the practices of many commons-oriented movements or, indeed, the great explosion of barter in the crisis and uprising of 2001–2002 in Argentina. Even so, it is hard to see how to separate the market from money, and how money can be separated from "amassing speculative revenue." Money destroys and divides; it is the great enemy of moral and political society.

Radha D'Souza, in her fabulous foreword to the previous volume of Öcalan's writings (a foreword subtitled "Reading Öcalan as a South Asian Woman," which takes a very different approach from the one advanced here) opens by saying, "As I write this foreword, I cannot help feeling how much more exciting my engagement with Öcalan's text could be if I could sit face to face with him and discuss, over cups of chai, as is common in the Eastern social settings, the issues he raises in this volume."[5] I would love to sit down and join that discussion, with Abdullah Öcalan, with Radha D'Souza, with David Graeber, who wrote a super preface for the first volume, with all the millions of people who have been inspired by this and the other volumes written by Öcalan. There would be so much to discuss, so many differences to air, so much to learn, so many voices in discordant harmony, a conversation between comrades who share the same hatred of capitalism and the same longing for a society based on the mutual recognition of human dignities.

The reality, of course, is much more brutal. Abdullah Öcalan is locked up in appalling conditions, while I sit comfortably in my professorial chair. We cannot meet to share a chai. What we can do and what I want us to do is to take his ideas seriously, to think about them, to discuss them, to disagree and agree with them, to take them into seminars and universities and assemblies and discussion groups. We are all participants in the same dialogue of "hope and despair," all joined in the determination that we will break the "civilization," the capitalism, that is destroying us.

ONE

Preface

This, the third major part of the main defense that I am trying to prepare for my case at the European Court of Human Rights (ECtHR), addresses the ruling that the case be reopened.[1] This volume both continues and complements the two previous volumes.[2] The overall aim of those volumes was to clarify the nature of power and capitalist modernity. *Power* was defined as *tools of force* based on human endeavor and essentially constructed with the intention to extort surplus product and surplus value. The apparatuses of power, comprehensively constructed in various forms, are ultimately repressive mechanisms constructed to control human labor. In the modern era, conceptualized as the capitalist system, society is confronted with these mechanisms in their most advanced form. In the current circumstances, the capitalist system, also referred to as globalization, constitutes a unique phase in what we call *the world system of power*, or *democracy*, in the model we are seeking to develop.

The reader might well wonder about the relationship between the European Court of Human Rights (ECtHR) in its institutional role—as a supranational judicial authority that only recognizes the right of the individual as a citizen to file an appeal—and a defense of this nature submitted by the individual named Abdullah Öcalan. There certainly is a relationship, a striking one at that. More importantly, without analyzing the civilization system based on Eurocentrism, we cannot analyze the ideological, political, and judicial system referred to as Europe's "soft power." In fact, we can only interpret this "soft power" accurately by examining the Eurocentric civilization system in full. We should always keep in

1

mind that the European civilization system has become the most advanced "world civilization system" of all time. Individual citizenship is one of the most important characteristics of this civilization. Never before in history were the concepts of *the individual, individualism,* and *citizenship* given as much significance within a society. The era that we are up against—capitalist modernity—is one where society is maximally dissolved into the individual and the individual into "symbolic society."

Thus, caught in a situation where escaping the reality of this era was very difficult (but not impossible), I fell into "major doubt" about my identity, constructed as a citizen of the Republic of Turkey. It is undeniable that this, in turn, brought me before the most severe judicial and penal system in history. The Republic of Turkey, a signatory to the European Convention of Human Rights (ECHR), refused to implement the ECtHR's retrial ruling. Furthermore, the Committee of Ministers of the Council of Europe, responsible for monitoring the execution of judgments, decided that the action taken by the Turkish judiciary complied with the requirements of the ECtHR's judgment.[3] This decision by the Committee of Ministers was not only a violation of the judiciary—it was scandalous. Several small states admitted during this process at the Committee of Ministers that they agreed to this decision under pressure from larger and more powerful countries, the US among them. This violation is clearly in conflict with their soft power theses. Therefore, for the past ten years I have been rendered "a person who cannot be tried." In this situation, as a "person who cannot receive a fair trial," I am still in the one-person İmralı Prison, Bursa, an island prison in the Sea of Marmara, where those sentenced to severe penalties have traditionally been held and left to die.

I have never doubted that the period from my arrival in Europe to my imprisonment on İmralı was planned and implemented with the collaboration of the US and the EU. Nor have I ever doubted that the role assigned to the Republic of Turkey was anything more than that of prison guard. While this is the stark truth, why the long and winding road? There may be some who think that I judge too harshly; however, the fact that on special orders from NATO all European airports were closed to the flight that was carrying me on February 2, 1999, provides convincing evidence of my abduction by these powers. The newspapers reported on it at the time.[4] Besides, the representative of then president of the US Bill Clinton openly stated that I was abducted and taken to Kenya, where I was held under customary supervision (all letters and cassettes belonging to me were confiscated at the airport) until I was handed over to Turkey, and that all this happened in collaboration with the US.[5] The unimaginable betrayal by the Greek authorities (especially the minister of foreign affairs, national security, the top officials at the Greek embassy in Nairobi, the emissary Major Kalenderidis, and Prime Minister Smitis) is an obvious fact that I find unnecessary to address. If it was my right to benefit from this European jurisprudence in terms of individual law, then why did those powers resort to such secret, obscure, and fraudulent means? What kind of bargaining was going on? Who participated in the bargaining process and to what end? Under the rule of Europe and the US, history has seen terrible colonial wars and witch hunts, denominational and national wars, class conflict, and ideological struggles. Perhaps my experience within this blood-soaked portrait of history is just a drop in the ocean, but it is important, and it does need to be clarified.

First, I must say that I reject the abstraction of individuals from their social identity. The right to an "individual complaint" that is so adamantly insisted upon does not have the meaning attributed to it. The idea of individuals isolated from their social identity is simply a fallacy of official Eurocentric epistemology, which sees itself as scientific. Besides, it is common knowledge that I am being tried on behalf of the Kurdish people, the most tragic people in the world, and not as the individual Abdullah Öcalan.

This brief enumeration of facts alone should provide a sufficient idea of the scope of my case. It is undeniable that all the system's powers played an active role in my arrest, trial, and conviction. No matter *how powerful* the central civilization system[6]—led by the hegemonic US and the EU powers—amid all the confusion, I clearly cannot be that easily eliminated. Furthermore, my people stood up en masse to oppose this great game. They protested against the conspiracy, with hundreds martyred and thousands arrested. They fully grasped the link between my trial and their own historical tragedy. They knew that their liberation demanded that this tragedy be brought to an end—and so they stood by me. The honorable task of explaining this, however, falls to me.

So, evidently, without clarifying all of the dimensions of my social identity—which forms the reality of our people, who have been subjected to perhaps the greatest tyranny and exploitation at the hands of a five-thousand-year-old central civilization system—I cannot easily elucidate the crux of my trial. The essential criteria for addressing my defense in such breadth lie buried in the facts I have presented above. I must now repeat something I have often said: there are moments when history plays out in an individual, and an individual makes history! Although it has been accompanied by a lot of pain, it is undeniable that this honor has partially been mine. I know that all the deceitful scheming behind my back is a result of the fact that I, unlike most others, strive to play a role beyond that of a mere "victim of destiny." This is why I chose the slogan "Freedom Shall Prevail" for this court case.

Overturning the repeated theme of fate in tragedies in favor of freedom is sufficient encouragement to make any pain bearable. In this play, in which my friends and I have our roles—the play titled *Reality*—defeat will this time be destiny's share.

It should now be clear why I have titled this volume of my defense *The Sociology of Freedom*. Each and every step toward freedom can only be an attempt. Thus, *An Essay on the Sociology of Freedom* might be a suitable subtitle.

No doubt, the hegemonic European central civilization is only one side of the coin. This civilization primarily represents power apparatuses that were built upon surplus value. The flip side, however, is the democratic face of civilization. The ideas at the base of this defense draw on the legacy of democratic civilization. From the trial of Socrates to mine, I am passionately devoted to the legacy of all the numerous fighters—including ours—who have struggled for their ideals and morals, for their peoples and communes. I hope to contribute to this legacy, even though it may be just a drop in the ocean. These monuments of humanity constitute the main building blocks for my defense. However, their true historical foundation is the five-thousand-year-old wisdom of the East and a tradition of democratic behavior. Without this background in mind, it is impossible to write a universal history of humanity or, more importantly, meaningfully evaluate the present.

The main theme of my defense is that the march of history and of society progresses more freely in the democratic civilization system, and that a life that rests on the right foundations is a better and more beautiful life for individuals.

It may be elucidating and encourage the reader to forgive some shortcomings if I say a few words about my writing technique. In solitary confinement, I am only allowed one book, one magazine, and one newspaper in my cell at any given time. Thus, it was impossible for me to take notes or to quote from sources. My main method has been to commit to memory the points that I found important and absorb them into my personality. I did not endure every prohibition slavishly. I responded by increasingly clarifying memory—the universe's store of knowledge—and by prioritizing vitally important ideas.

The greatest weakness of this method, however, is that human memory is doomed to failure. Hence, not being able to take notes was obstructive. As I was preparing to write this volume, a new ban was introduced: I was not allowed to have a pen. After this ban was lifted on the tenth day of a cell confinement penalty, I immediately began writing. This haste was necessary, because all the delays had prevented me from keeping my promise to write. In any case, as a result of being denied a pen I focused more intensely on my overall concept.

The next two volumes of my defense are intended as a kind of concrete application of my main ideas. I plan to call them *The Civilizational Crisis in the Middle East and the Democratic Civilization Solution* and *The Manifesto of the Kurdistan Revolution*. These volumes, which any intellectual could easily prepare with a certain amount of preparation, may, however, take me quite some time.[7] However, in a seething Middle East, and in the Kurdistan that has become its heart, discussing the present in the light of an analysis of historical-society is quite exciting—but it must be approached with a high degree of responsibility.

The past, present, and future have united to constitute a new sort of Gordian knot. To resolve this moment, through an anti-Alexander strike (like Alexander but with minimal physical effort; so that the *meaning* constitutes the most crucial aspect of the effort) is the most essential and sacred duty of all.[8]

TWO

Introduction

The knowledge structure of the capitalist world system is in just as big a crisis as its apparatuses of power and production/accumulation.[1] However, their very nature renders knowledge structures more susceptible to free discussion, which creates an opportunity to extensively interpret the degree of the crisis in which science finds itself. The role of knowledge in social and power structures is more significant in this period than it has been in any previous period in history. There is an ongoing historical revolution within the knowledge and information tools of social life. Revolutionary processes, as crises, essentially also play the role of seeking regimes of truth. Hegemony not only takes place in the fields of accumulation, production, and power; we also witness fierce hegemonic struggles in the field of knowledge. Production, accumulation, and power structures that have not secured their legitimacy within the field of knowledge cannot ensure their permanent existence.

The positivist disciplines of science that reigned supreme until recently are not as anti-metaphysical and anti-religious, as has been claimed. There has been a growing recognition and discussion of the fact that they possess as strong a metaphysical and religious dimension as metaphysics and religion themselves. The triumphant natural sciences, attributed to Classical Greek society and the European Enlightenment, were dealt the most significant blows from within their own midst.[2] The weakest aspect of the positivist sciences is the postulation of continuous progressive and linear development—no such structure and purpose of the universe can be detected. Furthermore, neither the subatomic world nor the cosmological universe can escape the observer-observed dilemma—because human consciousness is also part of this process. It is impossible to predict how consciousness could assume a role beyond this scope. Unlimited differentiation potential itself requires new interpretations.

Sociology—a Eurocentric knowledge structure—cannot get beyond the claim of positivist science enthusiasts that society can be considered a phenomenon, just like the phenomena in the fields of physics, chemistry, and biology, and, as such, can be explained using the same approach. But the audacity of objectifying human society, whose nature differs from that of the abovementioned phenomena, does not aid enlightenment but leads to an even shallower idolization. Today's discussions about science make it sufficiently clear that the philosophical statements of the German ideologues (who were recruited to deliver knowledge structures to nation-states), the science of political economy developed by the English ideologues, and the sociology of French philosophers were legitimizing tools for the apparatuses of capital and power accumulation. They provided the knowledge structures of the nation-states. German philosophy, English political economy, and French sociology ultimately could not avoid providing the basis for the emerging nation-state nationalism. We can comfortably say that these Eurocentric sociologies are by and large knowledge structures of the Eurocentric capitalist world system.

However, saying all this does not resolve the problem. It is now sufficiently clear that even the socialism—or sociology—of Karl Marx and Frederick Engels, which emerged as the opposing worldview, is a very vulgar interpretation of society. In spite of all claims of opposing it, they could not escape serving capitalism—even more so than its official ideology, liberalism. This is sufficiently clear from the trends, movements, and state systems of real socialism, social democracy, and national liberation. Despite their highly noble traditions of struggle, if the abovementioned trends and movements, while acting in the name of oppressed classes and nations, have found themselves in this situation, this is closely related to their knowledge structures. The knowledge structures that they rely on—both in their positive and negative aspects—have produced overall results that have contradicted their intentions. These outcomes would not have emerged so easily if there were not a chain of serious flaws and mistakes in their fundamental paradigm and structures.

The extreme theories of relativism that impose themselves as another countertrend have also not escaped becoming the knowledge structures of the capitalist world system. But, perhaps due to their excessive individuality, ultimately, they ended up serving capitalism's individualism more than anything else. This includes anarchist approaches. Criticizing capitalism—turning this stark opposition to capitalism into a discourse, as is often seen—has become a very effective way of serving it. The inadequacies and errors in our knowledge structures and our paradigms play a fundamental role in all of this.

Physical sciences (including chemistry and biology) do not only relate to physical nature as claimed nor do the humanities (including literature, history, philosophy, political economy, and sociology) merely relate to social nature. A better approach would be to accept the concept of *social sciences* in a broad sense as the intersection of the two sciences—because *all* sciences must be social.[3]

Agreement on a common definition of the *social sciences* does not settle the problem. What is even more important is to determine the fundamental model. In other words, what unit will form the basis of our evaluation of society? To say that the fundamental unit is social nature as a whole does not mean much for the social sciences. Establishing which of the numerous social relationships are of crucial importance is the first significant step in developing a meaningful theoretical approach. The social unit chosen will be meaningful to the extent that it explains the overall situation.

Various models related to the social sphere have been developed. The most widely known and used unit is the state, more specifically the nation-state primarily based on the perspective of the bourgeoisie and the middle class. Within this model, history and society are examined in light of the construction, destruction, and secession problems faced by states. This tendency, which is one of the shallowest models for approaching the reality of historical-society, cannot play a role beyond being the state's official educational approach. Its real purpose is to produce an ideology that legitimizes the state. Instead of enlightening, it serves to conceal the complex problems of history and society. This is, therefore, the most discredited sociological approach.

The Marxist approach chose class and economy as the fundamental units and hoped to formulate alternative models in opposition to the approach based on the "state" unit. Choosing the working class and capitalist economy as the fundamental model for examining society has helped explain history and society in terms of economic and class structures and their significance. But this approach brought with it several important flaws. The fact that this approach considers the state and other superstructural institutions to be the product and simple reflection of substructures led to a slip into reductionism known as economism. Economic reductionism, like state reductionism, could not overcome the flaw of concealing the reality of historical-society and its highly complex relationships. In particular, deficiencies in the analysis of power and the state led to the oppressed working classes and peoples, whom Marxism claimed to have acted on behalf of, not having adequate access to ideological and political apparatuses. The narrow economic struggle and opportunistic state conspiracy—the idea that the state and power can be destroyed and then reconstructed—have served capitalism as effectively as its own ideology, liberalism. The Chinese and Russian realities make this perfectly clear.

We also come across perspectives that in interpreting history and society see nothing more than the ruling power and authority. This sort of approach is, however, just as flawed as one that chooses the state as its model. Although power itself is a more comprehensive unit of inquiry, even this approach alone is incapable of explaining social nature. This is an extremely important area of examination; the investigation of social power can contribute to understanding history and society. But reducing the issue to power has the same shortcomings as any kind of reductionism.

We also often encounter an approach that examines society as endless singular relational developments devoid of rules. This excessively relativistic approach, which can almost be called the descriptive literary model, can only cause us to lose our way in the complexities of social questions. The approach of excessive universalist models may appear to be the opposite of this, but it essentially plays the same role. Both approaches attempt to define society in its physical simplicity with one or two laws. This is probably the approach that contributes the most to clouding our vision and blinding us to the rich diversity of society. The positivist understanding of society deserves to be remembered as the most vulgar model, encompassing both excessive relativism and excessive universalism.

Liberalism, the official bourgeois ideology of the middle-class, presents itself as an eclectic amalgam of aspects of all of these models, establishing itself as a system by claiming to amalgamate the best aspects of each model. But what it actually does is to combine the most flawed aspects of all models, incorporating a few truths, and constantly presenting society with the most dangerous form of eclecticism as a model. It is the official perspective that colonizes and occupies the collective memory of society, thereby consolidating its ideological hegemony.

I had to present my first major defense, my work called *Prison Writings: The Roots of Civilization*, as it was, without doing much to develop it into a model.[4] That defense was prepared in a rush with little or no opportunity for extensive research. It wasn't my ambition to develop a model; I simply put my understanding of social reality in writing. Later, I had the opportunity to examine the models of Murray Bookchin, Immanuel Wallerstein, Fernand Braudel, and other important sociologists. In addition, I also had a basic understanding of Friedrich Nietzsche, Michael Foucault, and some other philosophers. The most important among them was Andre Gunder Frank, who compiled and presented the views of many thinkers in his monumental work *The World System: Five Hundred Years or Five Thousand?*[5] I came to view this book by a thinker I had not previously heard of to be the best possible presentation of my views. The fact that in recent years several thinkers have conducted similar research led me to think more about my own model.

Indeed, the essence of my defense already bore clear traces of Immanuel Wallerstein's analysis of the capitalist *world-system*, as well as of Fernand Braudel's integrative *historical time*. These works also contributed to my longtime effort to use a similar approach to explain the defeat of real socialism. Furthermore, not only did I have no difficulty in grasping both Friedrich Nietzsche and Michel Foucault's interpretations of modernity and power, but I found them extremely close to my own. I cannot continue without mentioning that V. Gordon Child's *What Happened in History*,[6] written on the basis of archeological work carried out in Mesopotamia, broadened my horizons. I also studied many other philosophical works, treating them as if they were reports, and I had to make some decisions but did not ultimately claim any of them as my own "*model unit.*" My decision to present this more advanced method of analysis as a model in this major defense should not be misunderstood. My real problem was choosing a historical and social unit of analysis that would be both holistic and conclusive. All existing models, as I have briefly mentioned, have some correct elements as well as some faults and contain errors that we must avoid taking on. I was able to identify common deficiencies in all of them. Even the work by Andre Gunder Frank titled *The World System*, which reflects the model I come closest to, seemed to contain a serious flaw.

It was clear that Sumerian society, on which we based our understanding of the world system, was the first society where capital was accumulated. I consider the view that this world system, mainstream civilization from Sumer to the present, represents a cumulative build-up to be highly accurate. And I agree that this accumulation also has a historical continuity of hegemony and competition, center and periphery, and rise and fall. It is perfectly clear that the three pillars of this accumulation would be its economic, political, and ideological and moral dimensions. It is in this sense that the modes of accumulation are more important than the mode of production, and that the hegemonic transitions produce more important results than the mode of production. Frank was right to criticize Wallerstein for presenting capitalism as the only world-wide system in his analysis of the Eurocentric capitalist world-system.

It was an exaggeration to claim that European civilization is exceptional. As an extreme civilization, it could even be considered marginal. In addition, Frank's analysis of fundamental social forms, including socialism, capitalism, slave-owning society, and feudalism, as ideological realities was an approach that came closer to the truth. He also pointed out that these concepts serve to conceal the truth instead of clarifying it. This is an observation the importance of which should not be underestimated and that certainly deserves attention. The search for *unity in diversity* could contribute to a solution, but alone it is inadequate. In addition, Frank clearly makes a richer contribution to the analysis of historical-society. I view his analysis as a system analysis with a small margin of error favoring a better and more beautiful communal life. However, its biggest flaw is that it risks presenting a closed loop that may seem impossible to exit. In the end, he approaches hegemonic power systems as fate, or, more precisely, he does not dialectically show a way out.

Immanuel Wallerstein's decision to base his analysis of the capitalist world-system on a period of five hundred years is inadequate; clearly basing it on five thousand years might have been more productive. In the book *The World System*, we see traces of this in the writings of the many thinkers. However, the major advantage of Wallerstein's thinking is that it provides a better analysis of the way out of the world-system, which makes it an important contribution.

Fernand Braudel's analysis of capitalism, as well as his holistic understanding of society, presented in the form of *historical terms*,[7] is an important contribution to broadening the horizon. That he sees capitalism as anti-market and emphasizes that power monopolies and economic monopolies have similar characteristics of accumulation is particularly significant.[8] One of my favorite sentences is: *Domination always secretes capital.*[9] Another important sentence for those who grasp its meaning is: *Power can be accumulated—just like capital.*[10] Immanuel Wallerstein and Fernand Braudel both see the failure of the socialist revolutions as in part due to their inability to surpass capitalist modernity, an extremely significant observation that is also very instructive. However, these two famous thinkers need to be examined in the light of "economic reductionism," something they themselves talk about.

I must point out once again that my understanding of the social sciences, which has been somewhat influenced by the key thinkers just mentioned and also shares the views of many other thinkers that go unmentioned here, is nonetheless unique in a number of ways. In this book, I go into more depth and systematize issues discussed in my second major defense *Beyond State, Power, and Violence.*[11] My basic conviction is that the existing epistemologies could not escape being integrated into the power apparatus—even if against their will. There can be no doubt that Karl Marx, a thinker who took a highly scientific approach, best determined the true colors of capital. However, this important contribution was not enough to ensure his break with capitalist modernity. The knowledge structures Marx relied on and his very life itself were tied to this modernity in thousands of ways. I am not accusing him of anything. I am just attempting to make sense of his reality. Similar things could be said about Lenin and Mao. The system they envisaged, along with its many premises (including the knowledge structures and perspectives on modern life), was dependent on capitalist modernity. For example, they thought they could conquer major phenomena, such as, industrialism and the nation-state, by introducing socialist content. However, these fundamental forms of modernity—both in form and content—are oriented toward capital accumulation. Those who choose to make them their basis will inevitably produce capitalism, even if they are opposed to it. In all of these respects, I have made my criticism of real socialism perfectly clear. However, criticism is not enough. What option do I have to offer? That was the important question. It is also the question that I have constantly focused on.

Presenting the option of democratic civilization—a seemingly simple name that can be used until a more appropriate name is chosen—as a model for a systematic approach seems necessary and offers the necessary response to these questions. First of all, this option offers an alternative to the central world civilization system. Democratic civilization is not just a present and future utopia; it also seems very necessary and highly explanatory for a more concrete interpretation of the historical-society.

It is a necessity of social nature that there is resistance and an alternative to capital accumulation and the resulting instruments of power whenever and wherever they exist. Never and nowhere have societies lacked resistance or ever been without an alternative to capital accumulation and the instruments of power. The reason why they have generally been defeated must be sought not in the absence of resistance and alternatives but elsewhere.

If we don't understand the preposterous stories of capital and power accumulation, then we will have difficulty in making sense of the concept of democratic civilization. The structures of knowledge have always vacillated between two types of errors: either they were completely absorbed by the knowledge and power structures, or they could not avoid being stunted sectarian denominations, because they were unable to independently choose scientific and political options and moral positions. No doubt, we must always remember the role of violence and the seductive power of capital. If we do not condemn these two notable views of knowledge structures, we cannot make the option of democratic civilization tangible. What we need to question is not the existence of democratic civilization but the knowledge and power structures and the deviant sectarianism, neither of which have been able to see it. These realities cannot be explained solely by inadequacies and errors in the narratives of historical-society and can only be transformed by a thorough revolution in the social sciences.

The power and state structures based on five-thousand-year-old capital accumulation know from their daily experiences that they cannot sustain their regimes without organizing ideological and knowledge structures on a massive scale. We have to understand that the social sciences cannot become meaningful truth regimes until they see that the hegemonic power apparatuses are constantly accumulating the two other components of their triad—surplus product/value and the tools of legitimation. It is not possible to revolutionize the social sciences unless we grasp that the structures of mythology, religion, philosophy, and positivist science are all tightly intertwined with the history of capital and power accumulation, and that they continuously reinforce each other to protect their common interests.

The second important conclusion to be drawn from the concept of democratic civilization is that it provides a very broad foundation for a revolution in the social sciences. My basic thesis is that all of the "barbarians," nomadic tribes, lumpen, clans, communes, heretical denominations, witches, unemployed, and poor of history always lack meaningful movements and systems; to claim this is their destiny is to do nothing but generate and produce knowledge accumulation apparatuses, along with mythological, religious, philosophical, and scientific structures, in the interest of those who accumulate capital and power. History does not only consist of the domination of capital and power. At the same time, the knowledge mechanisms (mythological, religious, philosophical, and scientific) and their domination are always intertwined and in constant unity of interest with the domination of capital and power. The main reason for the failure of many prominent oppositional social science structures, especially the Marxist social sciences, was that they were based on social science revolutions that remained rooted in the history of capitalism and power accumulation and, as a result, failed to develop an alternative civilization system. No doubt many of the aspects we have mentioned here have been widely criticized, but the next step of incorporating these criticisms into a narrative unit that could encompass the whole of history is yet to be taken. An understanding of the world system could not be established, and as such narratives about it have never gone beyond fragmented efforts.

The third important point about the democratic civilization system is that since the agricultural revolution it has had the power necessary to develop urban and industrial elements, without allowing the excessive capital, power, and state accumulations based on the rise of the middle classes that play the role of cancerous cells within the society to take over. So "yes" to the city and industry, but "no" to the cancerous cells within them.[12] If we look at the massive present-day urban industrial power and communication networks and consider in this context the terrible environmental destruction, women's status or lack thereof, and the catastrophic levels of poverty and unemployment, it becomes clear that the concept of cancerous growth within social structures is entirely warranted. Today's leading social scientists, including Immanuel Wallerstein, among others, along with the raiding barbarians (we shall discuss the concept of "barbarism" with a fresh eye), members of heretical denominations, rebellious peasants, utopists, anarchists, and, last but not least, feminists and the ever louder environmental movements have the potential to attain a holistic meaning and act against the threat of this cancerous growth within the social fabric. No society can endure the current accumulation of cities, the middle class, capital, power, the state, and communication apparatuses for very long. Even if society, tightly held within an iron cage, has failed in its efforts to break free, the daily SOS signals sent out by the environment clearly show that the problems have reached crisis and chaos levels because of the existing central civilization system. Thus, we think the way out of this chaos is to adopt an approach that is deeply rooted in the resources of historical-society and an analysis of the present in the light of the current state of these resources. Therefore, we assert that the future can only be secured through a *central world system of democratic civilization.*

In this defense, I focus on clarifying various dimensions of my main thesis. I try to understand history by grasping its universal dimensions, because I fundamentally believe that local histories are meaningless without a universal history—I believe this to be of principle value. Undoubtedly, even the most indistinct societies can be illuminated by the light of universal history. In addition, I also consider it an important principle that the present is history, and history is now. However, I must add the following to these two important principles of history: at the local level, the present does not just repeat history like a reenactment of tradition, rather, it plays its own important role in historical accumulation by adding its own unique features and distinctions. History is not just repetition: it repeats while accumulating new contributions of every place and time.

My approach will be clear as long as the shifts seen in my previous defenses and my other written and oral evaluations are considered against the background of these principles. Clearly my views cannot be interpreted either as dry repetition or as radically renegade. Anyone who is reasonably observant understands that development requires diversification, and that the primary principal of the universe is change through diversification. When one becomes two, this is not just simple quantitative accumulation; at the same time, two always becomes different to one.

Following the preface and introduction, the next section will focus on some methodological problems. I will emphasize the excessive internal fragmentation that has led to a crisis within the sciences that is linked to the overall crisis of the system, and I will discuss the need for a holistic approach to science.

I will also highlight another methodological issue, that of different natures, especially the diversity of social nature. I will explain why a return to nature (first nature) requires a radical approach and will address this in connection with the women's issue.

The subject and object separation will be approached with caution, and the problems it has caused, as well as possible remedies, will be discussed. Its link with capital accumulation system will be illustrated, and the need to transcend it will be emphasized.

It is important to remain open to new approaches, even to important methodological dualisms, such as universalism and relativism, circularity and linearity, globalism and localism. In addition, a reinterpretation of the dialectical method is essential.

Clarity in methodological concepts can facilitate the presentation of the other topics. That is why it seemed necessary to treat methodology in a separate section in this volume.

The fourth section is titled "The Question of Freedom." Since the democratic civilization system is closely linked to freedom, it is important that we clarify what we mean by freedom. The imperious nature of the central civilization system means that the libertarian characteristics of the democratic civilization should be at the forefront. In this section, the close link between equality and freedom will be analyzed. More importantly, the concept of equality—a genuine concept—will be interpreted on the basis of a respect for differences. Concepts of freedom and equality that are not analyzed in terms of their bond with the systems create significant problems within the social sciences. As such, the reinterpretation of these concepts in the light of our main thesis proves illuminating.

The fifth section deals with the critique of human reason. In attempting to define social reason, its functionality in terms of its theoretical and the practical, as well as its analytical and emotional dimensions, will be clarified. Where might the use of reason by world systems lead? Are there limits to reason as the tool for both creating and solving problems? How can we update Immanuel Kant? Such questions themselves are stimulating and indicate that the use of reason as a tool to solve problems can itself lead to serious problems.

In the sixth section, the emergence and development of the social problem will be examined. We assess the main source of the problem—the central civilization system—in different historical periods. The further ramifications of social problems are linked to the essence of the system, or, put another way, the accumulation apparatuses of capital and power are themselves the problem. We will, in a sense, sketch the history of the problem.

In the seventh section, we propose the democratic civilization system as an instrument for solving the problem. What meaning can we hope to find by re-envisaging history as social history? In response, we emphasize the unbreakable link between democratic society and history.

In section eight, a continuation of the seventh section, we define democratic modernity as an alternative to capitalist modernity. We will discuss why two different concepts of modernity are both necessary and possible in light of crucial lessons. In this context, we will reconsider the reasons for the defeat of contemporary revolutions.

In the ninth and tenth sections, we will analyze the systemic crisis of capitalism and consider a possible way out of this crisis. As capitalist modernity, the current state of the world civilization system, dissolves, what alternatives are there? How can we build democratic modernity? What are the obstacles, and what are the opportunities? What are the tasks of rebuilding? No doubt these important questions carry within themselves their answers.

Section eleven, which approaches the issue from various angles, is intended as a conclusion and offers a final comment on this overall undertaking. History neither follows a straight fatalist line nor moves spontaneously toward an expected goal. It is neither the sole source of all evil nor will it one day or another present us with everything good. Human sociality could make a beautiful life possible. Society itself is a tremendous source of solutions. But this will only be the case if we figure out how to protect ourselves from all the different deadly diseases, including the different types of cancer, understand our world, which makes a splendid paradise possible, and choose the beautiful life!

THREE

Some Problems of Methodology

Methodology, the shortest path to the target, is not a Western concept. It has been an aspect of the schools of wisdom in the Middle East since ancient times. The most suitable ways of accessing knowledge have always been tested, and those that have achieved the best results became fundamental methods. Usually schools of thought develop a logic and a methodology based on the concepts that they focus on most closely. When the hegemonic center of the world civilization system shifted to Europe, developments in many areas that would ensure superiority, for example, methodology in the scientific field, also emerged. The appearance of Francis Bacon, René Descartes, and Galileo Galilei in the sixteenth and seventeenth centuries, with each introducing significant methodological approaches, is closely linked to the shift of the hegemonic system to Europe.

The development of the subject-object distinction, one of the most important concepts of scientific method, is linked to the domination of nature. When the capitalist monopolies, the new accumulation instruments of capital and power, started to exploit physical and biological resources and the resources that belonged to social nature, they quickly understood how advantageous these could be for accumulation. Objectification of resources that belonged to both of these natures made ever-increasing contributions to capital and power accumulation. The intellectual counterpart to this material development is the separation into subject and object. While this was reflected as the distinction between the subjective and the objective in Bacon, it took the form of a sharp mind/body distinction in Descartes. In Galileo, mathematics appears as the language of nature and the most advanced criterion of the object. Following history's long Mesopotamian journey, a development similar to that experienced in ancient Greece repeats itself with unique differences in West Europe. In fact, Sumerian society had also carried the life experiences of Upper Mesopotamia, filtered through thousands of years, into Lower Mesopotamia, which then added its own distinct qualities to create an original form.

In the central civilization systems, the subject always stems from capital and power. It represents consciousness, discourse, and free will. At times, it is an individual, and, at other times, it is the institution, but it always exists. The objects are the barbarians, the peoples, and the women excluded from power. They are only thought of—as is the case with nature—when they serve the subject as a resource. Given the nature of things, no other meaning is imaginable for them. In Sumerian mythology, the creation story of the human being as a servant from the excrement of the gods and of the woman from the man's rib reflect the dimensions of objectification in the depths of history. The transfer of this subject-object approach to European thought required significant transformations. But it cannot be denied that the development unfolded in this way.

At present, the subject-object distinction has faded, due to the rise to prominence of the financial capital system. The symbolic hegemony of financial capital in the central civilization system has dissolved all the former subject-object states. The fact that everyone positions themselves as subjects sometimes and objects at other times, as appropriate, is closely linked to these new forms of capital and power accumulation. The capital and power apparatuses that originate from the snowballing reproduction of nationalism, religionism, sexism, and scientism, both in the real and virtual dimensions, have wrapped themselves around the society like an octopus. Under these conditions each individual and institution can duly end up in the position of a subject or an object. When the role of gods in Sumerian society was taken over by the ideological apparatuses, the transformation of the subject-object distinction was inevitable. At the same time, the new symbolic characteristics of the gods and their dominion obviously rendered the existing distinction superfluous.

The gradual fragmentation of knowledge and the loss of sacredness in the course of the history of the central civilization unfolded in a similar way. We can clearly observe in history that the reproduction of capital and power apparatuses caused an equivalent fragmentation of knowledge. In all clan and tribal societies, science is a whole, and its representatives are considered sacred. Divinity is attributed to science, and it is assigned to all according to their desire and effort. While this was the overall approach in mythology, in religion and philosophy it was the principle approach. The original fragmenting was mainly seen in the natural sciences and knowledge structures of Western Europe. The new organizations of knowledge (academies and universities) increasingly detached themselves from society, and serving the interests of the capital and power elites found themselves in the ranks of the favored institutions of the new state (Leviathan). The process of turning science into capital and merging it with power was, at the same time, the alienation of science from the society. The headquarters and temples of science that resolves problems were turned into centers for creating problems, effectuating alienation, and ensuring ideological hegemony. A scientific discipline developed for every natural and social resource. This reality alone proves the interdependence of science with capital and power. The field of science, which is sacred to society as a whole, has drifted as far away as possible from serving society. Scientific disciplines have become paid professions and have even become capital itself. They have become highly dangerous accomplices of power. We know very well that the production of nuclear weapons and many other deadly weapons, as well as all the processes that risk environmental destruction, have their origins in scientific centers. Those who work in these centers are not concerned with the truth (society's collective conscience) but have chosen to act as mentors facilitating the production of capital and power as efficiently as possible.

The first question that comes to mind when you talk about scientific work today is: How much money will it bring in? Society, however, expects science to respond to its fundamental concerns. Society, with its material and immaterial concerns, has considered science as a whole to be a divine profession and has, as a result, accepted it. The degeneration of the academy and the university is another cause of the crisis in science. The history of knowledge underwent a transformation related to the history of civilization and could not escape its share of the system's general crisis. Although intended as a tool for solving problems, science has become the key source of problems. The result is the fragmentation of science, its disintegration, and chaos.

A good grasp of different natures—in other words, the question of first, second, and third natures—is necessary. All nature, excluding human society, is distinguished as first nature. The concept of first nature is contradictory in itself. First of all, there are an infinite variety of distinctions, such as animate-inanimate, plants-animals, even physics-chemistry, and, if we take another step, visible-invisible matter and energy-matter become conceivable. Moreover, we can delineate a society for each distinction. When we look closer at ways of approaching the question of natures, we find that they are profoundly influenced by the subject-object distinction. It should be emphasized that these are not sound distinctions, or at least should only be made conditionally.

Human society, as second nature, no doubt represents a very important stage of natural development and has certain particularities. Rather than as a separate nature, it makes more sense to see it as a different stage of nature.

The most important distinguishing characteristic of social nature is the extent of its intellectual capacity, flexibility, and ability to construct itself. First nature no doubt also has intellectual capacity, flexibility, and the ability to construct itself, but compared to the functioning of the social nature, it is very slow, rigid, and arduous. It seems very important to me that the nature of society be theorized as a whole. Although this was the priority for early sociologists, over the course of time the analysis of parts and structures increasingly came to the fore: just as we have observed in the analyses of other natures. Furthermore, distinguishing between the base and the superstructure of society, partitioning it into economy, politics, and power, dividing it into strata and stages, such as primeval communal society, slave-owning society, feudalism, capitalism, and socialism or communism, can only produce meaningful results if we are extremely conscious of *diversity*. No analysis of a stratum, part, or structure can replace a holistic theoretical approach. We could say that no philosopher or sociologist has been able to surpass the holistic approach of Plato and Aristotle. Even the holistic interpretations of the sages and prophets with their roots in the Middle East, or the East more generally, are more instructive and socially useful than those of the philosophers and sociologists of capitalist modernity. These interpretations are valuable, because they represent a more progressive and sophisticated approach. We must particularly emphasize that the most important role in rendering the holistic theoretical approach ineffective is played by the apparatuses of capital and power accumulation.

There is an urgent need for a new methodology, a profound theoretical approach, that can be used to examine human society. In particular, we must understand that sociological methods—overwhelmed by the hustle of numbers—conceal the truth instead of revealing it. It should not be seen as exaggeration when I say that existing sociology conceals the truth more than mythologies ever did. Moreover, the meaning reached on the basis of sensing the truth in mythologies is more humane and closer to truth than that reached by the sociologies of capitalist modernity.

The social sciences are without a doubt important, however, it is difficult to call them sciences in their present state. The existing sociological discourse hardly expresses any meaning beyond the legitimization of official modernity. Therefore, there is a need for a radical scientific revolution and a methodological egress.

The stage called third nature, which we want to make sense of, is only possible because of this scientific and methodological revolution. Third nature, as a concept, refers to a state of restored harmony between first and second nature at a higher level. Achieving a synthesis of social nature with first nature at a higher level requires a revolutionary theoretical paradigm and a radical practical revolution. In particular, surpassing the capitalist world system, or capitalist modernity—the current stage of the central civilization system—would be a decisive achievement. To this end, albeit minimally, we must develop constructs of democratic civilization, take successful steps in developing the ecological and feminist characteristics of society, creating a functional art of democratic politics, and building a democratic civil society.

Third nature is not a promise of a new paradise or utopia; it is the renewed *participation* of human beings—whose consciousness of the natures has increased—in a grand harmony, while protecting their difference. This is not just a longing, an intention, and the promise of utopia but, rather, the art of good and beautiful living that has a contemporary practical meaning. I am not talking about biologism here; I am aware of the danger of such an approach. I am also not talking about the "godly" utopic paradise promoted by capital and power accumulation apparatuses. I can see what these mean and foresee the dangerous and destructive consequences their intentions will lead to. Vulgar communism, the paradisiacal promise of materialism, is also primitive and dysfunctional, a kind of extreme variant of liberalism. In any case, we can easily understand from our daily experience that every promise made by liberalism stinks to hell.

The realization of the third nature would require the *longue durée*. A democratic system—as a regime for the realization of first and second natures at a higher level based on diversity and the expression of equality and freedom—only becomes possible if it develops the internal qualities of an ecological and feminine society. The human being's social nature is such that we could reach this stage. Approaching the issue of different natures with this methodology could lead to more meaningful theoretical and practical results.

Another important methodological issue discussed recently is the relationship between universality and relativism. Interpreting this as either the universality of meaning or the particularity of meaning draws upon the same content. We are faced with a methodological problem that requires careful analysis. We could define this problem as a new level of the subject-object distinction. The rigid approaches of capital and power apparatuses are called *laws* as a result of the material conditions underlying these methodological problems. Calling the legalistic approach *universality* is closely related to its use as a tool for ideological legitimization. We must not forget that law is a product of power. We should also not forget that power is capital. The rule of power is called *law*. Law, on the other hand, becomes stronger, in fact, almost impossible to oppose, when it is *universal*. This is how it starts to build God from the image of humans. The human holding power cannot openly dictate, so he deifies his rule. He believes he can hold on to his power more easily by using this ingenious legitimizing tool. We must clearly understand that efforts of this sort have been a substantial source for all universalities.

Relativism is presented as the opposite pole but in essence is very similar to universalism. It denotes the state of the debased human being completely removed from any rules, approaches, or methodologies. Relativism leaves the door open to the extreme perspective that *there are as many rules, approaches, and methodologies as there are people*. Since this is impossible in practice, it is inevitable that relativism falls captive to the laws of universalism. While one view exaggerates the degree of intelligence in human society and pushes it to the level of a *universally valid law*, the other underestimates it to the degree that it reduces it to *everyone having their own law*. Social intelligence can be interpreted more realistically by treating universal laws and relativism not as opposite poles but as two intertwined states of natural reality. Taking this approach could lead to a more productive narrative. Unchanging universal laws lead to linear progressivism. That is the flaw of progressivism. Were it true that the universe was constantly moving toward a goal, it should have reached this goal long ago, given the concept of "past eternity," which includes infinity. In contrast, relativism includes the concept of *eternal cyclicality*, but if that were true then existing universal transitions and developments would not have occurred. This is why universal progressivism and cyclicality are methodological concepts that are too flawed to explain universal development, which essentially differentiates by unifying and changing—in short, both approaches are methodologically flawed. I believe the methodology that is closer to the truth must *enable change by differentiation and include both the present instant and eternity*. Just as progression is cyclical, cyclicality involves progression, and eternity is hidden and inherent in the present moment; while, on the other hand, the totality of instantaneous formations contain eternity. All of this offers a clearer and more understandable methodological approach to establishing a regime of truth.

It is important to address some aspects of dialectical methodology. No doubt the discovery of dialectical methodology was an extraordinary achievement. Close observation at any point reveals the dialectical character of the universe. The problem here is how to define dialectics. The difference between Hegel's and Marx's interpretations of dialectics is well-known, and both have had very unpleasant and destructive consequences. The Hegelian interpretation, which led to the nationalist German state, had horrific consequences with the rise of fascism. Although the results were different, the narrow class-oriented real socialist practices of Marx's successors also led to many negative consequences and much destruction. It would, however, be more correct to look for the errors made by those who misinterpreted these dialectics in major ways and not in Marx or Hegel. Furthermore, it would be wrong to attribute the origin of dialectical methodology to Hegel and Marx. Nor would it be entirely correct to attribute it to ancient Greek thought. Dialectical interpretations are abundant in the wisdom of the East. No doubt, however, significant additions were made both in ancient Greece and in Europe during the Enlightenment.

It is neither right to interpret dialectics as the destructive unity of opposites nor to interpret change as the becoming and the creativity of the moment in the absence of opposites. The first conception leads to a vulgar tendency to always see the poles as hostile, which results in nothing more than seeing the universe as unregulated and in permanent chaos. The latter approach leads to an understanding of development without tensions, devoid of opposites, lacking its own dynamics, and always requiring an external force that cannot be realistically validated as cause. We know that this is the doorway to metaphysics.

It is therefore of utmost importance to free the dialectic methodology by cleansing it of these two extreme approaches. We can observe a constructive rather than destructive dialectic in any development. For example, the human being represents a dialectical development that is possibly as old as the roughly determined age of the universe. Human beings not only consist of everything from subatomic particles to the most complex atoms and molecules but also carry all biological phases within them.[1] This marvelous development is dialectical, but it is undeniably a constructive and developmental dialectic. No doubt certain hostilities arise in the much debated class conflicts (to which we could add tribal, ethnic, national, and systemic conflicts), but it is possible to resolve these contradictions and find a solution in the spirit of dialectics by drawing on society's extraordinarily flexible intellectual power rather than by massacres. Society's nature overflows with examples of such solutions. In attempting to better explain these developments, ideologues—perhaps against their will—have been unable to avoid arriving at contrary results. The fact that they often find themselves in this situation indicates the ongoing importance of interpreting the dialectical methodology itself.

To avoid an incorrect understanding of dialectics, we must briefly interpret dialectics in comparison to metaphysics. Undoubtedly, the most unproductive approach of all time has been the metaphysical search for formation, from a creator, externally. The philosophy, religion, and positivist scientism arising from this approach have created a thoroughgoing system of "intellectual colonialism." Nature may not have needed an external creator, and, if it did require a creator, that creator would certainly be an internal one. However, we can easily argue that metaphysics imposes "intellectual colonial regimes" that resemble an external creator on the intelligence of social nature. In this sense, it is essential that we criticize and overcome metaphysics.

However, what I wanted to address concerns another aspect of metaphysics. I am talking about the fact that human beings cannot exist without metaphysics. The metaphysics I refer to here are human society's cultural creations—mythology, religion, philosophy, and science, as well as all types of art, politics, and production techniques. Feelings of goodness and beauty have no physical counterparts. These are human-specific values. Morality and the arts in particular are metaphysical values. What needs to be elucidated here is not the contradiction between metaphysics and dialectics but the distinction between good and beautiful metaphysical creations and bad and ugly metaphysical creations. Again, I am not talking about the dichotomies of religion and atheism or philosophy and science but about religious, philosophical, and scientific beliefs, truth, and facts that make life more bearable and attractive.

Let's not forget that nature stages a great play of vast splendor that unfolds before the very eyes of humanity. On this stage, human beings cannot play the same role as nature. They can at best arrange their lives through pieces they construct themselves. The description of theater as the mirror of life has its origin in this profound truth. What is important is that we reduce the bad and ugly aspects and the mistakes of this stage life to a minimum and maximize truth, goodness, and beauty. When we speak of good, beautiful, and true metaphysics, we are talking about this profound human quality not the metaphysics that make us blind, deaf, and numb. I am convinced that these clarifications are of great importance in the methodological comparison of dialectics and metaphysics.

FOUR

The Question of Freedom

I almost want to say *freedom is the goal of the universe*. I have often asked myself if the universe is not, in fact, in pursuit of freedom. The formulation of freedom as a profound quest unique to human society always seemed incomplete to me, and I thought there must definitely be an aspect related to the universe. When I think of the particle-energy duality that is the cornerstone of universe, I would without hesitation emphasize that energy is freedom. I believe that the material particle is an imprisoned packet of energy. Light is a state of energy. Can we deny how freely light can flow? If quanta are defined as smallest particles of energy, then we must also agree that they are now seen to explain almost all diversity. Yes, quantum motion is the creative power of all diversity. I cannot resist asking whether this is the God that humanity has been searching for all along. When they say the supra-universe is of quantum character, I again get excited and feel that this *could well be*. Again, as I said a moment ago, I can't help wondering if this is what has been called "the external creativity of God."

I think it is important not to be selfish when it comes to freedom and not to fall into reductionism that restricts freedom to humans. Can it be denied that the flutter of the bird in a cage is a flutter for freedom? What other concept could explain the twitter of a nightingale in a cage, more beautiful than any symphony, but the desire for freedom? If we go a step further, don't all of the sounds and colors of the universe make us think of freedom? Can the struggle of women, the first and last slaves, who have experienced the most profound slavery of human society, be explained by anything other than their quest for freedom? When a brilliant philosopher like Spinoza interprets freedom as a way out of ignorance and the power of intellect, isn't he saying the same thing?

I don't want to suffocate the problem in infinite detail, nor do I want to portray the situation as one of *being convicted* from birth. Apart from a few lines I scribbled in memory of Prometheus, I have never tried to write a poem, which in a way is also a quest for freedom, even one that has only an imaginary meaning. Nonetheless, is there any denying that I am passionately searching for the meaning of freedom?

As we problematize social freedom, this short introduction is meant to draw attention to the depth of the issue. Defining society as the nature with the most developed and concentrated intelligence also contributes to the analysis of freedom. The areas where intelligence is concentrated are areas sensitive to freedom. It is fair to say that the more developed the intelligence, culture, and reason of a society, the more that society will be inclined to freedom. Yet it is also true to say that the more a society deprives itself or has been deprived of these values, the more it is enslaved. When I think about the tribe of the Hebrews, two characteristics and survival strategies always come to mind. The first is a special relationship to making money. Jews sought financial influence at certain times and at times attained worldwide supremacy. This is the material side. However, I think it is more important that they master the second, i.e. the art of influence in the intellectual field, even better. Jews have achieved an outstanding intellectual and cultural position, first with their prophets and later with their scribes, then in capitalist modernity with their philosophers, scholars, and artists, with roots that go back almost as far back as written history. This is why I propose the hypothesis that there is no other tribe that is as rich and free as the Hebrews. Some examples of the situation of the Jews in recent times will confirm this. Many influential people in the field of financial capital, which dominates the global economy, have Hebrew roots and are, therefore, Jewish. If we mention names like Spinoza in the emergence of contemporary philosophy, Marx in sociology, Freud in psychology, and Einstein in physics, and add hundreds of theorists of the arts, science, and political theory, we would get a sufficient impression of Jewish intellectual strength. Can the dominance of the Jews in the world of intellect be denied?

But there is also the other side of the coin, the Others of the world. The material and immaterial wealth, power, and dominance of one side is realized at the expense of the poverty and weakness of the Others, as well as their transformation into a herd. Therefore, Marx's famous state-ment about the proletariat: "If the proletariat wants to liberate itself, it has no choice but to liberate the whole society"[1] also applies to the Jews, almost as if Marx had thought of them when formulating it. If the Jews want to ensure their freedoms—i.e., their wealth, intelligence and power of understanding—they have no choice but to enrich and immaterially strengthen world society in a similar way. Otherwise, they could be per-secuted by new Hitlers at any time. In this sense, the liberation of the Jews is only possible if it is intertwined with the liberation and freedom of world society. There should be no doubt that this is the most noble task of the Jews, who have already achieved a great deal for humanity. We can also learn from the terrible genocide of the Jews that wealth and immate-rial prestige based on the poverty and ignorance of others contribute no real value to freedom. Freedom in a true sense is the transcendence of the distinction between us and others that is characterized by being available to be shared by everyone.

When we evaluate the central civilization system on the basis of freedom, we see that there is an increasingly multifaceted slavery. Slavery is primarily sustained in three ways. First, ideological slavery is con-structed. The construction of frightening and dominating mythological gods is very striking and easy to grasp, especially in Sumerian society.[2] The upper floor of the ziggurat is considered the location of the gods that dominate the mind. The middle floors are the headquarters of the priests' political administration. The lowest floor, on the other hand, is the floor of the craftspeople and agricultural workers responsible for all aspects of production. This model has not changed in any significant way until this day but has, in fact, expanded and spread widely. This five-thousand-year-old narrative of the central civilization system provides the historical concept that comes closest to the truth; more precisely, it is empirically observed reality. Analyzing the ziggurat is equivalent to correctly analyz-ing the central civilization system and, thus, the current capitalist world system. One side of the coin is the continuous and cumulative develop-ment of capital and power, while, on the other, we find terrible slavery, hunger, poverty, and herdlike behavior.

This can help us to better understand the profundity of the question of freedom. The central civilization system cannot survive and maintain itself without gradually depriving society of its freedom and ensuring that society behaves in a herdlike fashion. The solution within the system's logic is to create more apparatuses of capital and power. This, in turn, means society will be even more impoverished and herdlike. The fact that the question of freedom grew to the degree that it became the fundamental question faced by every age is the result of the dichotomous nature of the system. We have used the example of the Jewish tribe, because it is highly instructive. Examining both freedom and slavery from the point of view of Jewish history is no less important now than it was in the past.

We can also better understand the traditional debate about whether money or consciousness provides more freedom in the light of this narrative. As long as money is an instrument for capital accumulation, for usurping surplus product and surplus value, it will always be an instrument of slavery. The fact that it even invites the massacre of its owners shows us that money cannot be a reliable instrument for achieving freedom. Money plays the role of the particle of matter, the opposite of energy. In this respect, consciousness is always closer to freedom. Consciousness about reality always expands the horizons of freedom. This is why consciousness is always described as the flow of energy.

Defining freedom as pluralization, diversification, and differentiation in the universe will make it easier to explain social morality. Pluralization, diversification, and differentiation, even if only implicitly, are suggestive of the inherent ability of an intelligent being to make choices. Scientific research confirms that plants have an intelligence that leads them to diversify. Humans have yet to replicate the formations in a living cell in a laboratory. Perhaps we cannot talk about universal intelligence (*Geist*) as Hegel did, but, still, it cannot be judged as total nonsense to talk about an intelligence-like being in the universe. We cannot explain differentiation in any other way than as the result of the existence of intelligence. Pluralization and diversification evoke freedom because of the sparks of intelligence that underlie them. As far as we know, the human being can be defined as the most intelligent being in the universe. But how did the human being attain this intelligence? I had already scientifically defined the human (physically, biologically, psychologically, and sociologically) as an epitome of the universal history. Here we further define the human being as the accumulation of universal intelligence. This is also why the human being is presented as a model of the universe in a number of philosophical schools of thought.

The level of intelligence and flexibility in human society is the real foundation of social construction. In this sense, it is also appropriate to define freedom as the force of social construction, or what has been called the moral attitude since the first human communities. Social morality is only possible with freedom. More precisely, freedom is the source of morality. Morality may be defined as the solidified state of freedom, the tradition of freedom, or the code of freedom. If moral choice is based on freedom, when the connection between freedom and intelligence, consciousness, and reason is taken into consideration, it becomes clear why morality can be called the collective consciousness (conscience) of society. Calling theoretical morality ethics is only meaningful in this context. We cannot speak of an ethics that is not based on the morality of society. Undoubtedly, a more competent moral philosophy, i.e., ethics, could be derived from moral experiences, but there can be no artificial ethics. Immanuel Kant put a lot of thought into this subject, and it makes sense that he referred to practical reason as ethics. Kant's interpretation of morality as the choice and possibility of freedom remains valid today.

The connection between social politics and freedom is also apparent. The political sphere is the key area where farsighted minds collide intensely, focus the most, and strive to attain results. In a sense, it is also possible to define this area as the space where the participating subjects free themselves through the art of politics. Any society that does not promote and develop social politics needs to understand that this will rebound against them as a deprivation of freedom, and they will have to pay the price. It is in this sense that the supremacy of the art of politics emerges. Any society that fails to develop its politics (the clan, tribe, nation, class, and even power and state apparatuses) is doomed to failure. In fact, not being able to develop politics means not knowing your own conscience, vital interests, and identity. There cannot be a greater failure or loss for any society. Only when they stand up for their own interests, identity, and collective conscience—in other words, when they are engaged in political struggle—can it be said that such societies demand freedom. Demanding freedom in the absence of politics is a catastrophic error.

To not distort the relationship between politics and freedom, it is necessary to carefully determine how they differ from the politics (or, rather, the lack of politics) of power and the state and clearly distinguish them from it. Power and state apparatuses can have strategies and tactics, but in the true sense they have no politics. In any case, power and the state only come into existence when the denial of social politics is ensured. Wherever politics comes to an end, power and state structures are at work.

Power and the state are the point where political word and, therefore, freedom ends. There is only dealing with the situation, obeying, and giving and taking orders; there are laws and statutes. All power and all states represent frozen reason. Both their strength and their weakness arise from this quality. Hence, the spheres of power and the state are not areas where freedom can be sought or found. Hegel's statement that the state is the true sphere of freedom forms the basis of all of modernity's oppressive views and structures.[3] Hitler's fascism is a good example of where this view can lead. In fact, even scientific socialism, with Marx and Engels as its masterminds, conceives of power and the state as fundamental means for socialist construction. This led them to—unknowingly—deliver the extreme blows to freedom and, thus, to equality. The liberals understood the truth behind "the more state, the less freedom" much better, and to this they owe their success.

Because of their nature, rulers and the state as instruments of domination do not signify anything but the surplus product and surplus values appropriated through coercion, i.e., a different variety of total capital. Capital creates the state, and the state creates capital. The same applies to any kind of power apparatus. Just as social politics breeds freedom, power and the state are spheres where freedom is lost. Power and state structures can perhaps make some individuals, groups, and nations richer and freer, but, as we have seen from the example of the Jews, this is only possible at the expense of poverty and slavery in other societies. The result has been all kinds of destruction, from wars to genocide. In the capitalist world system, politics suffered its greatest loss. It is possible to talk about the actual death of politics at the stage of capitalist modernity, which is the peak of the central civilization system. Therefore, today we are experiencing a political decline of incomparable proportions. While the decline of morality as an area of freedom is a phenomenon of our times, so is the decline of the political sphere. This is why if we want freedom we have no other choice but to use all of our intellectual power to find ways to restore and functionalize morality—the collective conscience of society—and politics—common reason—in all their aspects.

The relationship between freedom and democracy is even more complicated. There is a constant debate about which emerges from which. We can safely say that the intensity of their relationship means that they nurture one another. Just as we think of social politics in the context of freedom, we can also associate it with democracy. Social politics is at its most concrete as democratic politics. As such, democratic politics can be defined as the true art of freedom. Without democratic politics, neither politicization nor freedom by political means is possible for society in general or for peoples and communities in particular. Democratic politics is the true school in which freedom is learned and lived. The more political work creates democratic subjects, the more democratic politics will politicize society, ultimately leading to freedom. If we accept politicization as the main form of freedom, we must understand that we free society by politicizing it and, simultaneously, we politicize society as we free it. There are, of course, many social spheres that nurture freedom and politics, most particularly various ideological sources, but basically social politics and freedom produce and nurture each other.

In general, the relationship between equality and freedom is confused. The relationship between the two is at least as complicated and problematic as their respective relationships with democracy. We note that when complete equality is achieved, the cost is paid in freedom. It is often suggested that they cannot coexist, and that it is necessary to make concessions in one area or the other. Some argue that concessions in the area of equality are necessary to achieve freedom.

It is necessary to explain the difference between the two concepts and, thus, the difference in nature of these phenomena, if we are to correctly address the problem. Equality is more of a legal concept. It foresees individuals and communities sharing the same rights regardless of their differences. However, diversity is not only a fundamental feature of the universe but also of society. Diversity is a concept that is closed to uniform rights. Equality can only be meaningful when it is based on differences. The main reason that the socialist understanding of equality failed to gain ground was that it did not take diversity into account, and this contributed greatly to its ultimate downfall. True justice is only possible with an understanding of equality in diversity.

Once we understand that freedom is highly dependent on diversity, then a meaningful connection between equality and freedom can be established in the context of diversity. Reconciling freedom with equality is one of the main objectives of social politics.

We need to touch on the discussion between the advocates of individual freedom and the proponents of collective freedom. We need to explain the relationship between these two categories, defined by some as negative and positive freedom. Capitalist modernity promoted individual

33

(negative) freedom at a great cost to social collectivity. It must be stressed that today individual freedom causes the decline of social politics as much as does the phenomenon of power. The crucial issue in a discussion about freedom is to clarify the role of individualism in the destruction of society, particularly in negating morality and politics. When we say that a society that is atomized by individualism does not have the strength to resist the apparatuses of capital and power, we can perhaps better understand the cancerous threat this poses for the social problem. Identifying liberal individualism as the main cause of the decline of social politics and freedom could possibly provide a meaningful way out. Of course, we are not talking about individuality or the necessity to be an individual. What we are discussing is the role of the ideological idealization of individualism and liberalism that consumes social politics and freedom.

We have already discussed collective freedom. We must emphasize that freedom itself, like individualism, requires that every community (including tribes, peoples, nations, classes, occupational groups, etc.) define its identity, represent its interests, and take steps to guarantee its security. This is the only way for freedom to be meaningful. If individual and collective freedom can be reconciled in this way we will be able to talk about a successful and optimally free social order. Although defined as if they are opposites, the experience of the twentieth century has shown us that there is a strong similarity between the individualist freedom promoted by liberalism and the collectivist freedom promoted by real socialism. Both are liberal options. When we see how the games of statism and privatization are played by these two forces, the issues we are addressing here grow clearer.

Democratic society provides the most favorable ground for harmonizing individual and collective freedoms, something that has become particularly clear in the aftermath of the individualist (savage liberalism) and collectivist (pharaoh socialism) models that brought about such terrible destruction in the twentieth century. Arguably, democratic society is the most appropriate sociopolitical regime both for striking a balance between individual and collective freedoms and for achieving an understanding of equality in diversity.

FIVE

The Power of Social Reason

The opportunity to resolve problems affecting society cannot be adequately evaluated if the extent of the intelligence in the human species and its connection with its own social process is not understood.[1] Measuring the potential intelligence of the human species may seem a speculative endeavor from the outset, and it may even prove impossible. But if we look at the phenomenon of war in human history, which has brought our environment to the brink of total destruction, it becomes clear that we are faced with a very different intelligence. It is understood, perhaps even proven, that ecological and social destruction cannot be prevented by class analysis, economic prescriptions, political measures, or power and the state's maximum accumulations. It is clear that this problem needs to be addressed at a more profound level.

Throughout the ages, there has been a constant focus on the power of reason. I will not be saying anything particularly new on the topic. I would just like to point out that it is more important than ever to draw attention to a certain quality of reason. The connection between reason and society is obvious. Reason cannot develop in the absence of the development of society; this is something that any ordinary observer of history will note. What really needs to be grasped is the conditions under which social existence is legitimized by reason. The environmental disaster and social destruction caused by capitalist modernity, especially by the recent domination of global financial capital, in making enormous profits using *symbolic reason* cannot be legitimized under any circumstances. Clearly, no form of moral, free, and political society can agree to the profiteering of *symbolic reason*. So how and by whom, with what mentalities and tools, were the thresholds of social legitimization shattered and destroyed? Whose role is it to rebuild, repair, and heal society in the face of the destructive power of reason? Using which intellectual guidelines and what tools can they play this role? These are vital questions that need answers.

I very much appreciate the seriousness with which Immanuel Wallerstein examines the emergence of the order he calls the capitalist world-system. I also find Fernand Braudel's important and well thought out work on the issue extremely stimulating. Samir Amin's analysis of capitalism, in particular in relation to the destruction of the Islamic civilizations of the Middle East, is also at times very instructive. Many thinkers treat the subject thoughtfully. A common conclusion is that the factors that paved the way for capitalism to become the dominant system are the weakness of the state tradition in Europe, the dissolution of the Church, and the devastation of Islamic civilization by Genghis Khan's Mongolian tribes. Capitalism, likened to a lion in a cage, found an open door created by these circumstances and seized the opportunity, developed, and finally gained the upper hand, dominating Western Europe, before expanding successively throughout Europe and North America. To claim that it has now successfully completed its attack on the whole world would not be out of line. Thus, the power that was previously caged has become the ruler of the world, while the past rulers are now locked in an iron cage. Metaphorically, it has been said that society was placed in an iron cage by the Leviathan—as Max Weber famously said, capitalist modernity shut society inside an iron cage.[2] This is the gruesome social picture that all famous sociologists try to describe—not openly but with feelings of guilt, in a cowardly way, almost in a whisper.

I personally see the problem in a more encompassing manner in connection with the central civilization system. I even think that the problem should be addressed in the light of the historical development of symbolic and analytical reason. In the central civilization system, analytical reason has undoubtedly taken a giant step forward. However, all civilization structures have similar impacts. Another factor, as important as the civilization factor, is how human beings learned symbolic thinking and acquired the capacity for analytical solutions. In the end, it is analytical intelligence that opened the door to civilization.

All living beings, from the most primitive to humans, the most advanced living species, operate in accordance with unfailing principles of reason. This kind of reason, which can be called natural or emotional reason, is inclined toward instincts. It is characterized by sudden reactions to stimuli. The relationship between stimuli and reactions in plants and animals is quite instructive in this regard. Plants and animals live their lives, which consist of seeking nourishment, self-preservation, and reproduction, with instinctive reason in a perfectly learned manner. The margin of error is negligible. I favor extending the topic to the field of inanimate beings. For example, if we think of our world's gravity as an example of instinctive reason (and I do), each object, even each particle, experiences the impact of its attraction and repulsion in accordance with its strength. The possibility of escaping this impact is very limited. Only with the power of light is it possible to escape gravity's impact. In this sense, philosophies that consider the universe to lack principles and to be idle do not satisfy me. The view that the universe moves with a certain reason is something that we very much need to consider in detail.

The strange thing about human intelligence is its ability to violate universal reason. As with the example of light, this form of intelligence (analytical intelligence) can be seen to represent human superiority. But how can we then analyze the contradiction in which this same intelligence stands in relation to the much more weighty reason of the universe, which is there for the most part? Perhaps "chaos theory," by pursuing the order within great disorder, provides a partial explanation, given that order is impossible without chaos. It is undeniable that this approach has legitimate and useful aspects, but the problem that arises is determining where and for how long human life can be sustained in the event of social chaos (including periods of economic depression and crisis). Because there are limits to the time and place where society can endure chaotic periods, if the chaos lasts too long and there is an extreme destruction of place (ecological environment), this can easily bring the end of society. Many societies have experienced this in the past. We know that humans lived in this chaotic environment for the longue durée (98 percent of their time on earth) in primeval or very simple communities. Neolithic society and the orders of civilization amount to less than 2 percent of the total lifespan of the human species. While protracted periods of chaos have not completely ended life, the current danger is of quite a different order. There is a marked difference between chaotic periods before and after the beginning of civilization. Civilization, with its destruction of the natural environment, has dragged not only human society but all living beings to a dangerous precipice. Worse still, the capital and power at the heart of human societies has spread like cancer (excessive urbanization, a growing middle class, unemployment, increased nationalism and sexism, continuous population growth). If the current cancerous growth continues unabated, we will soon long for pre-civilization chaos. Instead of giving rise to new orders, the chaotic period that comes with this cancer may result in the death of society, and this is no exaggeration. Scientists and others who feel responsible for addressing the issue arrive at increasingly dire conclusions every day.

We might ask, "What is the relationship between these cancerous social developments and analytical intelligence?" Let's take a closer look at this form of reason. Analytical intelligence has played a leading role that is most evident in the transition from sign language (primarily body movements) to symbolic language. Now, instead of body movements, semantic links can be established between combinations of agreed upon sounds and the phenomenon described without there being any physical or biological connection. For example, let's focus on the *eye*. Even though the sounds of the word has no physical connection to the eye, all those who connect this meaning with the sound will visualize an eye when they hear the *eye* sound. This is how the construction of symbolic language began. Although anthropological studies connect the beginning of symbolic language with the last emigration of Homo sapiens from East Africa around fifty to sixty thousand year ago, they agree that symbolic language truly boomed in the Middle East. The developments in the Semitic and Arian language groups support this thesis.

The structure of symbolic language had a tremendous impact on thought. Getting rid of body language and thinking in words was perhaps the first of the great intellectual revolutions. This revolution accelerated the separation of the human species from the animal world and gave great impetus to the clustering of societies around established symbolic languages. Because those who share the same patterns of sound gradually formed units whose intelligence increased as they became more distinct. Symbolic languages formed the identities of societies, making a significant contribution to the Neolithic Revolution. It would have been difficult to reach this revolutionary stage with only sign language. I will not repeat here how the transition to civilization took place, as I have addressed it numerous times elsewhere. But it is useful to know that the foothills of the Zagros Mountain range and the Mesopotamian plains known as the "Fertile Crescent" were the cradle of these developments.

All of this reveals the positive impact of symbolic reason. Its drawback, however, begins with its rupture with the environment. Previous societies were societies tied to the natural environment. These societies existed in the embrace of nature that was like the relationship between mother and child. The power of symbolic thought weakened the need for that way of life, because the new society, with its own new language, named the environment and opened the way to a new approach to its use. This new way established far-reaching hegemony over the world of plants and animals. All forms of thought prior to symbolic language arose from emotional intelligence. Its most important characteristic was thinking in feelings as an indispensable component of action and reaction. It is sincere, does not lie, and knows no deceit. It is not often that we see a mother approach her child insincerely, in a lying and cunning way. The intellect of the plant and animal world works the same way. When the lion appears, we see the thinking of its prey reflected in its emotions. Neither animal deceives the other. However, with human symbolic language, cunning thoughts abound, overflowing with both lies and insincerity (and devoid of emotion). What a terrible danger this way of thinking entailed, the far-reaching destruction it would cause becoming apparent after the transition to civilization.

Analytical thought grew out of symbolic language, playing a decisive role in the accumulation of capital and power. This form of thought would become very skillful at capturing and exploiting society through the use of lies, cunning, and insincerity. To the best of our knowledge, the right and left frontal lobes of the human brain became functional in relation to the both types of intelligence. The lobe where analytical thinking occurs was the last to develop. All other parts of the body carry the traces of emotional intelligence. As analytical thought gained an edge it began to have an effect on emotional thought that bears the mark of the whole body. Gradually, this development increasingly reshaped the entire human character. Had the power of this analytical intelligence, an extraordinary development, been used positively, it could have turned the world into a place of constant celebration for humankind. But, used negatively, it made the world into hell for the overwhelming majority of people and all the other living beings. Analytical intelligence is like nuclear power—under strict control it may benefit society, but the destructive consequences of it getting out of control were witnessed in the Chernobyl nuclear power plant accident, which was not nearly as bad as the nuclear weapons used in war. I see a danger like that of an uncontrolled nuclear explosion in analytical intelligence.

It is not, however, simply a danger; I am convinced that the society and the environment are increasingly exposed to nuclear bombardment. Even without dropping an actual nuclear bomb, the world capitalist system with its arsenal of analytical intelligence bombs has already brought society and the environment to the brink of uninhabitability.

Obviously, symbolic language and analytical thought are not inherently negative, but they offer suitable conditions for the emergence of the negative. What really sets the chain of negativity in motion is the development of capital and power apparatuses. The capital and power accumulation system that we call civilization is necessarily deceitful, fraudulent, and lacking in emotional intelligence because of what it is at its core. Apparatuses of oppression and exploitation are built on the food and safety of others. It is only natural that these instruments and their actions meet with a reaction. Maintaining capital and power is only possible in one of two ways: either by achieving legitimacy using the soft power of ideology or by force of naked violence. It is a historical fact that control has generally been exercised in these two ways. Capital and power are phenomena that can only be expanded through the use of fraud, lies, and coercion. It is precisely at this point that the main part of the mind provides the necessary conditions. We could call this the distortion and deflection effect.

When we use this paradigm to look at the history of civilization, we see that the concentration of class, urbanization, and power gives rise to an extraordinary structure of analytical thought. There are several milestones in the development of civilization. The original civilizations, which emerged in the Sumerian and Egyptian societies of the fourth millennium BCE, built extraordinary structures of analytical thought that continue to enchant us today. All the intellectual frameworks developed throughout the history of the central civilization show traces of these two civilizations. Many examples of social activity that carries the imprint of civilization, from mathematics to biology, writing to philosophy, religion to the arts, can be seen in their original form in these two civilizations. During the Greco-Roman stage, civilization was further enriched and advanced by the forms of analytical intelligence that already existed within its structure. Analytical thought reached its peak during the European Renaissance, Reformation, and Enlightenment, which developed in the wake of the brief Islamic Renaissance.

Of course, in all these historical processes the contributions of other civilizations, especially the Chinese and Indian civilizations, should not be overlooked. The five-thousand-year-old civilization, by its logic, can be seen as the sum of the metaphysical forms that grew like a huge tumor detached from the dialectic of life. All developments that reflect the enormous scale of capital and power accumulation, in all structures from architecture to music to literature, from physics to sociology, from mythology to religion, from philosophy to science, are what is seen as history. Wars, these terrible exhibits of military plunder, are the foundation of this civilization. Reason that builds on this foundation is in reality nothing but the greatest unreason. A function of ideological hegemony is to conceal this unreason, this criminal reason, this bellicose reason, this deceitful and fraudulent reason—in short, the reason of the accumulation of capital and power—and to turn it upside down, to sanctify and deify it. If we carefully examine all the templates of analytical thought, forms of belief, and the arts that have developed over the course of the history of civilization, it will not be difficult to pinpoint evidence to the criticisms offered here.

Only in the light of these historical facts, can we make sense of how the capitalist monster (Hobbes's Leviathan) got out of its cage. I must strongly emphasize that more than the weaknesses of the sixteenth century were involved in this monster's escape.

I would like to conclude this section with an evaluation of the reality of women in relation to this issue. No doubt feminist movements have contributed significantly to uncovering women's reality. But I am convinced that feminist studies are mostly carried out in an environment where male reason rules. It is all highly reformist, and it is vital that this issue be approached radically, i.e., at its roots.

Biological research elucidates the position of women as the root of human species. It is not women but men who broke off from the trunk. Women's emotionality stems from the fact that they do not deviate to any great degree from the universal dialectic of becoming. That women have been kept at the lowest level, especially during the period of civilization, has contributed to maintaining the structure they find themselves in until today. Women's emotionally charged reason has always been presented as "inadequate" by male reason, and an effort is made to portray this "inadequacy" as essential to women's character. Male reason has conducted and continues to carry out a number of major operations on women.

The first of these operations was to make women the original house slave. This process involved terrible intimidation, oppression, rape, insults, and massacres. The role assigned to women was to reproduce the "offspring" required by the property-based system. Dynastic rule was very much bound to offspring. In this system, women were rendered absolute property. They were the property of and an honor for their owner to such a degree that they were not even allowed to show their faces to others.

Second, women were turned into sex objects. In all of nature, sexuality is related to reproduction. Its purpose is the continuation of life. Especially with the captivity of women, and most predominantly during the process of civilization, the main role given to men was sex and the distorted development and explosion of sexual desire. While the mating season for animals is quite limited (often once a year), men strive to extend it to a twenty-four-hour-a-day preoccupation in humans. Nowadays, women have been turned into an instrument of sex and sexual desire and a locus where the exercise of power is constantly tested on. The separation between homes, whether private or public (the brothel),[3] has become pointless, because every place is considered a home and brothel, and each woman a private and public woman.

Third, women have been reduced to unpaid and unreciprocated laborers. They are made to do all the heavy work. Their reward is being obliged to become a little more "inadequate." They have been humiliated so much that they have actually accepted their extreme "inadequacy" in comparison to men. They therefore wholeheartedly embrace the male hand and male domination.

Fourth, women have been turned into the most refined of commodities. Marx calls money "the queen of commodities."[4] In fact, under capitalism, it is women who play this role. In the capitalist system the real queen of commodities is the woman. There is not a single relationship in which women are not on offer nor an area where they are not used. One difference is that although every commodity has an accepted remuneration, the remuneration women receive consists of nothing more than complete disrespect, including that brazen lack of shame called "love" and the nonsense that a "mother's work can never be repaid."

Civilization has turned reason into a monster: the reason of a great many tricks, lies, the horror of war, and ideological distortion; in short, a reason that destroys society and the environment, an analytical reason that only makes hollow speeches. If men, who possess this reason, find the treatment of women, without whom they say they cannot live, acceptable, then what would they not do to human society or the environment!? Stopping this form of reason is only possible if, to begin with, the social morality and politics that it has destroyed regain their place. Better said; this must be the basis for a new beginning. The sheer scale of analytical reason and the role it plays in all this negativity is a further demonstration of the urgent need to build the system of democratic civilization.

Reason must be accorded its true value. Social reason is a fact. Society itself is the area where reason is concentrated. There is no point in feeling hopeless. There is another voice that flows from all that is holy and says, "I have given you reason, do not use it not for evil but for good. Then you will get everything you need." We should really hear and understand this voice. The voice of conscience, also called society's common sense, and the indispensable voice of morality say the same thing, as does the voice that wants to make the art of freedom—or social politics—heard and fulfill its promise. Democratic politics is the practical implementation of what this voice expresses. The system of democratic civilization is the theory of this voice.

In the following sections we want to look at the concrete sources of this voice (a voice born out of the collaboration of analytical and emotional intelligence) and illuminate the solutions it offers.

SIX

The Emergence of the Social Problem

Problematic moments in the dialectic of various natures are defined as the periods of a qualitative leap in quantitative accumulation. While theories of order and progress describe moments of transformation as very short intervals, chaos theories emphasize the centrality of the chaotic situation, with order and progress remaining limited moments. Thoughts about the continuity of the chaotic environment and ideas that advocate the continuity of progress have kept human reason busy. While there are those who think that human reason, like a mirror, would reflect reality, there are others who believe that the origin of all reason is to be found in humans.

It is not difficult to identify the universalist and relativist interpretations in these thoughts. To approach these issues more concretely, it is necessary to define and deal with the question of social reason. Therefore, my analysis up to this point—the groundwork providing a deeper understanding—is an introduction to the source of the social problem.

Throughout history, all important intellectual breakthroughs have emerged during one of two periods. When things are going well within the system, social prosperity is satisfactory, and there are no major problems, the result is intellectual development. The thought, which is progressive in nature, brings prosperity, does not give rise to significant problems, and tries to instill confidence in people, speaks of its permanence. It considers problems to be incidental and temporary. It mostly focuses on first nature and does not want to deal with social nature. The thought during other periods, when the system is overwhelmed, cannot carry on as it is, and is consumed with problems, is generally preoccupied with second

44

nature. It is during these periods that new religious and philosophical pursuits proliferate. The solution to problems is sought in new ideas, new religions, and new philosophical insights.

The intellectual flow during both prosperous and problematic periods, with their great intellectual leaps, can be observed in all civilizations. In the highly prosperous period of Sumerian society we witnessed a magnificent leap of mythological thought, which has influenced all major religions, philosophies, sciences, and schools of art. There are no major religions, philosophies, sciences, or schools of art that were not influenced by the emergence of Sumerian thought. Similarly, the intellectual leap attained in ancient Greece was also linked to a period of prosperity. The fertile land in Mesopotamia was at the heart of Sumerian prosperity, while in Greece it was the result of the fertile land on both shores of the Aegean. While the Sumerians developed a magnificent mythology, in Ionia, philosophical thought came to the fore. There were developments of a revolutionary magnitude in both science and the arts. A similar surge of prosperity in Europe led to a great intellectual leap that by sixteenth century had a worldwide impact.

It is noteworthy that the intellectual revolutions seen during all three periods of prosperity started with discussions of first nature. However, when prosperity slows and crises erupt, discussions about second nature begin to predominate, and new ideas fuel fresh exploration. Some thoughts long for the past, charged with the memory of previous prosperity and order, while the avant-garde complain about the disorder and the gravity of the crisis and produce utopian ideas. They talk abundantly of new social forms. The outcome of all this searching is the formation of numerous societies. Various social formations come into being, including religious and denominational communities, new emergent tribal clans, and even nations, as in the European example.

Approaching history as the history of thought brings us face to face with social problems, making it impossible not to actually sense the enormous dimensions of these problems in present-day society.

I am trying not to think in terms of Eurocentric social sciences. I am conscious of the need to think independently of the Western social sciences. Some may underestimate this approach and judge it to be a deviation from the social sciences, but that is of no consequence. The Eurocentric social sciences truly stink of domination. You either dominate or are dominated. What we need, however, is to be democratic subjects and share things justly. European social science is in essence liberalism, which is to say, it is an ideology. But it has hidden this reality so well that it has even had the power to assimilate the thinking of its greatest opponents, using its own outstanding eclecticism. I have no other option but to develop a distinct analytical approach if I don't want to fall victim to this eclecticism. My position, however, is not one of anti-Europeanism. Anti-Europeanism is also part of Eurocentric thought. I develop my position by discerning which of our values are universal, because Europe can be found in the East and the East in Europe. Many European values reflect the present and further developed state of our own values. More often than not, those who are most anti-European become the most backward proponents of European liberalism. The practice of real socialism and national liberation movements abound with examples.

Marx and Engels developed the concept of scientific socialism as a solution to the social problem of their time, and they truly believed in it. They believed that they had defined the problem correctly by conceptualizing capitalism as a system; so when it came to building the socialist system they were certain they would find a way—so much so that they believed the "scientific socialism" that they had developed guaranteed it. But history developed otherwise. Previous utopians had similar expectations, and Lenin hoped for different results from the Russian Revolution. Many French revolutionaries were also terribly disappointed. The revolution devoured many of its own children.[1] The depths of history overflow with similar examples. There is no question that those who wanted to solve the problem were fully committed and conscious of what they were doing. However, there was obviously something wrong and incomplete in their experience of defining and analyzing the social problem, given the huge deviations and contrary developments in practice. As has been frequently emphasized, the issue is not the lack of effort or of rebellion and war. These exist in abundance. For all of these reasons, I feel the definition and solution of the social problem must be approached with caution. If we know how to learn from experience and respect the memory of the great heroines and heroes, each step we take will certainly be rife with the lessons learned from them and charged with a deep respect.

Defining the Problem of Historical-Society

In the first two volumes of my defense, I focused on power in general and on the capitalist monopoly of power in particular. Although these books have many shortcomings, I believe I effectively demonstrated that the central civilization system constitutes a line. The important thing was to present the key links in its development. I identified the issues and analyzed the accumulations of power, including the cumulative accumulation of capital, in its successive development. When I was writing these two volumes, I had not yet read Andre Gunder Frank's *The World System*.[2] What I did, in fact, was a different recounting of the contents of this anthology, in which I was inclined to link the solution to a system—i.e., democratic civilization. Were I to write these books now, I could perhaps refine my argument, but, out of respect for history, it is more valuable to leave them as they are.

I will be addressing the social problem in a separate section. My aim is not to present a history of power and monopoly or to discuss the democratic solution. I am attempting to theoretically address the social problem in light of practical experience, as a contribution to solving the problem. It is not that I have not touched on this question until now. I have treated it in bits and pieces, but it would be more instructive to address it in an overall way.

The question of how to define the social problem is thought-provoking. Some currents of thought consider social poverty, while others think that not having a state is the social problem. Yet others think that military weakness is the key issue, or that it is the errors of political system, the economy, or moral degeneration that are central. Perhaps there is no single social arena that is not considered problematic. There may well be something in each of these points of views, but they don't reflect the essence of the problem. To me it makes more sense to present the trampling of the fundamental dynamics of society as the social problem.

I think *society deprived of being a society* is the fundamental problem. The first issue is the existence of values that determine a society and conceive and construct a social existence. I am referring to the aspect that we call existence itself. Second, I am referring to developments that do not allow this existence to be itself and destroy its basis. When these two things are intertwined, there is a major social problem. For example, if glaciation during the clan period eliminated all the clans, we cannot call this a social problem, because natural disasters occur beyond human will. To be considered a social problem, the problem must be created by the human hand. Even the ecological problem should be defined as a social problem when it is the result of human activity. Therefore, linking the fundamental social problem to the forces that unravel and destroy society at its very foundations will lead us to a correct definition.

I see the monopoly of capital and the monopoly of power to be at the forefront of these forces. Both are essentially forces that hollow out the foundations of society by usurping surplus value. From this point on, I will refer to these two monopolies simply as "the monopoly." Defining the problem-free, normal, and natural state of society will also shed more light on the issue and contribute to our ongoing evaluation. Regardless of the level and form of a community, if a society can freely shape its own moral structure and politics, then we can call it a normal or natural society. It is also possible to call it an open or democratic society. Because I will focus on my proposed solution in later sections, let me just briefly emphasize that I will not present the solution as either a fully liberal or fully socialist society, the nation-state society, the affluent society, or as a consumption-based, industrial, or service-oriented society, because any classification of society of this sort is largely speculative. These definitional categories don't have an equivalent in a real society. Calling them attributes related to society would be more accurate.

Therefore, depriving a society based on free politics and morality of these fundamental qualities can be regarded the beginning of the problem. Monopoly is the force that triggers the problem. Thus, we must also define the scope of the monopoly. A monopoly is formed when surplus value, whether accumulated privately or by the state, is amassed agriculturally, commercially, and industrially. Undoubtedly, the initial triad within the monopoly—priest + strongman + sheik—was hierarchical. They each benefited from the monopoly proportional to their power. This triadic monopoly would eventually splinter off into various institutions over the course of history. Each of these institutions would also split internally but would essentially be carried to the present by increasing their chain-like influence.

We should always keep in mind the cumulative and chain-like character of the historical flow of monopoly. The central civilization system is both the cause and the effect of the chain-like development of the monopoly—this must be emphasized. Today, modernity's way of thinking imposes a terrible time pressure and stifles everything into a compressed "now." But "now" is both history and the future. Modernity's massacre of history by imposing this way of thinking is not in vain; it is much easier to rule a society that is cut off from tradition however the ruler wishes. The history of monopoly is unique in that no other history had the opportunity of such an intense, chain-like, and expanding self-formation. While the monopoly creates its history in this way, it also finds it essential to render all communities in all societies history-less; or, put otherwise, their dissolution and colonization is of the utmost importance. To this end, it forms mythological, religious, philosophical, and scientific structures and makes an effort to undermine the morality of communities and render them incapable of politics.

While we often use monopoly as a concept, let's not forget that we use it in economic, military, political, ideological, and commercial contexts, because these groups share surplus value in one way or another. Whatever the form and the ratio, the essence of the division remains unchanged. Based on their importance at a given point, sometimes those responsible for economic efficiency will have a say in how surplus value is shared, while at other times it will be the military, the political class, the ideologues, or the merchant cliques. Wholesale concepts like class and state can blur reality. Monopoly plays a clearer role—it is the exploitative and oppressive enterprise. The class and state formation behind it are of derivative value; they are secondary births.

The construction of the city is the third of the monopoly births. The city raises its head as monopoly's oppression and exploitation headquarters. The city is intertwined with the temple to provide it with ideological legitimacy. And, so, the city, as historically eventuated, first and foremost, appeared as the nucleus of the temple, military headquarters, and living structures (palaces) of the bourgeoisie. (We can call all these exploitative *urban* circles bourgeois.) The surrounding masses play the role of domestic servants—as the second ring around the core of castles. They could even be called the slave class.

The fortresses and ramparts that are continuously encountered in history are the clearest evidence of the nature of monopoly's urban structure. The factors that give rise to the social problem are the city, class, and state structures that came into existence around monopoly's essence. In a sense, the history of civilizations is the expansion of this triad across time and space. The logic is simple: as opportunities for surplus value increase so do monopolies, leading to the construction of new city, class, and state structures. Simultaneously, these basic structures create very strict traditions. The city tales, state traditions, and dynastic histories are a never-ending topic of narration. Those who are clever and have oratorical talent provide the necessary daily ideological legitimacy as the army of ulema.[3] There is almost no room for new fairy tales or parables. From the construction of gods (city gods and war gods) to the creation of the devil and jinn, from portraits of heaven and hell to literary epics—there is no area where they have not invented something. The fear-inducing structures like the mausoleums, palaces, and temples, as well as the theaters and stadiums, constructed by surplus human labor, are like monopoly's show of power. Part of the monopolistic tradition is to eradicate whole peoples, tribes, cities, or villages with their entire population (excluding any captives who might prove useful) in horrifying wars. Besides, anything of economic value can already be found in monopoly's holy book as the plunder of holy war.

The type of civilization developed by the monopoly after the agricultural revolution, thus the derivative triad (city, class, and state), is relevant to our examination of the emergence of the social problem. The questions are: Was the transition from the Neolithic stage of society to civilization (i.e., the stages of development also called slave-owning, feudal, and capitalist society) unavoidable? Were there ways that Neolithic society could have made the leap to a higher stage without urbanization based on class and the state? If so, why didn't that happen? Although such questions address the hypothetical, they nonetheless touch upon important matters, which will be discussed in greater depth in the section dealing with the democratic civilization system. At this juncture, I will, nonetheless, briefly answer those questions as part of our examination of social nature. According to the prevailing paradigms of civilization, all developments were destiny and everything happened as it was meant to: according to destiny. Our fate has been realized. All metaphysical constructs are based on this idea.

The analysis of democratic civilization, however, makes for a different interpretation of civilization and its social forms and has a different approach to the continuation and transformation of Neolithic society. In short, social reality is not what Eurocentric social sciences claim it is. Interpretations that come closer to the truth are certainly possible. Society comes into being differently than we have been led to believe. Seeing the difference between the standard discourses and reality, as well as recognizing the link between these discourses and the dominant central civilization system, is of great importance. Many categorical evaluations that have been imposed as indisputable truth and presented on behalf of the social sciences are predominantly propaganda. They aim at concealing the truth. Many schools of social science—including those advanced by scientific socialism—have been heavily influenced by liberalism. These issues need to be clarified, at least to some degree, or the margin of error in any response will be relatively large.

Identifying social problems at their origin in this way will lead to a more realistic interpretation of their development. Instead of dividing them into basic categories, presenting them as key stages in a process is more instructive, because this addresses the problem in its totality.

The First Major Problematic Stage of the Monopoly of Civilization

The first major problematic stage of the monopoly of civilization can be placed between 3000 BCE and 500 CE. Monopoly is a large organization that extorts surplus value from society in different ways, depending on time and place. Beginning in 3000 BCE, the Sumerian, Egyptian, and Harappa societies attained extraordinary agricultural surplus product using a method of organization that could be called "pharaoh socialism." This is capital's first major model for accumulation. A much higher level of productivity was attained than had been the case in Neolithic society. This productivity gave rise to the city, class, and the state. The first major age of exploitation based on either violence or a trade monopoly began with the advent of the accumulation of surplus product that had already begun in Neolithic society. There can be no doubt that pharaoh socialism was based on the exploitation of subjects who were worked like a new type of animal in exchange for food. This was the first link in the chain of exploitation that has culminated in today's exploitation of the periphery by the center. Available documentation clearly shows all of these developments in Sumerian society.

Obviously, this mode of production and the seizure of surplus product led to severe problems—like a knife stabbed into the heart of society. Mythologies and religions abound with stories of such problems encountered in history. Among the available narratives are the Epic of Gilgamesh, the Genesis flood narrative, the legends of Adam and Eve and of Cain and Abel, the construct of heaven and hell, the clash between the god Enki and the goddess Inanna, and the conflict between shepherds and farmers. It is quite clear that these narratives are essentially meant to expose the ruthless stabs of the monopoly—i.e., the extortion of surplus product by seizing and working people like animals.

Of course, a complex language is used in the countless stories that deal with similar examples of horrific plunder and forced human labor. It is important to keep in mind that during this period, ideological domination was as effective as physical domination. If history was written in the language of the oppressed and plundered, we would inevitably encounter a very different past than the one presented to us.

Many millions of slaves worked to build the Egyptian pharaohs' pyramids. (These were the pharaohs' mausoleums. What must their palaces have been like?) These people were housed in congested stable-like structures and were not even fed as well as the animals. They were whipped, often to death, while they worked to build these terrible structures. While these animal slaves, treated as property, were being used and abused in this way, the monopoly's military wing mounted expeditions against other communities. They were not just satisfied with seizing goods and the land used by these communities but would take captive those seen as useful by the community and kill the rest. The magnificent castles, ramparts, mausoleums, arenas, palaces, and temples, which even today astonish the passersby, were built by these captives. If these millions of captives had not been forced to work in agriculture, which was further developed by the first irrigation canals, such a huge surplus product could not have been produced, just as these gigantic stone structures would never have been built. And, by extension, the heavenly life of the monopoly would not have been guaranteed.

To present this horrendous period differently, narratives (mythology, religion, philosophy, and various schools of the arts and science) with roots in the central civilization (stretching from the Sumerian hegemonic civilization of Mesopotamia to present-day US hegemonic civilization) and ideologies have been developed, alongside many equally grandiose superstructural institutions. Analytical reason, in particular, made the most progress. The priests, under the leadership of the monopoly, developed numerous responses, including mythological utopias and portraits of heaven and hell. If that was not sufficient, philosophical and scientific explanations, as well as knowledge and wisdom that would better explain the phenomena of nature, were developed. To rule with greater ease, the initial steps in developing writing, mathematics, astronomy, and biology were taken. The search for new medication to ensure the monopolistic strata's comfort resulted in the foundation of medical science. The most exciting part of the Epic of Gilgamesh is the search for the "Immortality Plant." Stone architecture developed techniques to build immortal structures for the immortals. When mythology proved inadequate, the era of more rigid and dogmatic religions was induced. To console the people who were condemned to a terrible life, images of gods that reflected the god-kings were created. Analytical reason probably presented its greatest masterpiece in the transition to monotheistic religions.

Not only did this result in the social problem, the problem was delivered in its most terrible form. The monopoly descended like a nightmare onto society's material and immaterial culture. Even at that early time, the Sumerian word *amargi* meant the "return to the sacred mother and nature." Degraded humanity could only crave for its past. To die as soon as possible in order to go to heaven reached the level of an ideology. The heavenly life that at times was imagined to have marked the Neolithic Age was being deferred to other worlds and had become the subject of utopias. Secular, worldly consciousness was replaced by a consciousness that focused solely on the afterlife. Faced with this terrible problem, the world lost its diverse richness and was seen as a place of torment.

Social morality and politics received their very first fatal blows at the hands of this monopoly problem. While the building blocks of communal society—morality and politics—were being smashed, a dominant morality (in fact, immorality) and politics (the divine state) specific to the narrow communities of the members of the monopoly held sway. It is perfectly clear that social morality and politics atrophied before they had a chance to develop. They were replaced by a divine order that consisted of the insane way of life of the rulers and their ideas of divinity. Society was only granted this right—the right to embrace these narratives as the holy belief.

The result was not just the creation of the social problem, but, worse, society was made to cease to be itself; it was being transformed into monopoly's "animal farm." Slavery and servitude came to be accepted as the natural regime. The enslavement of women, which has become the most far-reaching life problem, has roots dating back to this primitive hierarchical period. Regimes with dominant male gods were built, as if to take revenge on the Neolithic sacred mother society and matriarchal society. As traces of the goddesses gradually disappeared, the magnificent age of the domination of the male imaged gods began. Even at that time women found themselves forced into prostitution, both in the temple and in ordinary brothels, and were thus confined to "public homes and private homes."[4]

This fertile period, partially the result of the newly developed irrigation technologies, fell into severe crisis in late 2000 BCE. Both drought and soil salination played a role. It is only natural, however, that after a two-thousand-year hiatus, the effects of social practice would disintegrate their own founding principles. Harappa had already disintegrated and fallen silent, and internal contradictions were making Egyptian civilization increasingly unsustainable. The Sumerians, once the dominant ethnic group, had long since been replaced by other civilizations with different ethnic origins.

The central civilization system of this period made two significant attempts to solve the severe problems it caused. The first of these was outward expansion. The process of colonization and imperialism, something that will be frequently encountered later, offered a temporary solution to existing problems, but it could not avoid resulting in new problems. Problems were not solved; on the contrary, they became more prevalent and intensified. When the problems concentrated at the center, in the metropole, were exported, they multiplied and rebounded upon the center after a brief respite. This cycle appears often throughout history, with center and periphery constantly shifting.

In my view, the Sumerian metropole (center) exported itself in three cardinal directions, four if we include the sea. The product of its initial western expansion was the Egyptian Nile. It seems likely that Egypt first developed as a colony and continued to develop after independence. In the absence of external support, the development of a civilization in Egypt, in a geographically enclosed area, was an unlikely proposition. The fruit of the eastern Sumerian expansion was Harappa, on the shores of Sind. As with Egypt, without external support Harappa could only have been a miracle in the desert. It is reasonable to similarly explain the birth of the first kingdom in China around 1500 BCE. The center-periphery relationship is an essential feature of civilizational practice since the birth of civilization. Another important area of expansion to the east was the Elam civilization, today's Iran (with Susa as its capital, it was often referred to as Susiana), which neighbored Sumeria. The northward expansions, on the other hand, were carried by the Arian-Hurrians, the local communities of Upper Mesopotamia that had been the fundamental force behind the Neolithic Revolution, and Babel and Assyria, which were not far from the center.

The Sumerians, Akkadians (an ethnic group with Semitic roots), Babylonians, and Assyrians continuously tried to colonize the Hurrians. Perhaps the very first and greatest resistance in history was that of the

Hurrians against the forces of this original central civilization. This process of resistance can be seen in the Sumerian tablets. Even the Epic of Gilgamesh clearly explains how this first expedition targeted the northern forests. Contemporary Iraq (Uruk), still a boiling cauldron, dramatically mirrors the continuation of this reality and tradition. The conflict between the Kurds with Hurrian roots and the Arabs with Semitic roots arguably still bears these ancient characteristics. The only thing that has changed is the nature of the center and the periphery, who holds hegemonic power, and the different technologies available.

The Hurrians are the original tribes of the Fertile Crescent. They could resist and develop their own civilization, because they had been profoundly influenced by the agricultural revolution. Numerous archeological discoveries provide insight into the establishment of the first Hurrian urban centers around 3000 BCE, independent of any Sumerian center. The megaliths found near the city of Urfa (Göbekli Tepe, 10000–8000 BCE), which predate the Neolithic Revolution, are particularly important evidence of this region's civilizational roots, which have had ongoing repercussions in the world of science. I think that the Sumerians were colonies with Hurrian roots that first settled in Lower Mesopotamia. Thus, it is understandable that both the Hittites and the Mitannis, with their Hurrian roots, established empires in Central Anatolia and the southeast of present-day Turkey after 1600 BCE.[5] Other civilizations may also have developed in these areas. Analysis of Göbekli Tepe ruins might provide us with a different view of civilization. The expansion of the Sumerians via the sea (Persian Gulf) led to civilization colonies in what are today Oman, Yemen, and even Abyssinia (Ethiopia). A city as big as Harappa has been discovered in Oman.

The Babylonians and Assyrians developed a second method for overcoming the crisis. The Babylonians developed industry and science, while the Assyrians established a trade monopoly in a continuous effort to expand Sumerian civilization, while simultaneously attempting to resolve the serious problems it faced. In terms of science and industry, Babel was the true London, Paris, Amsterdam, and Venice of its time. In fact, during its ascension it was even more famous than today's New York. It was no accident that Alexander drew his last breath in a waning Babel. It could even be argued that Saddam was the last tragic victim of the love for Babel, alongside thousands of others who cannot be enumerated here.

When I try to unravel Assyria's trade monopoly, the trade monopolies of Venice, Netherlands, and England spring to mind. The Assyrian trade monopoly, along with the Phoenician monopoly, was perhaps the most enterprising and creative in history. It is undisputed that the Assyrians developed trading networks—the famous *karums*, places of profit, *kârhaneler*—from Central Asia (even, it is claimed, reaching China) to Western Anatolia, from Arabia to the shores of Black Sea.[6] There is no question that they founded the first major trading empire. This trading octopus can be divided into three periods: 2000 BCE–1600 BCE, 1600 BCE–1300 BCE, and, finally, 1300 BCE–600 BCE. In this sense, it is unparalleled. Nonetheless, apart from a limited capacity to expand and strengthen the central Sumerian civilization, trade offers little else of analytical value for an overall solution of problems. Moreover, the trade monopoly has always been a collaborator of the main monopoly—the priest + the soldier + the ruler. Disagreements among them never goes beyond struggles over higher profit shares. Yet the fact that Assyria was a vehicle for the Sumerian central civilization for 1,500 years should not be underestimated. It is one of the strongest links in the chain of civilization.

Harrappa, Oman, Hittite, Mitanni, and Egypt easily fell into internal decay, because they were unable to achieve a similar success. It is undeniable that the most decisive role in the uninterrupted reign of central civilization was played by the Phoenicians, the Medes-Persians, and the late Hittites, as well as the Assyrians, who influenced Greek civilization through trading contact. The trade monopoly did not solve the existing problems, but, by spreading products that aid development (including ideas and beliefs) everywhere, it facilitated the ongoing growth and survival of the civilization for a while longer. Otherwise, it would have inevitably shared the fate of Harappa. History may have repeated itself for several thousand years, but let's not forget that the trade monopoly is the cruelest form of capital accumulation monopoly, whose political representatives never hesitated to engage in the most brutal of practices, e.g., castles and ramparts built from human skulls. Moreover, it is well-known that trade monopolies use price differences and differences in the production costs of goods to attain significant profit with minimal labor.

Here, we are not talking about small commodity exchanges or trade for nonprofit purposes or consumption. We are talking about monopolistic profit-driven trade. It is very likely that Harappa collapsed because it was unable to expand outward and develop trade. The New Kingdom of Egypt (1600–1000 BCE), which failed to develop the skills necessary to establish a trade monopoly and open up to the outside world, withered away under the dual impact of internal struggles and external attacks. Our world might have been different had the New Kingdom of Egypt expanded as much as Sumer. China, on the other hand, did not see the need to overflow its borders, perhaps because it was already large enough. Clearly, the boom of the first central civilization reached another stage by spreading the grave problems it caused across the world.

There are intellectuals who postulate that for the first time in history the Anatolian, Mesopotamian, and Egyptian civilizations acquired a central and hegemonic character primarily by becoming intertwined between 1600 and 1200 BCE. Although it is not called a golden age, it is clear that there was a great leap in urbanization, trade, and the development of an aristocracy. Evidently, the spread of the problem has contributed to the frequent shift in the location of the central hegemony and prolonged the life of the system. The famous Treaty of Kadesh (an Egyptian-Hittite peace treaty concluded around 1280 BCE) reflects the reality of this period.[7]

The crisis of the central civilization from 1200 to 800 BCE eased as iron working techniques superseded bronze technology (3000–1000 BCE). While the developments in production and war techniques always contribute to any era's uniqueness, social development is undoubtedly the decisive factor, but this social development is closely linked to technology. The hegemonic center moved outside Mesopotamia for the first time, taking the initial steps in the shift to the West and toward Europe. In this shift, the Median-Persian Empire (600–330 BCE) by land and the Phoenicians (1200–330 BCE) by sea would constitute the transitional phase. The Urartu (850–600 BCE) would later play a similar role. Social crisis, although not completely overcome, was alleviated by iron technology and widespread secure trade routes sustaining civilization. The Median-Persian Empire (hegemony) initiated important trade offensives via the land and the Phoenicians via the Mediterranean Sea. The Greeks were a colony of these two civilizations for a long time. Western-centric history considers the Greek-Ionian civilization to be original, but more realistic research shows that this civilization acquired most of its features from the expansion of these two civilizations. When we add Egyptian, Babylonian, and Cretan influence to the Median-Persian and Phoenician influences, then it becomes undeniable that the famous Greek civilization is largely an imported product.

No doubt the Greek-Ionian synthesis cannot be underestimated, but it is clearly not original. In fact, none of the civilizations are original. They are all based on gathering Neolithic society's values, either by extortion or through trade monopoly, and often both. Alterations of these values may have led to new syntheses, but, as Gordon Childe points out, only the developments in Europe from the sixteenth century onward are comparable to Neolithic society's technological innovations in the Taurus and Zagros arc in 6000–4000 BCE. The construction of the central civilization began around this technology with the rise of the city of Uruk from 4000 BCE onward. The most fundamental factor in the conflict between the goddess Inanna and the god Enki is the *mes* (the Neolithic technology organized around women, with *me* meaning *technical invention*) that Enki stole from Inanna. Here the relationship between male supremacy, which develops parallel to civilization, and the control of technology is emphasized. This example alone indicates the great educational value of Sumerian mythology. Of course, the language of those days isn't that of today; it was charged with mythology.

The Greek-Ionian civilization (600–300 BCE), rising on both shores of the Aegean, was undoubtedly an important link in the historical chain. It marked a great breakthrough in social development, making significant contributions, both in terms of the mindset and in technical and practical areas. It also greatly improved upon the legacy of the Phoenicians in maritime transportation. It formed colonies all along the shores of Europe. By developing the technique of writing, again influenced by the Phoenician legacy, Greek-Ionian civilization made an important contribution to today's alphabet. In fact, it was responsible for revolutionary developments in all of the known sciences of the day, as well as a total revolution in philosophy. It put an end to the era of Sumerian gods with Olympian gods, while the works of Homer carried the tradition of the Gilgamesh Epic to its peak. There were similar revolutionary developments in theater, music, and architecture, with magnificent cities built. Building techniques for temples, palaces, theaters, stadiums, and assembly halls from that period continue to reverberate today. And neither the leap forward in production and trade nor the progress in industry should be downplayed. Historic examples of democracy were introduced in the political realm that proved the superiority of democracy over other forms of governance, even if within the framework of civilization. All of the above does not, however, change the fact that Greek-Ionian civilization is a link in the central civilization system that began with the Sumerians—it confirms it.

When we consider the role that Greek civilization played in solving the social problem, or, better, its part in the development of the problem, it becomes clear that there is no essential difference between this civilization and the ones that preceded it. All progress made, in particular by Athenian democracy, indicates that the problems of central civilization were aggravated—not solved. A few examples follow.

Women's captivity deepened. They were not only obliged to produce children and serve men at home like the lowest of slaves, they were banned from participating in politics, sports, science, or administration. They were obliged to do all the difficult production work. Plato was of the opinion that living with a woman demeaned a man's nobility, one of the reasons for the widespread homosexual relationships at that time. Slavery in general, not only women's, also expanded immensely during this period. For the first time, there was a large number of unemployed slaves. This was also when the military institution of mercenaries first arose. Not only goods but also slaves were widely exported. In contrast, the most parasitic class of masters sprung up, and the concept of an aristocracy came into being. The social sphere was overrun with parasitic elements. The segments of society closest to the bourgeois class were the product of the Greek civilization. In short, new problems were added to the already existing problems, and existing problems were aggravated.

Urban development attained magnificence and the city an organic structure, but these developments were achieved at the expense of further aggravating the social problem. It is almost as if the structures of ziggurats and pyramids were pulled to pieces only to be replicated in much greater dimension. The first phase of the city was the temple and its appendages, the second phase was the construction of the citadel and the surrounding inner and outer ramparts in its foothills, and in the third phase these divisions were removed, and, with new additions, the city attained the spatial richness and splendor. All of this ran parallel to the growth of monopoly. These developments didn't solve the problems but, once again, amplified them. The army of slaves exploded, and the number of unemployed slaves grew for the first time, as people found themselves redundant. This is as severe as a social problem can get. A system that produces unemployment is the cruelest of systems.

A similar growth can be observed in power and the state apparatuses. Power spread to occupy not only the upper floors of society but the lower floors as well. The state's domination of the society grew as it gained a stranglehold on the political sphere. A state bureaucracy was formed, and the military class reinforced its privilege. In general, a rise in power over women, children and youth, slaves, peasants, and craftspeople was palpable in the social fabric. The worst thing about Athenian democracy was the way the state blatantly hollowed out politics. The communal democratic tradition seems to have drawn its last breath with the help of the Athenian aristocracy, and this is surely the most important lesson to be learned from Athenian democracy.

The monopoly of Roman civilization (750 BCE–500 CE) is a continuation of the Greek-Ionian tradition and should be evaluated within that framework. It is an example of the transfer of civilization from one peninsula to another. The most important thing to be said at this point is that if the Greeks were this civilization's period of childhood and youth, Rome was its maturity and old age. What had been taken from the East was assimilated and synthesized by Rome in a way that gave this civilization an edge over the East for the first time. Another of Rome's successes was integrating parts of Europe into civilization through brutal occupation and colonization. In all other ways, Rome was little more than an overgrowth of the Greek touchstone. Nonetheless, class and power evolved to a fantastic degree in the city, and the kingdom was transformed into an aristocratic republic, laying the base for the most powerful and extensive empire in history. As the Roman way of life became fashionable everywhere, the Roman aristocracy, like the bourgeoisie of today's modernity, was the decisive power of the modernity of the time. Parasitic aristocracy and a lumpenproletariat were stark reminders of Rome's raging problems.

It can be said that the social problem reached its peak during the Roman period. Little wonder. There is a direct link between the cumulative growth of the central civilization's monopoly and the growth of the inherent problem caused by it. Despite the terrible punishments (crucifixion, being torn apart by lions, cities, including Carthage, razed),[8] the internal conquest of society by Christianity, the political party of the poor, and the flow of the barbarian clans from the outside into Rome meant an explosion of problems—in essence, an outburst of the spirit of freedom. It is clear that the true barbarian was Rome, and that its collapse was caused by the enormous and ever-growing internal and external social problems. The collapse of Rome marked not only the end of the Roman city, Roman power, and the Roman aristocracy but the decline of the civilization that had its roots in the emergence of the city of Uruk, with its characteristic structure of center-periphery, competition-hegemony, and rise-fall—indeed, it was the collapse of the world system itself. Thus, the most savage period in history came to a close as a result of the problems caused by this anti-society system and the internal and external resistance that developed against it.

From Rome to Amsterdam

The distinctive feature of the period from 500 to 1500 CE is the rise of the Abrahamic religions. They emerged with a message meant to solve the existing problems and left their mark on this period. It is necessary to elaborate on the role of the Abrahamic religions, because, although they hoped to offer a solution, in the end, they created additional social problems.

The social message of the Abrahamic religions suggests that the problematic material structure of the central civilization system was transformed into a problematic immaterial structure. In other words, the problems of the material culture echoed in the problems of the immaterial culture. The holy books clearly state that the prophet Abraham fled or emigrated from the tyranny of Nimrod, the Babylonian representative in Urfa, and the increasing problems that tyranny gave rise to. His survival and escape from being burned is presented as a miracle of divine origin.[9] The fact that he was searching for a new god is also presented as a clear sign. We could interpret the search for God as a search for a new regime. The narrative also presents many other features of the severely problematic structure of that period. Abraham's hegira is estimated to have occurred around 1700 BCE. This hegira takes Abraham from a civilization with Mesopotamian roots to one with Egyptian roots. This suggests that passage between the two civilizations was possible. It may be that Abraham was looking for sanctuary and a new ally. His life in Canaan (present-day Palestine and Israel) confirms this thesis. He and his family left a small tribe and formed a new one in Canaan. His grandson Joseph was sold into slavery in Egypt, where his talents saw him rise to the position of vizier in the pharaoh's palace. It is worth noting that women played an important role in palace life and in his rise. In Hebrew history, women always played important roles.

A Hebrew tribe was also formed in Egypt but lived in semi-slavery. Tribe members suffered greatly by this. Nimrod was replaced by the pharaoh, whom he, for his part, had hoped to get rid of. It was at this point, around 1300 BCE, that Moses led the hegira. The narrative of this journey and its many miracles is recounted in the Holy Scripture. It is similar to Abraham's story, with a return to Canaan. Compared to Egypt, Canaan was a sort of "promised land." The God they sought on Mount Sinai called out to the tribe more clearly with the Ten Commandments, effectively the principles of organization and the political program of the tribe, gained from lengthy experience. The tribe firmly abandoned the religions of Nimrod and the pharaoh and established its own ethnic religion (worldview and program). The story of the later periods is presented in a divine voice at length in the Holy Scripture, not as mythological stories, as was the case in Sumer and Egypt, but as religious rules understood as absolute truth (orthodoxy).

This is a major revolution in the history of religion and a great intellectual revolution in its time. Research shows that the Hebrew tradition is one of the Middle East's most sophisticated sources of memory. I believe that the Hebrews transformed the essence of Sumerian and Egyptian mythology into a form of religious discourse (rhetoric). Throughout the historical process, the Bible was continuously developed with additions drawn from Zoroastrianism and from Babylonian (especially during the exile of 596 BCE), Phoenician, Hurrian, and Greek sources. Let's not forget that the Bible was first assembled between 700 and 600 BCE, and there are no earlier written sections.

It bears saying that throughout history, the Jewish people have not only accumulated capital and money but also most impressively ideology, science, and knowledge. They transformed their numerical inferiority into worldwide strength with the help of these two strategic accumulations. The Jewish ethnic group (initially as a tribe, nowadays as a nation) has been able to hold on to a relatively superior level of life at the margins and in strategic positions of power—not only today but throughout time—because of these two accumulations. But the catastrophes and the terrible problems they faced were also closely related to this. When analyzing history and present developments, if we proceed methodologically from the presumption that capital and knowledge equal might and power, and that power equals monopoly over capital and knowledge, then the social problem can be understood more clearly and realistically. Here I will confine myself to a brief examination of how the Abrahamic religions caused even more complex historical and social problems, as I will examine their role in solving these enormous problems in greater detail in the section titled "Envisaging a Democratic Civilization System."

The Old Testament presents the post-Moses period in the form of leaders, priests (Levites), prophet-rulers, prophets, and writers. It is possible to add to this intellectuals, scholars, and other similar categories for later periods. It seems that all the wisdom (priestly innovations) originating in Sumerian and Egyptian mythologies were treated as prophetic in the Old Testament. The main task of the prophets was to solve the unprecedented social problem created by a civilization based on monopoly. If we bear in mind that surplus product and capital accumulation were procured through forced labor on the basis of enslavement and by military means, what lies behind the enormous accumulation of problems becomes clearer. Prophecy reflects the impact of this reality on the social sectors experiencing severe problems. Grasping its institutional character in this manner opens the way to a better understanding of history.

We observe that Moses's ideological and political program gave birth to a small state around 1000 BCE, approximately three hundred years after his death, under the reign of the prophets Saul, David, and Solomon. The solution they found to the severe social problem they faced after all of these struggles was to develop a state apparatus and rule of their own. It is clear that this state was not as democratic as the Athenian state, was a lot weaker, and had fewer options to offer than the Egyptian and Babylonian-Assyrian traditions in which the Hebrew tribe had lived for such a long time. Given this, why was the Abrahamic tradition so state-focused? Because the state was the invention of the prophet, and his followers were provided the lands in Canaan as the "promised land."

The first Jewish state quickly collapsed as a result of familiar power struggles and occupation (i.e., the power struggle between the sons and grandsons of David and Solomon and Assyrian threats and occupation). It is comparable to the Israel founded in the same place three thousand years later. However, we should pay attention to this prophetic construct, which, with the help of ideological and monetary capital, exerted great influence on the powers of central civilization throughout history.

The prophet Jesus's tradition is the second most important Abrahamic religion. Its message advances a solution to the entangled problems resulting from the destructiveness of the occupying Roman forces. Jesus is called the Christ, the Messiah (the Redeemer). It is befitting that this movement, which initiated the Gregorian calendar, has been described as the first ecumenical (universal) party of Rome's lumpenproletariat and poor. It is far from the militant character of the Mosaic movement. It can be said to have grown out of the lower segments of the Hebrew tribe and to be the product of the circumstances (objective conditions) in which tribal organization lost its ability to resolve problems, while the emergence of classes, urbanization, and attaining power had eroded communal values. This is the basis for its universal and class character. At the time, there was an acceleration in the dissolution of many other tribes and peoples in the Eastern Mediterranean. The Greek, Assyrian-Babylonian, and, finally, Roman colonial movements exposed the unemployed and poor masses who had broken away from their tribes to hunger and homelessness, creating an intense search for a master and a messiah. It is clear that Jesus's movement is the collective expression of that search. In fact, he calls himself the "Message," and the Old Testament is renewed as the New Testament (the Bible). The civilizational culture and language at the time were Assyrian-Aramaic, Babylonian-Chaldean, Greek-Hellenic, and Jewish-Hebrew. Roman-Latin was a recent arrival. It is said that Jesus spoke Aramaic, while Hellenic became quite widespread in the region during the Hellenic era. Aramaic had been the language of trade and culture in the region for around a thousand years. Hellenic would later attain that status. Hebrew, on the other hand, as far as we know, was the language of the sacred text, with Latin finding its place more generally as the new language of ruling.

No traces of Arabic had yet been encountered. Arabic was widely used among the dessert tribes, becoming a civilizational language with the urbanization on the Arabian Peninsula. Arabic was to conquer the region only with the onset of the Islamic revolution. Although traces of Persian dialects can be found, their advanced forms are only encountered within the Taurus and Zagros Mountain systems and in the Persian-Sasanian civilization centers. Furthermore, numerous languages and cultures, especially Sumerian and Coptic (Egypt), were vitiated and eliminated by the influence of the central civilization. Armenian was also becoming an influential language in the region.

The conflict between the two hegemonic powers over the region, with one identifying its origins in the East and the other in the West, continued at full speed: the Iranian and Caucasian–centered Sasanian Empire and the Italian and Roman–centered empire. The Mesopotamian-centered civilization, which shifted out of the region for the first time following its establishment three thousand years earlier, continued the legacy shared by these two great hegemonic civilizations. The extremely violent wars between them were in essence about the legacy of Mesopotamian civilization. Perhaps history's most constant and intense hegemonic struggle was experienced in this period. Alexander's attacks and the resulting situation can be interpreted as the first round of this battle, but it would still be a long time before the center of civilization shifted to the West. Nonetheless, it was clear that the first steps in this direction had been taken.

We can also see that Greek philosophy within the Roman Empire and the Zoroastrian doctrine (more secular and moral) within the Persian-Sasanian Empire did not solve the problems stemming from both civilization monopolies. The war between the two was in fact a reflection of this deadlock. The limited potential surplus value makes the war between the monopolies—the most popular method of accumulation—grow in number and quality. War, in essence, has been the historical means to accumulate capital and power in civilization. It has nothing to do with the stories of legendary heroes. That is the propaganda aspect. The most meaningful description is clearly that wars, including those today, are, in the final analysis, the means by which capital and power change hands. Therefore, when reading history, we need to always keep in mind that wars take place and play a role at the center of the most fundamental forces of production and their relations. In comparison, defensive wars aim to protect the land and other forces of production and their relations and freedom—in a nutshell, the identity of society—and, to this end, its moral and political structure and its democracy, if it exists. Defensive wars owe their legitimacy to this fact.

Monopoly wars are often seen as the engine in the history of civilization. This is correct insofar as war has resulted in technological advances and organizational and operational innovations. However, we must not forget that wars are essentially the most antisocial, even the most unnatural, phenomena and beyond brutality. Yet they have their origins in society, since they act as a means for monopolization. In order for the society to cease being a society, they suck up these resources.

The phrase *turning the other cheek* attributed to the prophet Jesus no doubt expresses the search for great peace. It is clear that wars mean a loss of production, while peace means a substantial increase in production. Peace played a major role in Christ's movement, because it was clear that the massive unemployment and poverty at that time stemmed from the endless wars. This movement would retain this quality for three hundred years, infiltrating everywhere the Romans and Sasanians went, and reverberating as far away as China and India. The Manichaean movement, similar in nature but primarily Sasanian-based, appeared during the same period and also deserves attention. The Prophet Mani said, "I will personally go all the way to Rome and make peace with the Sasanians possible." If the Manichaean movement, a doctrine that combines aspects of Christianity and Zoroastrianism with a number of deeper qualities, had not been crushed by the tyrannical Sasanian rulers it would perhaps have led to a new Renaissance in the Middle East.

Christianity (it may be more fitting to speak of one denomination among a number claiming the name) became an official religion during the construction of Constantinople (İstanbul), and from that date (325 CE) onward rapidly became the official ideology throughout Eastern and Western Rome. While our subject is not the history of Christianity, the relationship of Christianity to the social problem and power monopolies is an aspect of our subject. Just as the original Mosaic movement ended in a state, its renewed version, Christ's movement (at least the majority tendency) also ended in power and the state. This movement not only became the official ideology of Byzantium, it became a powerful state in Rome by around 1000 CE. It indeed became much more than that; it came to be the sum of thousands of extensive and powerful society-based apparatuses of power, perhaps best referred to, both in symbolic and official terms, as the state.

For our purposes the internal strife within Christianity, conflicts between the Catholics and Orthodox and the rise of other famous denominations, are only important for indicating how problematic Christianity had become. While Christianity aimed to be a religion of peace, it became so militarist that it even adopted burning people at the stake, which shows us how deeply the essence of the central civilization runs. How else are we to explain the fact that Christianity has been the source of more wars than the war ideologies of mythological origin? The crusades against Islam in the East, the suppression of tribal religions and witches in Europe, later internal denominational fighting, and its role in colonial warfare in the Americas, Africa, Australia, and Eastern Asia led Christianity to completely stray from its aim. Assyrians, Armenians, Chaldeans, and Anatolian Hellenes, who were the earliest peoples to accept Christianity, clung to this religion, because they thought it would be a remedy for the profound social problems they faced, but they too fell victim to the religion's ultimate ties to the central civilization. Christianity, which they interpreted as some sort of nationalism, rapidly brought them face to face with the power monopolies of other peoples. While Western Christianity achieved power at the cost of its essential message, Eastern and Anatolian Christianity were crushed by forces that put on the masks of both Judaism—the initial Abrahamic tradition—and Islam—its third version, and then were totally wiped out by other nationalisms (Arab, Turkish, Kurdish). Here we are confronted with striking examples of how the social problem is augmented.

I must repeat my thesis: the Abrahamic tradition, inter alia Christianity, represents the immaterial culture that reflects the material culture of the central civilization. More precisely, it aims to solve the grave social problem that this material culture, namely, monopoly, has caused, just as real socialism (scientific socialism) sought to solve the problem originating in capitalism. But because the science and ways of life they developed to do so did not in fact subvert the relevant patterns of the era and of modernity, they could not escape becoming a new version of the central civilization—i.e., either a new hegemon or a dependent weaker power. Those who insist on remaining radical and sincere in their assertions cannot avoid being eliminated, although they will leave behind an important legacy. For this reason, I always compare the Abrahamic tradition to the social democratic movement of our time. Just as social democracy didn't go beyond patching up the grave problems caused by capitalist civilization, Abrahamic religions that played a more universal role over a long historical period were also content with some reforms, which were treated as the solution to problems caused by the central civilization that left masses unemployed, suffering, and hungry. In the final analysis, they were also unable to escape becoming a problem. The Abrahamic tradition, as an ideological and political program, is worthy of careful analysis, an analysis that is essential if we are to understand the capitalist world system in its entirety. These analytical efforts are of great value, both in connecting Immanuel Wallerstein's world-system to the five-thousand-year-old central civilization system and for understanding how real socialism collapsed from within.

When we analyze Islam, which is the third important Abrahamic religion, we can see the essence of this tradition more clearly. Islam represents a more proficient ideological and political orientation. When I look at the reality of the Prophet Mohammad, I always see him as the greatest representative of the last generation of the Sumerian priests who constructed the first great divine concepts. Behind the Sumerian priests, who constructed gods based on mythological concepts, are the most advanced religious and mythological traditions of that period. We need to keep in mind that the Prophet Mohammad internalized—albeit in a limited way—the religious, mythological, and even philosophical and scientific knowledge that was available in his own time and place. Just as he knew about the tribal systems, he got to know the civilization from the reflections of the two global hegemonic powers, the Byzantine and Sasanian Empires. Mohammad diagnosed the grave problems both systems inflicted on society. In addition to the corrupting effects of Arab tribalism, he experienced firsthand the oppressive and exploitative structure of Byzantine and Sasanian power monopolies that blocked society's development and dismantled it. It is thus understandable that he sought a radical break with both systems. Like Jesus, he was closer to the lower social strata. He did not hesitate to sympathize with both slaves and women. Although he was influenced by the Mosaic and Assyrian priests, he was also a witness to their inability to solve the problems within their societies. He considered the pagan religions (the idols in Mecca) to be outdated traditions that had long ago run their course. The message of the "last prophet" of the Abrahamic tradition was one of the things that most attracted his attention. Under these circumstances, he did the best he could by daring to make the third major reform (which could also be called a revolution) in the Abrahamic tradition.

The position taken by Marx and Engels on the utopians and Mohammad's position regarding the Mosaics, Christians, and even the Sabians (a group that also believed in one god) are similar. While Marx and Engels drew a distinction between genuine socialism and utopian socialism, Mohammad updated the outdated Abrahamic traditions in the form of a new truth. In other words, he provided a more realistic religious interpretation. The Koran and the hadiths are there; they emphatically preach not only an ideological and political program but also a new morality. They also have their own economic principles. Mohammad even restructured the rules of war. I will analyze his method, which can be called "the prophet's way," more comprehensively in the section that deals with science. For now, I will make do by saying that it is a good tradition.

It could easily be argued that Islam, which has more advanced views than original Christianity and Judaism, is civilizational. Within ten years of its emergence, it had succeeded in becoming the heir to all of the previous civilizations in the Middle East. Islam was able to establish the most powerful hegemonic ruling system in the region in 650 CE. Although the point here is not to address this particular history, we will continue to examine it in relation to social problems in the region, as well as in the world overall (because it presents itself to the world as the "good news").

We can be certain that the Prophet Mohammad's understanding of Allah is a social abstraction of the highest order and an expression of social identity. I think Islamic theologians have been very lazy in this regard and are unworthy of Mohammad. The richness and evolution of theology in Christianity has almost been suspended in Islam. I won't go into this any further here, as I will be returning to it later. It is nonetheless important to understand why Mohammad focused so heavily on the concept of Allah and charged it with such an enormous degree of sacredness. As I see it, Mohammad was not addressing a theoretical discussion about the existence of Allah but rather dealt with the social essence of Allah. He poured a lot of energy into this, which is reflected in his exhaustion and fainting when delivering the hadiths. This should be taken seriously. Allah, referred to with ninety-nine names, represents a more comprehensive social utopia and program than the most advanced social utopia, and, in this regard, Mohammad is both realistic and responsible in his deference. The misfortune was not only the ignorance of those after Mohammad, but also that they were rapidly taken by a lust for power.

Islam, as a revolution, is perhaps one of the most betrayed revolutions in this regard. Aside from not implementing the Prophet Mohammad's perspective, program, and way of life, the leaders after him, including the caliphs, failed to understand them and betrayed them in what they did implement. We cannot predict how well the Prophet Ali might have implemented the Prophet Mohammad's ideas, as he was unable to conclude his efforts. The interpretations and praxis of all denominations, especially Sunnism, are far removed from Mohammad's teachings. To put it baldly, the sultanate traditions that began with the Ummayads are nothing more than power monopolies that are much worse than the ones that preceded them.[10] I am sure that radical Islam is a disease of power that, far from reviving Islam, does it undeserved harm. It is most befitting to refer to these ignorant Islamists as provocative Islam.[11] If there is a message that can be taken from Islam, it would only make sense under a different name and in a different form. I leave further thoughts on this topic for later.

I attach importance to the real monopoly of power in the name of Islam but not as Islam, because Islam ceases to exist in this monopoly of power. It is nothing more than state symbols and rulers that follow in the footsteps of the Assyrian, Persian, Roman, and Byzantine lineages. I say this in relation to Islam as power. As an element of immaterial culture, there are, of course, areas where it is influential. I should emphasize that I do not see the utility of naming societies after ideologies. For example, calling a society Christian, Islamic, or Hindu reduces society to religion and leads to numerous inadequacies and errors. These concepts prevent an understanding of the actual nature of society. The same applies to concepts such as capitalist and socialist society. I will return to this topic at a more appropriate point. The most befitting and meaningful concepts would be democratic civilization society and monopolistic civilization society, because that makes the whole of society visible.

The central civilization systems had hegemony in the Middle East, which was by and large under Islamic rule from the fifth to the fifteenth centuries. Islamic rulers further expanded upon and further entrenched the power they inherited from the Byzantines and Sasanians, and society was being ruled in an unprecedented way. There was an increase in the number of big tribes, dynasties, and states controlled by these rulers. As a result, there was no decrease in the pace of wars for power; in fact, the increase continued. The military monopoly held the real power, but there were also developments in the trade monopoly. Islam is predominantly an ideology of military and trade monopolies. Cities grew, while developments in agriculture and industry were much more limited, as was also the case in the arts—it certainly failed to surpass what was achieved by the Greeks.

The period of Islamic rulers and Islamic states marks the end of the Middle East's hegemonic power. By the end of fifteenth century, the hegemonic core of the central civilization had shifted from Venice to Western Europe, and from there to Amsterdam and London. The Middle East was the Neolithic center between 10,000 and 3000 BCE and was the central civilization for 4500 years, from 3000 BCE to 1500 CE. Thereafter, under the weight of the enormous problems of civilization, the Middle East was worn out, had exhausted itself in attempts at self-renewal, and became, so to speak, a social wreck.

When we evaluate the role of the Abrahamic tradition within the central civilization system in terms of problems, we see that it was unable to limit power; on the contrary, it further amplified it. States increased in numbers and grew in size. Therefore, the problems arising from monopoly of power and the state multiplied, and war continued to be the far preferred means for securing monopoly. Concepts of democracy and the republic were unknown. For the most part, traditional rule by a dynasty persevered and became more common.

Second, the society grew weaker, while power and the state became stronger. The area of social morality and politics narrowed considerably, with denominations developing largely in response to this. Male dominance over women and youth grew apace. While the forms of slavery associated with pharaonic power disappeared, new forms of slavery (especially of Africans and northern Slavic people) became commonplace. The city and commerce grew but continued to lag behind their former glory and never reached the level seen in the Greco-Roman city or its commercial life. Nor were there agricultural or industrial advances worth noting.

Third, and perhaps most negatively, it gave rise to problems—which reached genocidal levels—based in the prevailing tribal and peoples' nationalism within the Abrahamic tradition. The expression "the chosen servant and people of God" lies at the root of this nationalism. Initially, the Hebrews were considered "the chosen people of God," and then the Arabs took the title of the "noble people" for themselves. The Turkic tribes went a step further, and the rubric of Islamic heroism turned being Islamic into a deep-rooted identity. Assyrians consecrated themselves as the very first people to embrace Christianity, while Greeks and Armenians would later insist that they were among the initial sacred peoples. The spread of Christianity to Europe played an important role in accelerating nationalism rather than ecumenism (universalism). Russian nationalism is also, in a sense, the product of Orthodox Christianity.

Along with such an influence on tribal nationalism, the Abrahamic tradition didn't simply drown the ancient peoples of the Middle East in problems, it brought them tragedy and disaster. The most ancient peoples to become Christians, including the Assyrians, Armenians, Pontus, and Ionians, were brought to the brink of social extinction by the Islamized Arab, Turkish, and Kurdish rulers. The role of Judaism in this cannot be underestimated either. The elimination of Armenians, Assyrians, Ionians, Pontus, and Yazidis, as well as other non-Muslim peoples and their cultures, rendered the Middle East in general, and Anatolia in particular, cultural desserts. With the decline of these peoples, who carried with them the oldest known cultures, the region they had inhabited fell into extreme backwardness. This was a tragic loss for all the peoples of the region, as the elimination of these peoples and their cultures not only aggravated the social problem but also substantially undermined attempts to find a solution. Without these peoples and their cultures, which had been leaders of development in many branches of science and the arts, society in the region lost its artistic and scientific memory and ability.

In the name of Christianity, similar tragedies were delivered upon the Native peoples in North America, the Aztecs and Incas in South America, the Indigenous people of Australia, and the Inuit. Even when they have religious attributes, regimes that are charmed by power and lust will commit any villainy and cause all sorts of problems and tragedies. I must emphasize that the perspective, program, and practical life of the Abrahamic religious tradition, under the significant influence of the material culture of the central civilization, is not attempting to surpass this civilization but rather to mitigate it and make it fairer. The Abrahamic religious tradition sought a reform to allow them a share of the surplus value and the right to join the monopoly. They offered their ideology to legitimize power and, in exchange, demanded their share from those in power. If their demand was not met, they instigated resistance, falling silent when their demands were finally met—something that we also see with European socialism. And, as we shall see, there is a continuity between the two. They have both undoubtedly played a major role in the maintenance and universalization of this ancient civilization. In the end, the Abrahamic religious tradition failed to reduce the ancient social problem of oppression and exploitation. To the contrary, both oppression and exploitation increased and were perpetuated.

Eurocentric Civilization's Hegemonic Rule

Since the 1500s, the European civilization that has been on the rise worldwide has been consistently referred to as capitalist. It has been asserted that it is unique and unprecedented. The ways in which it is unprecedented are continuously emphasized (the nation-state, industry, and informatics).[12] Its intellectual hegemony means that the claims made by the Eurocentric social sciences are presented as positive facts. These positive facts, which it is hoped will be accepted as strict and absolute facts—even more so than religious facts—are at heart the dogmas of the new modernity.

It cannot be denied that the structure of European civilization under-went a transformation into something different. But throughout history, the central civilization has evolved, getting to know many places and time. The form taken by the central civilization in one time and place was not identically reproduced in other times and places; differentiation has been continuous. Furthermore, this development is in keeping with universal flow. But the claim that European society is unprecedented is exaggerated. The fundamental characteristics that have marked the central civiliza-tion from its very beginning and determined its character have remained essentially unchanged for five thousand years. Administration may take different forms, and there may be differences in proportion, technique, organizational structures, issues of efficiency, and questions of ideology. But the one characteristic that remains stable whatever the differences or the forms adopted is the monopoly's hegemonic control of surplus product. The content may change, but the monopoly itself doesn't. The triad of priest + soldier + regent always exists. Their significance may vary at different times and in different places, but monopoly requires the con-tinued existence of these groups. The methods of appropriating surplus product or values may differ, but the principle never changes. Surplus product may be accumulated either through increased efficiency within agriculture or industry or through trade or military conquests. There may be times when particular methods are central, but accumulation is always the result of the sum of these methods.

We must take care to understand the monopoly. It is neither purely capital nor purely power. It is not exclusively formed in the areas of trade, military, and administration. It is the consolidated expression of all these values and areas. In fact, monopoly is not the economy either. It is the power to use organizations, technology, and violence to secure its extortion in the economic area; it is the company. This is not a traditional company but, in the final analysis, a corporation to accumulate capital. Sometimes it appears as a power apparatus that has not yet become the state, while at other times it appears as the state itself. Nowadays, it often takes the title of "business enterprise." As I have already mentioned, rather than seeing it as part of the economy, it makes more sense to describe it as "an enterprise intent on extorting the economy." It sometimes projects itself in the military form but generally prefers merchant's union and industrial monopoly. Like an octopus, a monopoly can have many arms. At times, it may emerge as the combined effect of different forces and potentials. Whatever the case may be, the key thing is that surplus value accumulates in its hands as capital. This is the fundamental unchanged and uninterrupted reality that has grown cumulatively over the past five thousand years. The competition and hegemony, rise and fall, and center and periphery in different times and places all serve the continuity of this reality and act to ensure that it carries on like the links in an unbroken chain.

It must be pointed out that concepts such as capitalism and the capitalist system are used for propaganda purposes. In terms of contents, we can determine corresponding parallels for these concepts. However, if they are interpreted as phenomena, incidents, and systematic relations, they are very likely to distort the nature of society and its problems. Social life unfolds differently. The dimension of the resulting social problems makes clear that this flow requires a new language and a new science.

If capitalism is a system of capital accumulation, then it has been proved that this form of accumulation was first comprehensively achieved in the Sumerian city-states—although in a relatively primitive form, capital with its enterprises, money, warehouses, organization, and administration formed the foundation of these city-states. Perhaps the city itself is the initial capital enterprise, the monopoly itself. The army of merchants, military men, scientists, and artists, together with priest-rulers and worker-slaves, were the fundamental social classes, even back then. The temple (ziggurat) is at the same time a factory, a place to take shelter for worker-slaves and the headquarters for ruler-military commanders and priests. Of course, the top floor was used by the gods for surveillance and supervision. All of these were arranged perfectly, one within the other. I find such a configuration marvelous and see the ziggurat as the womb in which our civilization with all its state, class, and city structures was formed. The tale of the five-thousand-year-old central civilization is nothing more than this temple having grown and spread across time and space.

I do not believe that a more perfect and original capitalist monopoly, enterprise, and company than that organized within this temple is possible. Just as the source of all cells is the mother cell, the mother cell of all these monopolistic structures is this temple, as is confirmed by the archeological excavations in this region to date. Archeologists agree that the latest discovery, the structure to which the t-shaped monoliths at Urfa-Göbekli Tepe belong, is the oldest temple we know of at this point (a temple of the hunter and gatherer societies that preceded the Neolithic Age around 10,000–8000 BCE).[13] Each new excavation confirms that this is the original source of capital accumulation.

It cannot be denied that Eurocentric "capital" represents both the latest form and the absolute culmination of monopoly. This capital clearly differs from its predecessors in many ways, ranging from accumulation to production through organizational and administrative structures and military organization to monopoly of the arts, technology, and science. But it would be a huge exaggeration to say that this is unprecedented. Frankly speaking, this is Eurocentric propaganda; put another way, it is a claim made by the new class of modern temple priests of Europe (the army of the university, academic science, and the arts). We can easily say that these modern priests serve to legitimize the new "capitalist system" even more than do the Christian churches.

The objective here is not to write the history of the emergence of European civilization and its roots in the "capitalist system." It is, however, one of the most clearly established facts of recent historical work that this civilization rose through the theological, commercial, scientific, technological, and administrative practices of fifth- and sixth-century Christianity and of ninth- and tenth-century Islam (especially, in the latter case, via the Iberian, Italian, and Balkan peninsula). After 1250, there was a shift in the center of hegemonic civilization, and as civilizational centers in the East went into decline, those in Europe were on the rise. The thirteenth century is, of course, also recognized as the beginning of the commercial revolution. With Venice, Genoa, and Florence leading the way from the eleventh to the fifteenth century, not only were material goods brought from the East but so were the traditions, ideas, and techniques, processes and methods of a civilization that was thousands of years old; in short, all significant social values were imported in this way. It is equally clear that this played an important role in shifting the center of the civilization. Christianity, Greco-Roman civilization, and, further back, the Neolithic Revolution (5000–4000 BCE) were all undeniably transferred from the East to Europe. I believe that bringing the fifteen-thousand-years-old social cultures from Asian continent, especially from the Near East, to the European peninsula led to the most magnificent synthesis of the last five hundred years. In a nutshell, this is my interpretation of history!

I am not here being either pro-Oriental or pro-Occidental. My main concern, my objective, and the point of this undertaking is to correctly interpret the totality, continuity, and differences in the maintenance of historical-society in its entirety.

It is clear that more than just the fundamental methodology and structures of central civilization were transferred to the West. The social problems were also transplanted. I briefly touched on what Christianity brought with it. The East's material civilizational values (trade, production, money, and the state) were as problematic as its immaterial values (Christianity, science). Europe, in a way, was immersed in these problems. Thus, it is not difficult to imagine the earthshaking impact of introducing the East's complex and contradictory social nature into the still stable and young Neolithic agricultural society of Europe. The competition for shares among monopolies had led to thousands of years of warfare in the East. Europe was caught unprepared (preliminary work by Christianity was inadequate), which would, of course, later lead to much greater disaster and destruction. Conflicts that flared up within the system from the sixteenth century onward carried the mark of an Eastern legacy stretching back thousands of years. The conflicts experienced in the aftermath of the Roman Empire also carried the marks of this culture. I can say, without exaggeration, that the positive immaterial and material values of the central civilization were not all that was brought to Europe. Grave contradictions, problems, conflicts, and war arrived as well. The traces of the Eastern civilizational tradition can be very clearly seen in the disastrous genocides Europe is responsible for. Assyrian kings boast about building castles and ramparts out of human skulls. The Eastern despots enthuse about the many tribal, village, and city communities they annihilated and the people taken captive in the process—in so-called heroic stories!

European social scientists have not scrutinized the East without reason. I find their efforts valuable. But the Orientalism involved means they do not even come close to presenting the facts. Again, when compared with what has been produced by petrified Eastern minds, I have to acknowledge that we owe European social scientists a debt of gratitude. Even if their work had precolonialist intentions, it would still be more accurate to say that their real aim was to understand the story of how Europe was civilized. For the only way to understand Europe, including its contradictions, problems, and wars, is by analyzing the Near East. My efforts should be understood as a modest contribution to the subject of means and method.

The majority of the people in the East consider Europeans self-confident and very intelligent. I, however, found the Europeans that I met very naive and incredibly fragile, gullible, and unequipped to live in Eastern culture.

I believe European Neolithic social tradition had a huge influence on how Europe became civilized after the sixteenth century. At the beginning of sixteenth century, all the traditional European communities had embraced Christianity. But Europe also incorporated its own theological interpretations to all the developments in this process, including the urban revolutions after the tenth century. This led Europe to the Renaissance, the Reformation, and the Enlightenment, as well as to scientific and philosophical revolutions. The East, in the face of the spread of Islam—the most recent civilizational tradition of Near East, was not able to show any development similar to that of Neolithic society. No doubt there were many successful Turkish, Persian, and Kurdish thinkers, scientists, and artists. There was even a limited Eastern Renaissance from the eighth to the twelfth century. However, the fossilized structure of traditional Eastern despotism was quick to dominate any society that it penetrated to the point of saturation. This was another very important aspect of the intra-Islam struggles. Of course, the real point was to secure a monopoly. Besides the society based on the Eastern Neolithic tradition had by this point lost all of its previous vibrancy and was worn out. It had fallen into ignorance and despair. On the other hand, Europe's Neolithic tradition was youthful, free, and much more creative, because, unlike the Eastern societies, Europe didn't face a five-thousand-year-old despotism. In addition, as previously mentioned, it was able to absorb the positive aspects of the great Eastern experience. These two fundamental issues are key to understanding the historical emergence of Europe.

Immanuel Wallerstein and social science groups closely associated with him analyze the "capitalist world-system" that began to develop in the sixteenth century. However, the above very short explanation serves to show that their assessments, which fail to integrate the actual historical basis of this development or the fact that capital is a very ancient invention, have, to say the least, many shortcomings. Moreover, his comments on the intensification of accumulation of capital in the Venice, Amsterdam, and London triangle show similar weaknesses. In the absence of pressure applied to Italy, Netherlands, and England throughout the sixteenth century by Charles V and his son Philippe II, would it have been possible for money-capital to be so intensely invested in manufacturing and agricultural production?[14] Was Amsterdam not the site of the national insurrection and the progress that Venice was unable to achieve, and wasn't it London that was able to use internal political and military resistance against external political and military pressure to reach a successful conclusion? The response to both of these questions validates Fernand Braudel's statement: intensifying power and the state secrete capitalism.[15] I want to take it a step further and say that power and the state are monopolies and capital in themselves. Indeed, if they were not a capital monopoly, it would not be possible for them to secrete capital. Just as you cannot milk a male goat, you cannot milk capital from power and state apparatuses that are not monopolies.

The factors that actually led to the rise of Netherlands and England were external power, state pressure, and internal state resistance. The Spain-centered empire recognized the dangers it faced. After it suppressed the ascending cities in Italy (Machiavelli's prince would not succeed in his resistance), it set out full throttle to eliminate the new nationalist monopoly formations in the Netherlands and England. Their success would have meant its own disintegration. The resistance of Netherlands and England was profound and protracted in areas including diplomacy, economics, military technology, trade, science, and philosophy, and even religion (the Protestant movement). It is widely accepted that this comprehensive strategic resistance, which led to military technology and strategic and tactical organization, to Calvinism and Anglicanism—radical Protestant interpretations of Christianity—to the technological and organizational advances that facilitated enormous economic productivity, and to the farsighted diplomacy, which included an alliance with the Ottomans and another with the Prussian state, not only scored a victory but also shifted the new hegemonic center of civilization to Amsterdam and London.

In the meantime, the activities of capital multiplied and money-capital began to play a dominant role for the first time in history. (The effect of the flood of gold and silver played a major role in money gaining global leadership.) Some families with money at their disposal (including many of Jewish origin) accumulated huge reserves of capital by making the state their debtor. All such developments played a crucial role in the organization of the bourgeoisie as a class. Moreover, it should be noted that a social layer similar to the working class also took shape during this grand national resistance. I am not suggesting that the working class was entirely the product of this national resistance, only that its contribution cannot be denied. It also cannot be denied that the economic boom that occurred amid these fevered developments led to both the East and West Indian Companies (state monopolies and the state itself). Are the economic base (infrastructure) or political and military structures (superstructures) primary? This is not a meaningful question. The ideas of bourgeois political economy (Marx's *Capital* included), with their whiff of propaganda, conceal the truth rather than revealing it. It is past time that we stop being instruments of this propaganda.

The emergence of European civilization in the sixteenth century was clearly systemic and hegemonic in the history of civilization. The center has clearly shifted from Venice (besides all Italian cities, Lisbon and Antwerp also belonged to it) to Amsterdam and London, with the original nation-state models developing under the leadership of England and Netherlands. It is unquestionable that the new rising civilization was different from all that preceded it and entailed a huge transformation. But we cannot imagine all these developments separate from the five-thousand-year-old history of the central civilization. For example, could we talk about the existence of a European civilization if we were to separate the Akkadians from the Sumerians, the Assyrians and Babylonians from the Akkadians, the Median and Persians from the Assyrians, Egyptians, Hurrians, and Hittites from Mesopotamian civilization, the Greco-Roman civilization from the sum of these developments, and, of course, the Abrahamic religions from all of them? Could the miracles of Amsterdam and London have occurred if transportation pioneered by the Italian cities from 1000 to 1300 had not occurred and spread from Italy to the shores of Western Europe (1300–1600)?

Historical-society theses and social science analyses and theories that overlook the totality and continuity of the world civilization system cannot escape major shortcomings and errors. While even first nature requires a holistic historical explanation, the analysis of the intertwined nature of society—like a sequence of key links in a chain—with a much stricter holistic approach with regard to its historical, philosophical, and scientific aspects is indispensable. The hegemony of European social sciences may have served the hegemony of the civilization by applying a rigid positivist metaphysics and denying this reality for far too long, leading to widespread chaos in the social sciences. Those who have analyzed capital have a huge responsibility in this respect. The many problems we face clearly show that not only were the majority of these analyses far removed from any attempt to explain capital and the capitalist system but, in fact, served to obscure reality.

There is a general agreement that during their European phase monopolies of civilization, which were hegemonic, crisis-ridden, and central throughout history, developed following a path through Venice in the fifteenth century, Amsterdam in the sixteenth and seventeenth centuries, and London, in particular, during the eighteenth and nineteenth centuries. The French civilizational monopoly waged war to snatch hegemony from Spain, Netherlands, and England from the fifteenth to the eighteenth century but failed. Germany underwent a civilizational ascent toward the end of nineteenth century that ended nightmarishly, culminating in its 1945 defeat. The US began its civilizational ascent in the twentieth century, consolidating its predominance after 1945. Its hegemony is now (since the early years of the twenty-first century) beginning to crack. Soviet Russia's attempt to become a hegemonic center from 1945 to 1990 was not terribly successful. For now, claims that China will be the future hegemonic center are little more than speculation. As has often occurred in history, a multicentered hegemonic reality may shape the near future. The US, the EU, the Russian Federation, China, and Japan all have the potential to become assertive centers. For the time being, however, it can be comfortably said that the US is the hegemonic superpower.

Earlier, I briefly examined the argument advanced by Anthony Giddens, the English social scientist, that European modernity (which can also be called civilization) is unprecedented. In short, this assertion is excessively Eurocentric and detached from reality—which I will address in more detail later under the heading "Social Problems." In what I call his interpretations of capitalist modernity, Giddens presents capitalism as an entirely European system, with industrialism even more specifically a European revolution, and the nation-state as the system's third pillar as a completely new order and experiment. At the risk of repetition, I must emphasize that capitalism has been observed in all civilizations, and that in all civilizations there have been, to a greater or lesser extent, industrial developments and revolutions. The nation-state, on the other hand, can be defined as the form of dynastic and tribal states at the stage of nation-society. Such categorization may prove very useful for understanding social nature, as long as it is not exaggerated.

The social problems of European civilization, or, more correctly, the European civilizational phase, which have unfolded as major contradictions, conflicts, wars, and even genocides, have peaked along with all the other areas of development. The epic proportions of the intellectual, ideological, political, economic, military, and demographic problems, together with sexism, nationalism, religionism, and ecological problems, are the main concern of the social sciences. In the last four hundred years, Europe has experienced more wars than the sum of wars in previous history. Every kind of war has been experienced: religious, ethnic, economic, commercial, military, civil, national, class-based, ideological, sexist, political, state-based, social, systemic, bloc, worldwide, and so on—there is almost no imaginable type of war that has not taken place. Records in the number of dead, the suffering, and the material losses have been broken across the board!

All these facts cannot be the product of the last four hundred years alone, which is a short time in the long historical march of humanity. Our short examination confirms this. The most correct and more useful interpretation of these wars is probably that the problems accumulated in the Neolithic Age and in civilized societies over the last fifteen thousand years exploded in the society of the European peninsula. Although it has not been completely successful, European society has fought the tangled problems handed down from the old society with superior skill, gaining a good grasp of these problems, and thereby struggling against them more meaningfully. To this end, Europe has undergone the Renaissance, the Reformation, and the Enlightenment, made amazing scientific discoveries, developed philosophical schools, and experienced profound periods of democratic constitutional development. It has established and subverted kingdoms and built republics. It has organized economic systems of unparalleled productivity and carried out the biggest industrial revolution. It is unrivaled in the arts and fashion. It has built amazing cities and established magnificent scientific and medical centers. It has spread the civilization system across the world. In short, it has constructed the most comprehensive world system in history.

However, despite these far-reaching developments, it is clear that instead of resolving social problems Europe has made them more complex. Leaving aside the current systemic problems around the world, including unemployment, conflicts, and environmental destruction, this fact can even be seen with more superficial problems, primarily because these problems have five-thousand-year-old civilizational roots—with civilization itself being a huge tangle of problems. I consider the greatest success of Europe to be its ability to hold the mirror of science up to the gigantic civilizational problems—even though the mirror was blurred and misleading in many respects, this mirror has made it possible to look at the problems more closely. Of course, the great contributions of the courageous fighters cannot be overlooked (even if the ideologies at play have often been illusory). The heroines and heroes of the battles waged in the name of equality, freedom, and solidarity are the genuine contributors.

We should not downplay the necessity of defining the fundamental social problem. For thousands of years societies have fought and have been obliged to fight. It is a sad fact that these societies did not know who they were fighting for. They were not only forced to work for their tyrannical exploiters, they were also annihilated in numerous wars.

Eastern sages were no doubt aware of the social problem. That is why they developed grand teachings, moral systems, religion, and denominations. For a long time, they preferred *aşiret* and tribal life to the state and civilization.[16] The main body of Eastern society has been alien to the state and civilization, gigantic ramparts and castles raised between them. Eastern songs and epics express all of this with artistic grace. The human in the East was so estranged from the civilized world and felt so hopeless that the goal became salvation in the afterlife. The supremacy of European society was based on its capacity to absorb the positive aspects of civilization without hesitation while resisting the alienating aspects. Europe did not solve the social problem, but it also did not allow the social problem to completely defeat it and render it helpless.

Adding our present-day problems and the traditional problems of Chinese, Indian, Latin American, and even African societies, to this branch of mainstream civilization will not change their nature. Some noteworthy problems of form can at best strengthen our narrative. In fact, the current world system (a multicentered system with the US as the super hegemon) has systematized and totalized not only its problems but the problems of all of the societies in the world.

I hope to present a summary of the historical and social problems from a new perspective, with a view to complementing the discussion and making it more concrete.

Social Problems
The Problem of Power and the State
I am frequently compelled to emphasize that just as history is "the present," any component of the present is also history. The very first thing each new

emerging civilization does is to make sure that history and the present are disconnected, using propaganda that aims to ensure its legitimacy and to present it as "past-eternity and post-eternity." In the real life of a society there is no such disconnection. Furthermore, without a universal history, no local or singular history would make sense. Therefore, the problem of power and the state—which has existed since they first appeared—is also, with a slight difference, a problem at present. These differences result from temporal and spatial changes. When we look at the concepts of differentness and transformation this way, we increase the degree of accuracy of our interpretations. We also need to consider the drawbacks of underestimating differentness, transformation, and development or of regarding them as trivial. Just as our thinking atrophies if it is not based on universal history, evaluating historical development without considering differentness and transformation and treating it as nothing more than repetition obscures the truth to a similar degree. It is quite important not to fall into either of these forms of reductionism.

Our first finding related to power and the state is that they have increased their capacity both over and within society. Until the sixteenth century, domination was primarily built outside of society and was both glamorous and intimidating. Civilization has taken numerous such striking forms through the ages. The state, as the official expression of power, had drawn firm lines, hoping that the sharper the distinction between the state and society, the more it would benefit. In terms of power, these lines were quite explicit as an intra-society phenomenon. The lines separating women from men, youth from the elderly, members of the aşiret from the head of the aşiret, faithful laypeople from the representatives of religions and denominations, were determined in keeping with clear rules and customs. From tone of voice to the way of walking and sitting, the authority of power, of dominating and being dominated, was firmly established with detailed rules. It is perfectly clear that to make power and the state tangible and present—as they were still the minority—required that their authority be established in this way. These rules served as tools of legitimacy and indoctrination.

The reason for the radical transformation of the authority of power and the state in European civilization was the need felt to more quickly infiltrate every nook and cranny of society. Two fundamental factors arguably played a role in the vertical and horizontal expansion of power. The first was the enlargement of the masses to be exploited. Without a corresponding expansion of the administration, exploitation would not have been feasible. Just as a growing herd requires numerous shepherds, the growing population required substantial growth in state bureaucracy. We must also consider the need for rulers to internally suppress society as a corollary of the massive growth of their external defense forces. Wars have always created bureaucracy. The army itself is among the largest of bureaucratic organizations. The second factor was the increasing consciousness and resistance in society. The fact that European society had not experienced profound exploitation and had continuously resisted it meant that extensive power and a large state were essential. In Europe, the struggle of the bourgeoisie against the aristocracy and that of the working class against both of them necessitated the construction of far-reaching power and a pervasive state. Perhaps the fact that for the first time the bourgeoisie, in the form of the middle class, constituted the state made for a new kind of power and state. This bloc, arising within society and becoming the state, with the inevitable increase in power, found itself compelled to organize within society.

The bourgeoisie is a such a huge class that it could not simply dominate power and the state from the outside. As this class became the state, it inevitably found itself enmeshed in internal social strife. The notion of class conflict makes this clear. Liberalism, a bourgeois ideology, beats around the bush looking for a solution to this problem. But what has, in fact, happened so far is further growth of power and the state and a cancerous bureaucratization. The more power and the state grow within the society, the more civil strife there is. This has been the fundamental problem within European society from the outset. The great constitutional, democratic, republican, and anarchist struggles are closely related to the way power and the state are structured. Our current preferred remedy is fundamental human rights tied to strict constitutional rules, the rule of law, and democracy. Instead of a permanent solution, the state and society are coerced to find a compromise around power and leave behind the great stormy past. As such, the problem of power and the state has not been resolved but has been removed to a level where it is sustainable.

If we look closely we can see that the intertwinement of society, power, and the state has been developed using nationalism, sexism, religionism, and various scientisms, whereby, to sustain the nation-state, everyone is drawn into a paradigm where "everyone is both power and society and the state and society." In this way, it is assumed that the bourgeois nation-state solution will be found by suppressing the internal class struggle and by the defensive position always remaining in place in the exterior. This is one of the main methods used worldwide to suppress the problem rather than resolve it. The fascist quality of the nation-state as the maximum power and state could be seen most clearly in German fascism.

The first example of the nation-state arose during the resistance of Netherlands and England to the Spanish Empire. The nation-state legitimized its rule by mobilizing the entire society against an external power that it called the enemy. Initially, the development of national society in Europe had relatively positive elements. But it was clear that this development, even at its birth, acted to conceal class exploitation and oppression. The nation-state definitely bears the mark of the bourgeoisie. It is this class's state model. Later, Napoleon's military expeditions strengthened this model in France and spread it across Europe. The German and Italian bourgeoisie were underdeveloped and had difficulty in creating national unity, which led them to adopt more nationalist policies. The bourgeoisie was compelled to embrace a chauvinist-nationalist state model because of the external threat of occupation, as well as the continuing internal resistance of the aristocracy and the working class. Defeat and crisis—these are the two things that brought many countries, especially Germany and Italy, at a crossroads "either a social revolution or fascism," with the fascist state model prevailing in this dilemma. While Hitler, Mussolini, and their like were defeated, their systems were victorious.

The nation-state can essentially be described as society being identified with the state and the state with society, which also constitutes the definition of fascism. Naturally the state can no more become communal than society can become the state. Only totalitarian ideologies can assert such a claim. The fascist character of such claims is obvious. Fascism, as a form of state, always has the seat of honor at the bourgeois liberal table. It is the form of rule in times of crisis. Since crisis is structural, so is the regime; called the nation-state regime. It is the apex of the crises of financial capital era. Capitalist monopoly's state, which has currently peaked globally, is also generally fascist during its most reactionary and despotic period. Although there is much talk of the collapse of the nation-state, claiming that democracy will be constructed in its place is simple credulousness. It may be that both macro-global and micro-local fascist formations are on the agenda. Developments in the Middle East, the Balkans,

Central Asia, and the Caucasus are noteworthy. South America and Africa are on the eve of new experiences. Europe seeks to distance itself from nation-state fascism with reform. It is unclear what will happen to Russia and China. The US, the super hegemon, is in an exchange with every form of the state.

Clearly, the problem of power and the state is in one of its worst phases. The dilemma of "either a democratic revolution or fascism" is on the agenda and is still vital. The system's regional and central UN organizations are no longer functional. Financial capital, which peaked during the most global phase of civilization, is the section of capital that most fuels the crisis. The political and military component of the financial capital monopoly is the intensive war on society. This is what is being experienced on many fronts around the world. Determining what political and economic formations might arise from the world system's structural crisis requires intellectual, political, and moral work not prophecy.

During the financial capital era, the pinnacle of the virtual capital monopoly of capitalist modernity, society is at risk of disintegrating as never before in history. The political and moral fabric of society has been smashed, leading to a social phenomenon that even goes beyond genocide: "societycide." Virtual capital's domination of the media provides it with a weapon for executing a societycide worse than that of World War II. Up against the cannons of nationalism, religionism, sexism, scientism, and artism (sports, soap operas, etc.), with which the society is being battered twenty-four hours a day by the media, how can the society be defended?

Media are effective in society like a second analytical intelligence. Just as analytical intelligence is neither good nor bad, in and of itself, media too is a neutral tool. Just as with any weapon, whoever is using it determines the role it plays. Just as hegemonic powers always possess the most effective weapons in the literal sense, they also have the dominant control over the media as a weapon. Because they use media as a second analytical intelligence, they can very effectively neutralize society's power to resist. With this weapon, they are building a virtual society. Virtual society is another form of societycide. You could also consider the nation-state a form of societycide. In both cases, society is prevented from being itself and transformed into a tool of the controlling monopoly. Just as it is very dangerous to treat social nature simplistically, preventing it from being itself exposes it to unclear dangers. The age of the virtual monopoly, like the financial capital age, is only possible in a society that has ceased to be itself. Thus, it is no coincidence that both appeared during the same period, since they are linked. The society (thinking it is the nation-state) that the nation-state has deprived from being itself and that the media has seduced is a totally defeated society. From the rubble of societies like this the hegemonic powers are building something new. There can be no doubt that this is the social age in which we find ourselves.

We are not only living in the most problematic societies to date but in societies that offer nothing to individuals. Our societies have not only lost their moral and political fabric, their very existence is under threat. Our societies are not just experiencing some random problem; they face the threat of destruction. If the problems of our age continue to grow and become more profound and cancerous, despite the effectiveness of science, societycide is not just a hypothesis—it is a real danger. The claim that the rule of the nation-state protects society creates a huge illusion and only makes this danger gradually come true. Society is not only facing problems, but its own destruction.

Society's Moral and Political Problem

I am aware of the dangers that result from partitioning the social problem into individual problems. This methodological approach developed by Eurocentric science using analytical reason unconditionally may seem to have led to some achievements, but the danger of losing the totality of truth cannot be underestimated. I will, nonetheless, use this methodology, always bearing in mind its flaws and the risk that comes with treating a singular social problem as if it were a series of discrete "problems." And in the epistemology section I will discuss other approaches.

There is a reason for power and the state to be the first social problems addressed, not least because they are at the main source of all social problems. The power and state relations and apparatuses, which, with all their gravity, initially became effective over the society, and since the sixteenth century within society, essentially function to prepare a weakened society, deprived of its ability to defend itself, for monopoly exploitation. This makes it important to define the role of power and the state correctly. Describing power and the state as no more than the totality of the apparatuses and relations of coercion is seriously inadequate. I believe that the most important role played by these apparatuses is to leave society weak and deprive it of its ability to defend itself, by ensuring that society's moral and political fabric, i.e., its very means of "existence," is continuously weakened until it can no longer play its role. Society cannot maintain its existence if it cannot form the key areas of morality and politics.

The fundamental role of morality is to equip society with the rules necessary to continue existing and provide the capacity to implement them. Any society that loses the rules governing its existence and the ability to implement them becomes nothing but a herd of animals—and can then be easily abused and exploited. The role of politics, on the other hand, is to provide society with the necessary moral rules and, through a process of continuous discussion, to decide on the means and methods needed to meet society's fundamental material and intellectual needs. Social politics leads to a more lively and open-minded society by continuously developing discussion and the decision-making skills necessary to meet these needs; this constitutes society's most essential area of existence, giving it the ability to govern itself and handle its own affairs. A society without politics will slip and slide from one extreme to another, running around like a chicken with its head cut off before its death. The most effective way to leave a society dysfunctional and weak is to deprive it of politics (including its capacity to develop politics, the Islamic term is sharia),[17] an imperative factor for the discussion and decision-making necessary for existence and for meeting fundamental material and immaterial needs. Nothing could be worse for society.

This is why, historically, power and the state apparatuses and relations have always instituted "law" in place of social morality and imposed "state administration" in place of social politics at the first opportunity. The fundamental duty of power and the state is to prevent society from using its moral and political power, the two fundamental strategies for its existence, and to replace them with law and rulers at all times. This is necessary to ensure the accumulation of capital and the monopoly of exploitation. Every page of the five-thousand-year-old history of civilization overflows with examples of how to break society's moral and political capacity and replace it with law and administration by the capital monopolies. This is the history of civilization at its bluntest and with its true motives, and, if it is to be meaningful, it must be written correctly from this point of view. This is the truth hidden at the heart of every social conflict throughout history. Will society live by its own morality and politics or be turned into a herd subjugated to law and to the administration imposed by unrestrained exploitative monopolies? When I say the main source of problems is the unreasonable cancerous growth of power and state law and administration, that is what I mean.

It may be beneficial to elaborate on another issue. When hierarchy is established for the first time and "experience" and "expertise" become important for the benefit of society, whether we call them state or authority, we expect them to be beneficial. The fact that society has not regarded the state and authority (power) as entirely negative is presumably due to these expected benefits. Society expects experience and expertise from the state and authority, believing this will facilitate its affairs. These two factors are the reasons why society puts up with the continued existence of the state. Not everyone has the necessary experience or an area of expertise. Throughout history the state and authority have taken advantage of this legitimate expectation to staff its administration with people who are the most clumsy, inexperienced, and lacking in expertise. As a result, administration became an arena of scheming rather than one that implemented the law, for dawdling instead of providing work based on expertise. The terrible degeneration and disasters we are witnessing are closely linked to this huge distortion and eversion.

The bourgeoisie, an expression of the cancerous development of the middle class, has historically placed itself at the center of society, at its "core," and presented its most selfish interests as "law" and its most degenerate methods as "constitutional administration," and to do so it has multiplied power and the state, divided into an unlimited number of "apparatuses" and so-called areas of expertise. This has been a total disaster. Society jumped out of the frying pan into the fire. The far-reaching liberal perspective that developed—the bourgeois refined reason—on topics such as the "republic," "democracy," "downsizing the administration," and "restrictions on power and the state" not only conceals the truth but is imbued with contradictions. The bourgeois middle class no longer has the ability that it had in antiquity to downsize the administration and restrict power and the state by developing a constitution, a republic, and a democracy. It is the material structure of the middle class and its way of existence that render these noble concepts dysfunctional. If the society could not sustain a king or a dynasty in antiquity, how is it supposed to sustain the burden of an unlimited bourgeois apparatus and the accompanying bourgeois family and dynasty? I intentionally use the term "bourgeois family and dynasty," because they both stem from the same source. The bourgeoisie got its art of administration and rules from the nobility and monarchy that preceded it. It has no capacity for self-creation. The cancerous effect of power and state relations on society stems from the class nature of the middle class, which is imbued with fascism.

Consequently, one of the most fundamental problems is that the bourgeoisie cripples and renders society's moral and political fabric dysfunctional. Obviously, the moral and political fabric of society cannot be completely eliminated. As long as society exists, so shall morality and politics. But because power and the state are no longer areas of expertise and experience, morality and politics can no longer fulfill their creative and functional capacity. It is crystal clear that nowadays power and the state apparatus and relations (such as media, intelligence services and specialized operational units, ideological teachings, etc.) have infiltrated every nook and cranny of society, stifling it. Society has fallen so far that it no longer recognizes itself and can no longer implement any of its moral principles, engage in any political discussion about its most basic needs, or make any decisions (the essence of democratic politics). In addition, the fact that "global corporations," the "past-eternity and post-eternity" monopolies—the much discussed and true ruling powers of our times—have experienced the greatest capital boom in history in this era is closely linked to the fact that society has been put in this position. Without the decay and fragmentation of society, it would not be possible to earn money from money by virtual means, which is to say, without involving in any way the means of production. The profits made by the monopolies throughout history and today's exorbitant profits made without working, as if money grew on trees, are attained by extracting from society's existence and brainpower, because, in fact, "money does not grow on trees"!

I must emphasize that it is not only the unlimited expansion of power and the state apparatus and relations that puts society in this position. The media is the other key effective source of hegemony, facilitating the ideological conquest of the society. Society cannot be brought down by the imposition of power and the state apparatus and relations alone; it needs to be stupefied with distractions like nationalism, religionism, scientism, and the industrialization of the arts and sports in particular. In the absence of virtual global corporations (i.e., financial capital, or money-capital, is meant here), the historical monopolies would be unable to prevent society from being itself and to subject it to unlimited exploitation—to the point of societycide.

Society's Mentality Problem

As we've established, one of the primary conditions for opening up a society to exploitation is to deprive it of morality and politics, which requires the collapse of society's mentality—the intellectual basis of society's moral and political fabric. This is why, throughout history, the rulers and the exploitative monopolies have first and foremost constructed "hegemony over mentality" to attain their goals, for example, the way the Sumerian priests first built the temple (ziggurat) to increase the productivity of Sumerian society, i.e., opened it up to exploitation. It is quite important to bear in mind the function of the Sumerian temple, as this (with its ongoing effects) is the oldest known example of distorting and conquering the social mindset.

I have emphasized that social nature is formed by the most flexible mental structures. If we do not truly apprehend that society is the most intelligent nature, we cannot develop a meaningful sociology. Therefore, tyrants, rulers, and the crafty make it their fundamental duty to undermine society's intelligence and capacity to think, making the original monopoly the monopoly of mentality, i.e., the temple. This original temple had two functions. First, it was a tool for intellectual domination, a hegemonic tool of the utmost importance. Second, it was the best tool for severing society from its essential intellectual values.

The concept of society's own mentality needs to be well understood. When a human being first picked up the stone and stick, it was the result of thought. What we have here is not instinct but the first seeds of analytical thought. As experience was accumulated, society developed, which, in essence, was the result of this concentration of thought. The more experience a society gained and the more focused this thought became, the more ability and strength it gained, with the result that it was better able to feed, defend, and reproduce itself. This process clarifies for us what social development is and why it is so important. Once society constantly makes itself think, its moral tradition—common sense or conscience— that is its collective thought begins to take shape. Morality is the greatest treasure of a society, and therein lies its central importance. It is the fundamental organ for accumulating experience and the reason a society survives, sustaining and further developing its life. Because of its life experience, any society understands full well that if it loses its moral base, it will crumble. To a certain degree, every society has a sharp, deep-seated instinct about the centrality of morality for its survival. In the old clan and tribal societies, the punishment for not abiding by moral rules was death or being banished from society and left to die. "Honor crimes," which still continue in the most distorted ways, are rooted in these moral rules.

While morality represents the tradition of collective thought, the function of politics is a little different. Discussing and making decisions about daily collective affairs requires the power of thought. Politics is necessary to daily creative thinking. Society knows very well that without morality, the source and accumulated thought, there can be neither political thought nor practical politics. Politics is an indispensable area of action for daily collective affairs (serving society's common good). When there are differences of opinion or even objectionable ideas, discussion is the key to making decisions about society's affairs. A society that lacks politics either adheres herdlike to rules imposed by others or loses all sense of direction, as in the example of the chicken with its head cut off. The power of thought is not a superstructural institution; it is society's brain with morality and politics as its organs.

Society's other organ is, of course, the temple as a sacred site. This temple is not the temple of hegemonic power (hierarchy and state), but society's own sacred site. Society's sacred site has a place of honor in archeological discoveries. It is perhaps the most important structure that has survived into the present. This isn't incidental. Society's first sacred site is the location of its past, its ancestry, its identity, and what is common to them. It is the site of collective remembrance and worship. It is the place of self-remembering, a sign of creating something rich for the future, and an important reason for being together. Society was aware that if the temple was built in a place that was remarkable, splendid, and worth living in, then it would be better able to symbolize society and would have greater value. For this reason, splendor was displayed most at temples. The temple—as can be seen from the Sumerian example—was also the laborers' living quarters and the storage site of means of production, which is to say, it was the locus of collective work. It was not only a place of worship but also of collective discussion and decision-making. It was a political center, the home of craftspeople, and the site of inventions. It was where architects and scholars tested their skills. It was the first example of an academy. Not surprisingly, temples in ancient times were also centers of prophecy. All these factors and many more are what make the temple important. It would be entirely reasonable to call this institution the ideological core of society's mentality.

The megaliths found amid the ruins in Urfa are twelve thousand years old. When this temple was constructed the agricultural revolution had not yet occurred. But it is clear that the stone carvings and the erection of t-shaped stone pillars required advanced skills and, thus, an advanced society. Who were they? How did they talk, feed themselves, and reproduce? How did they think, and what were their customs? How did they provide for themselves? We do not yet have answers to these questions. The only traces that remain are the megaliths and what are most likely the ruins of a temple. Since ordinary peasants today would not be able to carve and erect stone pillars like these, the people who did this and their society were clearly no more backward than today's peasants and village communities. We can only make assumptions about such issues. Although distorted, the sacred nature of Urfa may be like a flowing river filtered through a tradition that predates written history. This is why I am not discussing the existence and importance of the social temple but the hegemonic temple's existence and its key function.

Egyptian priests played at least as big a role as Sumerian priests in the formation of the hegemonic temples, and Indian Brahmins didn't lag behind the Egyptian priests. The temples of the Far East were in no way inferior to the Sumerian and Egyptian temples. South American temples also played a hegemonic role. The youth were not sacrificed in these temples on a whim. The dominant temples of all the eras of civilization served hegemony—like copies of the original. The main function of these centers was to prepare society to serve the rulers. The military wing of the monopoly sowed terror by severing opponents' heads and using their skulls to build castles and ramparts, while the spiritual wing completed the job by conquering minds, and both served important roles in enslaving communities. One generated fear, while the other convinced. Who can deny the continuity of this aspect of civilized society stretching back thousands of years?

European hegemonic civilization changed its form in this respect dramatically. But it preserved its essence. This change was not sufficient for the gigantic nation-state apparatuses that encompassed society, so they took steps to make society, whose very core they penetrated, dependent on them. What the centers for forming mentality, such as the universities, academies, colleges, high schools, primary schools, and preschools, begin, the churches, synagogues, and mosques complement and the military barracks refine. Is this anything short of the conquest, occupation, and assimilation of the remains of society's mindset, its moral and political fabric? When certain esteemed commentators claim that turning society into the multitudes amounts to turning the people into herds, they are not, in fact, talking nonsense. Furthermore, the memory of how such a colonization of the mind leads to fascist society is still fresh. The bloodbath of our recent past too is the outcome of this conquest of mentality.

It doesn't hurt to repeat that if you are the one waving the icons of nationalism, religionism, sexism, sportism, artism (the industrialization of the arts) you move society—or, rather, the herd—toward your desired target. The conquest of the mind is what opened society to the current dominant global financial capital. No use of force would have been as effective. Yet again, we should salute the Sumerian priests and the temples they invented! You were such great conquerors that five thousand years later your current representatives, in today's temples, can generate the largest accumulation of capital in history without lifting a finger! Even the most powerful images of gods and their shadows (Zillullah) could not yield as much profit.[18] Therefore, the continuous and cumulative accumulation of capital is not an empty concept. Distorting the intellect is not a simple operation. Dr. Hikmet Kıvılcımlı,[19] and the Italian thinker Antonio Gramsci, defined hegemonic conquest similarly while they were in prison during the nation-states' glory days. What both Gramsci and Kıvılcımlı knew was based on their experiences. I too, at the end of the day, am a "prisoner" of global capital. Failure to recognize it correctly in my own mind (identity) would be a betrayal of the very mind of society.

Society's Economic Problem

When there is a talk of economic problems, I always think of ant colonies. If small creatures like ants have no economic problems (since economy for each living being is about food), then how can creatures like human beings, with such advanced reason and experience, have serious economic problems or such an embarrassing situation as unemployment? Is there anything in nature that human beings, with their intelligence, cannot turn into work? The problem definitely has nothing to do with the natural functioning of things or the environment. The arrant wolf of humanity lies within it.[20] All economic problems, foremost unemployment, are linked to capitalization of society.

No doubt, Marx's analysis of capital is valuable. He tries to explain unemployment during periods of crisis. But sadly, the disease of positivism caught him in a very bad way, and the disease of scientism prevented him from a more profound analysis of historical-society. What I am trying to do is to show that capital is not the economy; on the contrary, it is the most effective tool for undermining the economy. I say this primarily because profit and capital have never been the goal of society's development and, thus, never had a place within society, as such. A rich and prosperous society is conceivable; morality and politics leave room for this. But when society suffers from need and unemployment, focusing on wealth and capital goes beyond being a crime; it is associated with societycide. We see civilization as an entanglement of problems, because it rests on the monopoly of capital.

When Rosa Luxemburg connected capital accumulation to the existence of noncapitalist society,[21] she was wandering at the edge of a very important truth. Had she walked right in, she would have concluded that capital accumulation is not simply dependent upon the existence of a noncapitalist society, this accumulation is also made possible through seizure of society's values, by bloodsucking ticks. She would have seen that the worker has become an accomplice, drinking a drop of the blood that is his share. Let me be clear, I do not deny the worker's labor, but the formation of capital is only dependent on the worker's labor to a very small extent, and when considered philosophically, historically, and socially, this small extent also loses its meaning. Current ecological problems make it increasingly clear that industrialism is a tool for usury at the expense of society and the environment. No person with knowledge and understanding can deny that business managers and skilled laborers have become society's most privileged strata, with an equivalent snowballing growth of unemployment as its counterpart. The advanced industrial strata, the monopolistic commercial and financial strata—i.e., capital monopolies with their "multi-stakeholder partnerships"—have further rendered the concept of *worker* meaningless. It is important to acknowledge that the worker has been reduced to a belt that ties society to the monopoly of capital. Just as real socialism, or state capitalism, is a system that rests on the "concessionist worker," classic private capitalism also has its concessionist workers. They have always existed in society side by side. The remaining society, the noncapitalist society, is what Rosa Luxemburg was thinking about.

What we are discussing here, if one notices, is a distinction made between capitalist and noncapitalist. For Luxemburg both are forms of society. I see it differently. I see capitalism not as a form of society but as an extensive network, an organization that has established itself above society and extorts surplus value, drains the economy, generates unemployment, amalgamates with power and the state, and uses the powerful tools of ideological hegemony. Recently, the concessionist workers have become a part of this organization. I hope to dispense with a number of misunderstandings by defining the essence of the monopolistic network. Above all, I hope to uncover the trap implicit in the concept of "capitalist society." Defining capitalist monopoly as a society is excessively gracious. Capital might form networks and organizational networks. Indeed, even the mafia must be seen as a gainful network of capital. The only reason that the network of capital is not called the mafia is because of its hegemonic power over society and its relations with the official power. Otherwise, it too would have remained nothing but a network, lacking even the ethics of the mafia.

I must add that I do not consider the medium-sized industrialists, merchants, or farmers capitalists. They are social strata that, for the most part, try to produce to meet genuine economic needs, even if they are being squeezed by capital from every direction. In addition, I do not consider exchange of small goods at the market capitalism or those who produce these goods at their small shops capitalists. Obviously, various professions cannot be considered capitalist. All workers who are not concessionist, peasants, students, civil servants, craftspeople, children, and women form the backbone of society. I aim to develop a definition of noncapitalist society. When I speak of noncapitalist society, unlike most Marxists, I don't mean a society that is defined as feudal, or one in which the Asiatic mode of production prevails, or one that is semifeudal. I am convinced that these concepts conceal rather than reveal the truth. Furthermore, my analysis not only addresses the capital networks that were centralized in Europe after sixteenth century but all of the capital networks (commercial, political, military, ideological, agricultural, and industrial monopolies) that have extorted surplus value throughout history.[22] It doesn't take a lot of study to see that present-day global financial capital verifies this analysis in striking ways.

It is essential that the anticapital character of social nature is recognized. Throughout its millennia-long march, society has always been aware of the highly corrupting nature of capital accumulation. For example, almost every religion has condemned usury—one of the most effective methods of capital accumulation.

It is not enough to say that capital is currently developing a massive growth of unemployment to create cheap and flexible labor force. While this is partially true, the main reason is that capital constrains society to profit-oriented activities. However, activity for the sake of profit and capital does not meet society's fundamental needs. If the production to feed the population does not create profit, then even if society wallows in poverty and starves to death—indeed millions of people are currently living and dying in just such conditions—capital will not budge. If a small portion of the capital available was invested in agriculture, the problem of hunger could be eliminated. But, instead, capital is continuously dismantling and destroying agriculture, because the profit ratio in agriculture is negligible to nil. As long as capitalists can earn huge sums of money from money, they will never think of agriculture. Such thinking would be meaningless to capital. In the past, the state as a monopoly considerably subsidized agricultural producers, receiving produce or money taxes in return. The present capital markets have rendered such state activities inconsequential. As a result, states that consider contributing to agriculture face bankruptcy.

This means, therefore, the increasing unemployment and impoverishment of the main body of society is not the outcome of capital's temporary policies but, in fact, stems from its structural characteristics. Even if people agree to work for the lowest possible wages, society's unemployment problem cannot be solved, as simple observation should make clear, even without further investigation. Let me say it one more time: we cannot free society from unemployment and poverty without abolishing policies and systems of maximum profit based on surplus value.

For example, why is there such widespread unemployment, hunger, and poverty in the Mesopotamian meadows that mothered Neolithic society for fifteen thousand years and nourished numerous societies through the ages? With a nonprofit production initiative, even by today's standards these meadows could feed twenty-five million people. Thus, what these people and meadows need is not the hand of capital that prevents work, but for that hand (whether private or state), which is the sole reason for unemployment, hunger, and poverty, to leave them alone. The only thing needed is to link the land with the hand of the true laborer, which would require a revolution in society's mindset. This, in turn, would mean social morality and politics resuming their function as the fundamental structures, or organs, of society. For this to happen, democratic politics must rush to this task with all its heart, soul, and real brains.

Society's Industrialism Problem

The Industrial Revolution, which was as important as the agricultural revolution, has carried on with ups and downs, experiencing a qualitative leap in the late eighteenth and early nineteenth centuries, based on thousands of years of accumulation. It is impossible to guess where, when, and how it will stop or be stopped. This revolution has a characteristic akin to analytical reason; it is, in fact, the product of this reason. And it is under the absolute domination of capital. There is no doubt, however, capital itself is not the creator of most industrial tools. However, capital has focused on turning them into profitable tools and taken possession of those it considers essential. Cheap mass production offers a major opportunity for the development of society. As with reason, industry that served society's needs would be valuable. The problem is not with industry itself but with the way it is used. Industry is like the nuclear option. When it is used by the monopolies it can be an unparalleled threat to life, portending both ecological disaster and war. Indeed, its use for making profit has become increasingly evident, accelerating environmental destruction. Industry is rapidly moving society toward virtual society. Humans are increasingly being replaced by robotics. If this continues, it will not be long before humans themselves are redundant.

There is consensus that the current state of the environment not only threatens society but all life on earth. I must emphatically stress that holding industry solely responsible for this would be an aberration. On its own, industry is neutral. An industry in harmony with society's existence can play a decisive role in developing the world into a third nature, not only for humans but for all lifeforms. It is possible, and if it were the case, we might even consider industry a blessing. But when industry is controlled by capital and is profit-driven, it can make the world hell for all of humanity except a handful of monopolists. In fact, that seems pretty much to be our current situation. Humanity is undeniably extremely alarmed by the current course of events. The industrial monopoly has established genuine empires ruling over society. For a single US hegemon, there are tens of industrial hegemons. Even if political and military hegemons could be stopped, the industrial hegemons couldn't be easily halted, because they are now global. If a country serving as the center begins to become precarious, then another location and/or country can be turned into the center. Who is to say that one of the US's industrial empires won't choose China as its center tomorrow? Why not, if the conditions are more suitable? We can see that this is gradually becoming an option.

Industrialism shot agriculture in the heart. Agriculture, a necessity if human society is to exist, faces rampant destruction at the hands of industry. This sacred activity, which has nurtured humanity for the past fifteen thousand years, was left adrift, and preparations are now being made to turn it over to industrial domination. Contrary to popular opinion, the involvement of profit and capital driven industry in agriculture is not an opportunity for mass production. The industrial monopolies' use of genetically modified seeds is making the soil like a mother bearing a child by artificial insemination. Just as healthy pregnancy and maternity are not possible through all kinds of artificial intervention, it is also not healthy to inseminate the soil with genetically modified seeds. Industrial monopolies are preparing to engage in just such madness in relation to agriculture. Humanity will, and has even begun to, experience its worst counterrevolution in the agricultural area. The soil and agriculture are not just any mode of production or relationship; they are inseparable existential aspects of society that cannot to be tampered with. Human society is primarily built on the basis of the soil and agriculture. Detaching it from this space and production would be a huge blow to its existence. The cancerous growth of the cities has already begun to clearly exhibit this danger. Liberation would probably largely mean moving in the opposite direction: from the city back to the soil and agriculture. I imagine the main slogan of this movement would be something like: "either agriculture and soil for existence or extinction." The drive for profit and capital do not allow for industry to unite with the soil and agriculture and link them together by a friendly and symbiotic relationship but instead piles up enormous contradictions and creates hostility between them.

The class, ethnic, national, and ideological contradictions within society may lead to conflict and war, but they are not impossible to resolve. They are constructed by the human hand and they can be dismantled by the human hand. However, humans cannot keep the conflict between industry, and the soil and agriculture under control, because industry is the tool of capital. The soil and agriculture arose ecologically over millions of years. If they degenerate they cannot be reconstructed by the human hand. Just as manufacturing soil is impossible, agricultural products or other living beings, including plants, are not likely to be created by humans at this point. This is not something we can expect. This potential has been fulfilled in the realization of the human being. It is neither meaningful nor possible to repeat what has already occurred. This is a profound philosophical issue, so I won't delve into it too deeply here.

However, just as the pharaohs tried unsuccessfully to prepare for the future with their pyramidic mausoleums, industrialism will also prove unable to create a future where life is worth living with its robotization. Its very approach is disrespectful to human beings. With so magnificent an entity as nature, how meaningful and important can robots or copies of the natural world possibly be? We are once again confronted with capital's mad drive for profit. Let us assume that robots offer the cheapest form of production. If there are no humans to use them, what good would they be? This aspect of industrialism is the main source of unemployment and is capital's major weapon against society's productivity. Capital uses industry as a weapon to manipulate the market both by employing the fewest possible workers and by enforcing price cuts. Monopolistic prices cause crises (of overproduction)—the main factor behind unemployment. Rotting goods and millions of unemployed, starving, and poor people are the victims of these crises.

Social nature can only be sustained by a tight connection with the environment, which is the product of millions of years and a favorable setting. No industrial creation can replace the environment, which is the fantastic creation of the universe. Land, air, sea, and space traffic have already reached disastrous levels. Industry constantly consumes fossil fuels, poisoning the environment and undermining the climate. The payoff for these disasters is a mere two hundred years of profit accumulation. Is this accumulation worth all the destruction, which is far greater than the sum of the destruction rendered in all of history's wars, with the loss of lives greater than the sum of total of lives previously lost to human violence, natural disasters, and all other causes?

Industrialism, as a monopolistic ideology and tool, is one of society's fundamental problems. It should be deeply questioned, and the danger it gives rise to is sufficient reason to do so. If this monster continues to grow and gets out of control, it will make any examination and possible safeguards "too little, too late." If we are to prevent society from ceasing to be itself and becoming a virtual society, now is the time to take this monster from the hands of monopolies, first to make it harmless, and then to make it a friend of society.

As we struggle against industrialism, there is a need to distinguish between monopoly's ideological approach to industrial technology and the way it is currently used and a form of industrial technology that is in harmony with the general interests of society. This is the most important aspect of any scientific work done and of any ideological struggle. Groups that claim to struggle against industrialism as humanists (philanthropists) independent of social and class issues cannot be expected to produce anything relevant. These groups cannot avoid coming into conflict with their own goals and ultimately rendering a service to industrialism as a monopoly. Contrary to popular belief, industrialism has an ideological, militaristic, and class-based character, with science and technology as the material form of its ideology. In fact, it represents the most dangerous dimensions of existing science and technology. The industrial monster did not appear entirely of its own volition. Let's remember that when the English bourgeoisie embarked on its historical imperialist project on the island, on continental Europe, and around the world, it was this class that organized most quickly to make the most comprehensive possible use of industrialism. Later industrialism became a common weapon of the bourgeoisie in every country. This is evident given that bourgeois domination around the world materialized at the point where industrial development—part of the triad of finance, trade, and industry—marked the nineteenth and twentieth centuries.

By declaring noncapitalist society reactionary and entering a strategic alliance with the industrial bourgeoisie the real socialist movement unconsciously but completely contradicted its own goals, leading to a more tragic outcome than that experienced by any other movement that has objectively fallen into betrayal. One example would be Christianity, which was a religion of peace for three hundred years, and then entered into an alliance with power and the state, leading it to objectively, and for the most part consciously, contradict and betray its own goals. The point is that Christianity also came into conflict with its initial goal, because it gravitated toward the monopoly of power and, as a result, could not escape becoming a civilization religion. In Islam, this happened while Mohammad was still alive. In the end, they all ultimately succumbed to the power industry.

While today all of humanity is crying out against environmental destruction, as if the judgment day were near, it is important to understand the historical, social, and class dimensions of the devastation caused by industrialism in the light of similar movements, to take up the struggle against industrialism as a society's movement of existence, and to inevitably wage a struggle in the style of a new sacred religious move- ment. Just as it is impossible to fight fire with fire, life lived in the swamp of industrialism must be questioned and abandoned if we are to wage an ecological struggle. If we do not wish to live new tragedies like those of Christianity, Islam, and real socialism, then we need to learn the lessons they offer and approach scientific-ideological and moral-political strug- gle correctly.

Society's Ecological Problem

Clearly the problem of industrialism is both part of the ecological problem and its essential source. Thus, there is a risk of repetition as we assess this fundamental problem under a different heading. But the ecological problem makes more sense than the problem of industrialism, because it is a social and problematic issue. Although the concept encompasses environmental science, it is essentially a scientific analysis of the tight relationship between social development and its environment. It basically became an issue of concern when environmental problems raised the alarm about a rapidly approaching disaster. A branch of research arose as a result, although not entirely without undesirable implications. Because, like industrialism, the ecological problems were not created by society but are the latest feat of the monopolies of the civilization—a comprehensive problem that encompasses history and is now number one on the agenda of the world—and society.

Perhaps no other problem has been either as severe or as important for revealing the true face of profit and capital systems (organized networks) and putting them on the humanity's agenda as the ecological problem. The balance sheet of the civilization system of profit and capital (the sum of all military, economic, commercial, and religious monopolies throughout history) is not only the disintegration of society in every respect (immoral- ity, lack of politics, unemployment, inflation, prostitution, etc.) but also the far-reaching threat faced by all life-forms and by the environment. What could prove more strikingly that monopolism is anti-society?

Although human society's intelligence and flexibility mean that it is recognized as of the highest nature in comparison to all the other living beings, in the final analysis, it too is a living entity. It is of this earth, the product of a very precisely regulated climatic environment and the evolution of the flora and fauna. Our world's atmosphere and climate and the plant and animal world are essential for human society as well, given that it constitutes the total sum of all. These worlds are highly sensitive and are closely connected. They are in essence a chain, and just as a chain ceases to work when one of its links is broken, when an important link in the evolutionary chain is broken, all of evolution is inevitably affected. Ecology is the science of these developments, and that's what makes it important. Humans can always reregulate the internal order of society, because social reality is a human creation, but the same is not true of the environment. If important environmental links are broken as a result of the actions of some groups organized around the profit and capital monopoly operating above the society from which it emerged, evolutionary disasters in a chain-like reaction might expose the environment and society to mass destruction.

Let's remember that the environmental links are the result of millions of years of evolution. The general destruction of the last five thousand years, the last two hundred in particular, has broken thousands of these evolutionary links in record time. We are witnessing the beginning of a chain reaction that threatens a final breakdown. No one has any idea how to stop it. The atmospheric pollution created by carbon dioxide and other gases will take hundreds, even thousands, of years to clean up. We are probably not yet fully aware of the devastation this has caused the plant and animal world. It is, however, clear that, like the atmosphere, both of these worlds are steadily emitting SOS signals. The pollution of the seas and rivers, as well as desertification, hover at the edge of disaster. Nonetheless, everything suggests that the end of the world will not occur as a result of the disruption of the natural balance but at the hands of some groups organized in networks. Of course, nature will inevitably respond, because it is alive and has an intelligence of its own and a limit to what it will endure. It will resist when the time and place are right, and when we arrive at that time and place, it will show us no mercy. We will all be held responsible for betraying the skills and values bestowed upon us. Is this not what the end of the world will look like?

I don't intend to add anything to the already existing disaster scenarios; but, according to our abilities, each of us must do and say what is necessary as responsible members of society. This is our responsibility and our moral and political duty, the very reason for our existence.

Throughout human history much has been said about the fate of Nimrods and pharaohs who withdrew to their castles and pyramids—for obvious reasons. Each of these Nimrods and pharaohs, whether as individuals or as an order, was a *monopoly* that laid claim to divinity. They were, in fact, the most sublime example of capital monopolies chasing profit during antiquity. Oh, how they resemble the monopolies that have withdrawn to the shopping malls in the cities! There are, of course, differences between them, but their essence remains the same. Despite their magnificence, castles and pyramids cannot compete with the present-day shopping malls, certainly not in numbers. The historical Nimrods and pharaohs don't total more than a few hundred. But the number of contemporary Nimrods and pharaohs is already in the hundreds of thousands. In ancient times, humanity was unable to endure the weight of a few Nimrods and pharaohs and complained bitterly. How much longer will it be able to endure the hundreds of thousands of them who have inflicted upon us far-reaching environmental devastation and the disintegration of society? How will it soothe the pain and agony of the war, unemployment, hunger, and poverty they have caused?

In the light of evolutionary development, these facts must be emphasized, as they clarify what we mean when we talk about historical-society as a totality. Are these facts somehow trivial and insignificant?

The science of capitalist modernity, with its positivist structure, was quite self-confident. It assumed major factual discoveries were everything. It regarded absolute truth to be a superficial knowledge of facts. It was sure that we had entered the age of infinite development. How are we to interpret its inability to see the environmental disaster under its nose? How are we to understand the fact that it was unable to address and remedy the social disasters of the last four hundred years, which exceed in sum all previous historical disasters, including, most notably, war? Let's put aside the prevention of war, which is power that has infiltrated into all the nooks and crannies of society. How do we explain the fact that science has been unable to correctly evaluate this as the case? It is clear that science, especially during the era when the dominant monopolies were at the peak of their hegemony, did not, as expected, answer these questions, because it came under the most intense ideological siege and structurally conformed in the way that best served the system. Science, whose structure, goal, and manner are announced and organized to legitimize the system, has proven to be even less effective than religion. However, it is also clear that if science is not ideological it cannot exist. It is essential that we recognize the knowledge and science that are the ideology of a certain society and class and hence determine our positions accordingly. If ecology, as one of the newer sciences, positions itself correctly within this framework it can provide the ideal capacity for resolving not only the environmental problem but also those of social nature.

Social Sexism, the Family, Women, and the Population Problem

The perception of women as a biologically different sex tops the list of the fundamental factors that result in complete blindness to social reality. The existence of different sexes in itself does not cause any social problem. Just as the duality in each particle in the universe is not seen as a problem, the duality in human existence should not be treated as a problem. The answer to the question "Why is existence dual?" can only be philosophical. Ontological analysis may search for a response to this question (not problem). My response is: the existence of a being is impossible in the absence of duality. Duality is what makes existence possible. Even if women and men were not as they are but were asexual (without a counterpart), they would not have escaped this duality. This is what androgyny must be. We should not be surprised. However, dualities always tend toward different formations, and proof of universal intelligence (*Geist*) can also be sought in this tendency to dualism. Neither part of the duality can ever be good or bad. It can only be, and must be, different. If dualities become identical, existence ceases. For example, you also cannot resolve the question of the reproduction of social being with just two women or just two men. Therefore, the question "Why women or men?" is pointless. Any response would ultimately be philosophical in nature: "It is because the universe *needs to be/has to be/has a tendency to be/has the intellect to be/desires to be* formed as such."

Therefore, it is not only meaningful to examine women as the point of concentration of social relations; it is, at the same time, very important for addressing and overcoming the entangled social problems. Because the dominant male view has become effectively immune to challenge, breaking down the blindness about women is like splitting the atom; it requires a great intellectual effort and the smashing of the dominant masculinity. In relation to women, it is necessary to unravel and demolish the socially constructed woman—this construction has been transformed into something almost existential—to an equal degree. The disappointment encountered in the failure to implement the utopia, program, and principles underlies the success and failure of all struggles—for freedom and equality, as well as democracy, morals, politics, and class-based struggles. This disappointment carries the traces of the relationship of domination (power) between men and women that has not been destroyed. It is this relationship that lies at the root of all of the relations that maintain diverse inequalities, enslavement, despotism, fascism, and militarism. If we want to validate concepts like equality, freedom, democracy, and socialism in a way that won't prove a disappointment, we need to disentangle and tear apart the web of relations around women that are as old as the relationship between society and nature. There is no other road to true freedom, equality (in diversity), democracy, and a non-hypocritical morality.

Ever since the emergence of hierarchy, sexism has been the ideology of power. It is closely linked to class division and the rise of power. All the archeological and anthropological evidence, along with current research and observation, indicates that there have been extended periods over a long term when women were the source of authority. This authority was not the authority of power based on surplus product. On the contrary, it stemmed from productivity and fertility and was a form of authority that served to strengthen social existence. Emotional intelligence, which has more influence on women, has strong ties to this existence. That women are not distinct participants in power struggles based on surplus product is related to their emotional intelligence and the nature of their social existence.

Historical findings and current observations clearly show the leading male role in the development of power linked to the hierarchical state order. For this, it was necessary to overcome and smash women's authority, which was substantial until the final stage of Neolithic society. Again, historical findings and current observations verify that major struggles, differing in length and form, were waged to achieve this. Sumerian mythology in particular, is quite illuminating in this regard, almost acting as the memory of historical and social nature.

The history of civilization is also the history of women's defeat and disappearance. This history is the history of the consolidation of the male dominant personality, with its gods and servants, emperor and subjects, economy, science, and arts. The defeat and disappearance of women is a major defeat that indicates the decline of society. Sexist society is the result of this defeat and decline. The sexist male was so willing to construct his social domination over women that he turned all normal contact into a display of domination. Even a biological phenomenon like sexual intercourse was turned into a consistent nexus of power relations. Men approach sexual contact with women as if they are scoring a victory. This is so deeply ingrained that it has given rise to numerous euphemisms and insults: "I got my end," "I finished her off," "her belly should never lack a colt and her back some lashes," "if you leave it to your daughter, she will run off with the drummer,"[23] "bitch," "whore," "marry her off immediately," or "a girl like a boy." This clearly shows how influential the relationship between sexuality and power is in society. Even today, it is a sociological fact that every man has countless rights over women, including the "right to kill." These "rights" are acted on every day. Relationships between men and women are overwhelmingly characterized by harassment and rape.

Within this social context, the family is built as man's small state. In the history of civilization, the institution called the family has been continuously refined due to the great force it gives to power and the state apparatuses. To begin with, the family centered around the man gained power and became the stem cell of state society. Second, the family ensured the unlimited and unremunerated labor of woman. Third, the family served to raise children, meeting population needs. Fourth, as a model, the family propagates slavery and decay throughout society. This family is, in fact, ideological. It gives form and functionality to dynastic ideology. In the family, every man perceives himself to be the ruler of a khanate. Dynastic ideology accentuates the perception that the family is very important and influential. The more women and children in the family, the greater the security and honor for the man. It is also important to consider the present-day family as an ideological institution. If we were to pull women and the family away from the civilization system—power and the state—little would be left of the system. The price paid to maintain the civilization system is the aggrieved, impoverished, decayed, and defeated existence of women in a constant state of low intensity warfare. A second parallel chain of monopoly, similar to the monopolies of capital maintained over society throughout the history of civilization, has been the "male monopoly" over women's world—the oldest and most powerful monopoly. Interpreting women's existence as the oldest colonial realm will allow for more realistic conclusions. It is more correct to call women "the oldest colonized people who are not a *millet*."[24]

Capitalist modernity, despite all of its liberal adornments, has not shattered the inherited status and made women free and equal; on the contrary, it has made their situation worse by loading them down with additional responsibilities. The cheapest worker, the houseworker, the unpaid worker, the flexible worker, the maid, and jobs of a similar status indicate the increasing harshness of her situation. On top of that, her role as the most important magazine staple and the major tool of advertising makes her exploitation even more profound. Even her body, a tool for a wide range of exploitation, is rendered a commodity that capital has no intention of giving up. She is the constant provocative tool of advertising. In short, she is the most productive representative of the modern slave. She is both a tool for unlimited pleasure and the most profitable slave. Is it possible to imagine a more precious commodity?

The population problem is closely linked to sexism, the family, and women. The larger the population, the greater the capital. "Housewifery" is the population factory, making it the factory that produces the most precious of commodities, "the offspring" that the system needs. Unfortunately, this is what the family has become under the monopolistic domination. While women are made to pay the bill for all the hardships, the value of this commodity is a most precious gift for the system. Population growth is most destructive to women, just as was the case under dynastic ideology. Familism, as the key ideology of modernity, is the final dynastic stage. All these issues have been increasingly integrated into nation-state ideology. What could be more precious than continuously raising children for the nation-state? The larger the population of the nation-state, the more powerful that state is. This means that underlying the population explosion are the critical interests of firmly organized capital and male monopolies. Hardship, grief, sorrow, accusations, poverty, and hunger are a woman's lot, while all of the joy and profit go to "her man" and the capitalists. No other era in history demonstrated such power or developed the practice of using women as such a multidirectional tool of exploitation. Women, as the first and last colony, are passing through the most critical moment in their history.

Whereas a joint undertaking of a life reorganized with women, based on a deep-rooted philosophy of freedom, equality, and democracy, could allow us to attain the most perfect level of beauty, goodness, and righteousness. I personally find living with a woman under the current circumstances not only very problematic but even ugly, negative, and wrong. I never had the courage to live with a woman under the current conditions. In my life I tried to question even such a powerful urge as the sex drive. The sex drive exists to sustain life. It is a natural wonder and should be treated as sacred. But capital and the male monopoly have contaminated women so completely that this capacity like a natural wonder has been transformed into an institution that is more like a "seed factory"—the most debased institution producing commodities. With these commodities, society is being ransacked and the environment is gradually collapsing under the weight of the population (it's currently 7.5 billion; let's consider what will happen to the environment with a population of 10 or 15 billion). No doubt being with a woman and having a child is a very sacred experience; it is an indication that life will not come to an end. It makes eternity tangible. Is there a more precious feeling? All species experience the excitement of being embraced by eternity under these circumstances. For the present-day human being, in particular, this situation could not be better summed up than by a wandering minstrel singing, "Our seed has become troublesome to us."[25] Once again it is undeniable that we face the far-reaching immorality, ugliness, and fundamental wrongness of the capital and male monopoly that contradicts both first and second nature.

Anything built by the human hand can be demolished by the human hand. What we are experiencing is neither a law of nature nor our destiny. These are the modifications made by the monopolies—the hands of the cancerous and hormone-injected life of the crafty and the strong man, i.e., the network. I always felt the need for women and men, the most wonderful pair in the universe (as far as we know), to achieve a profound understanding. I had the courage to prioritize my relationship with women in this manner, because it is important that above all we can think together, discuss where, when, and how much distortion has occurred and overcome it. One of the cornerstones of my philosophical pursuit is undoubtedly women, who think deeply and who can make good, beautiful, and right decisions, thereby winning my admiration as they surpass me and as people I can relate to. I always believed that the secrets of the flow of life in the universe would be more meaningful, good, beautiful, and true with such a woman. But I was different from other men in embracing a morality that led me to reject a life under the sway of the commodity of "capital and the male," Hürmüz with ninety thousand husbands.[26] In this case, perhaps "jineolojî" (where jin is the woman and jineolojî the science of women), which goes beyond feminism, is a concept that might serve our purpose.

Society's Urbanization Problem

Madaniyya is another name for civilization, literally meaning *urbanization* in Arabic. There are more than a few problems stemming from urbanization, and they are no less important than the ecological problems. At present, urbanization is one of the fundamental threats to social life. What has made the city like this?

Briefly, we could say that the formula city = class = state offers a simple explanation for the urbanization problem but lacks depth and prevents flexible thinking. Humanity thought that cities, like villages, would suit the nature of society and went about building them. The city is a key site of concentrated social intelligence, provoking and revealing the intellectual ability of human beings. Reason has developed in a close relationship with the city. The city is where human beings began to recognize the breadth of their capacity. Cities also provided security, those who are confident think more rationally. This development in thought resulted in new inventions. The city also developed methods and techniques for increasing production. The humans who experienced this saw the city as the source of light and always stretched toward it. Unsurprisingly, the city developed around the temple, because at the time the temple was where sacred reason and spirit gathered, making it a site where society discovered and created its own reason and identity. What we are emphasizing here are the assumptions in favor of the city.

As with everything, since its birth there was another side to the city: class division and the formation of the state. The material base of class division, no doubt, was rising productivity. Some of those who possessed the city's developing reason learned from experience that an increase in the number of people working the fertile land would mean more people could be fed. Once this became clear, the challenge was to develop the necessary mechanism for achieving it. The mechanism that arose was the state, which is a sort of monopoly. This organization of a new order, albeit at the city level, clearly took the form of an agricultural monopoly. Sumerian cities make all of this clear. Many civilizations, including Egypt and Harappa, were agricultural monopolies at their birth and were the apparatus that organized production from the outset. When production reached a level at which there was surplus product—at least twice what the existing population requires—the material basis for the state was in place. In fact, the state could be described as those who live off of surplus production. It might be more meaningful to call it an organization that amasses surplus, with the city the most suitable location for doing so, given that such relations were difficult to establish in tribal or village societies. Tribal and village structures simply did not allow for it. This is the basic reason that the state first arose in the city, and this is why humanity first encountered exploitation—a form of relationship previously unknown—in the city. The name of this new art was "statism." Whoever controlled the state would be capable of anything! It is an enormous apparatus for advancing interests. Even the slave laborer understood that unemployment under a state would be more comfortable and secure. It would, however, be an exaggeration to say that the laborer worked solely because of force and violence. This is more or less the story of the birth of the city.

Although it led to problems (e.g., the organization of exploitation and the powerful), it is clear that the city was a revolutionary step in the rational development of society. Aristotle considered a population of around five thousand to be ideal for a city. When cities first emerged, their population were generally around that number. The city did, however, signal a new social composition, one that surpassed the tribal community. Urban citizenship unites those coming from different tribes and lineages—"people of the city," "hemşehriler," and "bajariler."[27] This shows how the city enriched society, how it was, at that point, a tool for development. It was not yet the source of any serious problems. Throughout antiquity, excluding some periods in Babylonia and Rome, there is no evidence of a city with a population problem. The social superiority of life in the city meant that it continuously grew more popular. As the Sumerian model spread, Egypt began to construct contained cities. Indeed, Egyptian civilization is unique in having been part urban and part peasant. Historians tell us that there were at least ten villages for every city, but there was a symbiotic relationship between them, which meant that at this juncture there was not yet any problem between the city and the village. Nonetheless, trade and craftsmanship were highly developed. Roads, architecture, the arts, and palace structures, as well as other structures around the temple, expanded and reconfigured the city. Many cities were also built around military posts. Roman military posts in particular formed the nucleus of cities.

Rome, the last magnificent city of the archaic age, probably carried within it all of the problems of its era. This made Rome alternately civilization's most magnificent and its most problematic city. All classes and communities could be found in it (the aristocracy, the bourgeoisie, slaves, the lumpenproletariat, all of the different ethnic groups and races, and every belief system). The remnants of the old classes and communities and the embryo of the new ones were both present. It was also possible to note a range of morality and politics and distinct styles of administration. Every form of monarchy, republic, and democracy was being experimented with somewhere in the empire. Both the remnants and embryos of all of the different examples of science, the arts, philosophy, and religion were on display. Rome was a truly ecumenical city. This is another sense in which "all roads lead to Rome" was a reality. Rome represented the peak of the 3,500-year-old central civilization. Even its collapse reflected its magnificence. The two major forces that undermined Roman civilization were the Christians, who made up the poorer classes, and those groups that preserved strong ethnic characteristics (referring to them as barbarians is to fall into the trap of civilization's terminology). They attacked in waves, one internally and the other externally, and would finally bring the city down. The year 476 CE not only marked the fall of a city—the fall of Rome—but also the decay, decline, and collapse of antiquity and the archaic age of civilization.

At no point during the Middle Ages did civilization again attain the level of urbanization it achieved during antiquity. Initially, the cities, castles, and ramparts of the Middle Ages were relatively small and simple. These cities were little more than small emirates and feudal headquarters. They began to expand when craftspeople and palace servants first gathered around them. Although the merchant class provided the impetus for growth and greater magnificence, there were very few new cities that could hold a candle to older cities, such as Rome, Iskenderiya (Alexandria), Antakya (Antioch), Nusaybin and Dara, and Urfa (Edessa). They may have had larger populations, but in terms of architecture and amenities (temples, theaters, assembly halls, agoras, hippodromes, amphitheaters, public baths, sewage systems, workshops, and the like) they lacked the splendor of the old cities. The civilization of the Middle Ages was more makeshift, with its cities built on the ruins of antiquity and the archaic age. The life of the city in no way surpassed that of rural and village life. Cities were essentially islands in an ocean of villages. The cities were the site of power struggles and class conflicts, but they did not yet pose an environmental threat. In general, the civilization system, in particular due to capital monopolies, eroded the environment gradually—for example, salination was the work of agricultural monopolies. This situation continued until the end of the eighteenth century, with the problems being increasingly aggravated.

The real crisis of urbanization emerged with the nineteenth-century Industrial Revolution. This was no coincidence but was an aspect of the antisocial nature of industrialism. The primary responsibility for the ecological problems created by the city lies with its fundamental detachment from the environment. The village had a one-to-one relationship with the environment and recognized its total dependency on the environment and that it was, in fact, a product of the environment. It lived as if in a direct dialogue with the environment and the animals and plants— its common language being agriculture. Village society formation was heavily influenced by this language. The situation was quite the opposite in the city; the city gradually broke with agriculture and the environment. It developed a new language—the language of the city. It was based on a different rationale, and its attachment to environmental reason grew increasingly weak. The language of the city was more about trade, crafts, industry, and money, which constituted their reason and science and was, therefore, ultimately constituted by them. This was a new dialectical development of language. Clearly, language and mentality are laden with contradictions and alienation. At this point, urbanization was the result of the interplay of the widespread dialects and cultures of the clans, tribes, aşirets, peoples, and village societies of both the old rural society and this new social system. This new system also gave rise to a distinctive science, arts, religion, and philosophy. From a class perspective, two other major categories came into being—the aristocracy and everyone else. The city dweller had not yet attained new and independent characteristics, remaining at this point little more than an extension of general society.

This historical equilibrium was completely undermined in the nineteenth and twentieth centuries. Obviously, this was not an abrupt development. The renewed rise of the city between the tenth and sixteenth centuries on the Italian Peninsula (Venice, Genoa, Florence, Milan, etc.) denoted the spread of the commercial revolution from Italy to the rest of Europe, beginning in the late thirteenth century. The Italian cities led this process, attempting to replicate the growth of Rome. This resulted in intense inter- and intra-city competition, part of a struggle to gain leadership of this new phase of civilization. It was as if the old life had been revived, but the new conditions would inevitably transform that life. A new Rome could not be created by imitating the old one. That would only result in indistinct copies of Rome. Its attempt at establishing a central monarchy and the nation-state would not be successful either. Nonetheless, it is beyond dispute that the Italian cities of the Renaissance led European civilization during tenth through the sixteenth centuries, under the combined leadership of the church (Ecumenical Catholic) and secular tendencies.

The Hanseatic League (c. 1250–1450) launched the German urban revolution, with its constituent towns later undergoing their own commercial revolutions.[28] The rise of manufacturing that was set in motion marks the second period, with an intense struggle against centralization based on the confederalism of the towns. The struggle and rebellions, involving many peasants and various semi-working-class groups and craftspeople, lasted for around four hundred years. After a bloody period, for a variety of reasons (ideological, organizational, and matters of leadership) these early experiences of town and rural democratic confederalism were defeated by the centralized monarchies and the arising nation-states. Had they not been defeated, the history of Europe would have been written differently. The current Federal Republic of Germany is going through a very slow evolutionary transformation from bourgeois nation-state fascism to this older model, but as bourgeois federalism rather than democratic confederalism.

The real boom occurred in the towns in Netherlands and England. The fact that they had been the centers of three intense revolutions played a role. The commercial, financial, and industrial revolutions attained their true victories in Amsterdam and London. Communal federalism was easily suppressed in both of these countries, but this did not mean that all rural or urban people quickly succumbed to the center and the nation-state. It took the sixteenth- and seventeenth-century revolutions in Netherlands and England to accomplish this. Amsterdam was the leading city during the seventeenth and eighteenth centuries, while that honor fell to London in the nineteenth and twentieth centuries. Both of these cities were world centers of this modern age. They administered the central world civilization system as hegemonic powers during this huge transformation, and, as a result, both their population and their contradictions grew rapidly. It was during this period that the truly cancerous nature of the city began to become apparent. Its diseased structures were subsequently transported to France, the US, Eastern Europe, Russia, the Far East, Latin America, the Middle East, and Africa. The twentieth century is the "term" where the city begins to gain the edge over the rural in history.[29] The capitalist urban paradigm, alongside the old civilization, began to replace the paradigmatic world of communal rural society, which had played a key role for the previous twelve thousand years. The city was no longer just the center for commerce, finance, and industry but became the hegemonic center of a particular worldview. This new paradigm established itself through the universities and academic centers for science, as well as through hospitals and prisons and the new class structure and ascendant bureaucracies, and tried to assert control over the old eschatological worldview, replacing it with strict positivism.[30] In this sense, positivism became the new bourgeois religion. In the end, it found it more practical and effective to put on the mask of "scientism" and benefit from the extraordinary growth in the importance of the sciences.

Society had truly grown cancerous because of the structure of these cities. Aristotle, for example, had never imagined a city with a population of ten thousand people. Cities have grown steadily in population, from one hundred thousand to one million to five million to fifteen million to twenty million people, and now we can foresee cities with populations of twenty-five million or more! If this is not cancerous growth, then what is? Just feeding such a city could wipe out a mid-sized country and its surroundings in no time. Such growth is irrational and can only lead to the destruction of the nature of society and the city, along with first nature. No country and its population can environmentally sustain such growth for very long. This cancerous growth is the fundamental basis of the current environmental destruction. The city occupies, invades, and destroys, and in the process essentially colonizes its country and its people. The city is the new colonial power, the center of global commercial, financial, and industrial monopolies, with its bases in the shopping malls. The fact that the security precautions taken in these shopping malls are in every way equivalent to the measures taken at the old castles and ramparts confirms this.

Twenty-first-century imperialism and colonialism occur not outside of but inside countries. The colonizers are not foreigners but more like their partners. It is not only capital monopolies that became global but also power and the state. There is no longer a distinction between the inside and the outside of global power. They are all partners, therefore the nation they belong to is no longer of any importance. Making military, economic, and cultural distinctions has also become meaningless.

English is their common language, and Anglo-Saxon culture the common culture, NATO, the military organization, and the UN, the international organization. There is no longer a single New York, the hegemonic center of the US that took over from London in the 1930s, but multiple New Yorks and Londons. We have arrived at the age of global cities. The cancerous growth of the cities in the global age, with their rapid spread is not just destroying the environment. The mentality and way of life of urban dwellers would make even a Martian seem relatively earthly and less bizarre. The underdeveloped nobility of urban dwellers became obsolete before it was even born. It attempts to conceal its true monstrosity by presenting itself as modern and fashionable. The real barbarian (with its fascism, genocide, including unlimited cultural genocide, and finally *societycide*) is no longer rural-based but is city-based—it is indeed the city itself. All the barbaric individuals and groups (virtual simulacra and media-hyped society, sports fanatics, music groups with their frenetic but meaningless blowouts, exterminationist bureaucracies, and market profiteers, those with no discernible moral principles, and those who have become robots) make us miss the old barbarians (although I do not in any way believe that the migrant tribes were actually barbarians).

The Babylonians of the modern age are on the scene (let's have a little sympathy for Babylon, because until its collapse it was noble and sacred, and its degeneration was limited). The end of this age cannot be estimated, but all of the scientific data show that our planet cannot bear this world (this monstrous world that has betrayed its own interests and is intent on destroying its own ecology). Even if they were to retreat to the rural areas, they are infected from head to toe. It is very important to understand that city society is wandering at the edge of *societycide*.

No doubt class power and statist structures are responsible for the situation that has befallen the city. The incredible rentier from the city has turned city dwellers into merciless barbarians and created the city monster (the new Leviathan). City dwellers and society alone cannot be held responsible for this. Sometimes the innocent suffer along with the guilty. The slum dwellers—the new Christians of the city—must find a way out for themselves. Otherwise, they are condemned to face much worse conditions at the hands of thousands of Neros than anything a single Nero was responsible for.[31]

We should consider how to rescue the limited remaining beauty, morality, and reason in the city. Every social project needs to put the problems arising from urbanism (which long ago became a disease) at its center. We need to be aware that this is the only way we can hope to find meaningful solutions to all our current social and ecological problems. There's no need to look for other reasons for the approaching collapse of the world and society; problems originating in the cities are already sufficient cause for concern.

Society's Class and Bureaucracy Problem

Those who view class division and bureaucracy as requirements for social existence may find this problematization odd. Some people may assert that class division and bureaucracy may cause certain problems, but as entities they do not constitute a problem in and of themselves. However, these structures are as problematic as the city itself. Like the city, class division and bureaucracy may not have constituted much of a burden or problem during the initial stages of civilization, but their problematic nature has become more evident recently. Class division and the corresponding bureaucratization are problematic realities that do nothing to serve social morality and politics. Society has a long history of widespread opposition to these two developments, raising rigorous resistance and making their imposition less than easy.

The diversity in social nature, which I will elaborate on in later sections, can vary greatly and attain new forms. This is normal and in keeping with the spirit of nature. Just like some tissues in plant and animal species that are undeveloped and do not need to be developed, in the nature of society too—apart from quite limited, temporary, and functional classes and stratifications (including bureaucracy) that would make variety and diversity meaningful and would be a component of them—extremely permanent, nonfunctional, and useless classes and stratifications that penetrate the social fabric like a tumor are nonessential. The class-based development of the priest, the aristocracy, and the bourgeoisie that was to some degree useful for a while can be tolerated conditionally. However, these are the ideological, political, economic, and military hegemonic powers seen throughout the history of civilization. From the point of view of social morality and politics, it is impossible to accept them with their permanent excessively oppressive and exploitative characteristics. The contradiction is antagonistic from this point of view, because the very nature of class and bureaucracy amounts to a negation of social morality and politics. The condition I suggest is very important. A class and bureaucracy that is diverse or encourages diversity is certainly possible. For example, we cannot consider the temple created by the Sumerian priestly class completely dysfunctional. The priests laid the main foundations of science, efficient production, urbanism, religion, craftsmanship, and order. This is not unique; the priestly class played a similar role in the emergence of numerous cultures. Any conditional understanding shown to the priests must be understood in the light of their positive contributions. But the legitimacy of class and bureaucracy in their calcified, dysfunctional, and excessively overblown state is always controversial and must be overcome.

Much the same is also true of the aristocracy. Aristocrats also made contributions to social development in various areas, including order, effective work, administrative elegance, the arts, and science. This framework creates a certain tolerance for the aristocracy. But the familiar calcification, despotism, dynasties, and kingdoms, and even the deification of themselves, are all a disease that cannot be accepted. Social morality and politics are antagonistic to these developments. A struggle to overcome them is required if true morality and politics are to emerge.

All of this is even truer for the bourgeoisie. The development of this class and its bureaucratic apparatus has contributed to social development during revolutionary periods. Commerce and currency tools (like money and bonds), taking the initiative in developing industry, periodically experimenting with democracy, and making limited contributions to science and the arts are aspects we can tolerate. However, the excessively permanent structure of the bourgeoisie, which has led to more class division and bureaucratization over the last four hundred years to a degree unsurpassed in the previous history of civilization, exacerbated their cancerous growth making it larger in numbers and more dangerous than any other upper class. In my paradigm, the bourgeoisie and bureaucracy that occupy the center in the history of class division act like a cancer. Social nature simply cannot sustain such class division and bureaucracy. If forced to do so, I would call it "fascism." I believe that fascism expresses the ill intent of the middle class—the sum of bureaucracy and the bourgeoisie—toward society. What this indicates is that society and the middle class cannot coexist. Some intellectuals present the middle class as the class base of republican and democratic regimes. This projection is among liberalism's worst and falsest propaganda. The middle class has played the key role in the negation of the republic and democracy. Other classes play a more limited role and are generally unrelated to fascism. The middle class, with this particular feature, plays the same role as excessive urbanization—cancerous growth. And the tight organic and structural ties between the two should not be overlooked. The city acquires its disease from middle-class greed and growth, while such cities themselves inevitably foster the growth of middle class.

The middle-class mental framework is positivist. This class has the most superficial structure, lacking essence and depth, and cannot, in fact, will not, see all aspects of a phenomena beyond evaluating them on the basis of self-interest. Although it presents positivism disguised as "scientism," it is the most pagan class in history. For example, the number of commemorative statues has exploded under this class. In appearance, it is secular and worldly, but, at its core, it is the most religious and impulsive power. The religious aspect in this case is its bigoted "positivist" beliefs and thoughts. We know that positivism never rests on the totality of truth. This class, rhetorically secular but essentially anti-secular, shamelessly imposes the most delusionary projects (its otherworldly projects) on society. It is the class that has developed capital's economic, political, military, ideological, and scientific monopoly at a global level, making it the most anti-society class. Its anti-society nature expresses itself in two ways: genocide and societycide. It was the bourgeois class character that made it possible to annihilate a people or a community because of its descent, race, or religion. Societycide, however, is worse. It occurs in two ways. First, it imposes its nation-state ideology and the institutionalization of power as militarism and war penetrating all of the nooks and crannies of society. This is an all-out war on society carried out by power amalgamated with the state. The bourgeoisie knows full well from experience that there is no other way for it to rule society. Second, virtual society, arising from the "media and informatics" revolution of the second half of twentieth century, has replaced genuine society. Or, more precisely, we have a form of media-hyped, computer-based bombardment warfare. In the last half century, societies have been successfully ruled by this second form of warfare. When the imaginary, virtual, and simulacra society is substituted for genuine society, or is assumed to have been, it engages in societycide.

I favor a different approach to the categories of slaves, serfs, and workers—the exploited and oppressed classes of history. Such class divisions have a limited role in determining the subject and in democratization, because they are completely within the intellectual and structural framework of their masters and have been turned into an insignificant extension or appendage. No class in history has ever become its own subject and toppled its masters. This reflects a very important reality. Even in the case of the oppressed and exploited, class divisions can be viewed as branches at varying distances from the trunk—society. No matter how much the branch droops, or even if it breaks off, it will not affect the trunk, or, when it does, its impact is limited. That is why terms like slave and master, serf and aristocrat, or worker and bourgeois society are faulty. Social sciences must develop new names and descriptions. Just as we cannot describe a tree by its branches, we cannot identify a society simply on the basis of the classes that have emerged within it. More importantly, as we have seen from many examples in the history of both real socialism and anarchism, subjectivizing, praising, and charging these classes (slave, serf, worker, petit bourgeois) with central revolutionary roles has not worked out all that well. As I see it, this is because this is very much the wrong role to give them. The correct approach is to oppose all class division. The slaves, serfs, and working class (mostly semi-rural and craftspeople) may, indeed, have played a positive, subjective, revolutionary role during transitional periods. But they too degenerated and became dysfunctional as they grew, became permanent, and reconciled with the upper classes.

More importantly, a libertarian, egalitarian, and democratic worldview would not subjectivize or give moral and political value to either side of any class division, except in the instances I mentioned above. Such a worldview must struggle against class division and see it in contradiction with social nature and as anti-society regardless of the classes involved. Just because the classes we mention have existed does not make them legitimate or representative of true social values. A tumor cannot be considered a normal part of the body, and we can see social phenomena in the same way. Besides, all of the oppressed and exploited lower classes have arisen as a result of the force and the hegemonic ideologies of power and the state. The slavery, serfdom, and labor that arose under those conditions can only be condemned. To say "long live the glorious worker, serf, and slave!" is to objectively praise and approve the existing forces of hegemonic power. This approach to class by many schools of thought, including those of Marx and his successors, is the main reason for their failure. The upper classes may be meaningful to a certain degree, but because the classes that do the great bulk of the labor with much blood and sweat were formed through violence and ideological persuasion, it is best to continuously condemn such class stratification, never praise it, and struggle to overcome it. Classes are given the honor of being agents for change when they cannot be, and, although it is evident that they cannot make a revolution, they are given such a role, and, as is frequently seen in the history of social struggles, they cannot escape being defeated. The reason for the defeat lies in a faulty understanding of the problem and in attributing the wrong role to class stratification. The social struggles of the new era (the twenty-first century) will only be successful if they do not repeat this fundamental error.

It is true that the bourgeoisie has aggravated the class problem. It is also true that its class interests have acceded to power (acceding to power is effectively waging war on society) in every nook and cranny of society, and it has formalized this with the state, thereby, reaching its most advanced stage. Under the aegis of "capital partnership," it is abundantly clear that they have instrumentalized many social segments, concessionist workers in particular. The bourgeoisie has almost absorbed society. Even so, it is the most problematic class that has ever arisen, and it has vastly multiplied society's problems.

Bureaucracy, the ruling class's institutional instrument of implementation throughout history, has become increasingly ubiquitous with the formation of the nation-state over the last two hundred years, almost playing the role of an independent class and increasing its influence over power and the state. In fact, it can comfortably be said that it considers itself to be the state. It is hard to refute that it has become a primary power for caging society and has secured this role by seizing control of all social areas (education, health, jurisdiction, transportation, morality, politics, the environment, science, religion, the arts, the economy). In our present society (capitalist modernity), it is not only the state bureaucracy that has become monstrous but the world of monopolies that follows in its footsteps. The monopolies are the result of a decision to "become professionally managed companies rather than family businesses," massively increasing bureaucracies in this domain as well. This new reality of large corporations clearly contributes to the excessive growth of bureaucracy. In a certain sense, this is corporations "becoming states." In reality, when nation-states prove inadequate and the establishment of a new state form is on the agenda, there is an increasing tendency for global and local corporations to become more like states.

The problems of society resulting from the grip of class and bureaucracy are the current reality. It is—so to speak—the "now" of all history. Furthermore, it can be said that this pair have social nature (traditional society) in the stranglehold of their octopus-like arms and dissolve it. The conclusion that we can draw is that we are going through the most chaotic and crisis-ridden period of history. Social freedom, equality, and democracy will only be possible in a system with democratic civilization structures, and this in turn requires that we struggle to build it on the basis of a rectified science.

Society's Education and Health Problems

It may look like an unnecessary issue, but it is important to grasp the problems caused when the areas of education and health, as was the case for science, are monopolized by power and the state. Just as science that has become state science is the most effective tool for ideological hegemony, the same is true when education and health are integrated with power.

Education can be defined as society's effort to pass on its experience in the form of theoretical and practical knowledge to its members, particularly its youth. Children's socialization is ensured by society's educational activities. Because children and the youth belong to society, their education is society's most important duty and not the duty of power and the state. It is both a right and duty for a society to raise children and youth according to its own traditions and social nature. This is vital—a question of survival. A society cannot share with another power its right to exist, and to this end the duty to educate its youth, not even with the state or another apparatus of power. If it does, it will be surrendering itself to the ruling monopolies. The sacredness of the right to education stems from existence itself. No other power, including a child's parents, can be as close or feel the need to be as close to children and youth as society does. One of the most anti-society aspects of civilization throughout history is depriving society of its children and youth. The statist civilization system achieves this in one of two ways: either by annihilating the elders and enslaving the children and youth or by educating them to make them useful to the upper levels of the ruling power.

One of the most important purposes of war is to set up *devshirme* centers where children and young women and men—as the most precious goods—can be assimilated.[32] This is how the foundation of primitive bureaucracy is established. In a way, the history of civilization is the history of using this method both to weaken society and to constitute the power of the bureaucratic apparatuses—thereby establishing a society to counter society: the society of power and the state to counter natural society. In this establishment, children and youth who have been isolated from their own society are taught a completely different language, culture, and history. The fundamental goal of this education is to alienate children from their essence, and ideologically and materially inculcate them with the most statist identity possible, making it impossible for them to live without power. Power and the state are turned into the only valid framework of existence. Those recruited consider themselves to be power and the state, and thus are pitted against natural society. Sometimes state society and social nature are treated as equal. This is incorrect and contradictory. The history of civilization is built on this contradiction. These historical realities are the underlying reason for the rulers seizure of education. Beyond that, they do not care about the task of education for society. Just as a capitalist educates his workers, rulers similarly educate those they dominate—as their servant-workers. Even the members of the bureaucracy, from the highest to the lowest, are educated as servants.

The nation-state powers in particular secure their monopoly of society's children and youth through education. Imbued with the rulers' historical perspective and understanding of the arts, as well as with their religious and philosophical mindsets, these children and youth are no longer members of their families but are now the true children and goods of the rulers. This is how such profound alienation is institutionalized. The bourgeoisie is the class that has accomplished the most far-reaching monopoly over society in terms of education. When primary and secondary school were made compulsory and those wishing to find a job were reminded that they needed a university degree, the clamps of alienation and dependency imposed on society's youth, as well as the process of being caged, became compulsory. Force, financial power, and education have become the irresistible weapons with which society is colonized.

Throughout the history of civilization, education has been used to deliver the heaviest blow in the war that power and the state have waged against society. A society's right to education is one of the most difficult of its rights to accomplish. Society must control education if it is to secure its existence against the burgeoning nation-state and the economic monopolies. In this sense, society has entered the most difficult period of its history. Ideological hegemony colonizes not only militarily and economically but, more recently, is greatly facilitated by the communications revolution and the media war—intensely focused and very surreptitious—waged against the whole of society, facilitating a more successful renewed cultural colonization. Society's only way to freedom and emancipation is to resist this cultural conquest and colonization with its most fundamental tools for existence: moral and political struggle. A society that has lost its youth or, inversely, a youth that has lost its society, is beyond defeated; it has lost and betrayed its right to existence. Decay, disintegration, and annihilation will follow. The fundamental duty of society in response to this is to develop its own educational institutions as the main tools for securing its existence. Revolution of meaning will be successful when society's educational institutions interpret scientific, philosophical, artistic, and linguistic content in a way that removes them from the alliance of the science-power structures. Otherwise, there will be no way of ensuring that society's moral and political fabric functions.

Therefore, while addressing the question of education requires moral and political institutions (the fabric of society), the true objective of morality and politics is social education. A society that fails to educate itself will be unable to develop and sustain its own morality and political organizations, and such a society cannot avoid constant danger, decay, and eventual disintegration.

The health of members of society is also an issue every bit as important as education. The foundation, existence, and freedom of a society that lacks the means to sustain the health of its members is at risk, if not already lost.

Dependency in the field of health is a sign of overall dependency, whereas a society that can address the physical and psychological problems of its members autonomously has what it takes to achieve its freedom. The health problems that sweep through colonized societies are linked to the colonial regimes they live under. Establishing health institutions and training specialists must be seen as both a fundamental right and an essential duty of society. Power and the state strip society of this duty and monopolize it; this is a huge blow to social health. To struggle for the right to health is to respect yourself and understand the essence of freedom.

In capitalist modernity, nation-state control of education and health is considered vital. Without taking control of these two fields, upon which society's existential, healthy, and open-minded development depends, and constructing monopolistic domination over them, it is extremely difficult to maintain an overall hegemony and exploitation. Control of education and health is extraordinarily important to the monopolies, since they understand that they cannot make society their property by military force alone.

Once again, we see that the monopolistic power and state lies at the heart of all of society's existential problems. Profit and capital cannot be sustained without the power monopoly. It is equally true, however, that without a systemic struggle for a democratic civilization none of society's problems can be permanently resolved.

Society's Militarism Problem

Militarism is the most advanced form of antisocial monopolism. It is not unrealistic to assume that the initial effort to establish authority over social nature to oppress and exploit people was the result of the analytical thought and action of a "crafty strongman" from a hunting tradition. Essentially, he attempted to establish his authority over two key groups: the hunters at his side and the women he was trying to confine to the home. Along the way, as shamans (proto-priests) and gerontocratic elements (groups of elders) joined the crafty strongman, the first hierarchical authority was formed in many societies in various forms. With the transition to civilization, the crafty strongman, and his entourage—now the official power—institutionalized themselves as the military arm of the state (the initial monopoly of the economy based on the usurpation of surplus product). The three successive dynasties of Ur that followed in the immediate wake of the priest-king period of Sumerian society reflect this development, and many other communities had parallel experiences. In the Epic of Gilgamesh, it is possible to follow step-by-step the way the kingdom was clearly detached from the goddess Inanna tradition (the tradition of goddess-priestesses) and the way priestesses were weakened and confined to houses (both public and private).

If we see Gilgamesh as symbolic of the first commander in history, we can better analyze the rise of the militarist tradition. This tradition's task was to hunt down people to meet the city's need for slaves. With the help of the collaborationist Enkidu, who is mentioned in the Epic of Gilgamesh, they hunted the so-called wild barbarian tribes (practitioners of the Humbaba religion) living in the north of present-day Iraq. It is obvious that the tyranny of the city was the real source of barbarism and savagery. The word "barbaric" in the Greek cultural tradition was developed by the

city as diversionary propaganda and a lie to establish ideological superiority. The rural tribes, which were weak and disorganized compared
to the city, could not have been barbaric in the sense that official society
claimed. The concept of barbarism is one of the most important diversionary lies in the history of civilization. The second task of the town bully was
"security." To this end, the most common method was to erect castles and
ramparts and develop ever more powerful and deadly weapons. To do so,
millions of people were enslaved, turned into serfs, or proletarianized,
with those who did not accept their new status being killed, and, undeniably, all of this has been mirrored as history to us.

In keeping with its power, the military appropriated for itself the
largest share of the economic value extorted, as is clear from the many historical expeditions with no other purpose than plundering. Furthermore,
property was the basis of the state, and military conquest and seizure was
clearly the source of property. Whoever conquered it owned it, declaring this to be a natural and inalienable right. It is the sum of property
(especially land) and plunder (transportable possessions) that has been
conquered and seized by the forces of power and the state. The principle
that "all Ottoman land and people are the sultan's," for example, is nothing
other than the continuation of this foundational tradition concerning the
relationship between the state and military expeditions. Tradition was
established in this way and sanctioned in every newly built state. This is
why the military sees itself as the true custodian of the state, and, thus, of
property. And, in defining itself as such, it takes this historical tradition
into consideration. The fact that it is the strongest arm of the monopoly
accords with the nature of power and the state. Indeed, the humanpower
and weaponry it possessed was sufficient to achieve its goals. In this light,
the fact that military coups are the response to the occasional efforts of the
civil bureaucracy to increase its share of the monopoly is hardly surpris-
ing. The role of ideological and bureaucratic monopolies, also called the
ilmiye and *kalemiye* classes,[33] in the establishment of power and the state
was unquestionably indispensable but not as decisive as the role of the
military. Even the most superficial examination of past and present power
and state apparatuses confirms this.

First, what really matters for our purposes is that the military is the
most advanced and decisive monopoly. The soldier and the army are not a
source of glory, honor, and heroism (this is ideological propaganda meant
to mask and distort the essence of things) but are an essential element of

the monopoly of power. Their essence is economic. The army relies on the economy. It positions itself over it and at a distance from it, but, at the same time, takes the steps necessary to guarantee its income (salary) above all else. It is the monopoly sector that is the most difficult to oppose and the one that all other segments of the monopoly must compromise and share surplus value with, a practice that has an extensive historical basis and is, as such, a deep-rooted institutional tradition. In essence, it is the monopoly of the class (bureaucracy) that is most closely interested in economic development, but feels the most pressing need to keep its distance. To achieve this, it projects an image of itself as the power that is most remote from society, while in reality it is the monopolistic sector that has equipped itself with the most advanced economic and military weapons. Without a correct analysis of the military, we can neither fully understand what economic monopolism or power and state monopolisms are. The three of them comprise a whole. They feed on the same substance; the surplus values of society. In exchange they claim that they take care of society's security, education, health, and productivity. This is how statism—the ideological state—presents itself. But this is not the truth; the truth is as we just described it.

The military is the most sharply organized arm of capital and power. Thus, it follows that it is the institution that ultimately subjugates and cages society. The military has always been the power that has penetrated, controlled, and subjugated society regardless of the form of the state, but it reached its apex in the era of the middle class (bourgeois) and under nation-state monopoly. The defining characteristic of the nation-state is that in the name of creating an official army the rest of society was officially disarmed and the monopoly on arms was transferred to the state and the army. At no time in history was society as disarmed as it has been under bourgeois rule. The reason for this extremely important development is the intensification of exploitation and the resultant rise of far-reaching resistance. Society cannot be ruled if it is not thoroughly and continuously disarmed, opened up to the infiltration of power, and subjected to constant surveillance. Society cannot be dealt with unless it is confined in the "iron cage" of modernity.[34] In addition, society cannot be ruled if it is not confined and besieged by the media army of the global monopolistic financial age. Formation of the ideological-media monopolies, as well the bureaucratic-military monopolies, replicates the aspects of exploitation monopolies. Not only are they inseparably bound together, they also condition each other. The most recent major central civilization, the super hegemon, together with other regional hegemons, including all of their local collaborators, is based on militarism and a gigantic arms industry, both above and within society. The priority given to this monopoly over any other stems from its historical and current position. In this light, identification of militarism with the fascism of capitalist monopoly makes perfect sense.

Of course, during the era of natural society and throughout written history various forms of society have engaged in wholesale self-defense against the militarist evolution of civilization, developing a variety of forms of resistance and engaging in numerous uprisings, participating in institutionalized guerrilla and people's defense armies, and waging great defensive wars, all based on a tradition of self-defense. Of course, defensive wars and militarist monopoly wars are not equivalent. There is a difference in both quality and essence. While one is anti-society, colonialist, corrupting, and destructive, the other favors and protects society and strives to free society's moral and political capacity. Democratic civilization protects and defends society, engaging in systematic self-defense against the central civilization's militarism.

Society's Peace and Democracy Problem

Under the previous eleven headings I tried to briefly describe the problems plaguing social nature. Any paradigm or social science will only be of use if it is based on an analysis that takes into consideration the issues raised here and develops responses. Otherwise, there will be nothing to distinguish it from traditional or liberal rhetoric (the art of words that conceal domination). The general conclusion I have reached is that the source of social problems lies in the combined effect, domination, and colonization of the oppressive and exploitative monopolies. They exploit social nature (society's existence) and in particular the economic resources that generate surplus value. The problems do not arise from nature (first nature) or any social factor (second nature).

Societies cannot survive without social morality and politics, which are factors necessary to their existence (their social fabric) and for addressing society's common affairs. The natural state of society, its existence, cannot be immoral and apolitical. If a society's moral and political fabric has not properly developed or has been undermined, distorted, and paralyzed, then it can be argued that society is occupied and colonized by various monopolies, capital, power, and the state among them. To sustain this sort of life is a betrayal of and alienation from its own existence; it is to exist like a herd, like goods, commodities, and possessions under monopoly domination. Under these conditions, society has lost the natural essence and proficiency of a natural society or become obsolete. Such a society has been colonized or, even worse, has become property in every way, leaving itself to decay and poverty. There are numerous societies that fit this definition, both historically and currently. Those that have decayed and been annihilated far outnumber the survivors.

When a society can no longer create and run institutions that provide meaningful moral and political guidance, that society has succumbed to oppression and exploitation. It is in a "state of war." It is possible to define history as a "state of war" waged by civilizations against society. When morality and politics are dysfunctional, there is only one path open to a society: self-defense. A state of war is nothing more than the absence of peace. As such, only self-defense will make peace possible. A peace with no self-defense can only be an expression of submission and slavery. Liberalism today imposes on societies and peoples peace with no self-defense. The unilateral game of democratic stability and reconciliation is nothing but a fig leaf on the bourgeois class domination achieved by the armed forces. It is nothing but a covert state of war. The major plank in capitalist ideological hegemony is the idea that a true peace is a peace that requires no self-defense. "Sacred concepts" have been used throughout history to express this idea. Religions, in particular civilized religions, overflow with an abundance of such concepts.

Peace is only possible and meaningful if society can defend itself and protect its moral and political character. Peace, particularly the peace that Michel Foucault worked so hard to define, could in this way acquire an acceptable social expression. Peace understood in any other way is nothing but a trap and an implicit state of war on all peoples and communities. In capitalist modernity, the word *peace* abounds with pitfalls. Using the word without correctly defining it has many drawbacks. Let us redefine peace: peace is neither the complete elimination of the state of war nor stability or the absence of war under the supremacy of one party. There are different parties to any peace, and the complete dominance of one party over another does not and cannot denote peace. Furthermore, weapons will fall silent only when there is acceptance of the functioning of society's moral and political institutions. The three conditions mentioned immediately above must be met for principled peace. Any other peace would be meaningless.

Let's elaborate on these conditions; first, a complete disarmament of the different parties is not on the table, but the conflicting parties must vow not to attack one another regardless of the dispute. Military superiority will not be pursued. All sides must accept and respect the right of the other to maintain the means necessary to ensure its security. Second, the ultimate superiority of one party over the others is not at stake. While it is possible to achieve stability and quiescence under the rule of the gun, this cannot be called peace. Peace is only on the agenda when all sides agree to stop the war without one of the parties achieving armed superiority, regardless of whether they are right or wrong. Third, again regardless of the positions of the various sides, they agree to respect the moral (conscience) and political institutions of societies when addressing the problems underlying the conflict. This is the framework of what we call a "political solution." A cease-fire that does not include a moral and political solution cannot be called peace.

Democratic politics is a central issue for a principled peace. When society's moral and political institutions are functioning, the natural outcome is the process of democratic politics. Those who want peace must understand that peace can only be attained if politics based on morality play a part. To attain peace, it is essential that at least one side acts on the basis of democratic politics. Otherwise, the sole result will be a "peace game" played in the interests of the monopolies. In that situation, democratic politics plays a vital role. Only dialogue among democratic forces can stand up to power and the state forces and achieve a meaningful peace process. Without such a peace, even if the warring parties (monopolies) silence the weapons for a time, the state of war continues. Of course, there is war fatigue and economic difficulties arising from logistical needs, but as long as these difficulties can be resolved, the war will continue until one side attains unchallenged superiority. The silencing of weapons in this context cannot be called peace but, rather, a cease-fire that portends a fiercer war to come. For a cease-fire to lead to genuine peace the three conditions we have outlined must be met.

On occasion, the side engaged in self-defense (the side in the right) may attain conclusive superiority. This doesn't change the three conditions for peace. As was seen with real socialism and many legitimate national liberation struggles, immediately establishing your own rule and state to secure stability cannot be called peace. This is just replacing an external monopolistic force with an internal force (state capitalism or a national bourgeoisie). Calling it socialism does not change the basic sociological reality. A principled peace is not something that can be attained by the superiority of power and the state. If power and the state, whatever they call themselves (bourgeois, socialist, national, non-national) do not share their advantages with the democratic forces, then peace will not be on the agenda. In the final analysis, peace is the conditional reconciliation of democracy and the state. History overflows with stories of the many attempts at such conditional reconciliations. There have been principled examples that have endured and others that have collapsed before the ink dried on the treaty. Societies do not only consist of the establishment of power and the state. No matter what restrictions are placed on society, unless it is completely annihilated, it will continue to live in keeping with its own moral and political identity. Although not a focus of written history, this is the essential reality of life.

Society should not be seen as a narrative about power and the state. On the contrary, seeing society as the decisive nature would contribute to the formation of more realistic social sciences. No matter how big or wealthy power and states may become, including capital monopolies (like the pharaoh and Croesus) or their present-day beast-like heirs (the new Leviathan), they can never eliminate society. Because, in the final analysis, it is society that determines them, and those who are determined can never replace those who determine them. Even the present rulers' spectacular and unsurpassed media propaganda cannot obscure this fact. At the end of the day, they are the most miserable and pitiful of forces playing at being giants. In contrast, human society cannot be stripped of its meaning as the most wonderful creation of nature.

The system of democratic civilization—our main paradigm—is a system in which society, both in its historical and present form, is interpreted, scientifically explained, and reconstructed. That is the subject matter of our next chapter.

SEVEN

Envisaging the System of Democratic Civilization

Ever since I began to know myself, doubt has never let go of me—it has followed me like a ghost. The depths of my skepticism would be like an affliction at times. When any of my dogmatic beliefs were shaken, it felt like my weakest moment. At the time, I was lackadaisical in life. The most important contribution of this skepticism, which even reared its head around issues that we cannot seriously consider defending, was that it taught me how elusive "the truth" is. I believe that my decision to problematize everything, including the instincts that drive me, finally gave me the strength to break with the dogmatic thinking that is still very strong in the social traditions of the Middle East. The fact that, in the final analysis, the Eurocentric hegemonic way of thinking still holds a certain sway over modernism's dogmatic positivism and the postmodernist system of thought illustrates the importance of the issue. I tried to determine where I stand by comparing the East's faith-based intellectual quality with the West's inquiry-based intellectual power but could not find my place on either side. Naturally, the result of such thinking on my part meant that the gap between my life and these forms of thought deepened every day.

Neither form of thought ever really satisfied me, primarily because of the major role these systems of thought play in the development and growth of the social problem. This both encouraged and required me to adopt a position critical of both the East's faith-based system and West's rational system.

A second aspect is that my awakening consciousness never detached from my social practice. In this regard, a quality of my personality showed itself quite early on. Even when I was walking to and from primary school (it was a school in the neighboring village of Cibin), I would memorize a few prayers and pretend to be the imam of a small group of students. I took it quite seriously, like a role in a play. I think my motivation was to prove myself by sharing with other children the few suras I had memorized with great difficulty;[1] hence the self-respect I felt due to having started to think: "What you have learned is difficult and important, so it must be shared!" Obviously, I was being introduced to a serious moral principle here. In earlier volumes of my defense, I shared a short version of how I experienced the first glimmers of clarity about modernity. I stopped when I truly realized that capitalist modernity had laid waste to my frantic marathon of thinking. Ironically, smashing the gods of the four-hundred-year-old capitalist world-system gave me the emotional strength that I imagine felt similar to the joy of the Prophet Abraham from Urfa when he emerged as an iconoclast. I was both able to easily take control of my skepticism and to engage in a meaningful way with the "truth" I was pursuing.

It is painful to observe that humanity, weakened in every way, has let its contact with truth decline to the most instinctive level. Today, there is almost no one who is not ready to capitulate in return for a life with a partner, a child, and a regular salary. I don't deny this reality. To worship this material life in the name of rational thought, substituted for philosophy, brings nothing but complete misery. This is the world that the nation-state god has bestowed upon its happy servants. Can we realistically deny that we live in a terribly restricted world? Personally, I would find it a thousand times more meaningful and sacred to live under the symbolic god of ancient times than under the present nation-state divinity. I know, of course, that I am talking about the hollowest theism of the capital monopolies. It pains me to see that even those who receive the hardest of blows remain under the influence of this divinity and cannot think of breaking away. I am also quite aware that this is humanity's current situation. This is best reflected in the Holocaust, which reveals the tragic levels that this situation has reached. Unfortunately, the Hebrew tribe, whose story we have told, has an important part in both the formation of that situation and the countless victims. Jewish power of thought has a hegemonic quality. I do not deny the reflection of this power of thought on my own personality, as a result of things ranging from memorizing prayers to iconoclasm, or underestimate its importance. But the tragedy of the Holocaust alone indebted the Jewish people to profoundly question themselves—as Adorno did. I too, proportionate to the degree that I have been affected, focused on the "democratic civilization system," in the hope of paying my share of this debt.

At this point, we are Abrahamic. But when we have some Zoroastrianism in our heads the need to think differently grows. The dominant understanding of history in the form of narratives of civilization has developed significant fault lines. It is now generally accepted that while the march of power and the state may be the official history, it is not the history of society. Narratives about the formation of power and the state should be treated as a faint symbolic endpoint of historical truth that are only useful to capitalist monopolies. It is precisely these sort of marginal narratives that make history boring by not encompassing social tradition. It is clear that given the essentially antisocial nature of this history, it cannot address the society as a tradition. On the contrary, it will obscure and distort it in a multitude of ways. Dynastic stories fall into a similar category. Religious historical narratives, whose social representation is extremely shallow, are nothing more than the history of power and the state, especially when they enter the process of becoming civilized.

Class and economic interpretations of history, which detach social reality from its totality and are close to being reductionist, resemble state histories albeit from a different angle. A partially positivist point of view lacks the capacity to understand history even more than most religions. Although it may look as if they are in conflict with one another, all of these historical narratives are united by having originated in civilization.

I don't believe that the history of social nature has been properly understood in both a paradigmatic and empirical sense. Historiographies that are called social history have little to offer and are nothing more than the most fragmentary parts of positivist sociology. They are no more than a depiction of the frame, i.e., a depiction of one part of the totality. I could say more about all of this, but it wouldn't usefully contribute to our discussion.

At the risk of repeating myself, the reason I focus on history—as the narrative of democratic civilization—is because of the stalemate in solving social problems, which I still find difficult to grasp. This stalemate is not only found in daily life, the narrative is also overladen with it. The combination of these two conditions make the official narrative of civilization insurmountable. Squeezing in some bits about social history only serves to complicate matters.

I frequently say that scientific socialism clarified some facts by using the class character of history to explain this situation, but it could not solve the problem and, in fact, could not even avoid becoming part of the problem.

It is for this reason I often say that if we don't completely overcome the capitalist modernist paradigm, grasping historical truth is unthinkable. On the contrary, the modernist paradigm will act to conceal the truth and deem it absurd even more effectively than religion. The historical consequences of Marx's paradigmatic view can be better understood today. An incorrect grasp of history leads to an incorrect practice. If the paradigmatic and empirical approaches of civilization generally and capitalist modernity particularly are not overcome, a paradigmatic and empirical approach based on social nature will remain out of reach. I am attempting just that here, albeit without sufficient preparation.

Definition of Democratic Civilization

The school of social science that postulates the examination of the existence and development of social nature on the basis of moral and political society could be defined as the democratic civilization system. The various schools of social science base their analyses on different units. Theology and religion prioritize society. For scientific socialism, it is class. The fundamental unit for liberalism is the individual. There are, of course, schools that prioritize power and the state and others that focus on civilization. All these unit-based approaches must be criticized, because, as I have frequently pointed out, they are not historical, and they fail to address the totality. A meaningful examination would have to focus on what is crucial from the point of view of society, both in terms of history and actuality. Otherwise, the result will only be one more discourse.

Identifying our fundamental unit as moral and political society is significant, because it also covers the dimensions of historicity and totality. Moral and political society is the most historical and holistic expression of society. Morals and politics themselves can be understood as history. A society that has a moral and political dimension is a society that is the closest to the totality of all its existence and development. A society can exist without the state, class, exploitation, the city, power, or the nation, but a society devoid of morals and politics is unthinkable. Societies may exist as colonies of other powers, particularly capital and state monopolies, and as sources of raw materials. In those cases, however, we are talking about the legacy of a society that has ceased to be.

There is nothing gained by labeling moral and political society—the natural state of society—as slave-owning, feudal, capitalist, or socialist. Using such labels to describe society masks reality and reduces society to its components (class, economy, and monopoly). The bottleneck encountered in discourses based on such concepts as regards the theory and practice of social development stems from errors and inadequacies inherent in them. If all of the analyses of society referred to with these labels that are closer to historical materialism have fallen into this situation, it is clear that discourses with much weaker scientific bases will be in a much worse situation. Religious discourses, meanwhile, focus heavily on the importance of morals but have long since turned politics over to the state. Bourgeois liberal approaches not only obscure the society with moral and political dimensions, but when the opportunity presents itself they do not hesitate to wage war on this society. Individualism is a state of war against society to the same degree as power and the state is. Liberalism essentially prepares society, which is weakened by being deprived of its morals and politics, for all kinds of attacks by individualism. Liberalism is the ideology and practice that is most anti-society.

In Western sociology (there is still no science called Eastern sociology) concepts such as society and civilization system are quite problematic. We should not forget that the need for sociology stemmed from the need to find solutions to the huge problems of crises, contradictions, and conflicts and war caused by capital and power monopolies. Every branch of sociology developed its own thesis about how to maintain order and make life more livable. Despite all the sectarian, theological, and reformist interpretations of the teachings of Christianity, as social problems deepened, interpretations based on a scientific (positivist) point of view came to the fore. The philosophical revolution and the Enlightenment (seventeenth and eighteenth centuries) were essentially the result of this need. When the French Revolution complicated society's problems rather than solving them, there was a marked increase in the tendency to develop sociology as an independent science. Utopian socialists (Henri de Saint-Simon, Charles Fourier, and Pierre-Joseph Proudhon), together with Auguste Comte and Émile Durkheim, represent the preliminary steps in this direction.[2] All of them are children of the Enlightenment, with unlimited faith in science. They believed they could use science to re-create society as they wished. They were playing God. In Hegel's words, God had descended to earth and, what's more, in the form of the nation-state.[3] What needed to be done was to plan and develop specific and sophisticated "social engineering" projects. There was no project or plan that could not be achieved by the nation-state if it so desired, as long as it embraced the "scientific positivism" and was accepted by the nation-state!

British social scientists (political economists) added economic solutions to French sociology, while German ideologists contributed philosophically. Adam Smith and Hegel in particular made major contributions. There was a wide variety of prescriptions from both the left and right to address the problems arising from the horrendous abuse of the society by the nineteenth-century industrial capitalism. Liberalism, the central ideology of the capitalist monopoly has a totally eclectic approach, taking advantage of any and all ideas, and is the most practical when it comes to creating almost patchwork-like systems. It was as if the right- and left-wing schematic sociologies were unaware of social nature, history, and the present while developing their projects in relation to the past (the quest for the "golden age" by the right) or the future (utopian society). Their systems would continually fragment when they encountered history or current life. The reality that had imprisoned them all was the "iron cage" that capitalist modernity had slowly cast and sealed them in, intellectually and in their practical way of life. However, Friedrich Nietzsche's ideas of metaphysicians of positivism or castrated dwarfs of capitalist modernity bring us a lot closer to the social truth. Nietzsche leads the pack of rare philosophers who first drew attention to the risk of society being swallowed up by capitalist modernity. Although he is accused of serving fascism with his thoughts, his foretelling of the onset of fascism and world wars was quite enticing.

The increase in major crises and world wars, along with the division of the liberal center into right- and left-wing branches, was enough to bankrupt positivist sociology. In spite of its widespread criticism of metaphysics, social engineering has revealed its true identity with authoritarian and totalitarian fascism as metaphysics at its shallowest. The Frankfurt School is the official testimonial of this bankruptcy. The École Annales and the 1968 youth uprising led to various postmodernist sociological approaches, in particular Immanuel Wallerstein's capitalist world-system analysis. Tendencies like ecology, feminism, relativism, the New Left, and world-system analysis launched a period during which the social sciences splintered. Obviously, financial capital gaining hegemony as the 1970s faded also played an important role. The upside of these developments was the collapse of the hegemony of Eurocentric thought. The downside, however, was the drawbacks of a highly fragmented social sciences.

Let's summarize the criticism of Eurocentric sociology:

a) Positivism, which criticized and denounced both religion and metaphysics, has not escaped being a kind of religion and metaphysics in its own right. This should not come as a surprise. Human culture requires metaphysics. The issue is to distinguish good from bad metaphysics.

b) An understanding of society based on dichotomies like primitive vs. modern, capitalist vs. socialist, industrial vs. agrarian, progressive vs. reactionary, divided by class vs. classless, or with a state vs. stateless prevents the development of a definition that comes closer to the truth of social nature. Dichotomies of this sort distance us from social truth.

c) To re-create society is to play the modern god. More precisely, each time society is recreated there is a tendency to form a new capital and power-state monopoly. Much like medieval theism was ideologically connected to absolute monarchies (sultanates and shāhanshāhs),[4] modern social engineering—as re-creation— is essentially the divine disposition and ideology of the nation-state. Positivism in this regard is modern theism.

d) Revolutions cannot be interpreted as the re-creation acts of society. When thusly understood they cannot escape positivist theism. Revolutions can only be defined as social revolutions to the extent that they free society from excessive burden of capital and power.

e) The task of revolutionaries cannot be defined as creating any social model of their making but more correctly as playing a role in contributing to the development of moral and political society.

f) Methods and paradigms to be applied to social nature should not be identical to those that relate to first nature. While the universalist approach to first nature provides results that come closer to the truth (I don't believe there is an absolute truth), relativism in relation to social nature may get us closer to the truth. The universe can neither be explained by an infinite universalist linear discourse or by a concept of infinite similar circular cycles.

g) A social regime of truth needs to be reorganized on the basis of these and many other criticisms. Obviously, I am not talking about a new divine creation, but I do believe that the greatest feature of the human mind is the power to search for and build truth.

In light of these criticisms, I offer the following suggestions in relation to the social science system that I want to define:

a) I would not present social nature as a rigid universalist truth with mythological, religious, metaphysical, and scientific (positivist) patterns. Understanding it to be the most flexible form of basic universal entities that encompass a wealth of diversities but are tied down to conditions of historical time and location more closely approaches the truth. Any analysis, social science, or attempt to make practical change without adequate knowledge of the qualities of social nature may well backfire. The monotheistic religions and positivism, which have appeared throughout the history of civilization claiming to have found the solution, were unable to prevent capital and power monopolies from gaining control. It is therefore their irrevocable task, if they are to contribute to moral and political society, to develop a more humane analysis based on a profound self-criticism.

b) Moral and political society is the main element that gives social nature its historical and complete meaning and represents the unity in diversity that is basic to its existence. It is the definition of moral and political society that gives social nature its character, maintains its unity in diversity, and plays a decisive role in expressing its main totality and historicity. The descriptors commonly used to define society, such as primitive, modern, slave-owning, feudal, capitalist, socialist, industrial, agricultural, commercial, monetary, statist, national, hegemonic, and so on, do not reflect the decisive features of social nature. On the contrary, they conceal and fragment its meaning. This, in turn, provides a base for faulty theoretical and practical approaches and actions related to society.

c) Statements about renewing and re-creating society are part of operations meant to constitute new capital and power monopolies in terms of their ideological content. The history of civilization, the history of such renewals, is the history of the cumulative accumulation of capital and power. Instead of divine creativity, the basic action the society needs most is to struggle against factors that prevent the development and functioning of moral and political social fabric. A society that operates its moral and political dimensions freely, is a society that will continue its development in the best way.

d) Revolutions are forms of social action resorted to when society is sternly prevented from freely exercising and maintaining its moral and political function. Revolutions can and should be accepted as legitimate by society only when they do not seek to create new societies, nations, or states but to restore moral and political society its ability to function freely.

e) Revolutionary heroism must find meaning through its contributions to moral and political society. Any action that does not have this meaning, regardless of its intent and duration, cannot be defined as revolutionary social heroism. What determines the role of individuals in society in a positive sense is their contribution to the development of moral and political society.

f) No social science that hopes to develop these key features through profound research and examination should be based on a universalist linear progressive approach or on a singular infinite cyclical relativity. In the final instance, instead of these dogmatic approaches that serve to legitimize the cumulative accumulation of capital and power throughout the history of civilization, social sciences based on a non-destructive dialectic methodology that harmonizes analytical and emotional intelligence and overcomes the strict subject-object mold should be developed.

The paradigmatic and empirical framework of moral and political society, the main unit of the democratic civilization system, can be presented through such hypotheses. Let me present its main aspects:

a) Moral and political society is the fundamental aspect of human society that must be continuously sought. Society is essentially moral and political.

b) Moral and political society is located at the opposite end of the spectrum from the civilization systems that emerged from the triad of city, class, and state (which had previously been hierarchical structures).

c) Moral and political society, as the history of social nature, develops in harmony with the democratic civilization system.

d) Moral and political society is the freest society. A functioning moral and political fabric and organs is the most decisive dynamic not only for freeing society but to keep it free. No revolution or its heroines and heroes can free the society to the degree that the development of a healthy moral and political dimension will. Moreover, revolution and its heroines and heroes can only play a decisive role to the degree that they contribute to moral and political society.

e) A moral and political society is a democratic society. Democracy is only meaningful on the basis of the existence of a moral and political society that is open and free. A democratic society where individuals and groups become subjects is the form of governance that best develops moral and political society. More precisely, we call a functioning political society a democracy. Politics and democracy are truly identical concepts. If freedom is the space within which politics expresses itself, then democracy is the way in which politics is exercised in this space. The triad of freedom, politics, and democracy cannot lack a moral basis. We could refer to morality as the institutionalized and traditional state of freedom, politics, and democracy.

f) Moral and political societies are in a dialectical contradiction with the state, which is the official expression of all forms of capital, property, and power. The state constantly tries to substitute law for morality and bureaucracy for politics. The official state civilization develops on one side of this historically ongoing contradiction, with the unofficial democratic civilization system developing on the other side. Two distinct typologies of meaning emerge. Contradictions may either grow more violent and lead to war or there may be reconciliation, leading to peace.

g) Peace is only possible if moral and political society forces and the state monopoly forces have the will to live side by side unarmed and with no killing. There have been instances when rather than society destroying the state or the state destroying

141

society, a conditional peace called democratic reconciliation has been reached. History doesn't take place either in the form of democratic civilization—as the expression of moral and political society—or totally in the form of civilization systems—as the expression of class and state society. History has unfolded as intense relationship rife with contradiction between the two, with successive periods of war and peace. It is quite utopian to think that this situation, with at least a five-thousand-year history, can be immediately resolved by emergency revolutions. At the same time, to embrace it as if it is fate and cannot be interfered with would also not be the correct moral and political approach. Knowing that struggles between systems will be protracted, it makes more sense and will prove more effective to adopt strategic and tactical approaches that expand the freedom and democracy sphere of moral and political society.

h) Defining moral and political society in terms of communal, slave-owning, feudal, capitalist, and socialist attributes serves to obscure rather than elucidate matters. Clearly, in a moral and political society there is no room for slave-owning, feudal, or capitalist forces, but, in the context of a principled reconciliation, it is possible to take an aloof approach to these forces, within limits and in a controlled manner. What's important is that moral and political society should neither destroy them nor be swallowed up by them; the superiority of moral and political society should make it possible to continuously limit the reach and power of the central civilization system. Communal and socialist systems can identify with moral and political society insofar as they themselves are democratic. This identification is, however, not possible, if they have a state.

i) Moral and political society cannot seek to become a nation-state, establish an official religion, or construct a non-democratic regime. The right to determine the objectives and nature of society lies with the free will of all members of a moral and political society. Just as with current debates and decisions, strategic decisions are the purview of society's moral and political will and expression. The essential thing is to have discussions and to become a decision-making power. A society who holds this power can determine its preferences in the soundest possible way. No individual or force has the authority to decide on behalf of moral and political society, and social engineering has no place in these societies.

When viewed in the light of the various broad definitions I have presented, it is obvious that the democratic civilization system—essentially the moral and political totality of social nature—has always existed and sustained itself as the flip side of the official history of civilization. Despite all the oppression and exploitation at the hands of the official world-system, the other face of society could not be destroyed. In fact, it is impossible to destroy it. Just as capitalism cannot sustain itself without noncapitalist society, civilization—the official world system—also cannot sustain itself without the democratic civilization system. More concretely the civilization with monopolies cannot sustain itself without the existence of a civilization without monopolies. The opposite is not true. Democratic civilization, representing the historical flow of the system of moral and political society, can sustain itself more comfortably and with fewer obstacles in the absence of the official civilization.

I define democratic civilization as a system of thought, the accumulation of thought, and the totality of moral rules and political organs. I am not only talking about a history of thought or the social reality within a given moral and political development. The discussion does, however, encompass both issues in an intertwined manner. I consider it important and necessary to explain the method in terms of democratic civilization's history and elements, because this totality of alternate discourse and structures are prevented by the official civilization. I will address these issues in subsequent sections.

The Methodological Approach to Democratic Civilization

The universalist linear progressive approach in the social sciences leads to at least as many problems as religious dogmatism when it comes to how truth is perceived. There is no discernable difference between its judgments and religious certainty: the universe is in an eternal state of progress, and everything predicted in the Levh-i Mahfûz is coming true.[5] In other words, "what is taking place is just what should take place." Everything is unfolding as foreseen. Contrary to popular belief, positivism is not anti-metaphysical and anti-religiosity, it is an absolutely vulgar materialist religion with a light polish of science. In fact, it is the idolatry of modernity. The basic similarity between both dogmatic methods is the idea of the existence of a force called law that rules nature. God's laws have been replaced by scientific laws. The rest of the narrative is similar. The most serious problem with the positivist methodology of thought is that its conclusions have the power of law. There is no room for interpretation. A deduction that is considered conclusive and objective and implicitly the view that everyone must hold is also essentially anti-science. The fact that positivism bases itself on a sharp distinction of subject and object also fails to leave room for a margin of error.

The efforts of the bourgeois class to present medieval theology with a polish of positivism as a secular and scientific philosophy is understandable. It will, of course, bear the marks of the social reality it grew out of. If we do not free ourselves from all the imaginary approaches that have been imposed upon our thinking since the Middle Ages—indeed throughout the history of civilization—it is inevitable that a wave of positivism will capture our minds, so to speak. This did not allow for any other development other than the endless repetition of clichéd thoughts and the belief that a hollow and dry rhetoric reflected reality. It amounts to the replacement of "whatever the imam says is right" with "whatever the teacher and the philosopher say is right." This is what lies at the core of our intellectual infertility. As such, we were even deprived of our right to address our own social nature. This is a very grave situation; it is cerebral blunting and enslavement. At least religious dogmatism, as a kind of conveyor of tradition, resonates with certain historical facts. The same cannot be said about positivism. Positivism raises a huge dam of alienation between us and our reality. As the ideological hegemonic power of the West, it would like to seize control of its opponent without, so to speak, firing a shot (i.e., without using its brain). Clearly, without breaking through this dogmatism, it is impossible, generally speaking, to analyze official civilization and specifically break with the capitalist modernist paradigm. Therefore, it would have been difficult to attain the capacity for free interpretation. I am convinced that ideological weapons play a more effective prohibitive role than military weapons.

When I first asked myself, "Can democratic civilization be systematized?" I struggled quite a bit to free myself from these methodological chains. Even more challenging and difficult, however, was smashing the dogma surrounding scientific socialism, which I had totally believed in.

To free yourself from the prison of dogmatism, you must struggle with yourself. Then again, I had been doing that for most of my life.

I was also wrestling with a paradox: on the one hand, I was still under the influence of a culture that stretched back thousands of years (to 10,000 BCE) in the homeland of the agricultural revolution; on the other hand, I had begun the struggle for a postcapitalist society. How were we to establish a new society without resolving the gap between the two that stretched back at least twelve thousand years? Our system of thought had turned into a kind of science of the afterworld. Obviously, there was not yet a fecund intellectual method that took hold in my mind. This disease of being unable to think even an inch outside of the margins of what had already been written can only be explained by the effect of dogmatism. Before we were free of the clamor of the religious patterns, we were bombarded with a "domineering" official positivism. I grasped that the true protective force of any system is its ideological hegemony. That is why I understand Nietzsche's struggle against the official German ideological power to the point of going mad. If we know even a few simple truths about the West, we owe them to this frantic struggle.

The very first dogma that I firmly shed was scientific socialism's thesis that primitive communal society was imperatively followed by slave-owning and other forms of class society in a necessarily consecutive way. I had treated this dogma like it was a law for a very long time. It didn't take me long to break a second dogma that was intertwined with the first, that of identifying society with a class. Calling society slave-owning or feudal conceals the most sensitive of truths about its nature and identifies society with its masters. It was clear that such designations are a remnant of the dominant structures. Addressing the third dogma, which is intertwined with the previous two, was fairly straightforward. I refer to the dogmatic belief that different stages of class society are both necessary and progressive. I came to understand that these stages are neither inevitable nor progressive; I recognized that these stages were the most reactionary and enchaining development. The end result was to grasp that a way to formulate a historical discourse that brought us closer to truth was possible. Instead of shying away from a multidirectional analysis, it was obvious that this would be a more appropriate methodology for uncovering deeper layers of meaning. Obviously, when dogmatism (presupposition) is smashed in a wide range of areas, this opens the way to greater interpretive power and the development of a wealth of meaning.

I can clearly state: no matter where people are and what conditions they are living under, if they are unable to resolve the problems they face, the main reason will be that they lack the courage to move beyond their primitive way of thinking and smash the thousand-year-old dogmas and instincts that underlie their behavior. Behind any cowardice lies the fear of thinking.

While I was intellectualizing democratic civilization, a second important point caught my attention: the amount of concrete empirical material available to me. The examination of history shows the widespread availability of this sort of material, which begs a couple of questions: Why are dynasties, plunder of surplus value, and power structures treated as a system, while the family, the tribe, the aşiret, the non-power classes (both in villages and cities), non-statized peoples, and nations—the stem cells of society—go systematically unevaluated? Why are the latter not seen as constituting ideologically and structurally meaningful systems?

There must be a reason why those in whom we invested our hopes were unable to adequately answer these questions. Nonetheless, it is clear that these are not pointless questions that lack truth. Although the answers have not been systematized, there are many fragments of the answers available to us if we know where to look.

As we tend toward a different civilization and a different modernity, a third factor is the potential of freely building social nature. If there are massive and piled up problems, and if people are exhausted due to unemployment and starvation, then construction of systems (not in terms of creation or social engineering) is both possible and an imperative moral obligation. As a matter of fact, the very dimension of our problems raises the need for a revolution, and revolution puts the structures that provide answers on the agenda.

The fourth factor driving my quest can perhaps be summed up in the question: If the dominant system does not provide hope or treat you like a human being and does not show any interest in resolving the simplest of problems, such as that of identity, then what is required of a human being is to conjoin self-esteem and hope with the capacity to build your own system. Otherwise, at the table of the wolves, you may not get to pick the bones but instead might become the prey.

The final driving factor might well be somewhat personal, but it probably also has a more general resonance. No matter who it is—even your mother—you invested your hopes in, if they were unable to offer you much, you should not hesitate to trust in your own strength. You should also not surrender for any other reason or because of any drive. If there is no possible life worth living for you, don't forget that you have the capacity to display the intelligence and will necessary to build the good, the true, and the beautiful!

According to the linear interpretation of history, the city society that emerged after the agrarian-village society is the "last word," and narratives of civilization developed around the city are truth itself. The force—dominant class—that seized control of the city and organized it as a religious state is the motor of history. Everything they did was right and holy—the realization of destiny. To this end, divine ideological hegemonies were exalted. Each and every dissident sound was considered treason against the word of past-eternity and post-eternity and its expression of life and felt "God's wrath." Rationalizations for all of the dishonorable activities of the despots, their most vile oppression and their systems of exploitation, poured from the lips of the priests as the most holy word of God or the gods. Once the servants surrender to the gods' laws, they no longer feel the pain.

In its original form, the city-centered civilization—as an organization of capital and force—has been presented to us in the ramshackle narratives of mythology or religion and carried into our present times through a series of transformations. The shine has come off this civilization, whose essence remains the same but whose rhetoric and form has regularly changed and shifted as it sought new ways to present itself. Despite its lack of luster, it is not shy about declaring itself post-eternal in the form of a rigid nation-state fascism. The bureaucratic iron cage, as the city's organization of capital and force, multiplies AIDS and biological cancers along with its contents. But what is worse is that we have entered an extremely serious stage in our development; social nature, with all its internal structures and its natural environment, has entered a cancerous phase. To understand that there is no exaggeration in the facts we have schematically advanced here, we only need to look at war and colonialism—the war that has spread throughout society over the past four hundred years of the world system (and, indeed, the past five thousand years), as well as at our current environmental disaster.

When we look at all forms of liberal ideological hegemony and more particularly at their official spheres (state ideologies), we can see that this is their end of history. In other words, the capitalist system, which is at the peak of the global age, presents itself as the post-eternal form of the final word. This is nothing new; the end of every significant age of capital and tyranny has been accompanied by declarations of "post-eternity." This is the truth that the five-thousand-year-old "sciences" of civilization have cloaked in thousands of different disguises and turned into a methodology. Methodology has become the truth, and the truth has become methodology.

When one whispers that other worlds, sciences, and methods are possible, along with discourses about deserving hell for heresy and infidelity, unlimited forms of "terror" (from being beheaded to crucifixion, from being burned at the stake to being hanged, from being sentenced to a lifetime of labor to torture, from being worked to death to languishing in prisons, from being made a housewife to colonization and assimilation) come into play.

We see that the central civilization, which acted against agrarian-village society as if it were taking revenge, attempting to destroy it for the last five thousand years, has, since the early twenty-first century, been taking steps to completely subvert this society and to eradicate its remaining traces. Environmental destruction is, in fact, the final form of revenge upon agrarian-village society. Interestingly, it is not social nature that has been silenced but first nature that responds to this disaster with various catastrophes (climate change, drought, rapidly melting glaciers, rapid extinction of various species, flooding, and cyclones, to mention but a few). Humanity (silenced humanity) can at times become the most voiceless form of nature. While it hurts to acknowledge this, who can deny that it is true?

The key shift in the paradigm of looking at history must be in relation to the understanding that the city-based capital and power monopoly could not have developed without agrarian-village society (10,000 BCE to date). This opens the way for a fundamental methodological change. Rosa Luxemburg stated, in a very broad manner, that "capitalism, accumulation of capital, and monopoly cannot exist in the absence of a noncapitalist society."[6] Expanding this definition to all of history and all forms of capital is a more accurate narrative; it provides an adequate analysis of capital throughout the historical-society. The most fundamental mistake Karl Marx made was to develop the model of pure capitalist society. Such a society is neither theoretically nor practically possible. Proving this is simple: let's say we have a society with capitalists (including bureaucrats) and workers (including the unemployed) only. Pure capitalist society requires this. Let us assume that in total one hundred units of a particular good are produced. If twenty-five units are sold to the workers and another twenty-five units are left for the use of the capitalist class, what will then happen to the remaining fifty units? The rest would either have to be left to rot or distributed free of charge. No other approach is possible in a purely capitalist society.

From this point of view, when Rosa said that if this fifty units were sold to a noncapitalist society for a profit, then the system could function, she was wandering the shoreline of truth. Social reality is a lot more comprehensive though. In addition, we should always clearly keep in mind that profit and capital accumulation based on profit are unpaid social surplus. What is a noncapitalist society? It is above all the historical agrarian-village society, the society of women confined to their homes, of the craftspeople who live off their own labor, of the poor and the unemployed of the city (who live through subsidies). If we look at the reality in this way we will be able to better analyze the five-thousand-year-old civilization and its last four hundred years as the capitalist world system—its most systematic period. Most probably the network (aristocracy, lords, bourgeoisie) that have organized themselves as capital and power throughout history have never amounted to more than 10 percent of the population.[7] Therefore, the main body of social nature has always been above 90 percent of the population.

In that case, let me ask a question about the methodology employed: Is it more scientific and correct to historicize and systematize this 10 percent, making it the main object of thought, as opposed to the 90 percent? We need to examine this. Perhaps others might say, "No other approach is possible, because thought, science, and methodology are monopolized by this 10 percent." But isn't this monopoly, in the final analysis, built on extortion and erosion of social surplus? Does being the best organized ideological group justify such privilege? Even if it were only 1 percent, the well-organized might of 1 percent can be used to dominate and rule over millions. They can set fundamental terms of science and methodology as they wish. But can this substitute for truth? Who declares such a handful of tyrants and monopolists as the truth? Can those who do—presenting it as mythology, religion, philosophy, science, and the arts and becoming wedded to the rule of capital's tyrannical network—change social truth (the truth of the 90 percent)? The reason why this problem must be addressed in this

manner is fairly obvious. No ideological, scientific, religious, philosophical, or artistic hegemony has or should have the power to alter this reality.

When we examine historical-society structurally in the light of this
main method and express it through various forms of thought (mythological, religious, philosophical, and artistic) the dimensions of truth will
be easier to see and will make more sense. Democratic civilization could
have a much more systematically advanced form of this two-directional
(within its structuralism, objectivity, and subjectivity as a way of expressing itself) narrative of historical-society. It is both possible and necessary
to more comprehensively systematize the historicity and totality of social
nature. A systematic analysis of this sort should be part of the paradigmatic basis of the scientific revolution and the social sciences.

This approach to the question of methodology would allow for a more
accurate presentation of social nature, with all of its historical richness
and totality. At first glance it would seem that:

a) A society without capital and power is possible, but capital and
   power without a society is not.
b) An economy without capital is possible, but capital without an
   economy is not.
c) A society without a state is possible, but a state without a society
   is not.
d) A society without capitalists, feudal lords, and masters is possible,
   but capitalists, feudal lords, and masters without a society are not.
e) A society without class is possible, but classes without a society
   are not.
f) Agriculture and the village without the city are possible, but a city
   without agriculture and the village is not.
g) A society without laws is possible, but a society without morality
   is not.
h) It is possible to put society in a situation where it lacks politics or
   morality. In that case, society is being torn to pieces and swallowed
   by the new Leviathan (nation-state fascism). And, indeed, this is
   the moment when the death of society and humanity becomes
   a huge spectacle. This is the moment when genocide is carried
   out. The moment that Michel Foucault proclaimed is the death of
   man.[8] This is the moment when, according to Friedrich Nietzsche,
   society and humanity have been castrated, dwarfed, and reduced

to worker ants and have, in fact, become a herdlike multitude. This is the moment when, Max Weber declared, society has been confined in an "iron cage"!

The democratic civilization paradigm must and needs to come into play at this moment:

a) Since society cannot be sustained without agriculture and the village, throughout the history of civilization the segments of the society living in these areas have always been exploited and oppressed. Their resistance through the ages will only achieve its goal if they transform themselves into political society.

b) The existence of the city is still possible, if it does not become the base of capital and power monopolies. True liberation of the city, which has been obliged to act as the base for exploitation and oppression throughout the history of civilization, requires it to become a political urban society and to install democratic governance. The cities, which have very rich appearance in history, can only be saved from becoming mass cancerous structures by further developing democratic and confederalist governance.

c) If the capital and power monopolies built above the economy are not restricted and eliminated, then economic crisis will not end and other problems cannot be solved. The main cause of unemployment, hunger, and poverty, as well as environmental destruction and all types of unnecessary class division, social diseases, and war, is the struggle of capital and power groups to snatch shares and increase their share of societal surplus value. Social nature is equipped with a flexible membrane against all these problems and diseases. If capital and power apparatuses are restricted, the free pursuit of development will become possible. If history is to be understood economically and from a class perspective, this paradigm offers a way to attain true meaning.

d) Without the capital and power monopoly, moral and political society is the natural state of society. All human societies must have these qualities from their birth to their decay. Slave-owning, feudal, capitalist, and socialist society molds are like clothes they hope to put on social nature; they do not express the truth. In spite of what they claim, there are no such societies. These societies, whose original state was moral and political, were unable to fully develop, because they were continuously oppressed, exploited, and colonized by the capital and power monopolies.

e) The main task of democratic politics is to restore the free functioning of moral and political society. Societies like this are transparent and democratic societies. The more developed democratic politics, the more functional moral and political society. It is the art of democratic politics that is responsible for keeping such societies functional. It is not the task of democratic politics to "socially engineer" societies. Attempts at social engineering are part of what liberalism does to create capital and power monopolies.

f) All kingdoms, empires, republics, city-states, and nation-states established throughout history in the name of civilization, whether separately or collectively, reconciled or competitive, hegemonic or equally powerful, are essentially the forms of capital that have become power and the state.

Moral and political society can never seek to become a monopoly. It can either live independent of them or in conditional peace and reconciliation with them. There are various ways for democratic civilization and the civilizations of official power to reconcile. Because peace rests on these conditional reconciliations, all other times would mean a continuous state of war within or above society.

g) Since society does not rest on the continuous exploitative monopolist wars (internally or externally) it needs to develop various forms of democratic civilization in the agricultural villages and among the city's laborers. History is not the tool of inhuman and fusty structures and warfare or the sum of power and states alone; there are far more unrecorded examples of democratic civilization: the family, tribal and aşiret systems, confederations, city democracies (as far as we know, the most striking example is Athens), democratic confederations, monasteries, dervish lodges, communes, egalitarian parties, civil societies, denominations, religious and philosophical communities that have not been absorbed by power, solidarity among women, and numerous communities and assemblies based on solidarity. Unfortunately, the history of these communities has not been systematically recorded. Nonetheless, the true history of humanity can only be the systematic expression of these groups.

h) While the civilizations of official power have been sustained by capital and arms monopolies intertwined with ideological hegemony, the ideology of democratic civilization has always remained weak and unsystematic, and thus have been continuously oppressed, distorted, and, more often than not, eliminated. The countless sages, scientists, philosophers, religious leaders, denomination members, and artists who did not surrender and listened to the voice of their free conscience were severely punished and silenced. The fact that the history of all of these people has not been written does not mean they did not exist. One of our primary intellectual tasks is to make sure that democratic civilization is expressed systematically as historical-society.

i) In response to capitalism's four-hundred-year ideological, administrative, military, nation-state civilization system (in the form of the monopoly of economics and power), there have been city democracies (in Italy) and confederations (in Germany), peasants' rebellions and communes, workers' rebellions and communes (the Paris Commune), the experiences of real socialism (in one-third of the world), the process of national liberation (their non-power and the non-state mode of being), numerous democratic parties, civil society movements, and, recently, ecological and feminist movements, democratic youth movements, arts festivals, and new religious movements that do not seek power. As can be seen, democratic civilization is based on a broad spectrum of movements and has a system—although not fully integrated—that should not be underestimated.

j) Although the present-day nation-state is experiencing grave systemic problems and its cracks are multiplying daily, it still has the strongest system in the national, regional, and global arena. Nation-states, numbering over two hundred, are represented by regional unions (particularly the European Union, NAFTA, which consists of the US, Canada, and Mexico, APEC in Southeast Asia) and by the United Nations globally. The democratic civilization system is represented by loose and formless forums like the World Social Forum and by non-state and non-power unions of laborers and peoples that are inadequate. Their inadequacy is ideological and structural. In order to address this inadequacy, world democratic confederalism—local and regional democratic confederations with their political parties and instruments of civil society—must be developed.

A Draft of the History of Democratic Civilization

The most basic feature of free human nature is that each person can choose their own history and know how to live by history. History is the interpretation of existence—the process that has been realized to date. The more diverse the forms of existence considered, the more histories we will have. But diverse histories do not mean that there is no historical unity. In the absence of unity, diversity is meaningless. Diversity exists only in connection with unity. The important issue is to determine what will represent this unity. In the case of the human species, intelligence and the ability to use tools provide a possible basis for unity. Without these abilities, there is no difference between them and other living species. There can, of course, be different bases for unity, including the state at times, and at other times democracy, the moral and political dimension of society, mentality, and the state of the economy. The important thing is to determine what sort of diversity can be developed on the basis of the unifying factor chosen.

We consider moral and political society to be the fundamental basis of unity in a democratic civilization. To clarify what we mean, we have defined it and tried to determine its methodology. Now, I would like to draw a brief outline of its historical development:

a) We know that close to 98 percent of social nature's life occurred in units of twenty-five to thirty people—what we call clan society. The clan can be defined as the stem cell of society. Clan society has carried on within all societies that have formed throughout time, including the family, the tribe, the aşiret, the peoples, and the nations, in a manner similar to cell differentiation. According to our basic definition of social nature, clan society is a moral and political society; whether they use sign or symbolic language is not so important. Of course, the morality and politics that exist within a clan are very simple, but the important thing is that they exist. Just because it is at a simple level does not diminish its importance.

On the contrary, it proves its importance. It may even be said that the strongest expression of morality is seen within clan society. It seems almost instinctual. Living according to morals is the sine qua non of existence. A clan that has lost its morality is a clan that has been dispersed, dismantled, or destroyed. That morality can be expressed in simple rules indicates its vitality. In comparison, today we can see that the impact on society of the frequent violations of the rule of law is negligible. Given conservative nature of law, such violations may even play a more positive role. The deterioration of rules within the clan, however, means the end of the community.

It is much the same for politics. A clan has two very simple jobs; hunting and gathering. Hunting and gathering are vitally important to all clan members. Surely, they would have many times over discussed, consulted, shared experiments, and appointed members to form and implement the best and most efficient policies for hunting and gathering, otherwise life would not have been possible. The most fundamental political issue was what to gather and eat, and this was collective work. Politics is defined as collective work, which means that clan society was a very simple but vital political community. If a clan society ignored politics even for a day, it would have died. Politics are, as a result, of great structural importance. In most other ways the human clan might have resembled other primates. The only significant difference between them was that the clan developed a simple moral and political social fabric. In this sense, even the development of tools come into play when there is a political dimension. Likewise, the development of language requires morality and politics. We should never forget that the discussion and decision-making to get any job done accelerated the need for the ability to speak. I find it pointless to argue that the nutritional needs of the clans gave rise to morality and politics. Surely an amoeba—a single-cell living entity—also has nutritional requirements, but we cannot speak of the morality and politics of amoebas. What makes a human being distinct from an amoeba is that morality and politics enter into the way humanity meets its nutritional requirements. In this sense, the Marxist statement "economy determines all" doesn't explain much. The important thing is, in fact, how the economy is determined. For humans to resolve this, society requires a moral and political fabric and, thus, a social sphere.

It is this feature that places clan society at the origin of the history of democratic civilization. In this respect, the history of democratic civilization is the history of 98 percent of humanity. In addition, as we mentioned, the clan continues to exist as the mother cell of the family, the tribe, the aşiret, the peoples, and national and international society, as well as of transnational communities.

Around twenty thousand years ago, as a result of glaciers melting in the fourth glacial period, Mesolithic (c. 15,000 to 12,000 years ago) and Neolithic (c. 12,000 years ago to date) societies formed, most spectacularly in the Taurus-Zagros ecosystem. These societies were substantially more advanced than clan society. They had advanced tools and settlement arrangements. Indeed, the first agrarian-village revolution occurred during this period. While the Taurus-Zagros social system was predominant, similar formations started to appear wherever human communities lived at the time in Africa and Eurasia. I believe that this development was the result of the spread of Neolithic society of Taurus-Zagros region. This is a great epoch in the history of social nature. Many developments, such as the symbolic language that is still used, the agricultural revolution (conscious cultivation and harvesting and the domestication of animals), the formation of villages, the origin of trade, the transition from a mother-based family to tribal and aşiret organizations, occurred during this historical stage. No doubt the fact that this period was called the New Stone Age refers to the appearance of sophisticated stone tools. There was also a remarkable evolution of human intelligence. All tools and equipment that have left their mark to date— including principles of their usage—seem to have been invented back then. It is the second extended period of history. One percent of the remaining 2 percent reflect this period. Society was still essentially a moral and political society. There was still no law and no state. Power had not yet arisen. The mother was seen as sacred, and the goddess image was elevated. The transition to the period of sacred temples and mausoleums also occurred during this period. Life was lived in such direct contact with history that the living shared their space with their dead. The ruins of temples and mausoleums are a glaring example of this. We are faced with real and genuine people not primitives.

The second main period in the history of democratic civilization can be described as expressing the pure values of democratic civilization. As symbolic language and intelligence developed, moral and political society experienced democracy in the most spectacular manner in the villages and tribes. This may seem odd, but it is the truth. This was the period when morality and politics were the purest democracy. The gradually increasing surplus product led to systematic oppression and exploitation by the hierarchical powers and later city-based civilization forces that existed above society.

b) Civilization narratives called written history (all types of mythological, religious, and scientific discourse) begin history with the command of the creator. The history we are talking about is that of the last five thousand years. With my sociological analysis as a starting point, I can say that such historical narratives are ideologically bent upon sanctifying oppression and exploitation. What all of the scientific schools, including so-called political economy, do, is develop an ideology based on surplus value—even on all values of life—of the society that has experienced a qualitative development in the productivity of its labor practices. Hiding the truth required an enormous ideological effort and a lot of force. Construction of the city, the class, and the state occurred at the same time as the major ideological constructs arose. The main function of these ideologies was to depict creation and formation in a different way, project it as the successful work of the priest, the strongman, or the ruler wrapped in divine imagery.

Democratic civilization must first sweep aside these ideological veils and barriers. Only then can we better understand not only the family, agrarian-village society, and tribal and aşiret structures, but also the class nature of the city-based state, the ongoing established hierarchical power, and the original colonization of women. Such a paradigm shift would greatly improve our understanding.

There is no doubt that aside from the triad of city, class, and state—the monopolist capital groups that are effectively the criminal gangs of civilization—there is also the democratic civilization that continues in a new phase even though it has profound contradictions with this civilization.

While contradiction arose between rural and urban areas, the tendency for the rural and urban areas to complement one another outweighed the tensions. Just as democratic civilization had its urban extensions (slaves, craftspeople, women), the cities also had their rural extensions. In particular, hierarchical structures that grew strong in rural society became the collaborators of the city-state rulers. Nonetheless, the contradictions and conflicts took place between these two social blocks, whose material interests differed. Intense ideological, military, and administrative conflicts between democratic civilization—representing the communal, moral, and political society's forces—and the civilization based on capital and state monopoly—establishing itself above the city's slave labor, plundering the tribes and villages in the rural areas, and looting—did occur. There was also warfare among city rulers, as they sought to increase their shares. The lamenting and melodies that can be found in Sumerian epics in relation to the city make the intensity and severity of these conflicts apparent. It is possible to deduce that to a large degree the tribal and aşiret structures arose in response the attacks of city-based civilization. The ethnic structures we begin to see around 4000–3000 BCE must also have been a product of this period. We know that it was the Sumerians and Egyptians who named the varying ethnicities. The Sumerians called those to the north and northeast the Aryans (descendants of hill and mountain farming people). Those to the west were called the Amorites (people with Semitic roots, proto-Arabs who had not become Sumerian), the Gutians, and the Kassites. The Egyptians called those who came from the deserts of the Sinai Peninsula the Apiru (*the dust-covered men and tribes from the east*). It is generally accepted that *Hebrew* is derived from Apiru (or Habiru). The ramparts erected around the cities and towers provide the best evidence of the existence of an opposing society.

The intensity of the clashes makes it clear that society did not easily accept class-based civilization. Archeological records prove that numerous villages and even some centers of civilization were burned to the ground. Mesopotamia is full of multilayered mounds that were settlement areas that were burned down numerous times. Mythology and literature from this period also reflect this. Homer's *Iliad* is a thirdhand version that reflects the epic tradition with Mesopotamian origins. Hesiod created a similar version that transformed the pantheon of Sumerian gods into the Olympus pantheon. That wars were the wars of gods personified by kings is a factor in all of the epic traditions of that period. It is quite clear that kings were identified with gods. The titles of Nimrod and the pharaohs are striking examples of that identification. While economic plunder and the enslavement of village societies were the anticipated result of war, there were also similar expeditions against the tribes to loot and take captives. Civilizations also considered plundering one another and taking slaves a significant source of wealth. Material interest continues to be a basis for conflict and reconciliation to this day. Everything was based on a calculation of "who is stronger." The unity of the celestial gods is clearly understood as the symbolic state of the largest kingdom on earth. That the Ottoman sultans called themselves Zillullah proves this.[9]

It would be a major shortcoming to present narrow class contradiction as fundamental during this historical period. Evidence suggests that the slaves at that time were entirely obedient servants of both their masters and the temple. They essentially acted as extensions of their masters' bodies. It was the villagers and the tribal and aşiret communities that resisted and refused to be enslaved. There were also frequent battles among the monopolies as each attempted to increase its share. Around 1500 BCE a struggle for hegemony began, with the Hittites and the Hurrians and Mitannis on one side and Egyptian civilization on the other. In the Middle East, the central civilization first formed around 1500 BCE, with significant evidence of competition and the ultimate rise to hegemony of the history's first magnificent cities from 1500 to 1200 BCE. This is considered a very vibrant and glorious period in history. Tribal, aşiret, and village communities continued to develop. Trade became so important that for the first time empires began to be built around it. Assyria and Phoenicia essentially gained power through their trade monopolies. Around 1500 BCE, when Chinese and Indian civilizations were taking their first steps, Europe, other parts of Asia, Africa, and America were beginning to enter the Neolithic Age. My greatest interest lies with two historical periods: 6000–4000 BCE and the rise of Neolithic agrarian-village society and the city life of urban society from 1500 to 1200 BCE. The originality, creativity, and rate of development and the epic narratives of these periods are most interesting. I believe that epic heroism and ideas about divinity primarily arose during these periods.

In outline, my analysis of the temporal and spatial spread and development of civilization is as follows:

1) Agrarian-village society began right after the magnificent hunter and gatherer society (the Göbekli Tepe temple in Urfa is illustrative of the process) around 15,000–12,000 BCE in the area where the Tigris and the Euphrates are fed by the Taurus-Zagros Mountain system that converges with the lowlands, where there was an abundance of plant and animal species and a climate that provided natural irrigation. This agrarian-village society was in its infancy, its transformation to sedentary life only occurring around 6000 BCE. From 6000 to 4000 BCE agrarian-society experienced its most creative period. From 5000 BCE on, it began to spread everywhere. There was little emigration, the spread primarily took the form of cultural export. The Ubaid culture, which began its ascent with irrigated farming in Lower Mesopotamia around 5000–4000 BCE grew strong enough to start colonizing parts of Northern Mesopotamia. Archeological remains attest to this culture's colonial spread in Upper Mesopotamia around 4000 BCE.[10] But at the same time, that region predominantly maintained its own culture. The Uruk period emerged between 4000 and 3000 BCE. It represents the birth of the city. The subject matter of the Epic of Gilgamesh is this magical development. A similar

northward expansion occurred during the Uruk period. Both periods of colonial expansion were likely the result of growing efficiency in weaving, pottery making, and agricultural production. The period from 3000 to 2000 BCE is the period of the classic Ur Dynasties. Its distinctive feature is an increase in the number of cities and the intense and continuous conflicts among them, each hoping to increase its share. We can also call these wars for parceling out domination among early monopolists.

2) The Neolithic Revolution, with its center in Mesopotamia, can be thought to have spread to China, India, all of Europe, and the north and east of Africa around 4000 BCE, settling in these areas between from 4000 and 2000 BCE. The Neolithic societies with European and Caucasian roots grew stronger and reversed the flow after 2000 BCE. This wave of onslaughts of the first large tribes from the north, who were on the offensive, which stretched from Anatolia to India and reached the civilizational centers of Mesopotamia and Egypt, led to an important historical upheaval. In addition, around 4000–2000 BCE, both the Arab tribes with Semitic roots and the mountainous Aryan tribes also attacked these civilizational centers in waves.

Both types of civilization were observed to have developed within these initial expansionist colonial and anti-colonial movements. While the upper tribal strata began the process of transformation into a state, many of the other tribe members were incorporated into the slave class. There is dissociation within the ranks of the tribe and the aşiret. While, on the one hand, new city civilizations were springing up, on the other hand, tribal and aşiret organization was increasing and solidarity among them was growing.

3) The period from 2000 to 1500 BCE marked the end of the Sumerian and Egyptian classical periods, with relations with Babylonia, Assyria, Mitanni, the Hittites, and the new Kingdom in Egypt deteriorating and conflicts becoming more intense. The era of the central hegemonic civilization had begun, a particular period of globalization was occurring. The northern tribes were using civilization's technical knowledge and practices against the centers of civilization, and the mountainous and desert tribes of

the Middle East were continuing their uninterrupted attacks. It is also important to note that iron replacing bronze led to many new developments in arms technology. This is also the period when mineral exploration and trade became of central importance for the first time, with trade rising to previously unseen levels. The breathtaking rise of Assyria and Phoenicia was the product of commercial monopolies. In this context, there was a huge increase in construction of castles and ramparts. In the end, however, between 1500 and 1200 BCE, civilization was dealt a major blow by the attacks of the Scythians and Dorians from the north and Aramaic warrior tribes from the south, resulting in a period of decline from 1200 to 800 BCE, with the Assyrian Empire the only power to survive.

4) It is as if Greco-Roman civilization—the last great civilization of the classical era of antiquity—absorbed the legacy of the two previous civilization systems (Mesopotamia and Egypt). This civilizational process lasting from 1000 BCE to 500 CE continued to expand across Asia, Africa, and Europe, giving rise to an additional classical era, thereby effectively contributing to the civilization. As the mythological era faded in importance, a new and original religious, philosophical, and even scientific development began. The Roman Empire constituted the summit of capital and power monopolies. However, in good time, under the blows of democratic civilization forces—Christianity, as the party of the poor within the empire, and the resistance and attacks of the tribes and peoples on its borders—brought the empire, and with it antiquity, to a close.

c) The Abrahamic religious tradition is the most difficult to place in the historical civilizational process. The nature of the civilization these three major religions belonged to remains a controversial issue.

After much thought and on the basis of my analysis of civilization, I define the Abrahamic traditions as eclectic and typically conciliatory movements that try to find a middle way between the two main forces of civilization (like today's social democratic movements). Although, I symbolically call them movements under the leadership of the Hebrew tribe, instead of addressing the racial basis of these religions, it would be more accurate to evaluate them as movements with a powerful ideological under-pinning. Although the Abrahamic tradition is presented as tribal, it is essentially a centrist movement between the democratic civilization of Middle Eastern origin and statist civilizations. It is not exactly a class or a tribal movement. Furthermore, it is neither completely ideological nor completely moral and political. It is centrist in all respects. The tradition in question has maintained this quality since the Prophet Abraham's appearance around 1700 BCE (if we take it as far back as Adam and Eve, then its roots stretch back to the origins of the Sumerian and Egyptian civilizations). This tradition has been a constant source of inspiration for both democratic and statist civilizations, while at the same time it has severed the ties of its affiliated forces (both material and immaterial) from the legacy of these civilizations, with the consequence that attracting both their friendship and animosity resulted in historical developments.

The Abrahamic religions ended the mythological era of the civilization and took leadership of the religious era. They may be more easily understood in the light of our new civilization paradigm. The most prominent narrative of the mythological era is that of the god-kings. It should not be forgotten that storytelling in antiquity was loaded with mythology. It is futile to look for present-day rationality in this manner of storytelling. All facts are delivered and all events described using mythological language. The mythology of the Sumerian era was deeply influenced by animism (the idea that all of nature is made up of living beings and spirits). This era initially transformed this belief system (which could be called the religion of the clans) in some small ways, for the first time making a distinction between a "divine and non-divine nature." The essence of all of the Sumerian priests' inventions came from Upper Mesopotamian Neolithic society, and, instead of a mother-goddess narrative, they favored a father and male-god mythology. The great material transformation of society took place thusly; first came the male-dominated hierarchical order, followed by and in parallel with the birth of authority in the form of the state. We can find its reflection in the new religious mythology from the outset with the emergence of Enki, the crafty god. The struggle between the Uruk goddess Inanna (her roots go back to the Mother Goddess Ishtar, which means *star of heaven*) and the Eridu god Enki (the first male god of a city) around this issue is quite striking. Inanna tried to prove that all divine rights belong to the mother-goddess and claimed that out of the famous 104 mes, 99, things like virtue, talent, invention, and the arts, were created by women. Enki tells Inanna that her claims are no longer important and tells her to submit and listen to her father. Here, while declaring himself the father, man, and god, he reduced goddess Inanna to the position of his daughter and wife. Oh, how this resembles all of present-day secular, religious, and scientific preaching! I personally believe that Enki is the initial god of all of them. Enki is the original; all the others are adaptations and copies. The gods of Olympus in particular are the third or fourth version of Sumerian mythology. The mythological narrative finally dies out with the onset of the Roman gods.

According to the story, Abraham, who smashed the idols of gods in the pantheon of Urfa, was thrown into the fire by Nimrod, but a divine miracle occurred where the fire burned and a sacred lake was formed. Abraham then migrated to the Canaan provinces (from an area controlled by Babylonian civilization to an area under Egyptian control), because it became difficult for him to find shelter in areas controlled by Nimrod. In fact, it was a typical case of asylum. It was probably while he was the leader of a local tribe that he came into a conflict with Nimrod, the ruler of the city. It is clear that the dispute was about property, merchandise, and trade. At the time, there was both rivalry between the Babylonian and Egyptian civilizations, and the first period of very lively commercial trade had begun. This rivalry seriously impacted the traditional interests of thousands of people like Abraham. This was the material basis for hegira and asylum. The lands of Canaan lay between the two civilizations and were to some degree semi-independent. Abraham migrated when hegemonic power began to target him. It is quite likely that this hegira incorporates the stories of thousands of migrations into a single narrative in the language of the time. All indications point to the fact that story in question tells of the contradictions and conflicts experienced by the local tribe and principalities, whose interests were submerged during this period under the weight of the two great civilizations (the new Kingdom of Babylonia and Egypt). Not only did these forces reject the Nimrods and pharaohs presenting themselves as gods, they also actively protested whenever they got the chance by smashing the representative idols. In short, the conflict over material interests was reflected as an ideological struggle.

It was not easy to struggle against a god-king ideology that was at least three thousand years old; it required enormous courage and ability. This is why Abraham's act of resistance in Urfa has taken on such miraculous significance and why it was so important. Servants for the first time opposed god, and that was an unprecedented and miraculous development. There is both the material aspect—smashing the idols—and the new ideological quest. How and where to find the new god, and, in a sense, how to create his own ideological construct, was still an open question—a question that was discussed for centuries thereafter. Abraham claimed he found his god by calling out to the voice that had inspired him "Wa hewe"—"He is (Yahweh)." Jehovah is the name of Abraham's first god; it seems very likely that the word has Aryan cultural roots. The transition to the theism of El, Ula, and Allah occurred long after Abraham went to the Canaan provinces.

El has Semitic roots and reflects the features and the longing for similarity and unity of tribes living in the extensive desert environment. The second major inspiration found its expression in Moses and his Ten Commandments. In fact, meeting God on Mount Sinai represents Moses's search for a solution to the worsening problems of the tribe he leads. If we keep in mind that the Ten Commandments are typical rules governing the tribe, we should be able to further develop our analysis. The tradition was to be renewed by Jesus, and Mohammad would have a similar experience in Mecca (on Mount Hira, where he received his first revelation from God). Many holy books include narratives about the contact of various prophets with God. It is clear that these were traditional narrations of guiding ideas and actions during important stages of that time. This is the nature of the narrative. The holy text reflects the natural and social (first and second nature) facts and events in the language (rhetoric) of the time, which I call the prophetic style.

We can easily say that this tradition represents a historical stage relevant to our topic:

1) It opposed history's and that period's first two major civilizations ruled by god-kings. This was the very first rebellion of servants against God.

2) A new ideological expression was created: a discourse that said the god-kings were simple human beings, but God was not human. He was the true creator of all things (the famous saying "He is" is the product of this great inspiration), and only He can be God and Rabb (The Lord).[11]

3) You could only submit to Him not to god-kings.

These were the main principles of the new ideology. These three points are the basis shared by this marvelous tradition called the Abrahamic religions. After many historical experiences, widespread sections of society gradually came to oppose the upper layer who did not contend with monopolization and deified themselves. This meant that these large sections of the society developed a sacredness and divine discourse that were more beneficial to them.

It is far more important to explain the change that occurred in relation to moral and political society. In the previous two millennia (3500–1500 BCE), moral and political society had been dealt a major blow. A very important development was the replacement of the "deities of nature"—which signified the sincere, equitable, and living relationship of nature with the mother-goddess culture and all of the clans and tribes—with the servant-god duality (essentially the slave and master class structure) expressed strictly through the domination of mythological male gods who are the creators of the land, the sky, and the sea. This is a clear indication that the ideological aspect of moral and political society has also been dealt a major blow. A major transformation in material and immaterial culture was taking place. Mythological narratives overflow with expressions of this.

It goes without saying that in this long historical period, the triad of priest, king, and commander, who are organized as a sprawling network of material interests over social nature and hidden behind an ideological mask, dealt a major blow to moral and political society. When we start from this paradigm, we can understand the society of this two-thousand-year period a lot better. The crafting of a concept is very difficult and requires a great endeavor. The paradigm of the Abrahamic tradition undoubtedly reconceptualized at least two-thousand-year period of the Nimrods and pharaohs, as well as bringing about the transition to a more humane and reasonable narrative and religion. The new religious narrative was, of course, also metaphysical and differs by far from today's rationality and social sciences. Yet it was still a very important historical development. It did not constitute a complete return to the moral and political society of the old times, as is clear from the Ten Commandments, which present morality exclusively as religion. Moses's Ten Commandments are obvious moral principles in religious garb. Elements of faith are secondary and weak. Therefore, substituting religion for morality was a very important transformation of moral and political society. The simpler moral and political life of the past was covered with a god that pervades all. In effect, life is wrapped in the cloak of a more advanced religion.

What most requires investigation is whether this religionized morality and politics was opposed to civilization (statist, classed, and urban) or constituted a new civilization in itself. This is the historical past of the present ongoing debate about secularism and Islamic civilization, particularly in Turkey and the Middle East. Considering the evolution of the Abrahamic religions to date, it is possible to give a dual response.

The tendency that resonates with the upper layer is the stratum (similar to right-wing social democrats) that seeks to create kingdoms and principalities based on maintaining the power of the Nimrods and pharaohs under fresh ideological cover (instead of being God, being God's messenger, shadow, or representative) and has done so since the religion's emergence. Abraham, for example, continued to trade while leading his tribe, which tells us a lot about his position. It is not difficult to establish that he sought a local principality or kingdom. He does not wish to remain as a simple servant of Nimrod. He found this religiously, as well as morally and politically, distasteful. It is highly likely that Moses was a dissident prince in Egypt. He rebelled against the pharaoh, representing the Hebrew community (the word *Hebrew* is derived from the word *Apiru*, which means *the dust-covered men and tribes from the east*), who were poor, lived in semi-slavery, and had not fully integrated into Egypt but had preserved a distinct character. The Holy Scripture tells us that following very difficult negotiations with the pharaoh he decided to leave Egypt. His exodus from Egypt (the Prophet Mohammad has a similar exodus) with the Hebrews he has organized in complete secrecy was successful. The story of his forty-year struggle in the desert depicts his endeavor to establish a new principality or emirate. He develops rules. He is searching for an imagined "promised land." As we know, this utopia was achieved around 1000 BCE in today's Israeli-Palestinian territory by the prophets Solomon, David, and Samuel. The true ideological leaders are the Samuel-like priests. After 1000 BCE, many similar principalities that evoke the example of the establishment of small nation-states and kingdoms were formed, taking advantage of the conflict between the two major blocs, the East and the West. Today, a similar, although somewhat different, trend continues to exist, particularly in South America but also in many other countries around the world.

Second was the anti-civilization tendency of the poor and radical sections of society. These sections understood that becoming civilized would aggravate their problems. Even in the first kingdom of Israel and Judah this was an intense contradiction. This is partly reflected in the fierce opposition of the Samuel-like priests to the leaders who became kings. The emergence of Jesus would make all of this even clearer. During this period, class division had deepened among the Hebrew people. The representatives of the upper layer, the owners of the Kingdom of Judah, who were Roman collaborators, accused Jesus of undermining their power and had him seized and crucified (with the help of Judas Iscariot, the thirteenth apostle, a Jewish informant who collaborated with the authorities). The governor who represented Rome did not insist that Jesus be crucified; it was the representatives of the Kingdom of Judah who demand crucifixion. It is clear that Jesus was regarded as a symbol of the first great inter-people's party that represented the poor, not only of the Hebrews but of all peoples (especially the Greeks, Assyrians, and Armenians, who were all peoples that had established civilizations at the time) impoverished by the Romans and the Persians. This was a new movement developing against classical civilization. The members of this movement lived an anti-Roman and anti-Sasanian underground life for three hundred years, running the risk of all types of hunger and torture. Later, the senior management (e.g., the council of priests and the consul) of the politicized movement officially collaborated with Roman emperor Constantine, becoming the ideological organ of the second largest Eastern Roman Empire built during the Byzantine era.

In contrast, the poor and the radical sections linked to different denominations displayed a fierce resistance that lasted for centuries. The resistance displayed by the Arianists, Assyrians, and Gregorians is important. Clearly, class struggle, and even the struggle for a moral and political society, carried out by the oppressed tribes and peoples under religious cover has continued unabated for centuries. The major factor in the formation of denominations within Christianity is the debate about whether Jesus was created from divine nature or human nature. Its roots go back to Sumerian mythology. The upper stratum declared itself the descendants of gods, asserting at the same time that it was impossible for lower strata to be god's descendants (the myth about how they were created from God's excrement addresses this). This discourse profoundly affected the Abrahamic religions as well. Mohammad's attitude is clear: man is not God but a messenger of God and can only be his servant. This is a contradictory issue within Christianity. Denominations that came out of the poor strata (Arianists) claimed that Jesus was of human descent, while those who were eyeing possible collaboration with the rulers tended to claim that he was God's descendant. In essence, the issue is about class formations. The anti-civilization struggle maintained by local and transformed official mythological beliefs had both class and ethnic characteristics in the period from 3000 to 1500 BCE. The aspiration for freedom is clear.

There are numerous examples to support this argument. The tribes and aşirets with Aryan roots in the Taurus-Zagros area waged a mighty struggle and destroyed the Akkadian Empire in 2150 BCE, establishing the Gutian Dynasty. Later, in alliance with the Hittites who, with the Kassites, occupied Babylonia in 1596 BCE, they formed the Mitanni confederation in 1500 BCE, with Serêkani (Ceylanpınar) as its center and all of the Egyptian and Mesopotamian cities acknowledging its power.

The Abrahamic tradition of resistance developed after this historical phase and has been quite effective in a variety of ways within different historical formations to date. Still, it would be wrong to entirely detach the Abrahamic tradition from mythology. The majority of events taking place in all three holy books (in particular the story of Adam and Eve) can also be found in Sumerian and Egyptian mythology. The difference is primarily related to God and the transitions underway in different periods. The important thing is that moral and political society imposed itself through strong local ideological and religious expressions. Religion is largely moral resistance. The Zoroastrian tradition in particular denotes a more radical transformation. This tradition, a very influential source for the Abrahamic religions, is the semi-philosphical and semi-religious moral and political teachings of the Zagros Mountains–based agricultural and animal husbandry society. The Zoroastrian questioning of the God with Semitic origins with the famous question "Tell me, who are you?" reflects a radical rupture. By replacing "sanctity" with "good" and "evil," as well as the concepts of "light" and "dark" for the very first time, they paved the way for the later Greek ethics (the science of morality) and philosophical movements. It is possible to deduce from the Herodotus's Histories, which are primarily stories about the Medians, that the Greeks owe much to Zoroastrian tradition, which they encountered through the Medians. It can be argued that the Zoroastrian tradition continued to reflect the strong moral and political society of the mountain tribes and

Aryan agricultural society at large, which had not been colonized. Understandably, it expresses the moral and political reality of a society where slavery had not really developed, and there was still a substantial free social life.

d) The Greco-Roman civilization of the final period of antiquity encompassed all three traditions. On both peninsulas the period of traditional god-kings was the first phase. The Greco-Roman mythology is the last variant of the Sumerian and Egyptian originals. The mythological tradition (Zeus on Olympus, Jupiter in Rome) experienced its last great era during the Etruscan and Spartan Kingdoms. During the Roman Republic (508 BCE–44 CE) and Athenian democracy (500–300 BCE), the philosophical tradition came to the forefront as the mythological narrative died out. Socrates is the famous philosopher and Cicero the famous orator of this period. The Athenian and Roman citizens, who were not prepared to easily abandon their former free traditions, were still quite devoted to their moral and political society tradition. They struggled intensely against monarchy and imperial systems. This is reflected in the struggle between Athens and Sparta and the struggle of the leading figures of Roman aristocracy with Caesar. Socrates and Cicero were philosophers of morals and thought, and were important figures in the development of the early doctrines of ethics and democratic politics. Although not reflected in society as a whole, it is indisputable that the power of Athens and Rome stemmed from their still vigorous moral and political society tradition. The limited institution of slavery cannot be compared to the large masses of free citizens, both in urban and rural areas, and this makes their role in the development of doctrines about the republic and democracy important. The Roman Republic and Athenian democracy succumbed to the imperial experiments of Augustus and Alexander, which was a significant setback, given that most of the positive values left by the Roman and Athenian period were the product of the republic and democracy. For the first time in recorded history, we confront the fact that moral and political societies express themselves better, although not fully, with a republic and democracy. To fully express themselves, moral and political societies must move beyond representative democracy; they need direct participatory democracy.

Christianity, the third tradition, initially had a destructive role within the empire. Christianity and the offensive by the Germanic tribes were strong constituents of the democratic civilization before the collapse of Roman Empire (476 CE). With the rise of the Byzantine Empire, Christianity fell into the reactionary position of being a representative of the statist and official civilization. However, the representation of very strong oppositional denominations shows that Christianity continues to play a positive role in the development of democratic civilization.

As a result, the classical civilization system increasingly developed its hegemonic character based on the 3500-year-old city, class, and state triad (capital and power monopoly networks). However, despite this, it collapsed (the collapse of Rome was the collapse of antiquity) under the assault of anti-civilizational Christianity and anti-civilizational (Germanic, Hun, and Frank) tribal resistance and offensives—which should be considered democratic civilization's two main constituents—showing us very clearly the course of historical development. The degeneration of the upper layers and reproduction of classical civilization that occurs at the heart of democratic civilization forces does not change this fact. Let's not forget that classical civilization's territory and cities were still like islands in the sea of democratic forces (tribes and peoples, religion, denominations, the city, and craft organizations). Humanity had not abandoned moral and political society. Thousands of years of war reflected this. It was, in fact, the tendency toward freedom—related mainly to social nature—in the form of moral and political society that was trying to sustain itself in a religious disguise. It is very important that we understand this.

e) The main problem in relation to Islam, the last major Abrahamic religion, is whether it is a continuation of classical civilization or a strong voice for democratic civilization. I do not believe this debate is over. Mecca, the city the Prophet Mohammad emerged from, was a trading city. It had a vast hinterland in its own way. It was located at the intersection of north-south and east-west trade routes. It was also a central market, where Arab tribes met to trade. Ideas, god symbols, and slaves were available alongside commercial goods. This was the place where religions from Abrahamic tradition, as well as mythological and even the animist tradition all resonated. Hajj is the center of pilgrimage. When the Prophet Mohammad was born, the Byzantine Empire, one of two empires going through a transition from antiquity to the Middle Ages, reached Damascus in the north and carried with it the official branch of Christianity it controlled. Assyrian priests were mostly in the opposition and accelerated the Christianization of the Sasanians. The Sasanians, on the other hand, sought to expand their hegemony from the northeast to the Arabian Peninsula. In the southwest, the effect of Christian Abyssinia (present-day Ethiopia in Eastern Africa) spread into Yemen. The Jews, who represent the oldest part of the Abrahamic tradition, permeated the peninsula, benefiting from a wealth of property and trade.

The Arab tribes, the true original inhabitants of the peninsula, on the other hand, were in a deep socioeconomic crisis. The former frequent expeditions in all four directions were no longer possible because of the strength of the existing civilizations. Prior to the Sumerian and Egyptian civilizations, Semitic tribes attacked the fertile Neolithic areas and the later city civilizations. Amorit, Apiru, Akkad, Canaan, and Aramaic are names that were given to them in different periods. It was a period when the tribes were under extreme pressure and approaching the point of implosion. You might say that the Arabs were waiting for a miracle to realize their last major expansion. Islam was that miracle. It is clear that Mohammad understood his time and the conditions well. He embodied all of the characteristics needed for a new period of history. He did not become a disciple of any of the existing ideological traditions. He was influenced by Judaism and Christianity—calling them Religions of the Book—as well as by Zoroastrianism and Sabianism.[12] His attitude toward idols was similar to Abraham's; he understood that they would not serve his goals. His initial propaganda and military action were against the Mecca trade monopolies. He knew that if he did not break their influence, he could not benefit from tribal dynamism. His reinterpretations of the revelations about God were very similar to the tradition of the Ten Commandments. It is clear that he was trying to inculcate the tribes with a new moral and political perspective. If the essence of the concept of Allah can be analyzed on the basis of his ninety-nine names, then it becomes clear what kind of social utopia is being constructed. In Medina, where he held political power, he further clarified his utopia.

The success of his initial actions was seen as miraculous, which increased his self-confidence. The way that Mohammad worked in Medina is fairly important to our discussion. The mosque functioned as a democratic assembly. Initially, meetings to address social problems were held in the mosque, and until Mohammad's death the mosque continued to play this role. The rituals of worship (prayer, fasting, and alms) were part of educational activities aimed at strengthening the believer's personality. Nobody can deny that this was the nature of emergent Islam. Although under complete religious cover, clearly, a powerfully dynamic moral and political society was revived. Therefore, if we are to talk about a true Mohammedan movement and Islam, then we must say that it is "an undeniable fact that a moral and political society can only be rebuilt on the basis of participatory democracy and with the goal of overcoming fundamental problems." It is known that some actions were extreme, and that Mohammad preceded very hesitantly as a result—particularly relating to the Jewish people—especially around the issue of qibla,[13] as well as of the killing of all the men of the Jewish Qurayza tribe because of their collaboration with the Quraysh aristocracy. Had a suitable solution been found, perhaps the Arab-Hebrew contradiction could have been resolved at the time, and Islam would have progressed even further.

On the whole, Islam can be described as a movement that is close to being democratic, libertarian, and egalitarian. Its expansion in a very short time cannot be seen as the result of use of arms alone. Islam's misfortune was to become a tool of civilizational forces much more quickly than was the case for Judaism and Christianity. Less than fifty years after its birth, it was used like a patch to the classical civilizational force in the hands of the

Muawiyah Dynasty in Damascus. The massacre of Ahl al-Bayt was also the destruction of many of Islam's positive features. I would argue that it was the end of Islam. Denominations that were shaped by the followers of Ahl al-Bayt and Khawarij,[14] the Islam of the poor, are noteworthy traditions. The Shia branch of Ahl al-Bayt joined official civilization with the Savafid Dynasty in Iran, losing its anti-civilizational essence. The Alevis of Anatolia and Kurdistan, on the other hand, were ruthlessly oppressed by the Sunni tradition of power for hundreds of years and were only able to carry on their existence as a moral and political society, and as a result they failed to achieve systematic development. The situation was no different for the other branches. Khawarij, Qarmatians, and many other similar movements tried to develop Islam as a firm class movement of the oppressed, and they were eliminated with even greater ferocity because of this. The existence of such a rich legacy under Islamic cover requires examination. This is why there is a need for a democratic history. Mohammad's Islam was never to be. Islam during the Umayyad, Abbasid, Seljuki, Ottoman, Safavid, and Mughal periods cannot be called the Islam of Mohammad.[15] This is why so many sects and denominations arose. However, there was no serious success. What is presented as Islam's success is the massive growth of a crafty trade monopoly in Mecca under Muawiyah and the related far-reaching expansion of the trade and power monopolies controlled by tribal aristocrats (emirs and sheiks) made possible by the Mecca trade monopoly. This was clearly a betrayal of Islam.

We know that the Prophet Moses and the Prophet Jesus were also betrayed. But the betrayal of Mohammad was lot more comprehensive. England instrumentalized nineteenth- and twentieth-century Islam as part of its colonial expansion in the Middle East, and it was made to play an extremely reactionary nationalist role in a variety of nation-state formations (Arab, Iranian, Turkish, Afghan, Pakistan, Indonesian, and other nation-states). Currently, along with the ambiguous radicalism of the al-Qaeda variety, we have the efforts by formations like the Organization of Islamic Cooperation that have no clear presence (I am talking about a variety of organizations that carry that name. Their link to Islam is only in name; the majority are capitalist, modernist, and nationalist organizations) to establish Islam's place in the world, which indicates that Islam is in one of the least meaningful periods in its history. I take the Prophet Mohammad and his Islam seriously, but only if the debate unfolds around his approach to ideas, morality, and politics in particular and provided that all those involved are prepared to respect and honor the Mohammedan reality that will emerge from any honest discussion. I will expand upon this later in this book, when it is relevant.

The reader must understand why I analyze the Middle Ages (476–1453 CE) from the perspective of Islam and Mohammad. Because the Middle Ages is the age of Islam or the age of Mohammedans, but in terms of betrayal to Islam's name and essence not in terms of its actual implementation. The precursor to our present-day hegemonic system called capitalism is ultimately this Islam. This is the age when trade monopolies reached their initial zenith. The center of civilization was still in the Middle East, and this was the prelude period when all the games of capitalism were first invented and implemented. The Venetian merchants, in collaboration with these monopolies, carried the material culture of the Middle East into Europe over three hundred years, following in the footsteps of Christianity, which had already introduced the immaterial culture of the Middle East to all of Europe between the sixth and tenth centuries. The eighth to twelfth centuries, also called the Islamic Renaissance, were nothing substantial when compared to the thousands of years of civilizational tradition that preceded them.

I believe the current state of the Middle East, which is plagued with problems and has been in steady decline since the twelfth century, is closely linked to this betrayal in the name of Islam. Even when the starting point offers a golden opportunity, betrayal will only do the worst. What happened to Islam confirms this. I can't stress enough my certainty that if the followers of Mohammad had developed genuine theological, ethical, philosophical, artistic, and political debates, as was the case with the followers of Moses and Jesus, and shared the results with moral and political society, then the hegemonic center of classical civilization would not have shifted to the West. More importantly, rather than classical civilization, democratic civilization would have been the predominant development.

The Judaic and Christian traditions, which withdrew from the Middle East to Europe, were a lot more open to discussion. No doubt though, dogmatism, which is in the essence of any religious tradition, continued to pose a serious obstacle. But by spreading the far from insignificant immaterial cultural values of the Middle East to Europe, as dialectics would suggest, they accelerated the development of philosophy and science. What has never been done and is still not permitted in the Islam of the Middle East is to have just such a dialectical discussion and to respect its conclusions. This aside, the Middle East led Europe both in agricultural and commercial development for thousands of years and did not lag behind in manufacturing. In short, the Mohammedan movement could have shown a way forward that would have suited the history of Middle East. But the rather crippled tribal *asabiyyah*,[16] as Ibn Khaldun argued at the time, had already imposed something similar to the present-day nationalist fascist tendencies in the early days of Islam and wasted the Middle Ages. The central civilization system that went into decline in Middle East resumed its ascent in Europe from the fifteenth century onward. The accumulation of material and immaterial culture that formed during the ten thousand years following the agricultural revolution was to make its new offensive at this point in this new location.

My intention is not to sketch the history of democratic civilization but to attempt to define it, determine its location, and describe its historical function. I believe that history unquestionably needs this analysis, otherwise we would not find meaning in the so-called miraculous developments. How can we understand history without analyzing the resistance movements, wars, and communal structures that developed in opposition to those who tried to loot the material and immaterial values? We speak here of the upper layers that declared themselves gods for thousands of years in a very rich cultural atmosphere, while driving these people to extinction and imposing disreputable social structures like slavery, serfdom, cheap labor, and housewifery on them. How can we become familiar with our humanity if we don't understand history? If we respect what is socially indispensable, including politics, which is the art of reason, morality, and freedom, then we must ask and answer these questions. We will not arrive at a solution using narrow class tricks and tribal *asabiyyah*. In the absence of systematizing the tremendous movements in social nature's history and revealing how and why they emerged, as well as their consequences, we can't define our existence as humans. If that were the case, our life would be meaningless. The narratives of the civilization, supported by mass of propaganda, the essence of which is the networks that secure the monopoly of capital and power, do not constitute a meaningful history of humanity. Democratic civilization's initiative to build historical-society arises from the need to end the capitalist network's deceit—such as ideas about the end of history and a singular world—not only because we can imagine new worlds, but because they are absolutely indispensable.

Before it was possible to completely shatter the medieval dogmatism that destroyed the human being, the much worse dogmatism of the nation-state infiltrated people's minds. It is a thousand times worse than the chauvinism of the tribal asabiyyah. This, along with the establishment of national histories that blind people and lead them to disregard the facts, has created new deserts of the intellect. Blood has flowed like a river to create and validate this disgusting history. Nationalism and the nation-state are nothing more than the most reactionary idol running roughshod over the whole of humanity. I am making an attempt to formulate this history knowing that even the so-called darkest ages of social consciousness were not this barren and humanity had not yet fallen so far.

I must repeat: without knowing social nature's history we can never understand the reality. I will never forgive myself for evaluating history so bleakly for so long under the sway of capitalism. Without knowing history, which is a true apocalypse of humanity, and thus not being bound to the reality of moral and political society, we cannot avoid falling into the most disrespectful and unworthy of positions. The more historical you are the more you can understand the reality. History, on the other hand, can only establish a link with social reality if it is the history of democratic civilization.

Because of its importance, I will present my approach to the history of the democratic civilization as opposed to capitalist modernity under a separate heading in the next section.

Elements of Democratic Civilization

It may be instructive to elucidate what constitutes community in a moral and political society. Defining the diversifying social elements will also be necessary if we are to gain an understanding of its totality. Its totality can only have a meaning in diversity. We cannot consider the city, in terms of being the state, an element of democratic civilization. However, those craftspeople, workers, unemployed, and self-employed people who live off their own labor, even if they are from the city, are part of the democratic element, and we will be discussing them in further detail.

Clans

We briefly touched on the clan. It is the mother cell and spans 98 percent of humanity's long adventure. Life was extremely difficult for these groups of twenty-five to thirty people, who used sign language and lived on hunting and gathering. It was hard not to fall prey to wild animals and to find healthy food. At times, the climate was extremely cold; there have been five major ice ages. We should not underestimate our ancestors. If it wasn't for their great efforts we would not be here today. The totality should be sought here. Existent humanity is the result of their struggle for survival. History is not just the written parts. Real history must take into account the state of our social nature millions of years ago, if it is to become meaningful. The main features of clan society were, perhaps, the original form of a united humanity. We have tried to show that the clan was the purest form of moral and political society. These communities continue their physical existence in a number of places, as well as being the mother cell that lives on among all of the elements of developed societies.

The Family

Even if clans were not families, they were something close to that. The family was the first institution to differentiate itself within the clan. After a lengthy period of the matriarchal family and the experience of the agrarian-village revolution (c. 5000 BCE), a transition to the patriarchal family under male-dominated hierarchical authority occurred. Administration and the control of children were left in the hands of the male elders in the families. The ownership of women became the basis for the initial concept of property. This was followed by male slavery. During the civilization period, we come across large and long-lasting families in the form of dynasties. The simpler sort of family of the peasants and craftspeople have always existed. The state and rulers have equipped the father and/or male within the family with a copy of their own authority and gave him a role based on this. This made the family the most important instrument for legitimizing monopolies. It was also always the source of slaves, serfs, workers, laborers, soldiers, and all other service providers for the networks of capital and domination. This is what underpins the importance and sanctification of the family. The most important source of profit for capitalist networks is their exploitation of women's labor within the family. By disguising this fact, they put an additional load on the family. The family has been turned into an instrument for securing the system and has been condemned to live through its most conservative period in history.

A critique of the family is essential if it is to become a key element of democratic society. It is not sufficient to analyze the situation of women alone (the approach taken by feminism); we must analyze the family as the cell of power—in the absence of which the ideal and implementation of democratic civilization shall be deprived of its most important element. The family is a social institution that cannot be overcome but can be transformed. For this, hierarchical property claims on women and children must be abandoned, and no kind of capital and power relation should play any role between partners. Instinctive drives, such as the preservation of species, must be overcome. The ideal approach to the relationship between women and men is one based on a philosophy of freedom bound to moral and political society. A family that underwent a transition of this sort would become the most robust guarantee of democratic society and one of the most fundamental relationships within democratic civilization. Rather than simply being officially recognized spouses, it is important that couples become natural partners. Both parties in the relationship should always be ready to accept the right of the other to live alone. In relationships, we cannot act in a blind and slavish way. It is clear that in a democratic civilization the family will undergo a very meaningful transformation. If women, who have lost much prestige throughout the millennia, do not regain their esteem and power, there can be no meaningful family unit. A family built on ignorance is not worthy of esteem. The family has an important role to play in the reconstruction of democratic civilization.

Tribes and Aşirets

Families are inherent to two important social elements, the tribes and the aşirets. They share a common language and culture that primarily developed within the agrarian-village society. The tribes and aşirets are the necessary social units for production and security. When the family and the clan were no longer sufficient for solving the problems of production and security, the transition into a tribe became necessary. They were not units based solely on blood ties but were the core elements of a society assembled to meet these production and security needs. They represent a tradition that lasted thousands of years. One of the most far-reaching genocides of capitalist modernity was declaring these social structures to be reactionary and aggressively eliminating them. This was essential, because had people remained in these tribal units they could not have so easily have been turned into workers ripe for exploitation. The same was true for slave owners and feudal lords. Tribes were, in a word, the enemy. The tribe could not turn its own members into slaves, serfs, and workers.

Tribal life is closer to communal life. The tribe is the social form with the highest development of moral and political society. Tribes have always been seen as the merciless enemy of classical civilizations because of their moral and political features. Besides, it was impossible to conquer and control them; they would live free or perish. There have, of course, been tribal societies that were corrupted over time. Collaborators played a negative role in both the family and the tribe. The tribes, which were always first and foremost nomadic, were one of the most constructive of historical forces. The slave, serf, and worker have never given rise to anything like the historic resistance of the tribes, neither in term of rebellion nor in the freedom with which they lived lives. They have mostly (with exceptions) been the masters' most loyal servants. Perhaps if history were evaluated in terms of tribal resistance instead of class struggle a more realistic picture would result. One of the most important distortions of those who have constructed the history of civilization has been to downplay the role of the tribe, presenting their historical impact as negative or not considering their role at all.

The aşiret, a kind of federation of tribal communities, was even more important. Aşirets arose primarily in response to the attacks of slave-owning civilization. The need to unite and resist in order not to be wiped out led to the aşiret as an organization. It was a social formation where military and political organization rapidly developed; it was essentially a spontaneous military and political force. To function an aşiret needed a shared mindset and organizational unity. Aşirets carried with them a long history and culture. They were the headwaters of the *nation* cultures. As well, their contribution to production should not be underestimated. Their collective social structures made mutual assistance essential. Aşiret and tribal communities had a strong communal spirit, providing one of the positive qualities of national character but could pose a danger if collaborationism developed. Despite the efforts of historians of civilization to discredit the aşirets, they were one of the key motor forces of history. If they had not resisted in the name of freedom, communalism, and the democratic tradition, humanity would have been reduced to a servant masses or a herd. All of this made the aşiret a fundamental element of democratic civilization.

The history of democratic civilization, to a great extent, is the history of resistance, rebellion, and insistence on the life of the moral and political society of the tribes and aşirets in their struggle for freedom, democracy, and equality in the face of the attacks by the civilization. The best qualities of society are found in tribal and aşiret structures. The nation-state's sweeping destruction of the aşiret and tribal cultures to gain the dominance for an ethnic group was effectively an all-encompassing cultural genocide. Although this far-reaching genocidal attack on society has since been somewhat relaxed, it remains a major threat. In forming democratic nations, tribes and aşirets could make much more positive contributions than nation-states or state's nation. This should make clear why aşirets and tribes are seen as essential elements of democratic civilization.

Peoples and Nations

In democratic civilization, the way societies are shaped as peoples and nations, and their lives are different to those of classical civilization. In official civilizations, peoples and nations were conceived of as an extension of the ruling dynasties and ethnic groups. Thus, the history of the formation of peoples and nations was fictionalized to give credit to the ruling dynasty or ethnic group. In this fictional history, the state of natural society is obscured. Heroes were made of individuals, who were then declared by the dynasty or the dominant ethnic group to be the founding fathers of the people and the nation. This is the step after deification and the step before deification of founding fathers. History, in a way, is the art of manufacturing this deification and of creating founding fathers. The reality, of course, was different. Society advanced in the form of tribes and aşirets that developed language and culture as they adopted a more sedentary life. In maintaining its essential identity—moral and political society—it began the transition into becoming the people and the nation. Societies were not born with peoples or nations as their identity. However, in the Middle Ages they began to draw closer to an identity as the people and in the modern era as the nation.

Being a people is in a way the material necessary to form the identity called nation. In the modern era, peoples become nations in two ways. The official civilization transforms people's asabiyyah into modern nationalism, and then attempts to determine the state's, the bourgeoisie's, and the city's new society form as the state's nation. A dominant ethnic group generally plays a key role in this process, and its identity becomes the identity of the entire nation. Moreover, different tribes, aşirets, peoples, and nations with different identities are forcibly assimilated into this ethnic group's language and culture. This is the way of what could be called "savage nationalization." This approach of the official civilization meant the greatest of cultural massacres in all nations and of the languages and cultures of thousands of tribes, aşirets, peoples, and nations. These peoples and nations are the primary elements that we need most to focus as we configure the history and system of democratic civilization.

The second way of becoming a nation is to transform the same or similar language and cultural groups—which are part of moral and political society—into a democratic society on the basis of democratic politics. All tribes, aşirets, peoples, and even families play their part as units of moral and political society in forming such a nation. They transfer their linguistic and cultural wealth to this nation. This new nation will not allow any single ethnic group, denomination, belief system, or ideology to dominate. The richest synthesis is always voluntary. Moreover, democratic politics allows distinct linguistic and cultural groups to live together as democratic societies under the identity of *nation of nations*—the common über-unit of nations. This way is the most suitable to social nature. Whereas the state's nation method is the approach of capitalist modernity and is far removed from natural society and shaped as "one language, one nation, one country, one (unitary) state." This is the secular version of the former "one religion, one god" approach. Thus, it is the new form of capital and power monopoly and the state. The state's nation denotes how capital and power monopolies took their place at the heart of society at the stage of capitalist transformation and colonized society, dissolving it within itself. Maximum power is the form that allows for maximum exploitation. It is alienating society from its moral and political dimension, relinquishing it to death, turning individuals into worker ants, thereby creating a herd-like fascist society. Profound historical and ideological factors, as well as factors like class, capital, and power, play a role in this model, the model most contrary to social nature. Genocides were carried out as a combined consequence of these factors.

Within the democratic civilization system, nation formations and fusions are the antidote to capital and power monopolies. It is also the main way to eliminate the disease of fascism and genocide (the cancerous metastasization occurring within society), along with their root causes. Once again, we are confronted with the harmony of social nature with democratic civilization.

Village and City
Villages and cities will have a different meaning from a democratic civilization perspective (paradigm). Just as agriculture and industry are two necessary reciprocal fields of production within social nature, the same is true of the village and the city. The equilibrium between them must be protected. If it is undermined, we are on the road to ecological disaster, the ratcheting up of class and the state, and the monopolization of capital. Once price disparities begin to be exploited to maximize profit, trade becomes an increasingly illegitimate practice. Our watchword must be: "Yes to the city, but no to the monopoly of class, the state, and capital." These fundamental ideas lie at the base of any sound history of the development of the city and the village. It is incredibly ironic that the triad of city, class, and state are defined as civilization, while those communities living in harmony with true social nature, in a reversal of reality, are called "barbaric" and "savages." True barbarism and savagery are the plunder and destruction of social nature effected by the alliance of this

triad, represented as a single unit by the city. This irony shows us, once again, how ideological hegemony stands truth on its head. Throughout history, ideology has been important both for leading us to the truth and for steering us away from it.

Democratic civilization evaluates the city, class, and state triad as the real barbarity, hypothesizes that those who oppose this triad are the true expression of moral and political society, and ideologizes this.

Village community is important as the first example of settlement. It is an essential aspect of ecological life that must be renewed in the industrial era. The village is not just a physical phenomenon, it is a fundamental source of culture. Just like the family, it is a basic unit of society. This is not changed by the fact that the city, industry, the bourgeois class, and the state attack the village. It is also of the utmost importance, because it is the most suitable unit for implementing moral and political society. The city, on the other hand, will only play a positive role if it undergoes a clear transformation in terms of population and function to reestablish its equilibrium with the village. Only a radical transformation can stop it from being a center for exploitation and oppression and allow it to contribute meaningfully to social development. The city must stop being the site of the cancerous growth of the middle class and capital in the form of state and company bureaucracies. This is vital to the liberation of contemporary society. In their current form, cities—both in terms of their scope and their meaning—are the key centers for the rapid depletion of society (ecological destruction and societycide). All of this stands as unquestionable evidence of the failure of classical civilization. There was a single Rome, and it reigned throughout antiquity. As such, its collapse signaled the collapse of antiquity. It is the cancerous plurality of our present-day cities, on the other hand, that make society cancerous. Cities are centers for absorbing society, including rural and village societies. Humanity, as a society, must rid itself of this fallen city. Otherwise, the city will certainly wipe out what remains of humanity's social nature.

The harmonious unity of village and city is of the utmost ideological and structural importance to the democratic civilization system. Social nature can only maintain its existence safely on the basis of this harmony.

Mentality and Economy
The economic foundations of democratic civilization are in a perpetual conflict with the capitalist monopolies based on social surplus value.

Taking fundamental social needs and ecological factors into consideration still leaves a lot of room for the development of agriculture, trade, and industry. Aside from monopoly profit, all revenue should be considered legitimate. Democratic civilization does not oppose the market. On the contrary, because it offers a truly free environment, it has the only genuine free market economy. It does not deny the market's creative competitive role. What it opposes are techniques for amassing speculative revenue. Fecundity is the measure for the question of property. The role of monopoly, as property, always contradicts fecundity. Neither excessive individual ownership nor state property ownership are consistent with democratic civilization. Social nature stipulates that the economy be in the hands of the communities.[17] In the absence of monopolies, neither the individual nor the state have anything to do with the economy. Economies where individuals or the state make economic decisions will either generate profit or go bankrupt. The economy is always the work of groups. It is the true democratic sphere of moral and political society. Economy is democracy. Democracy is especially essential for economy. In this sense, the economy is neither the base nor the superstructure. It is more realistic to interpret it as society's most fundamental democratic action.

Both the analysis of capitalist political economy and Marxist interpretations that alienate economic relations are quite harmful. The action of the boss and the worker does not constitute the economy. I had to evaluate the boss-worker dichotomy to portray the monopolist thieves of the economy, which is the essential democratic act of social nature. If we include the clan and tribal periods, it is more appropriate to call the economy the essential activity of moral and political society. In this case, what I mean by a worker is the concessionist worker who, in the form of wages, receives a small portion of the value stolen from the other poor sections of society, in particular unpaid housewives and young women. Just as the slave and serf were the extensions of their masters and lords, the concessionist worker is always an extension of the boss. We should view slavery, serfdom, and becoming a worker with suspicion, oppose it, and, on that basis, develop our own ideology and practice—that would be the basic prerequisite for being moral and political. Just as the master, lord, and boss triad is worthy of no praise, the triad of slave, serf, and worker, as their extension, should also never be glorified. We should feel sorry for them, see them as degraded social sectors, and struggle for their freedom.

The economy is an essential action of historical-society. No individual (master, lord, boss, slave, serf, or worker) or state can be the proponent of economic action. For example, no boss, lord, master, worker, peasant, or individual from the city can remunerate the work of mothers—the most historical and social institution. This is because mothers carry out the most difficult but necessary act of society: maintaining life. I am not only talking about childbearing. I look at motherhood more broadly than that; it is a culture, a phenomenon that is in continuous state of emotional upheaval, with all mothers' actions charged with intelligence. I think this is the correct way to look at it. What sort of reason and conscience are compatible with treating women—who are constantly rebelling, full of emotions and reason, always obligatory, arduous, and active—as unpaid laborers? Marxism, the ideology that best represents the interests of laborers, did not consider the actions of mothers and other similar social sectors as falling within the scope of value, thereby legitimizing their unwaged status. This has placed the boss's servant in the seat of honor. How can an economic science of this sort claim to present its solution as a social solution? Sadly, Marxist political economy is a form of bourgeois political economy. Marxist political economy needs to critically examine itself. With its collapse and self-dissolution after seventy years, real socialism taught us that searching for socialism in the area of bourgeois profit and an alleged commitment to socialism that lacks courageous self-criticism provides a very valuable and unreciprocated service to the capitalist system. How right Lenin and others were when they said, "The road to hell is paved with good intentions!"[18] Could Lenin have imagined that his actions would confirm the accuracy of this saying? I hope to further develop this analysis in the relevant sections.

The economy can be thought of as the main moral and political act of historical-society that, should it prove necessary, could possibly be turned into an abstraction and a science. But to envisage Eurocentric political economy as a science is to intellectually fall prey to the second most exploitative mythology after Sumerian mythology. A radical scientific revolution is vital in this area.

We must insist that economic activity is the most moral and political of social activities. With this characteristic, economy must be the top priority of democratic politics. The democratic civilization system promises a true revolution and a correct interpretation of the economy of historical-society. This is a thousand times more important to the health of society than any medication could be.

Contrary to popular opinion, society's mentality is not a superstructural element far removed from the economy. In fact, this and other base and superstructure distinctions complicate our understanding of social nature. Intelligence in nature is most intense in social nature. To think of separate elements of mentality may be seen as out of place. But science has been detached from historical-society, put to service by official civilization, and has been reduced to the most efficient source of power for rulers. This is why it is important that we look closely at the mentality and structure of life in a democratic civilization. Opposition and the construction of alternatives to the mentality and structure—the ideological hegemony and science—of the official civilization have been constant. Movements based on ideological struggle and alternative science have never been absent. Classical civilizations have primarily exploited the analytical development of intelligence, and have used an array of deceptive, intimidating, and delusional fiction and symbolism to cover up this abusive reality. They have consistently advanced the idea that it is futile to search for other truths, using mythology, religion, philosophy, and science to assert that their material reality is coterminous with general social reality.

This suggests that the "monistic" ideal capital monopoly is the "only right path." They have attempted to reduce the extraordinary diversity of first and second nature to uniformity to prove that this is our only option. A small amount of the surplus value they have amassed was used as intellectual capital, assuring constant ideological hegemony. Schools and educational systems became locations and structures where their way of life was learned by heart. They have used the university not as a site for grappling with truth and social identity, but as an area of exclusion and denial. In the name of objectivity, the content and structure of science has been carefully designed to objectify the reality of historical-society and prevent it from acting as a subject. Mechanisms within a rigid civilizational line are presented as the ideal universal rules and forms.

The harmony of democratic civilization with that of social nature can be seen in the development of the mind. Even the clans, having a childlike mentality, were aware of their animate connection to nature. The idea of "dead nature" is betrayal and falsification on the part of civilization forces, with their mentality that is increasingly detached from nature. Today's global financial era fails to apprehend the vitality and divinity it sees in "money" in any natural formation. In this sense, the clans were more advanced in their understanding of nature's vitality and divinity than are present-day monopolisms. Tribes, aşirets, peoples, and democratic national structures have become the realm of existence of an animate mentality. For these social formations, intelligence and structure are for bonding with life. Analytical and emotional intelligence can only achieve dialectical unity within the democratic civilization system.

Democratic civilization's mentality has always included skepticism about official schools, academies, and universities, and throughout history it has developed alternatives, from prophets to philosophical schools, mysticism to natural sciences, and the many *maqam*,[19] dervish convents, *ocak*,[20] sects, madrasahs, monasteries, tekkes, mosques, churches, and temples. As we can see, a dual as opposed to singular existence of civilization is apparent in all areas of social nature. The issue is not to get bogged down by the official singular structure but to develop an analysis based on the naturalist side of this contradiction, and with it the diversity of free life that makes democratic civilization possible.

Democratic Politics and Self-Defense

Politics and security, as elements of democratic civilization, are essential to the existence of moral and political society. Another specific category of democratic politics would be extraneous, since society itself is understood to be political. However, there is a difference between the two. A political society is not necessarily synonymous with democratic politics. In fact, throughout history the official civilization has overwhelmingly imposed the domination of despotic kingdoms on political society. Political society does not disappear under the weight of this domination, but it cannot democratize itself either. Having an ear does not guarantee hearing; sound health is also required. Similarly, having a political social fabric does not guarantee that it will always function freely. The healthy functioning of these structures requires a democratic environment.

In general, a democratic environment and the political structure of society can be called democratic politics. Democratic politics does not just denote a way of doing things, it also indicates the totality of the institution. In the absence of political parties, groups, assemblies, media, meetings, and other such institutions and activities, a democratic politics praxis cannot develop. The true role of institutions is to facilitate discussion and decision-making. Life cannot continue in the absence of discussion and decision-making when it comes to all the common affairs of society.

The result will be either chaos or dictatorship. This is always the fate of a society that is not democratic. Such societies are always oscillated between chaos and dictatorship—it is one or the other. The development of moral and political society in that environment is unthinkable. This makes the primary objective of political struggle, which is to say, democratic politics, the formation of a democratic society and finding the best approach to common affairs through discussion and decision-making within this framework.

The primary goal of politics—deprived of its real function—in the environment and in the institutions of bourgeois democracy is, above all, to hold power. Power, on the other hand, is about getting a share from the monopolies. Obviously, this cannot be the objective of democratic politics. Even if democratic politics are to operate within the institutions of power (e.g., the government), their fundamental task remains the same. This task is not to seize a share of the monopolies but to arrive at and implement decisions that serve the vital interests of society as a whole. It is meaningless to say that "as a rule, we should not participate in bourgeois democracies." In fact, it is necessary to understand how to conditionally operate in that arena. Unscrupulousness can only benefit the pseudo-politics of the ruling class.

It is important to always keep in mind that democratic politics require competent cadre, media, political party organizations, and civil society organizations, as well as continuous education and propaganda. We could define the required features of successful democratic politics that attain results as based on an overall respect for diversity within society as a basis for equality and reconciliation, a rich and courteous open discussion, political courage, the prioritizing of morality, a good understanding of the issues at hand, a grasp of both history and the present, and a holistic and scientific approach.

Self-defense is the security policy of a moral and political society. More precisely, if a society cannot defend itself, its moral and political features become meaningless, and society is either colonized and goes into decline or must resist and try to regain its moral and political qualities and its capacity to function. This process could be called self-defense. A society that insists on determining its own course, that rejects colonization or any form of imposed dependency, must be capable of self-defense and have strong institutions. Self-defense is not only required to face external threats, conflicts and tensions will also occur within the structures of the society. Let's not forget that historical-societies have long been the subject of class division and submersed in power, which means that they will want to maintain these characteristics for a while. These forces will resist with all their might to protect their existence. Therefore, self-defense as a widespread social necessity will have an important place on the agenda for some time to come. In fact, to be effectively implemented, decision-making capacity needs to be reinforced with self-defense.

Moreover, power is not only external but has seeped into every nook and cranny of society. It is vital that self-defense takes places in as many of these nooks and crannies as possible. Societies without self-defense are societies that have surrendered and been colonized by the capital and power monopolies. Self-defense has always been an issue for all of the different historical social units, including clans, tribes, aşirets, peoples, and nations, as well as for the religious communities, villages, and cities. Capital and power monopolies are like wolves pursuing their prey; they seize what they want from those who lack self-defense—like grabbing a stray sheep from a disbanded flock.

It is imperative that self-defense be established and always be at the ready to defend democratic society and ensure its continued existence, at a minimum, inhibiting the attacks and exploitation of capital and power monopolies. It is important not to fall into either of two mistakes, since we will be living with capital and power apparatuses for a while. The first mistake is to entrust self-defense to the monopolistic order. We know of thousands of devastating examples of this error. The second mistake is to try to become a power apparatus under the rubric of forming a state to counter the existing state. Real socialist experience has sufficiently eluci-dated the consequences of this error. As such, meaningful and functioning self-defense will continue to be a factor in democratic civilization that cannot be ignored historically, at present, or in the future.

It is surely possible to increase the elements of democratic civiliza-tion and explain their essence, but I believe that this presentation is suf-ficient to make clear the importance of the topic.

EIGHT

Democratic Modernity versus Capitalist Modernity

The research methods used by the Eurocentric social sciences for investigating truth are quintessentially hegemonic. They make alternative paths of truth virtually impossible in two fundamental ways. The first is the monistic-universalist approach. Truth is always reduced to "one." The second is the infinite relativist model. To say that everyone has a truth of their own is essentially to say that there is no truth. This is like saying that everything changes in order to prove that nothing changes. It is clear that both methods have reductionism in common. They openly reflect their character by reducing truth to "one," whether through universalist "monism" or relativist "singularism."

Undoubtedly civilizational monopolism lies behind these methods. Its foundations date back to when the Sumerian priests constructed "En" as the greatest god. The reason for exalting "En" was the need to legitimize the emerging hierarchy and monopolism of the city, class, and state and to make them dominant and hegemonic in social mentality. "First cause" in Greek philosophy, God as the greatest invention (Plato and Aristotle's understanding of God), has the same source. In monotheistic religions, the form assumed by "En" is "Allah," the god of all worlds. "El" has its roots in "Elah."[1] "El" became "Jupiter" with the emergence of Rome. The attempt to use such religions or mythological concepts to legitimize the construction of god-kings and imperial regimes in any society can be widely observed. Almost all kingdoms, empires, and despotic regimes endeavor to use such concepts to exalt themselves and attain ideological hegemony. Without this hegemony, these regimes are unlikely to survive.

During its sixteenth-century ascension, European capitalist monopolism, as civilization's new hegemonic center and form, was clearly aware that it would not achieve dominance without a similar effort. Money-capital (a form of capital that differs from agricultural capital and commercial capital, as well as from capital as an instrument of power), which until then had hidden itself in the cracks and backrooms of society, began for the first time to rise above society as a hegemonic force and gradually infiltrated its every pore.

The search for new method by Roger Bacon, Francis Bacon, and René Descartes, who had their roots in Christian, and, therefore, Middle Eastern-Sumerian, theology, was closely connected to this material hegemonic rise. The truth they were pursuing, whether in method or content, had a share in this new kind of capital and its hegemonic rise. As capitalist monopoly consolidated its hegemony, it also consolidated and perpetuated its ideological hegemony. We can only provide a scientific explanation of the new revolutions in method, philosophy, and science by looking at the transformative effects of these material conditions. No doubt, attributing everything to capitalism leads to scientific blindness and would fall into a trap and into the most vulgar reductionism. But if we ignore the importance of connections between them, the exploration of truth will be crippled and lose its value amid metaphysical narratives.

In explaining the concept of modernity, it is necessary and very instructive to take the formation of this methodology and truth into account. *Modernity* as a concept means *time, the present.* There are different moderns, depending on the age. From Sumerian modernity to Roman modernity, and even before and after them, there have been and are many examples of modernity. Who could deny that at a certain time Roman modernity was proudly lived in all centers of civilization? Are we not in awe when the archeological records tell us that the Sumerians and, even before them, Upper Mesopotamians presented perhaps the most spectacular examples of modernity in terms of time and scope? Could we explain these revolutionary material cultures if they were not charged with meaning?

When Anthony Giddens emphasized the difference between capitalist modernity and all other modernities, he contributed to explaining the truth to a certain extent.[2] Obviously, it is possible to understand Giddens's perspective; he is, after all, a child of English hegemony. To claim that capitalist modernity is unprecedented is a sort of debt to or worship of their country and the new God, the nation-state, required of any contemporary intellectual. His description of the three pillars on which capitalist modernity rests is quite instructive. But he separates modernity from capitalism and treats it as a superior category. As a result, he clearly adopts the "singularity" attitude that dominates the methodology of social sciences. He does not want to give any other kind of modernity a chance. If there is a modernity then it is unprecedented; two kinds of modernity cannot exist simultaneously! This is the mentality that dominates all schools of the social sciences, whether left, right, or center. No leftist intellectual, including Karl Marx, doubted the singularity of modernity or that this modernity was European. Center and right-wing intellectuals, the liberal intellectuals, were sure that it represented the last word of truth (how very similar to the "last prophet" discourse of medieval Islam!). It is only recently that different postmodern discourses have begun to surface.

Nietzsche's critique of modernity is important. Religious critiques of modernity, on the other hand, are only possibly meaningful from the point of view of their own modernity (antiquity, which lags behind modern times). Michel Foucault's assertion that modernity results in the "death of man" is important but insufficient.[3] Real socialism, on the other hand, despite assertions to the contrary, never thought of representing a different modernity either theoretically or practically. While spokespersons for real socialism often claimed to represent a new civilization, they were referring to development and competition with capitalism in all areas. They thought they were closer to the basic templates and pillars of capitalist modernity (industrialism, the nation-state, and state capitalism replacing private capitalism) than capitalism itself, and thus declared it their primary task to overtake the capitalist system. The real socialist experiments, particularly in Russia and China, quickly proved to be the fresh blood needed by capitalist modernity. The primary goal of all of the national liberation movements, seen as the peak of success, was to catch up with the dominant modernity as quickly as possible, thereby achieving a happy life. No one really doubted this theoretical and practical orientation.

However, if the content and form of the last four hundred years of dominant modernity is examined, we will not only conclude that this is just the most recent manifestation of the times (modernities) of the five thousand years of civilization. At the same time, it will be easy to analyze once we see that they go hand in glove and are links in a chain.

With my defense, whether in this volume or in the two previous volumes, I tried to shatter this understanding of a singular universal modernity and to prove that an alternative to the dominant modernity always exists and, despite all attempts to suppress and disguise it, continues to exist in all its forms and contents as one side of a dialectical pair of opposites. Democratic civilization (given that civilization corresponds to the concepts of time, era, and modernity) may be inadequate as a name and could be criticized extensively. But when I considered the historical-society nature of society (Fernand Braudel's approach to this issue was encouraging) and visualized the movements that represent the carriers of the history of clans, aşirets, tribes, peoples, religious communities, and similar communities, I could neither emotionally nor intellectually designate these movements as "barbarian" or as "religious reactionaries." After I realized with a certainty that dialectics do not necessarily function through opposing poles bent on each other's destruction, it was no longer difficult (as observed in the universal becoming) to establish that civilization is not a monistic but a dichotomous process in the (mostly) non-destructive dialectical development of historical-society. Although under very difficult conditions and poorly equipped, I have attempted to present my ideas in these volumes. What both amazes and infuriates me is that despite being fully equipped to do so, Eurocentric social scientists have not tried to systematize this dichotomous state of civilization as two different modernities.

Let's take another look at what the three fundamental factors of Anthony Giddens's modernity entail and what responses its antithesis, the concept of democratic modernity, offers.

Deconstructing Capitalism and Modernity

According to Anthony Giddens, capitalism first appeared in Europe. An overwhelming number of Eurocentric social scientists hold a similar view. According to them, in no other period and location in history was such a development seen. The capitalism referred to here is the capitalism that rose as the world hegemonic power center in sixteenth-century Dutch-English capitalism, with Amsterdam and London as its hub. There is some truth in this, in that, subsequently, Amsterdam and London took over the hegemony of the classical global center of civilization from this century onward. The question of how this shift in hegemony occurred is the subject of an extremely large body of literature dealing with this phase of world history. I cannot and need not repeat all this here; I will simply remind you to keep it in mind. I touched upon these issues in the previous two volumes. What is more important is what remains incomplete and incorrect about this observation.

a) The assertion that capitalism is singular is simply incorrect. I have presented a comprehensive analysis that shows that the first capital monopoly arose in the Sumerian priests' temple (the ziggurat was perhaps the first bank and the first factory). In this context, we can comfortably conclude that we owe the formation of the city, class, and state triad as the first hegemonic monopoly to the Sumerians. After I encountered the views of Andre Gunder Frank and his friends who share his way of think-ing about central civilization and the world system,[4] I felt particularly strengthened in my views. But I emphatically argue that the monopoly of power represents another form of capital monopoly. I have stressed that the importance of grasping that power is one of the four main forms of accumulation. The first monopoly was established over agriculture, which was becoming more productive. The surplus product necessitated trade, allowing a trade monopoly to develop. In addition, the first indus-trial monopoly was established over craftspeople in the city and temple. The city administration, on the other hand, had taken on military and administrative tasks; it worked closely with three previously mentioned monopolies to form a strong monopoly of power. The unequal distribu-tion of power among them necessitated hegemonic relations. Initially the priests were the main hegemonic power, but that eventually changed. In short, both monopoly and a hegemonic character already existed in the founding phase. In the two previous volumes, I roughly traced the histori-cal course of these developments. Another very important observation is that no matter how much internal conflict exists among them, monopolies within civilization react to external forces (the forces of democratic civili-zation) in a united way and historically behave like the links of a chain. No civilization would have developed without the legacy of the previous ones. I am talking here about the central civilization system, not the Chinese or Incan civilizations.

I had also tried to present in detail the story of the formation of the European link in the chain. I especially emphasized its relationship with Eastern civilization (even the Neolithic Age of the East) and the role of Venice in transferring these values for over three centuries. It could be claimed that the highly advanced quality of money-capital was a singularity of European civilization after the sixteenth century. Undoubtedly from this century onward, the money-capital monopoly succeeded in establishing its hegemony in Europe. It is possible to speak of a singularity or being unprecedented in this sense. But clearly it is not possible to conclude that Europe is the homeland of money-capital, or that it emerged for the first time during this era. Other items that were used in a similar way to money existed long before the civilization. Experts researching antiquity agree that obsidian and other similar materials were the first to assume the role of money. Various valuable materials still play a similar role in primitive communal societies. We know that the first coins were minted by the Kingdom of Lydia, on the eastern shore of the Aegean Sea, around 560 BCE, and that they were made of gold and silver and bore the image of Croesus.[5] The same is true of money-capital accumulation. Accumulation is a very old tradition. Valuable metals and goods have been accumulated throughout history in this sense. Archeological records offer plenty of examples, and the old expression "as rich as Croesus" also bears witness to this reality. But nothing can tell the story of the use of money-capital to produce profit in such an original and attractive way as the Assyrian *karum* (simultaneously meaning money, trade, the market, and a warehouse).[6] There were many cities in the East that were home to money-capital thousands of years before Venice, Amsterdam, and London.

What is singular about European money-capital was its rise and its establishment of hegemony. For the first time, Karl Marx regards this kind of hegemony of capital as something positive and speaks of its favorable and progressive role in shaping modernity. Immanuel Wallerstein likens this hegemony to a lion breaking out of its cage, but he also feels the need to emphasize that its role is positive. When he links the emergence of the new hegemony to the weakening of the Church and the kingdoms, as well as to the Mongol invasion developing in the East, it is as if he is confessing that he is faced with great question marks. Ultimately, he concludes that this was not the best course for history to take. This is not the place to present the horrifying balance sheet of the last four-hundred-year reign of money-capital. However, it is not difficult to understand the kind of hegemony we are up against if we consider the number of people who have died or been wounded in wars, the number and duration of these wars, the devastating consequences of economic crises, the rates of poverty and unemployment, and, most importantly, its role in the ecological crisis.

b) That the modernity that rests on capitalism is singular is insufficient and incorrect. Nonetheless, this assertion by the Eurocentric social sciences is quite comprehensive and all-encompassing. And it is not so different from previous civilizations in claiming that its existence as a world-system and its all-encompassing reach mark "the end of time" and are "the last word" of truth. Furthermore, it makes this assertion even more absolute, using science as its weapon. Liberalism, having established its ideological hegemony, joins the media monopolies in claiming that this assertion is a common truth of all humanity. To this end, it makes an extraordinary effort to create ages within the age (e.g., the media age, the information age). Although it recognizes the importance of presenting the content and form of reality within its historical dimension, it does not refrain from constructing a futurology (the science of the future) detached from both the past and the present. It is amazingly concerned with the "now" and instills an ethos of "live the *now*; all else is meaningless" as a fundamental doctrine.

Neoliberalism, formed from all sorts of old and new ideas and ideological templates with an eclectic approach, smacks of the decline of Rome, only much worse. We are in a period where the three S's, sports, sex, and art [Turkish: *sanat*], have been maximally ideologized.[7] All three have been given a religious dimension. It is really difficult to find another religion today that is more of an opiate than soccer, which has been transformed into a fiesta in the stadiums. We are seeing a similar development in the field of art, which has been transformed into an industry. The most basic of natural instincts, sexuality, has been turned into the sex industry. Sex with its opiate effect has also been transformed into a religion on par with sports and the arts. It might be more appropriate to refer to this triad as the religious celebrations—the fiesta—of capitalist modernity. Even religious fundamentalism, which pursues the goal of the religious rule, is a current of modernity, no matter how anti-modern its façade.

When examined in depth, it would seem that the modernity influenced by capitalism is the most insecure of modernities. Its need for such broad eclecticism proves this. Although postmodernism was a product of this insecurity, it failed to provide an alternative to modernity. Its only goal was to open a window for all those intellectuals who were sick of modernity. In terms of its way of life, it was deeply immersed in capitalist modernity. A typical example would be the philosopher Theodor Adorno saying, "Wrong life cannot be lived rightly," in *Minima Moralia*.[8] He explained modernity in a very clear and concise manner but offered no alternative. This is among the reasons why the revolutionary youth turned against him. Neoliberalism actually wanted to renew the flaking varnish of modernity. But despite its add-ons and innovations, whitewashing the contradictions of the age of global financial monopoly and saving the system is no easy task.

Andre Gunder Frank came very close to discovering the truth when he determined the role and importance of European civilization within the five-thousand-year-old civilizational process. But he also profoundly regretted that, apart from some generalities, he could not develop and present an alternative or any solutions. But he retained hope. The formula of "unity in diversity" within the classical civilization is a correct but extreme generalization. There is no explanation offered of how to achieve this. His error, however, is the hope that a better and different modern life (in theory and practice) is possible within the system. Immanuel Wallerstein is positive and radical in this regard; he does not believe in a solution within the system. He repeats tirelessly that the current crisis is systemic and structural and suggests that we devote ourselves wholeheartedly to the intellectual, moral, and political tasks that he correctly defines. His shortcoming, however, is that he does not present a comprehensive answer to the question of what kind of system. However, he offers a sincere self-criticism when he says, "We have all drunk from the same cups in the sacred temple of the bourgeoisie."[9] At the same time as he metaphorically expresses his fear of the wrath of the gods, he talks about the ways in which intellectual capital is strongly dependent on capitalist modernity and how difficult it is to make a radical break. In short, he makes many points that provide necessary lessons.

On the other hand, my situation is best expressed in the saying: "It is of no use to try to escape death." I fled from capitalist modernity, but this flight was not enough to escape its clutches. Therefore, instead of dying in its clutches, I decided that trying out the alternative would be more realistic and courageous. Thus, I was neither content with speaking the truth like Nietzsche or announcing the death of humanity like Michel Foucault nor, like Theodor Adorno, did I resign myself to fate, sulking and saying, "What cannot be cured must be endured." I also did not find it sufficient to seek shelter under the slogan "unity in diversity." Moreover, contrary to Immanuel Wallerstein, I did not believe that it was sufficient to determine the importance of the intellectual, moral (ethical), and political tasks. However, these people of thought and virtue have doubtless made significant contributions to this attempt of mine and gave me courage. However, "wrong life cannot be lived rightly" is not something that could have been true for me. I never lived that way. I ran after it a lot, but neither my strength nor my faith was enough to grasp the capitalist modern life. But what is more searing is that the human who rebelled within me kept saying, "Don't sell us out; whatever you seek, find it within yourself." I am writing about my rebellions.

One might ask, "What can you do about the triad of forces of modernity that have taken root in every mind and soul for five thousand years and in the last four hundred years have seized every social value, whether inside or outside, from the highest layers of the air to the deepest layers of the earth, turning them into commodities to be bought and sold, and which have become a million times stronger than the orders of the Nimrods and the pharaohs?" But, of course, I am posing the question incorrectly, in a way that modernity wants. What I hope to show is that there is no positive value to such a question or the construct that lies behind it.

I have neither discovered nor invented democratic modernity. Although I have a few things to say about its reconstruction, that is not terribly important; to be more precise, the real important point lies elsewhere—and that is that democratic modernity has been dichotomous since the emergence of official civilization, whenever and wherever it arose. What I am trying to do, even if only in broad terms, is to give due recognition to this form of civilization (the unofficial democratic civilization; the name is not so important) that exists whenever and wherever official civilization exists and to meaningfully clarify its main dimensions in a way that arouses interest. Additionally, I will try to understand and define its basic forms of mentality, structures, and living society.

There is nothing incomprehensible about the fact that whenever and wherever the supposedly singular civilization (the modernity of different eras) existed, a counterpart has necessarily existed for dialectical reasons. It is rather incomprehensible that this natural consequence of the dialectical method has not been systematically expressed throughout the history of civilization and has not been given a voice. From Sumer to Egypt and Harappa, from China to India and Rome, when all these civilizations took form, was there no reaction, no ideas, and no social structures among the numerous tribes, aşirets, and religious communities that were oppressed and enslaved, but who rebelled from the Great Sahara to the deserts of Central Asia and from Siberia to Arabia? Could it be possible that nobody thought of this? Is it really possible that the agrarian-village communities fed all civilizations for ten thousand years but never raised their voices, never reacted, and never had counter-structures? Is that conceivable? Is it just? If they were exposed to all sorts of repression and exploitation by the rulers of the cities that they had built with their own hands for thousands of years, would the working peoples sit there quietly and be grateful for their fate? Is that really possible?

It is possible to ask thousands of questions about different areas and periods, and there are answers. What is missing is the weaving of a system of civilization (construct of thought, theory) from the answers to these questions. There are also counter-structures (the attitude of moral and political society). The level of interest shown for the despotic, imperial, and power and capital monopolies is not shown for the situation and development of moral and political society, the basic state of social nature.

Take Islamic civilization, with which I am quite familiar. Even the most minute details are recounted in the extensive stories of the caliphs, sultans, emirs, and sheikhs, but the stories of the believers, sects, and denominations spread across three continents, and their resistance, longings, and convictions are either not deemed worthy of a similar treatment or are distorted. Clearly there is an internal conflict and dichotomy within civilization, but while one side is exalted by boundless praise, its opponents are abased. I have witnessed this myself; I have observed Alevi Kurds, Sunni Kurds, and Yazidi Kurds. I can unequivocally say that the civilization of the Alevi and Yazidi Kurds, distilled over thousands of years, is more moral and political than the counter-civilization. But the classical discourses of civilization are full of unspeakable slanders against the Alevis and Yazidis. Of course, when I say that I am not talking about the laborers or tribal and aşiret cultures that belong to the Sunni faith. All these social sectors are part of democratic civilization. Examples of this can be shown at all times and in all places, but this will suffice to explain what I mean.

It is important to clarify another point about modernity. In a way, the term *capitalist modernity* is incorrect, and it should be noted that I use the concept conditionally. If the concept of capitalist society is ambiguous and risks obscuring reality, this is even more true of the concept of capitalist modernity. Modernity in general is a given era's social way of life. It is the material and immaterial culture that contains all the elements of technology, science, art, politics, and fashion that shape a certain period. In this sense, it is a grave mistake to attribute modernity to capitalism. In fact, many of its elements are overwhelmingly opposed to capitalism, which is essentially a monopoly. Moral and political society, which is social nature's main mode of life, is opposed to civilization in general and to capitalist civilization in particular, so it holds a similar position in modernity. Modern society is not a capitalist society. So why do I use the term *capitalist modernity*? Because capitalist monopoly and its hegemonic allies would like to shape not only society but the modernity that is understood to be the way of life of this particular time. Together with its ideological, political, and military allies, it systematically strives through education, military barracks, places of worship, and the media, to appear to be the creative force of the era's way of life. It creates a dominant mentality that reflects ownership of what does not belong to it. If its propaganda effort has been successful, then it has shaped society or modernity.

Anthony Giddens most probably does not realize that he is caught in a dilemma when he considers capitalism to be the most important pillar of modernity. The crucial question is which gave rise to or determines the other. It is unthinkable that modernity gave rise to capitalism; modernity is lived as an era specific to social nature. But when oppressive and exploitative monopolies took the form of the city, the class, and the state they tried to shape the way of life of that period and take credit for its development. We have to admit that they were mostly successful, but it was a propaganda success. An entire era has been attributed to impostors. When using the concept of capitalist modernity, we should always keep this in mind. But social nature never totally adopts the colors or way of existence of capitalism or any other monopoly as its own identity. It is also impossible for social nature, as *selfhoods*, to transform into a network of oppressive and exploitative monopolies. Just as we have shown that pure capitalism is impossible, it is also impossible to realize a pure civilization. We should ask those who think it is: When there remains no society to exploit and rule, how will the city, the class, and the state live on as they are? How will they even maintain something as basic as their material life? That, however, doesn't mean they can't shape and exploit the social nature of the period. If we speak of Europe, for example, we cannot attribute the Renaissance, the Reformation, and the Enlightenment to capitalism. The creators of the Renaissance were not the owners of money-capital and the rulers, who nonetheless hoped to use their money and their power to leave their mark on it, knowing they would earn even more money and power if they were successful.

Its counterpart, society, which is targeted by money-capital and the rulers, can also leave its mark on the way of life of an age, and there are a variety of examples of the various ways it has done so. The *selfhood* of social nature also tends in this direction. Society is overwhelmingly anti-capitalist, because it experiences the exploitation and domination of capital monopoly on a daily basis. Youth, women, the unemployed, colonized peoples, many religious communities, and all communities that live off their own labor are the main block (demos) of historical-society that give the way of life, the modernity of an era, its true color.[10] As a matter of convenience, we call all of these and similar groups the demos. Democracy is the expression of the self-governance of these groups. Although these are political concepts, "democratic society" and "democratic modernity" are closer to its essence, because the realm and the groups they cover constitute the main block of the society. Therefore, I ask that you bear with my frequent use of these terms. When I speak of the option of democratic modernity, this is what I mean. Therefore, both the concepts of a singular modernity and of modernity influenced by capitalism are quite dubious and contain a high likelihood of error.

What will determine any given modernity's color are the ideas, structures, and struggles of its opposing poles and the extent of their success. To call either pole entirely capitalist or entirely democratic is to fall into blind and crude reductionism. In any case, when we talk about society we should use the concept of "entirely" sparingly. Social nature is complex and never corresponds entirely to one thing or one color. We must not forget that contradictions require differences. Diversity is the meaning of life. The end of contradiction and differentiation would spell the end of life. Even death is nothing but proof of life. Can you imagine, for example, a life that has been condemned to last an eternity, a life with no death? Such a life would be great torture. If it is not for the purpose of crushing opponents, seeking similarity at all times is the negation of life. The efforts of fascism or capitalist modernity—besides fashion, what is called fashion is the most fraudulent art form invented by capitalism to conceal its hostility to life, demonstrated through the torture of making things similar—to liquidate all social differences and reduce them to a single color is more proof of its hostility to life.

In conclusion, although we describe modernity as a dubious concept, it is nonetheless important to determine its scope and duration. Reducing

it to singularity is rife with serious errors. Describing modernity as contemporary, as the present of the civilization, requires us to make careful
choices about its social context. The sweeping shortcomings and errors
of the social sciences in this respect are obvious. We can best explain this
by the pressure of the capital and power monopolies and the money on
which these sciences depend. Science breeds power and power breeds
capital, but the inverse is also true. Despite this, the main block of social
nature remains democratic in the age of capitalist hegemony. Therefore,
there is no reason to believe that modernity, which is the era's way of
life, cannot be democratized. The social scope of democratic modernity
exceeds that of the modernity of the capitalists and their collaborators
many times over. To understand this, we only have to learn to think
correctly.

The Industrialism Dimension of Modernity and Democratic Modernity

It is true that our era (our modern way of life) is unprecedentedly dependent on industry. It cannot be denied that the industrial revolution that
occurred in the nineteenth century is the second major social revolution
after the agricultural revolution. Just as was the case with the accumulation of capital, the assertion that industrialism is an unprecedented
aspect of our modernity is an exaggeration. There were several industrial
advances in social nature, in particular in Neolithic agricultural society
and later in societies of the civilizational period, although not to the same
extent as in the nineteenth century. Progress is continuous, because all
technical developments are in a way industrial achievements. During
periods of accelerated development, however, qualitative leaps have taken
place. Thousands of inventions can be listed in the field of industry, including the first pottery industries, hand mills, weaving looms, the wheel, the
plow, the hammer, the anvil, the ax, the knife, the sword, the mill, papyrus,
paper, and various metal tools. Of course, it is nonetheless indisputable
that at the beginning of the nineteenth century, under English leadership,
the most significant industrial revolution to date took a huge leap forward.
While this is an important feature of modernity, it does not guarantee
singularity. It merely describes a difference.

We have a different situation in the transition from industry to industrialism. Industrialism expresses the ideological character of industry.
The industrialism that developed to the detriment of agriculture and the

village, as well as traditional urban crafts, is at the root of all of the current diseases of modernity, in particular ecological disasters. There is no doubt that industrialism is the ideology of capital monopolies. At the end of the eighteenth century, the capitalist monopolies had large sums of money and capital but had limited (traditional) ways to use it. The reason they turned to industry was to prevent the fall in their rate of profit and instead further increase it (the law of profit). This is especially true of the textile industry. As mechanical production coincided with new energy sources (coal, steam, and electricity), a sudden explosion of production maximized the profit rates. The phenomenon of nation-states and the fierce competition between them are both related to these new rates of profit. Industrialism outperformed everything else. It became the most sacred doctrine of the nation-state. This race among nation-states continues unabated to this day, and it is generally agreed that the consequences have already reached drastic proportions—not only ecological destruction in the narrower sense but also the more profound and comprehensive cultural and physical genocides and local, regional, and global wars of an unprecedented dimension, as well as the use of ideological and metaphysical methodologies, along with the growing power of the nation-states, to increasingly detach society from its moral and political identity. In this sense, societycides are closely connected to the tendency or religion of industrialism. This is why the science and technology used by industry have attained a historically incomparable ideological quality.

Industrialism, as an unprecedented development of modernity, constitutes the greatest threat society faces and one that lies at its very heart. Industrialism is the essential factor for the constant growth of power, which destroys agrarian-village society, leads to the cancerous growth of the city, keeps the society under total surveillance and control, and seeps into all of society's pores without exception. The nation-state, as the fundamental form of industrialism's power and ideological hegemony, plays the leading role in all these processes.

Humanity, as a social nature, has long been under the "end of the world" threat of industrialism as one of the unprecedented developments of modernity. All the catastrophes that have flared up portend the danger to come. In the final analysis, capitalism, with its greed for constant accumulation and permanent growth on the basis of "the law of maximum profit," is synonymous with hostility toward society and plays an essential role in this hostility. To continuously impose the law of accumulation on social nature is societycide itself. Material and cultural genocides are the initial steps in this process. Scientists of reason and conscience agree that if measures are not taken we are on our way to the end of the world. Industrialism, the second unprecedented singularity of modernity, is therefore not simply content with shaping modernity with its "Siamese twin," capitalism, it also triggers economic crisis through modernity and is the main cause of the cancer eating away at all of the vital fabric and elements of society.

It is precisely here that the position of democratic modernity in social existence not only becomes clearer, its absolute necessity is obvious. Society shall either continue its gallop toward the end of the world or embrace democratic modernity and with a push for its reconstruction to stop this headlong plunge. The price of letting things drift is constantly and immeasurably rising every day.

These findings do not mean that industry is entirely negative; they draw attention to the disaster of profit-seeking industrialism. As with analytical intelligence, industry used for the benefit of moral and political society could lead to a paradisiacal life. An industrial offensive that goes hand in hand with ecology and agriculture will not only solve the most fundamental economic problems but could also turn all other side effects of the problems into positives. It isn't hard to see that halting the rampant automobile madness could have revolutionary consequences in many areas, from oil production to transport and from pollution to human biology. If we look at the acceleration of the industrialization of the seas alone, and the rate at which both the sea and the land are being devastated, we can see how vital it is to have a clear limit on the number of vehicles used for transportation. Of course, this is not the place to discuss at length the results of radical changes that would limit industrialism in countless sectors, from nuclear energy to cultural industrialism. I wanted to take the opportunity to draw attention to the consequences of limiting industrialism. Understanding its revolutionary implications is sufficient to demonstrate the great importance of the subject.

Bringing an end to the fixation on the law of profit would require far-reaching social action. Since the main driving force behind democratic modernity is not profit, it gains vital importance as the most appropriate option for civilization. The main concern of the moral and political social system not based on the system of class, capital, and profit is to safeguard its own identity and to bring to life the instruments of democratic politics.

Liberalism sets the goal of unlimited earnings and the passion for profit before the individual. To do so, it constantly propagates the idea that capitalist and industrialist modernity is the only possible way of life. A bit like the religions of antiquity, it finds it necessary to consecrate its system, so to speak. Cultural industrialism is the new form of this boundless consecration. Economic class struggle, all kinds of power struggle, and ecological and feminist movements will only be able to stop a modernity that has grown so enormous with an alternative modernity. Four hundred years of capitalist modernity make this clear.

We do not need to be great social scientists to understand that the dissolution of real socialism was the result of its inability to develop an alternate modernity. We may well assume that if real socialism had found a solution to the question of industrialism it could have maintained its superiority. If in the struggle against the capitalist hegemony that literally did everything to shape modernity, all of the forces with a real socialist line and all the other main opposition groups (utopian, anarchist, ecological, feminist, and national liberation movements) had determined at least one main theoretical and practical point of orientation in the struggle for their own modernity, the modernity of today's world would probably look quite different. Their common point of defeat was not asking "which modernity?" and jointly pursuing a theoretical and practical line in response; they were up to their necks in the way of life that capitalism and industrialism dictated and did not see any harm in this way of life.

Moreover, and most importantly, instead of criticizing state nationalism as an aspect of modernity, they accepted it as the main form of their way of life. Under these circumstances, it becomes difficult and doubtful for the opposition, particularly left-wing opposition, to present and attain its promise.

I am astonished by the slogan "another world is possible." The fact that this slogan is presented as if it were an important discovery only reinforces my astonishment. Now that the massive problems of modernity are out in the open, the ship of the system is already sinking and falling apart piece by piece, and even nature is rebelling, such a slogan, presented like a new discovery, leaves me speechless. Since the problems and madness (i.e., the way of life) of the ruling modernity (characterized by capitalism and industrialism) are now perfectly apparent, one should not be content with criticism of modernity's main elements but ask: "What alternatives can you come up with and actually build?"

In the past, religion, philosophy, moral teaching, virtue, and wisdom developed in response to the problems of modernity in their respective eras. Whether or not they were adequate responses is open to discussion. What's important is that there was never a lack of effort in the name of moral and political society. In the light of these experiences, democratic modernity only makes sense if it confronts capitalist modernity with comprehensive analyses and answers to specific problems. Contrary to popular belief, history and the present are not realms absolutely ruled by the forces of civilization, although a mass of propaganda asserts that to be the case. Just as not all histories written are true, not everything asserted by present-day social sciences about current modernity is accurate; it is mostly the rhetoric of ideological hegemony meant to confuse, dazzle, and establish dogmas. Democratic politics, in the narrow sense, is not only a means of making political society function, it is also the act of explaining historical-society in all its aspects. Moral and political society's great decision-making capacity and power to act is only revealed when its efforts to explain capitalist and industrialist modernity through democratic politics unite with truth. Then and only then will there be an adequate answer to the question: "What kind of a modernity and modern life?" The last four hundred years of experience with capitalist hegemony proves that no other approach is capable of producing adequate and promising responses. Democratic modernity would be a suitable response to this historical experience, both in thought and in practice.

The Nation-State, Modernity, and Democratic Confederalism

Modernity's third and most important discontinuity, the nation-state, is the most fundamental instrumental form of capitalism's action to conquer and colonize society. While liberalism presents itself as the totality of goals (the sum of ideas), the nation-state represents the fundamental form of power. The most far-reaching conquest and colonization that the society has ever experienced, both internally and externally, would not have been possible without the nation-state form.

The nation-state is also the subject around which the social sciences have created the most distortions, blindness, and dogma. We cannot really say that there has ever been a thorough analysis of the state. Even a Marxist like Lenin when he embarked on one of the greatest social revolutions failed to liberate "the question of power and the state" from the nation-state pillar of modernity in his attempt to analyze it.[11] And this is an understatement: he could not even refrain from assessing the rapid transformation of the soviets—an organization of democratic society— into a nation-state as a consolidation of the revolution, despite all criticism. The Chinese nation-state, which is currently of the greatest service to world capitalism, is nothing more than a sprawling example of the same approach.

There is some truth to Anthony Giddens's approach to the nation-state's singularity. However, this approach is highly inadequate in terms of the nations-state's chain-like dependence on the historical cumulative power monopolies. I tried to define the nation-state in detail in the two previous volumes. Here, I will illuminate the nation-state from different angles and extend the presentation by way of necessary conclusions.

Above all, the nation-state should be considered the maximum form of power. No other state form possesses the same power as the nation-state (it may be more correct to speak of a state-nation). The most important reason for this is that the upper echelons of the middle class have been increasingly involved in the monopolization process. We must never forget that the nation-state is the most developed and complete monopoly. The commercial, industrial, and financial monopolies are maximally allied with the power monopoly at the level of the nation-state. What we have is the most developed unity of all the monopolies. In this context we must also consider ideological monopoly an inseparable part of the power monopoly.

One of the areas where the social sciences are most misleading is in relation to monopolies. They attach great importance to positioning the power apparatuses as discrete from the supra-economic institutions, i.e., the commercial, industrial, and financial monopolies. Thus, they want to present power in general and the state in particular as if they are distinct from monopoly. This is one of the essential points that has crippled the social sciences. The difference between supra-economic monopolies and power monopolies is best explained as a division of labor. Apart from that, they definitely constitute a historical totality. At this point I must quote a sentence by Fernand Braudel that I find very impressive. Braudel says: "Power like capital can be accumulated."[12] It would seem that he has grasped the totality of the two. In any case, he is wise and has illuminated the subject in many ways.

Power is not simply accumulated like capital; it is the most homogeneous, refined, and historically accumulated form of capital. I would like to repeat this: power is the most homogeneous, refined, and historically accumulated form of capital. Other supra-economic capitals are accumulated in different ways; they change ownership and are organized. We regard them all as monopolies, because they are all supra-economic, and the seizure of social values in general and of social surplus values in particular make up their character. In short, whether in the form of taxes, profits from companies, or completely open plundering, all such extractions from society have a monopolistic nature. Therefore, the term *monopoly* is appropriate and should be well understood.

The historical peculiarity of the nation-state is its ability to unite all these monopolies within itself in a cohesive way. The nation-state is the maximum totality of capital, and this is the basis of its strength. It also follows that it is the most effective instrument of capital accumulation. It came as a surprise when, after seventy years, the nation-state built by the Bolshevik Party showed itself to be a gigantic totality of capital. However, if we look at the issue from the perspective of our nation-state analysis, this situation makes perfect sense. The nation-state is the most straightforward and typical organization of capital as a state. With the nation-state, it is not possible to organize socialism but, at best, capitalism at its purest. It is about as possible to make the nation-state socialist or to regard it as socialist as it is to turn a mule into a horse!

Nevertheless, we cannot explain the nation-state's singularity by separating it from historical forms of state. No matter how developed it may be in comparison to the earlier historical forms of the state, what is decisive is the historical accumulation of power. Let's have a look at England, the first country to have organized the nation-state. England was in the grip of the power of Spain, France, and the Normans at the beginning of the sixteenth century. Were it unable to organize itself as a nation-state, its liquidation seemed imminent. England was a kingdom. One after another, dynasties had risen and fallen. Its economy was built on migrations from Europe beginning in the Neolithic Age. What made it distinct from other European countries was that it was an island. It built its nation-state on the basis of these concrete historical conditions. History clearly shows how the increased strength of the sterling was accompanied by debt and maximum monopolization of the economy. It is well-known that England turned to industrial revolution to make a hegemonic leap forward. So without its basis in English history, and in particular in dynastic history, and without being dynastic itself, the English nation-state not only could not have been founded; it would have been unthinkable. Dynasties represent the longest lasting and most comprehensive state form in history, and this is why England still has not abandoned the prestige of the dynasty. Democracies and republics have been much more limited. Empires are an altogether different state form. In the absence of accumulation of power as monopolies filtered and refined over thousands of years, states in general and nation-states in particular would not have been possible.

I have only touched upon the link between the nation-state and theological sources, but this is an extremely important issue. Carl Schmitt elucidated another aspect of the reality when he said that all contemporary political concepts originate in theology (the science of god). A close look at sociology should make it fairly clear that religion, and with it the image of god, is the oldest form of social identity. Religion and god should not be understood as conscious fictitious identities, but as a necessity of the age of thought. Collective imagination led society to identify with the most sacred concepts. Society regarded this as a way of securing its survival. The roots of divinity lie in the sacralization of social existence. In time, as the divergence of power and the state from society accelerated, attributes such as holiness and divinity were removed from the collective identity of society as a whole and attributed to the owners of power and the state. Ideological hegemony plays an important role in this development. Establishing that power and the state are of divine origins opens the way for those in power and in the state to assert their holiness and divinity. From there, arriving at the concepts of *god-king* and *god-state* is not that difficult. The concepts of *God's messenger* and *God's shadow* would follow in due course.

Although the secular state acts as if it had nothing to do with this process, this is not true. Since secularism was a basic principle of the Masonic lodges, which rejected the influence of the Church, it is in the nature of things that it owes its existence to a large extent to this concept as an antithesis to the spiritual principle. We must emphasize that laicism is not as secular and worldly as is thought nor is spirituality otherworldly or focused on the great beyond. Both of these concepts are worldly and social. The great difference perceived between them rests on ideological dogmas.

It is therefore to be expected that the image of the divine origin of power and the state, which was present at all times, will also be reflected in our time. It is unthinkable that today's state remains unaffected by this.

The term was given shape throughout history. The concepts of secular power and a secular state are contradictory and dubious.

The nation-state is laden with more divine concepts than we recognize. It is subject to more consecration ceremonies than anything that preceded it. The concepts it rests upon and its chosen images, such as fatherland, flag, unitarianism, independence, and holiness, along with the national anthem and heroic stories, possess more divine prestige than was the case in god-kingdoms. No form of state has wrapped itself in so much ideological, legal, political, economic, and religious armor as the nation-state, primarily because it is the essential source of income for an increasingly inflated civil and military bureaucracy. When the state chair is pulled out from under it, the bureaucracy is like a fish out of water. For the bureaucracy, the state is a matter of life and death, and this is a key reason for wrapping the state in the highest level of divine prestige possible. If capitalist modernity, more than any other modernity, emphasizes the state and creates a tempest in a teacup around it, this is because of the change in class structure. There is a close connection between modernity and the nation-state and the pursuit of the "unitary state" and "unitarianism" and the concept of the unity of God in particular. Just as some tribes and peoples were eliminated from history or absorbed by the dominant tribe and people, so their gods were also eliminated or absorbed by and united with the dominant god of the tribe and people. If we look at the concept of the unity of God from this sociological perspective, it is easier to grasp its meaning. It contains colonialism and assimilation.

The unitary nature of the nation-state is historically rife with divinity. The complete disarmament of their subservient societies and the transfer of the complete monopoly of arms to the modern state has led to this unitarianism, but at its core there is a devastating monopolization of exploitation and colonialism. Theorists of sovereignty, in particular Hobbes and Machiavelli, by defining the modern state in the name of science, provided the greatest service to capitalist monopoly. The concentration of all weapons within a monist structure in the name of social peace led to an unprecedented political weakening of society and thus to the deprivation of its entire economic existence. Since power and the state will ultimately act like a monopoly, there is no social value that they cannot seize, given the armed forces concentrated in their hands. They will shape society as they wish and eliminate anything undesirable. This is, in fact, how history, including its unimaginable genocides, has unfolded.

The nation-state, as the common denominator of all monopolies, is not content with being built on the theft, conquest, and colonization of social material culture, it also plays a decisive role in the assimilation of immaterial culture. In the name of the "national culture" it usually gives official status to the cultural norms of a dominant ethnicity or religious community and declares war on the remaining cultural entities. Arguing that they are "harmful to national unity," all of the religions, ethnicities, peoples, nations, languages, and cultures that have preserved their existence for thousands of years are eliminated either by force or through material incentives. Languages, religions, denominations, ethnic tribes, and aşirets, along with peoples and nations, have fallen victim to these policies, or, rather, these genocides. Material genocides (physical annihilation) are only a drop in the ocean compared to immaterial genocide. Linguistic and cultural values filtered through the thousands of years are sacrificed together with the carrier groups in an act of madness consecrated to the sacred act of creating national unity.

The nation-state's concept of "fatherland" and "homeland" (*vatan*) is much more problematic. Territories that are put under state domination and monopoly, however this is achieved, are symbolically portrayed as the "holy homeland" or "holy fatherland." But these homelands have actually been turned into the common property of monopoly alliances. The system they built is a more profound form of colonization than that experienced in earlier colonies. While in the past there was a single type of colonialism for a given country, today, there are as many kinds of colonialism as the number of monopolies the modern nation-state establishes over its "holy homeland." Just as the colonized peoples were disarmed, the people of the "holy homeland" are similarly disarmed and rendered incapable of resisting any form of exploitation. Their labor in particular but also their material and immaterial cultural entities are subjected to multilayered exploitation. There is no other way to satisfy the cancerous growth of monopolies of bureaucracy.

Nation-state diplomacy is built to ensure coordination with external monopolies—the other nation-states—and to pursue the affairs of the global system of nation-states. Given the logic of the global capitalist system, if a nation-state is not recognized by other nation-states it cannot exist for even twenty-four hours. Without the consent of hegemonic power, the existence of a nation-state cannot be permanent. All of their stories are recorded in the hegemon's book. Those who break the rules will either meet Saddam's fate or be driven to bankruptcy and toppled by sanctions. It is assumed that every nation-state knows very well, either during its foundation or soon thereafter, that without the permission of a hegemonic power its existence cannot be permanent. Even the Soviet Union and the Chinese state were no exception to this rule.

Another fundamental feature of the nation-state is that, for obvious reasons, its structure is very much closed to plural or diverse political formations, because they would be an obstacle to monopoly exploitation within the given borders. It is in the nature of things that if moral and political society is constituted by various political structures, especially democratic political structures, the monopolists' area of domination will shrink considerably. Terms such as the *indivisibility of sovereignty, territorial integrity, unitary structure*, and the like were conceived for this reason. The intention is not to share the value of the country with its people and social groups. This, in fact, plays a major role in the destruction of the immaterial culture. Although political and democratic pluralism is the best regime for both freedom and equality in diversity, any act to achieve it is presented as dangerous and illegal, because it "puts the territorial integrity of the country and its regime in danger."

The nationalist identity so often used by the nation-state may have made it the greatest collaborationist representative of hegemonic power of all time. In a nationalist guise, it is the most loyal collaborator of the global capitalist system. No other institution is as dependent as the nation-state on the central power of global capitalism nor is any as great a lackey of that power. This character is the reason for the internal colonialism. The more nationalist the behavior of a nation-state, the more it serves the hegemonic power of the world system. To consider the nation-state that has been carefully prepared, formed, and systematized by hegemonic power over the last four hundred years to be the most nationalistic state is to have failed to learn anything from the terrible hegemonic power struggles of the world system.

When analyzing the concept *nation-state*, it is important not to confuse it with other issues and arrive at erroneous conclusions. First, it is necessary to clearly define the concept of nation-state. The states in history have generally defined and presented themselves as organizations limited to their members. They had to be accepted as cadre states, convincing, praising, ennobling, and even deifying each other. This approach changed with the onset of the nation-state. From then on, it had to present itself as encompassing the greatness, sublimity, and holiness of the nation-state god not only to the cadres of the state but to each of the individuals in society, called citizens, who are its subjects. The whole of society was virtually absorbed by the nation-state. This amounts to being confined in an iron cage. Until we grasp this fact, we cannot understand the nation-state or modernity. A primary difficulty in understanding the nation-state correctly is that it is always discussed in the context of the republic and democracy. The nation-state is not a republic and has, in fact, developed in opposition to the philosophy, basic institutions, and function of the republic. The nation-state is, in fact, the negation of the republic. The still influential view and official doctrine of the real socialist left for the past 150 years that "democracy and socialism cannot exist without a centralist nation-state" is a terrible self-deception. The grave consequences of this were particularly apparent in Germany with the assassination of Rosa Luxemburg and many other socialists and democrats. Another example would be the dissolution of the real socialist system. No other self-deception has done so much harm to socialism and democracy. The republic and democracy can only attain their true meaning through pluralistic and democratic political structures that are directed against the monopolism of the nation-state. Only then can a meaningful patriotism and a life of unity in diversity be realized through a pluralistic-democratic republican regime.

Under today's conditions, as the monopolies of global financial capital compete for hegemony, we observe their attempts to restructure the old nation-states. This tendency of neoliberalism is understandable, even if it is masked as other goals (especially the deceptive mask of democracy). In many respects national monopolism cannot compete with global monopolism, cannot meet the requirements of global policies, and cannot implement them quickly enough. Therefore, it leads to stagnation in the system as a whole. The efforts to rebuild are not meant to liquidate the nation-state but to subordinate it to the demands of the new global hegemonic financial capital.

The nation-state is not afraid to use four main ideological forms, intertwined and eclectically, in the service of the ideological hegemony with which it has imbued society. Nationalism, as the basic ideological form of the nation-state, has been given a totally religious essence. As much as the nation-state belongs to capitalist modernism, nationalism, likewise, is a modernist religion. It was cultivated as the social religion of positivist philosophy. We should think of patriotism as an expression of social nature, as the opposite of nation society. Nationalism, in this regard, is the most anti-nation ideology. Nationalism provides an unparalleled service to exploitative monopolies by placing the nation, which is a democratic phenomenon, under the ideological hegemony of capitalism. It turns the entire nation into the common property and a colony of the monopoly alliance (commercial, industrial, financial, and power monopolies), with nationalism in particular fulfilling this function in the garb of a positivistic and nationalistic religion.

Nationalism, as the religion of the nation-state, however contradictory this may appear, manifests itself as two phenomena that are basically the same. The first is the divinity of the "unitary state." Within the nation, it is very sensitive to the need for a one-god state. In the international arena, this one-god form expresses itself as the super-hegemon (the president of the US, the super-hegemon, George W. Bush claiming, "I am driven with a mission from God" proves this).[13] In Hegel's words, although he intended them for Napoleon and France, the super-hegemon is the "march of God on earth."[14] Second, every nation-state as God is a nation idol of the super-hegemon. Thus, the multiplication of the nation-state in this way does not mean that its unity is fragmented and that a transition to a polytheistic system occurs. It is rather the multiplication of idols. The source of this in philosophy is positivism. The nation-state's second most important eclectic ideology is positivist scientism. It is the ideological source closest to nationalism. They foster one another. Its founder Auguste Comte explicitly wanted to construct positivism as a secular, universal religion. However, positivism did not hold up as well as Marxism. Nevertheless, it remains the fundamental religion of secularism. Nietzsche hit the nail on the head when he correctly observed that positivism that claims to be the opposite of metaphysics is itself the most vulgar form of metaphysics. As one of the favorite ideological variants of modernity, it has become a hegemonic ideology that distorts, blinds, and idolizes the social sciences.

Positivism as a science (then called scientism) is the most vulgar philosophy of phenomena. A phenomenon is the visible part of reality; in positivism, however, the phenomenon is reality itself. Thus, if something is not a phenomenon, then it is not real. But, on the other hand, we know from quantum physics, astronomy, and biology, and even from the substance of thought itself, that most of reality occurs in worlds that cannot be seen by the naked eye. In the relationship between the observed and the observer, reality (truth) has assumed a highly mysterious character that eludes physical measurability and description. Positivism, in negation of this depth, most resembles the idolatry (paganism) of antiquity. The idol, which appears as a phenomenon, reflects the common link between paganism and positivism. Therefore, all brains washed by the religion of nationalism in the nation-state see the world as consisting of simple phenomena and perceive this as a kind of worship. The obsession of consumer society with the "object" is that worship itself. In this sense, the formation of consumer society as a product of the nation-state environment is highly important and easily grasped. On the one hand, this means that all individuals in society, as prisoners of the commodity (in the nation-state and in consumer society, the commodity has completely become an idol) and as extreme consumers offer the capitalist monopolies the possibility of extreme profit. On the other hand, a society that has been taken captive by consumerism, which has attained a sort of religious veneer, is turned into the most obedient, assimilated, and easily ruled society. The society that has fallen prey to a terrible nationalist mindset expresses this truth very clearly.

The third important ideological structure is social sexism. Sexism has been the weapon most often used by the civilization systems against moral and political society throughout history. The multipurpose colonization of women is a brilliant and exemplary narrative. Women produce offspring, are unpaid workers, do the most difficult work, and are the most obedient of slaves. They are permanent objects of sexual desire and a means of advertising. Women are the most valuable of commodities; indeed, we might say that women are the queens of commodities. They, as a constant tool of rape, appear as a factory for the production of men's power and potency. As pieces of jewelry with beauty and voices, they also immaterially uphold the male-dominated society. Nowhere have women fallen so deeply in every respect in male society as in the structures of the nation-state. Women, with the image of goddesses in nation-state society (the common conception or identity of women), appear at first glance as objects of worship. But here the attribute "goddess" signifies the deepest humiliation and is suitable for brothels. The woman as this goddess is a woman who has been most severely insulted and entirely humiliated. On the one hand, the sexism in nation-state society endows men with the maximum power (all dominant men play the sexual act in their heads as

"I have finished the whore" or "I am done"), on the other hand, through women it transforms the society into the deepest colony. In this sense, women in the nation-state are the most developed colonized nation within historical-society.

The nation-state does not refrain from using religion as a premodern tradition intertwined with nationalist ideology, because religion is still very influential in societies. Islam in particular is still very much active in this regard. But as a result of its use in modernity, the religious tradition is no longer the religion it once was. Whether in its radical or more moderate forms, religion, as used in modernity by nation-states, has been detached from its real social function (its important role in moral and political society) and presents itself in a castrated form. The role of religion in society is the role the nation-state allows. Major obstacles are placed in the way of religion that prevent it from continuing its positive function in moral and political society, laicism foremost among them. Thus, we should not be surprised when struggles occasionally flare up between religion and laicism. The nation-state does not totally abandon religion as an ancient tradition, not only because religion still has great weight in society but also because its structure is charged with nationalism and very suitable for its use. Sometimes religion itself assumes the role of nationalism. The Shi'sm on display in Iran is the Iranian nation-state's strongest hegemonic ideological weapon. This Shi'ism is an extreme example of religious nationalism, but there are many similar examples. In Turkey, Sunnism is the religious ideology that is closest to nationalism and the one that most easily becomes nationalist.

It will not suffice for the nation-state to solely use fascism, the most terrible form of violence, to secure the fourfold monopolistic exploitation it has taken over (trade, industry, finance, and power monopolies). This requires the hegemonic use of the four eclectic ideologies at least as much as the systematic violence of the fascist regime. The fascist regime cannot be maintained without ideological hegemony.

Democratic modernity responds to the homogenization (uniformization), herd-like, and mass-like society that the modern nation-state strives to achieve by adopting a universalist, linear-progressive, and deterministic (methods closed off to probabilities and alternatives) method with pluralistic, probabilistic methods that are open to alternatives and make democratic society visible. It develops its alternative through its ecological and feminist characteristics that are open to diverse multicultural, non-monopolistic political structures, as well as with an economic structure that meets basic social needs and is controlled by the community. Democratic modernity's political alternative to capitalist modernity's nation-state is democratic confederalism.

We can briefly describe the characteristics of democratic confederalism:

a) Democratic confederalism is open to different multilayered political structures. The complicated structure of contemporary society requires different horizontal and vertical political structures. It holds central, local, and regional political structures together in equilibrium. Pluralistic political structures are better suited to finding the right solutions to social problems, because they respond to specific conditions. Cultures and ethnic and national identities have the natural right to express themselves in political structures—or, rather, it is a requirement of moral and political society that they do so. It is open to a principled agreement with state traditions, whether in the form of the nation-state, the republic, or bourgeois democracy. They can coexist on the basis of a principled peace.

b) Democratic confederalism is based on moral and political society. Social forms that consist of capitalist, feudal, industrialist, consumerist, and other template projects based on social engineering are seen in the context of capitalist monopolies. While such societies don't actually exist, their propaganda does. Societies are basically political and moral. Economic, political, ideological, and military monopolies are apparatuses gnawing away at the fundamental nature of society, chasing after surplus value and social tributaries. They have no intrinsic value. Even a revolution cannot create a new society. Revolutions can only play a positive role as an operation to restore the worn-out and lapsed moral and political fabric to its proper function. Everything else will be determined by the free will of moral and political society.

c) Democratic confederalism is based on democratic politics. In contrast to the rigidly centralist, linear, bureaucratic understanding of the governance and administration of the nation-state, all social groups and cultural identities realize the self-governance of society in political structures that allow them to express themselves. Affairs are dealt with by leaders elected to office not appointed. The key is an ability to make decisions on the basis of discussions and at assemblies. There is no room for a leadership that acts as it wishes. From a general coordinating body (assembly, commission, congress) to local bodies, the democratic governance and supervision of social affairs are carried out by a bouquet of bodies that seek unity in diversity and are multi-structured in a way that suits the composition of all groups and cultures.

d) Democratic confederalism is based on self-defense. Self-defense units are the basic force, they are not a military monopoly but are under the tight control of democratic organs in accordance with society's internal and external security needs. Their task is to validate the will of democratic politics, i.e., moral and political society's egalitarian decision-making structure based on freedoms and diversity, and to render harmless any internal or external force that attempts to frustrate, prevent, or otherwise undermine this will. The command structure of the units is under the dual control of both the organs of democratic politics and unit members and can easily be changed, if necessary, by motions and their democratic approval.

e) Democratic confederalism leaves no room for hegemony of any sort, particularly ideological hegemony. While the principle of hegemony is active in all classical civilizations, democratic civilizations and democratic modernity do not tolerate hegemonic powers and their ideologies. If hegemonic powers and their ideologies cross the boundaries of different levels of expression and democratic governance, they will be neutralized by self-governance and the freedom of expression. Collective management of social affairs requires mutual understanding, respect for different proposals, and commitment to democratic decision-making. While the general governance concepts of classical civilization, capitalist modernity, and the nation-state overlap, there are major differences and far-reaching contradictions between these concepts and those embraced by democratic civilization and democratic modernity. Succinctly put, what underlies the differences and contradictions is bureaucratic and arbitrary governance, on one side, and democratic moral leadership, on the other.

There can be no ideological hegemony in democratic confederalism, instead pluralism is even valid among different views and ideologies. The leadership has no need of ideological camouflage to strengthen itself. As such, there is no need for nationalist, religionist, positivist scientist, or sexist ideologies, and the establishment of hegemony is rejected. As long as society's moral and political structure is not worn-out and hegemony is not sought, every opinion, idea, or belief can be freely expressed.

f) Democratic confederalism favors a World Democratic Confederal Union of national societies, as opposed to the union of nation-states under the control of super-hegemonic power in the United Nations. For a safer, more peaceful, more ecological, more just, and more productive world, we need a quantitatively and qualitatively strengthened union of much broader communities based on the criteria of democratic politics in a World Democratic Confederation.

Finally, we could continue to compare the differences and contrasts between capitalist modernity and democratic modernity endlessly. They exist not only as an idea, but concretely, as two vast, existing worlds. These two worlds, which have at times over the course of history mercilessly fought each other as dialectical opposites, as well as having often lived in peace, have a similar relationship and similar contradictions today, sometimes finding themselves in conflict and making peace at other times. The outcome will undoubtedly be determined by those who, in the present systemic, structural crisis, make the departure in favor of the good, the true, and the beautiful in the intellectual, political, and ethical spheres.

Jewish Ideology, Capitalism, and Modernity

A correct narrative of the development of historical-society would be difficult without a proper understanding of the past and present story of the Hebrews. To regard the Hebrews in history and Jews in the present simply as one of many ethnic communities or nations would be totally inadequate. It is particularly important to evaluate them as a fundamental source of culture with roots in the Middle East but having a major impact and influence on the whole world. Here I am not talking about culture in the narrow sense, I am talking about the totality of material and immaterial culture. There are two serious errors that we must guard against:

first, the overblown glorifying view that the Jews are a power that rules the world, which also includes the sobriquet "God's chosen people." The more we guard against such exaggerations, which are very susceptible to abuse, the easier it will be for us to grasp the subject realistically. The other view is one that demonizes Judaism, making it the scapegoat for all evil, as is often the case. This view, at least as much as the first, leads to faulty calculations, and staying clear of the effects of this view will better clarify the subject.

In the previous volumes of this manifesto, I have endeavored to present the Hebrews from different perspectives within the framework of the Abrahamic religions. Now, however, I will try to substantiate my view from other angles, essentially treating Judaism and the Jewish question in the context of capitalism and modernity.

The Jewish diaspora and its scattering around the world began after the second destruction of the Temple in Jerusalem around 70 CE and had significant consequences in the Middle East, Europe, and eventually the whole world. In fact, similar things had already happened. The problems caused by the exodus of the prophet Abraham from Urfa to the vicinity of Jerusalem have a continued and increased impact on a world scale. The Egyptian adventure of his descendants, the events surrounding Joseph, and the exodus of Moses from Egypt have left their mark on the world. The compilation of the Holy Scripture, even before that the establishment of the first Kingdom of the Hebrews, the Babylonian exile, and the relations with the Persians and Greeks that began at that time all had important consequences. All these developments together with their impact have their place in the history of civilization. The compilation of the Holy Scripture was a monumental undertaking in its own right, and it served to make the Abrahamic religions quasi-official. To have a book was an event of great historical influence.

From 70 CE onward, however, the diaspora had much more radical effects. It is not possible for me to write a comprehensive history here; I will have to content myself with a very brief assessment. It is generally accepted, for example, that as a result of diaspora and migration, there was a division into Sephardim in the East and Ashkenazim in the West.[15] The influences were correspondingly different. The Eastern Jews first spread to present-day Syria, Iraq, and Iran, the shores of the Caspian Sea, in Russia, and probably later to Central Asia, where they lived in significant colonies. There was also constant migration to and colony building in the West, in the sphere of influence of the Roman Empire, from North Africa to Eastern Europe, from the Iberian Peninsula to the Balkans. Anatolia, on the other hand, appears as the center where the division into Eastern and Western diaspora took place. Until the fall of Rome, the religious dimension of Jewish influence was decisive. Both as a Mosaic faith and in the form of the Christianity that developed from it, it undoubtedly had a leading influence. It established a kind of spiritual empire of its time.

This question of how the relationship of the Jews to money developed, how they turned it into a material force equal to their immaterial influence, would undoubtedly be the subject of a longer investigation. One strategic issue they tackled was immaterial culture, including religion, literature, and science, while their second strategic effort was at the level of material culture. Both are historically significant. I suspect that during these centuries, Jews were very conscious of the importance of strategic leadership at both levels and, therefore, actively sought to achieve it. The main reason for this was their concrete living conditions. Their small number, their position in the clasp of two civilizations, one with Western roots and the other with Eastern roots, and their awareness of themselves as "God's chosen people" (here we face a sharp ideological hegemony) required a constant strategic search. Their small population, their migration, their holy faith, and the constant threat of massacres sharpened their awareness of what they were doing and forced them to develop "liberation strategies"—oh, how this resembles revolutionary liberation strategies! Their way of life required them to think strategically and develop instruments of liberation. Otherwise, as happened to thousands of other tribes, they would have disappeared.

In this situation, their only salvation was constant resistance, which requires two things: faith and material means. Faith is the spiritual strategic element, money the material. Therefore, in Judaism, religion and money have become two indispensable resources that unite in the goal of liberation. If we look for the reason for the sovereignty of the Jews in questions of money and religion and meaning, the answer is clear: they have no other choice. Their circumstances require constant resistance if they are not to disappear, as well as to ensure a decent quality of life (because they believe they are God's chosen subjects). Without strategies for liberation (ideological leadership) and without money as strategic material potential (material leadership), continued resistance would be a difficult art. To resist without these resources, you have to either be in the desert like the

Arabs or in the mountains like the Kurds. The Jews have access to neither. What remains are ideological and material resources.

Although still debated, it seems quite clear that Christians within Rome played a major role in its collapse. In light of the Jewish roots of the very first Christian, Jesus of Nazareth, the role of a wing of the Jews in the decline of Rome is indisputable. In a sense, they took revenge for the double destruction of the Temple in the Jewish capital of Jerusalem. Also, the beheading of St. Paul (born in Tarsus, one of the first Christians, and the most important author of Christian doctrine) in Rome could not go unanswered. The fact that thousands of Christians were crucified or thrown to the lions was, so to speak, part of their resistance. The first successful offensive of the diaspora was to use Christianity as a strategic spiritual force. Objectively, therefore, we can confidently claim that the destruction of Rome from within was the consequence of the first major strategic spiritual offensive of the Jewish diaspora. Undoubtedly the attacks by the Germanic, Hunnish, and Frankish tribes also contributed to the fall of Rome. Nevertheless, the internal factors were decisive.

The next step in the development of Western Judaism after the fall of Rome took place on the material level with the founding of cities (the first European revolution from the tenth century onward) and the creation of markets around them. The increase in commodity, money, and trade relations provided the Jews with the opportunity to make a second move in which money was of strategic importance. Sovereignty over money meant having a role in the city, i.e., in the government of the new emerging states. But by the tenth century, the spiritual conquest of Europe—its Christianization—was complete. This conquest was to have a strong indirect influence on the Jews, both positively and negatively. The positive aspect was the conquest of Europe by an Abrahamic religion. The negative side was that the Mosaic faith, as a limited tribal religion, was increasingly cornered. From pagan tribal Europe to the times of Hitler and even until today, people have claimed that the spiritual power of the Mosaic faith and the financial power of Judaism is behind its many problems and crises. The decisions of the Third Lateran Council of 1179, which forced Jews into ghettos for the first time, were a consequence of this.[16]

From the tenth century onward, Judaism continued to develop as Europe's (including Russia's) strategic ideological and material force. In new cities, one of the rich and one of the intellectuals was often a Jew. This inevitably led to envy, contradictions, and conflicts. The formation of the first ghettos was a harbinger of future developments. In view of this new situation, Jews developed new strategies and tactics: conversion [*dönme* in Turkish] and the secular-laicist movement.[17] Both were to have profound consequences. With these two new strategic moves, however, Jews initially successfully emerged from the Middle Ages. We must not forget that Abraham and Moses had already used the strategy of formally turning away from an earlier religion. The exoduses of Abraham from Urfa and of Moses from Egypt can be seen as strategic spiritual offensives.

The Masonic lodges, founded by—among others—Jewish stone masons in the Middle Ages, can be imagined as the first secular-laicist movement.[18] In Amsterdam, one of the original temples of capitalist modernity, the great Jewish philosopher Baruch Spinoza became the mastermind of the first great secular-laicist philosophical awakening. Laicism is a hotly debated topic in Turkey and in other countries designated as Muslim. I think that terms such as *capitalist society* or *socialist country* are propaganda terms, and that terms such as *secular, Muslim, Christian,* or *Buddhist country* are also used with similar intentions. For societies, I find descriptions addressing whether or not they are "moral and political societies" to be a more realistic approach. Laicism in the sense of secularization has a positive function in creating a distance and liberation from religious dogmatism. However, if laicism is used in the sense of *laïcité* [France] or *laiklik* [Turkey], it can itself quickly become a dogmatic antipode. Laicism in this sense is no longer very different from other religionisms. The stronger anti-Judaism becomes, the more conversions (of faith) increase. Before I continue with the description of Judaism in the era of the nation-state, I must address the extremely influential and interesting events in the Middle and Far East.

Until the emergence of Islam, Jews had good relations with the Persian-Sasanian state. It is said that Jews had great influence in the palaces. Esther, the first prophetess mentioned in the Holy Scripture, was known to have played an important role in the Sasanian palace. It is likely that Jews were important for commercial and financial affairs, as well as for ideological developments in the empire. Cyrus, founder of the Persian Empire,[19] had liberated the Jews (exiled to Babylonia from 597 to 539 BCE by the Babylonian ruler Nebuchadnezzar), which served to create a strong tradition. In the history of Iran, Judaism has always been a force not to be underestimated. This is similar for Arabia, North Africa, and even East Africa, especially Ethiopia. The Jewish influence on all developments in material and immaterial culture should also not be underestimated.

At the time of the origin of Islam, the Jews emerged as a religious trading group with possessions in the fertile regions. They were apparently the most important of the non-Arab Semitic groups. The Assyrians found themselves in a situation similar to that of the Jews.

In a sense, with the Islamic awakening, the Arabs pursued, among other things, the goal of establishing their own trade and power monopolies opposing Jewish monopoly. That Islam is strongly influenced by Judaism only confirms this. We can compare this with the establishment of the nation-state in capitalist modernity. The Arabs responded to medieval modernity with Islam. This fact underlies the ideological and material conflict with Jews and Judaism. We must point out that the class dimension played a major role in the Islamic awakening, as did the ethnic dimension. The rapid spread of Islam and the harsh way the initial resistance of the Jews was crushed left the Jews fearing another catastrophe like that they had faced under Roman rule. They had two options: another exile or conversion. Some Jews probably fled to Iran, North Africa, and Anatolia. Others superficially accepted Islam but disguised themselves and practiced *taqiyya*,[20] thus going in the direction of becoming *dönme*. It is very likely that Jewish converts were involved in many uprisings and denominational movements against the chauvinist Sunni Arab rulers. The involvement of Jews in the emergence of a number of oppositional currents, particularly in Iran and Mesopotamia, is certainly a subject worthy of more research.

The most significant development was the founding of the Jewish state of the Turkic Khazars on the northern shores of Caspian Sea in a part of today's Turkmenistan and Azerbaijan. Seljuk Beg, the eponym of the Seljuks, is said to have held the position of a commander in this state. An important indication of a connection to Judaism is the fact that three of his sons had Jewish names.[21] Given this, we can assume that, as in many movements coming from Iran and directed against Arab rule, Judaism played a role in the Seljuk movement that should not be underestimated. This too is an important issue that requires further research. Anatolia was already an important center for Judaism in ancient times. Like the Greeks, Jews were also involved in founding many cities. There was a competitive relationship among them. Traditionally, Jews gathered in Anatolia when they were in trouble in the West and in Arabia. The fact that they considered Anatolia a second home after Israel becomes clearer from this historical perspective. Moreover, Anatolia has always been a large market for money and trade, as well as being central to ideological movements in which Jews played a role.

Jews who were expelled from Spain in 1391,[22] 1492,[23] and around 1550 settled in Anatolia in several waves of migration. When we consider the influence they gained in the Seljuk and Ottoman sultanates, we understand how firmly they were anchored. In addition, there were also a large number of dönme who converted to Islam. Within this dönme movement, Sabbatianism played a role from about 1650 onward (there was a strong dönme movement centered in the region of İzmir and Manisa).[24] Sabbatians gained considerable influence over Ottoman monetary and financial policies. Perhaps they were also teachers who helped the Ottomans understand the importance of money and trade. Although there were occasional serious conflicts and the confiscation of their property (müsadere),[25] their role in the appointment and removal of numerous sultans cannot be denied.

It turns out that conversion was the third strategic departure necessary for Judaism to survive. Without converting, the Jews could not have maintained their existence either within the Muslim majority in the East or the Christian majority in the West. Conversion should be seen as a survival strategy. As long as religious dogmatism persists and does not recognize freedom of expression, as with other similar ideologies, tendencies toward renegading and conversion will inevitably arise. With the help of these three strategies, the Jewish managed to survive the Middle Ages.

As well as in staying alive, their ideological power also allowed them to influence the spiritual sphere. The large number of Jewish intellectuals, writers, thinkers, ideologues, and scientists is connected with the intellectual leadership for which they always felt a need. That a number of religious, philosophical, and scientific movements developed in Judaism is an indispensable aspect of their survival strategy.

The conversion strategy would develop its true significance in the age of nation-states. England, as the first nation-state, is key to understanding this. The kings of the two great powers, Spain and France, who massacred and exiled both Jews and those who had converted from Catholicism to Protestantism, tried everything in the sixteenth century, including war, to neutralize England in Europe and prevent its rise. The Jews were safest in İzmir, Amsterdam, and London. They maintained close relations with each other, and there were also efforts to forge an alliance between England, Netherlands, and the Ottomans. In the sixteenth century, they increasingly made London their center, a position it continues to hold until this day.

It was in this century that the construction of the nation-state began in England. As pointed out earlier, the nation-state means that not only the cadres of the state but all citizens have a common ideological framework, as in a religion, with citizenship making every member of society also a member of the state. This means the further development of a characteristic that the Hebrew tribe has always had, first as a people [kavim], then as a nation-state. The Hebrews, first as a tribe, then as a people, and finally as a nation form a whole, both ethnically and religiously. More precisely, ethnicity is at the same time religiosity, and religiosity is ethnicity. Moreover, regardless of the division between those who rule and those who are ruled, they share a common goal. To put it clearly; nation-statism derives from Hebrew tribal ideology, which has been adopted in a modified and adapted form by all other peoples and nations. This is my personal interpretation, and I consider it important.

The modern capitalist state, organized on the basis of Hebrew tribal ideology presents itself as a nation-state (currently Israel). More importantly, in ideological—not racial—terms the core of any nation-state is of a Zionist character (Zionism as Jewish nation-statism). The nation-state is the state form that Judaism has taken as its model in capitalist modernity. Werner Sombart probably exaggerates when he considers capitalism to be a work of Judaism.[26] The great British philosopher of history R.G. Collingwood, on the other hand, when he remarked on the definition of nation-state nationalism—if I remember correctly—that "Jewish universalism has triumphed, but in the person of the one behind their genocide,"[27] wanted, in my opinion, to express just this fact. The nation-state has won; this victory is based on Jewish ideology (tribalism, nationalism, Zionism). But with the nation-state, it has ultimately created the perpetrator of the genocide of its own people. This statement is significant and explains a general characteristic of nationalism. Every nationalism is Zionist. So Arab nationalism is also Zionist. It is not wrong to define Palestinian, Turkish, Kurdish, and Iranian-Shiite nationalism as essentially forms of Jewish ideology primarily used by nationalist monopolies. Anyone who studies English and Dutch nationalism will find that Jewish monopolies played a major role in its development, not only theoretically but also concretely through the power of money and capital.

We must not consider this to be a conspiracy or to be motivated by any ulterior motive. Jews, as merchants and bankers, concentrated a lot of capital in their hands and made enormous investments in the construction of every nation-state, thereby gaining a place to live. The nation-state led to the rapid growth of Jewish capital. If Werner Sombart had described the role of the Jews in the development of capitalism in this way, he might have been closer to the facts. As Jewish capital grew around the world, it, of course, produced its own counterpart. That is the origin of the present conflict between national monopolies and supra-national monopolies. It is clear that while doing a historical service to the birth of the nation-state on the basis of their traditional ideological line, the Jewish accumulators of capital, always aware of their past dif-ficulties, objectively laid the foundations for the genocide that would target the Jewish communities, which were not aware of what was going on and cannot be blamed for it. This is in a way reminiscent of Jesus and Judas Iscariot, who betrayed him. The Jews, who for three hundred years mobilized their material and immaterial cultures (the talk of similarities between German ideology and Jewish ideology are not without reason), were convinced German nationalists until Hitler's period. The greatest Zionist nationalists were in various respects also the greatest representa-tives of German nationalism. Russia and the Ottoman Empire and Turkey are among the many similar examples that could be cited. The Jewish universalism of which Collingwood speaks (nationalism, positivism, reli-gionism) had triumphed, but only by simultaneously creating those who perpetrated the genocide of the Jews and committed physical and cultural genocide throughout the world.

Because of the importance of this issue, we must look at it more closely.

Judaism is perhaps one of the first examples of a historical-society identity in which ethnic and religious characteristics are ideologically intertwined. From Abraham to the present day, it has preserved this par-ticularity. If we add the belief that Jews are the "chosen people," the third important characteristic of this ideology appears to be that Jews consider themselves above all other societies. Historically, this concept of superior-ity has always carried with it the potential for conflict with other societies and has often led to conflicts that frequently reached the level of genocide.

Jewishness has always retained the special feature of being an ideo-logical society that developed in connection with this contradiction. As a natural consequence of the concept of the "chosen people," Jews were forced to develop strategies to protect themselves and the related tactical instruments. The strategy to protect themselves, because of its structure, had to be developed theoretically and ideologically. The tactical instruments, on the other hand, are more a matter of material strength and are mainly money and weapons. While money is earned through trade and banking, weapons tend to be further developed by technical innovations. Jews have demonstrated their abilities in both areas. Leaving aside their contributions in antiquity and the Middle Ages, developments in modern times will undoubtedly be closely linked to the Jews, as they are an experienced and organized people. When the capitalist world-system began its hegemonic rise from the sixteenth century onward in Western Europe, especially in the centers of Amsterdam (Netherlands) and London (England), the strategically well-positioned Jewish financial and ideological strength played an important role. Anyone who takes a closer look at this period can easily see that.

To claim that capitalism is an invention of the Jews, as Werner Sombart does, is certainly an exaggeration, but it cannot be denied that they played a significant role in capitalism becoming a system and attaining hegemonic power. Research on the subject shows that Jewish traders and bankers were numerous at all the major marketplaces, stock exchanges, and fairs, starting with London and Amsterdam. The fact that the representatives of political economy are silent about this and ignore it is due to the blinding role of ideology. The fact that the ethnic and national origins of capital accumulation are barely dealt with in the works of political economy, including Marx's *Capital*, is a significant shortcoming that at the same time makes one think. It is equally wrong to constantly rant that capital has no religion, belief, or nationality. Capital has a very close connection with religion, belief, and nationality. Those who belong to particular religions, hold specific beliefs, and are members of particular nationalities form a number of capital and power monopolies and colonize and exploit the majority. The bluntest example of this today is the US, whether in terms of religion, belief, or nationality, and it cannot be denied that most capitalists are from the US.

The role of the Jews cannot be argued away with a focus on the construction of the other two pillars of capitalist modernity: industrialism and the nation-state. The Jewish merchants and bankers, who emerged from the first urban revolution in Europe (1050–1350), gained importance in the era of commercial capitalism from the fifteenth to the eighteenth century. Similar developments took place in the cities of the East (Cairo, Aleppo, Damascus, İzmir, Tabriz, Antakya, Baghdad, Istanbul, etc.). When, with the Industrial Revolution, it became clear that industry was the most profitable sector, Jews did not hesitate to channel their capital into the industrial sector. We don't need to explain the reason for this in detail. Capital goes on the offensive wherever profit is high. Isn't that the so-called law of profit?

So how can we take lightly the leading role of Jewish capital monopolism in both commercial capitalism and industrial capitalism in the modern age and refrain from emphasizing it? Even if we do not assume a deliberate distortion, we can safely speak of it as the consequence of ideological blindness. Moreover, from a Jewish perspective, this role poses no problem. Trade and industrial monopolies can develop in any national, religious, or ethnic community. What is important here is the strategic role of Jewish trade and industrial monopolies. A Jewish monopoly has always existed in the financial sector. The fact that political economy avoids analyzing the connection between trade, industrial, and financial monopolism and ideology, especially nationalist, religious, scientistic, and sexist ideologies (liberalism is nothing more than propaganda), is not, as claimed, due to any desire to be "objective." On the contrary, political economy hides the religionist, nationalist, scientistic, and sexist identity of all monopolies, including the monopolies of power, thus showing that it is not an objective science, that it conceals concrete facts at vital points and declares them insignificant, and that rather than being a science, it is an instrument of ideological propaganda.

In a world system that has been hegemonic for four hundred years, the strategic position of Jews in commercial, industrial, financial, media, and intellectual capital monopolies continues to increase in importance. Without acknowledging this, we cannot theoretically analyze either a global or a local problem or solve it in practice. The role of Judaism, both as a strategic ideological and material force is even more evident in the construction of modernity and of the nation-state. Using the nation-state, Judaism brings to light the capitalist nature of modernity. It concretizes and fixes modernity as the nation-state, which constitutes the union of trade, finance, industry, and power monopolies. Of course, the Jews are not the god of the nation-state, but from the age of tribes to the present day, from its embryonic state to the present age and decay, they have masterfully developed it in their own sphere of influence.

I have no love for conspiracy theories. Certain allegations keep coming up to support such conspiracy theories: secret Masonic lodges that rule the world, meeting of the Bilderbergers or meetings in Davos, a "standing committee of the twelve" that rules the world, the UN and other entities as "Jewish tools." What all these theories have in common is that they exaggerate, lapse into dogmatism, and are unscientific, even if they contain assertions that are partly true. But the facts are obvious. The important role of the Jews in all three pillars of capitalist modernity is beyond question.[28] They have strategic, often even decisive, ideological and material influence in all these areas. Note the scope of these remarks: I am talking about the influence of the Jews in the field of capitalist modernity not about their place in democratic modernity, which is a wider historical and social reality. The Jews also exist in democratic modernity but have lost much of their strategic strength.

Before we move on to this topic, we should analyze the nation-state a little more. At the end of the Middle Ages, the Jewish ideology, in the sense of a survival strategy, always sought to neutralize its Christian and Muslim opponents. The nation-state, the concentrated form of all trade, financial, industrial, and ideological monopolies, as well as monopolies of power, together with the worship of the national god always contained within it (in Judaism Rabb fulfills this function),[29] confronts us here as the most suitable model for a survival strategy. In the nation-state, laicism fulfills the function of the Jewish national god Rabb. Concepts developed by Jewish freemasonry are significant in this regard. In this sense, the nation-state is Judaism's most important tool for universal governance.

To dissolve the French and Spanish empires through Anglo-Saxon monopolies, Jewish monopolies made effective use of the nation-state model. The French and Spanish empires had developed malevolent plans to subdue the other two powers, Netherlands and England. Netherlands and England were threatened with massacres and faced the danger of being effaced from history. The nation-state, as the most highly concentrated and unified monopoly power became the model for success in the fight against Spanish and French monopolism, which were not equivalently organized but tried to achieve their goals within the traditions of medieval empires. In his famous work *The Modern World-System*, Immanuel Wallerstein explains that the nation-state was the main factor in England's superiority over France, thereby highlighting the importance of this factor.[30]

When the Austro-Habsburg dynasty collapsed, the Allied Powers proposed the formation of Prussian nation-state, with the leading role in the unification of Germany being passed from Austria to Prussia. At the time of the French Revolution, London was the center of opposition to the French king, England's traditional enemy. The freemasons played an important role in the revolution in which the king lost his head. In the preceding revolutions in Netherlands and England there had been similar liquidations. The same game was played against the Prussian nation-state, which wanted to replace France as the new hegemonic power. Even Marx, an opponent, lived in London. During the two world wars, the Allies destroyed Germany's hegemonic claim. One reason Hitler carried out the genocide of Jews may well be that he believed that Jewish capital had used its strategic strength on England's side and played a major role in Germany's defeat in World War I. During the Cold War, the same alliance, in a new configuration, would also destroy Russia's hegemonic claims. There should be no doubt that if things continue in this vein, it is very likely that should China think of acting as a hegemonic power, as it is often imagined it eventually will, it will suffer the same fate.

Today, more than two hundred nation-states are represented at the UN, with its headquarters in New York City. It is widely known that the UN operates under the leadership of the same alliance, or at least that it does not make any decisions without the agreement of the alliance.

Let me make it clear once again: these two hundred nation-states are not run by Zionists or any other Jewish power, but they (including the mortal enemies of Israel, the nation-state of Iran and the Arab nation-states) were also founded on the basis of the Jewish nationalist paradigm, and, in the hands of the same core alliance, their threads have been interwoven over the course of four hundred years. Even if there is not a single Jew in a nation-state's elite, its scope for independent action is still extremely limited—either for paradigmatic reasons or because of concrete arrangements made by the alliance. As long as they act according to the traditional ideological and structural templates developed over the course of four hundred years of capitalist modernity, everything is fine, and they can carry on. But if a nation-state becomes, as one US president put it, a "rogue state," it will suffer the fate of Afghanistan under the rule of Taliban, Saddam Hussein's Iraq, and dozens of other states and powers before them. This is what is referred to as the international system or the UN status quo.

Even Soviet Russia was only integrated into the system after seventy years of existence, once it fully adapted to the demands of capitalist modernity. China was integrated earlier. Clearly, the system draws its strength from the two strategic forces that I outlined above. In both of these, Judaism is close to authoritative, both historically and presently. The elements of strategic-ideological power are the cultural industry, intellectual capital, and the media, which are religionist, nationalist, scientistic, and sexist in content. The elements of strategic material power are the monopolistic structures of trade, industry, finance, and power. The international alliances of nation-states, as state systems, represent the official structure. We must not confuse the two huge areas of strategic power with the states and their systems as their official expression.

At this point, I would like to add a brief and, as I see it, important assessment of the Anatolian Jewry. I have already briefly touched on the situation of Jews in the area in ancient and medieval times. Seljuk-Jewish and Greek-Jewish relations are important in this regard. The Eastern Jews spread from Andalusia to Central Asia in the Middle Ages, founding, for example, the Turkish Jewish state of Khazaria. In the Muslim states, conversion and the open practice of Judaism were not prohibited; the Jews, with their traditional ideological and material strength, were particularly influential in areas of strategic importance for power and states. Their position in trade and banking was in no way inferior to that of Jews in the West.

The Jews, who had longstanding conflicts with the Christians (e.g., around accusations that they had crucified Jesus and with the development of Christianity into the official religion of the West), were locked up in ghettos after the decision of the Third Lateran Council in 1179 and felt an increasing need for a home of their own after the pogroms of 1391 and the expulsion from Spain in 1492. The concept of the "promised land" was still alive. The relationships they established during the rise of the Ottoman sultanates and their circles proved useful. As banking and trade grew more important to the Ottomans, the Jews were further able to improve their position. The constant expansion of Ottoman power over Christian communities and the increasingly difficult situation Jews in the West faced in a Catholic and Orthodox Christian world led them to ally with the respective Ottoman sultans in much the same way they previously had with England. It is generally believed that this alliance grew stronger in the second half of the sixteenth century. During the same period, similar alliances developed in the Protestant countries of Netherlands and England. Exploring the relationship of Protestantism, capitalism, the nation-state, and modernity with Judaism would be a worthwhile undertaking.

The expulsion of Muslims and Jews from Spain and the Iberian Peninsula (completed in the seventeenth century), provoked the expulsion of Christians from Anatolia. As a result, the situation of some of the oldest peoples of Anatolia, with their strong history of material and immaterial culture, and who were Christianized early on, specifically, the Rûm Greeks, Pontic Greeks, Armenians, and Syriacs,[31] began to take a turn for the worse. The two Mediterranean peninsulas, Turkey and Greece, liquidated peoples and cultures piecemeal in a succession of mutual retaliatory strikes. The second Jewish maneuver—the first having occurred in the years 1550–1600—resulted in the Committee of Union and Progress, (CUP).[32] (The party was founded in the 1890s, at approximately the same time as the first Zionist Congress of 1897.)[33] At least one wing of the CUP, centered in Thessaloniki, which developed in collaboration with the conversion movement led by Sabbatai Zevi beginning in the 1650s, was Jewish. In the nationalism that they constructed (Moiz Kohen, Armin Vambery),[34] *Turkish* exists only as a word; in this Turkish national movement there were freemasons and converted Kurds, Albanians and Jews. This had very little to do with Turkishness as a sociological phenomenon. It was exclusively about a political Turkishness. Another important factor was that the Jews from Germany and England competed to theorize and frame Turkishness. However, the history is complex, and this is not the place for it.

After all, the Jews, whose existence goes back to antiquity, and who combined the lessons they learned in exile and their experience in building nation-states with their strategic, ideological, and material strength, played a major role both in founding of the Republic of Turkey and its rapid transformation into a nation-state (probably around 1926). They essentially repeated the role they had played in the seventeenth century in the Netherlands and England. To present the rapid transformation of the republic into a nation-state and the cultural liquidation of traditional Islam and the Kurds, which began after the (also physical) liquidation of Anatolian Christians, merely as a nation-building project of the Turks would be a serious mistake. The topic is more nuanced and is related to the fact that the Jews accepted Anatolia as their Jewish home before turning to Israel. The project of a Jewish home with a center in Thessaloniki or Edirne, which Jews urged Mustafa Kemal Atatürk to embrace, is a subject shrouded in silence. We can, however, say that it only faded in significance with the foundation of Israel. Nevertheless, Israel and the Jews still have a strategic interest in Anatolia and Turkey.

The role of Mustafa Kemal Atatürk in the establishment of the Republic of Turkey is beyond question. However, the fact that he was deified against his will is a fiction of Jewish ideology, one that has been applied in many times in different places throughout history. In Jewish universalism (levh-i mahfuz, fate, belief in law, determinism, belief in progress; the form of the Sumerian god constructions transformed into monotheistic religions) deification became a highly developed and frequently implemented concept. All literary utopias and spiritual concepts, including that of the Golden Age, and all theories, hypotheses, and laws, whether formulated by prophets or modern intellectuals, are closely related to this tradition. As long as we do not correctly analyze the role Jews played in developing the divine and secular hegemonic dogmas that were established over the Turks and over all peoples of the Middle East, any understanding of the region will be difficult to formulate and will remain deficient.

Of course, the Jews' material power was also strategically important. While I do not believe that Mustafa Kemal Atatürk capitulated to this current, I am also convinced that despite all his reading and research (it is not without reason that he went back to the Sumerians and Hittites), he did not fully analyze it. I have no doubt that he wanted to be a good republican and to develop the republic not as a nation-state but as a democracy. He was also not, as claimed, anti-Kurdish and anti-Islamic. However, it is clear that he could not persist with his initial liberal approach to the question of Islam and laicism (added to the constitution in 1937) or the Kurdish question. It should be noted that this was because he was thoroughly encircled by the CUP's convert cadres.

In my opinion, it would not be realistic to link the hegemonic conflict between the laicists and Islamists over the Republic of Turkey, which began as early as 1926 and is still being fought with full force today, to Mustafa Kemal Atatürk and to present it as something that was done according to his will. There are many indications and substantial evidence that he himself tended toward a democratic republic.[35] I don't think that this hegemonic conflict will end in the short term with the complete victory of one side or the other. However, I would like to reaffirm my growing confidence that in Anatolia, with its great democratic tradition, a strong breakthrough toward the goal of a democratic republic will be successful this time. I hope to be able to present some insights into the struggle for hegemony over Anatolia and Turkey in the section on the Middle East, which I plan to publish as a separate volume of this manifesto.[36]

It would be insufficient and wrong to think of Judaism only in connection to capitalism, modernity, and the nation-state. It also exerted a strong influence on democratic modernity. Even if this influence fails to match that of the power-oriented, statist wing (e.g., the Kingdom of Judah and the State of Israel), there has always been a strong Jewish wing of democratic civilization and modernity. Historical mention of the Judaism that lived in poverty and lacked strong tribal ties has been consistent. From the time of Ishmael, the son of the Prophet Abraham and his concubine Hagar, to Joseph, who was taken to Egypt as a slave, and from Miriam, the sister of Moses, through Mary,[37] the mother of Jesus, to the present, the list encompasses prophets, scribes, intellectuals, social anarchists, feminists, philosophers, scientists, and, together with its laborers, the other side of Judaism has produced great discoveries, inventions, theories, revolutions, and works of art in the struggle for democratic civilization and modernity. The Jews have not always devoted their ideological and material strength to the monopolies. They have also made significant efforts and achieved important successes for a more enlightened, just, free, and democratic world. What prophetic movement, what fraternity and solidarity of the poor, what utopian, socialist, anarchist, feminist, or ecological movement is conceivable without Jews? Likewise, philosophical schools, scientific and artistic movements, and religious denominations are hardly conceivable without Jews. How far could socialism have developed against capitalism, internationalism against nation-statism, communalism against liberalism, feminism against social sexism, ecological economy against industrialism, laicism against religionism, or relativism against universalism without Jews?

Clearly, Judaism is important for both worlds of modernity. At key periods in history, as well as today, Jews have retained their significance. Nevertheless, the Jewish question still exists. As mentioned above, either considering the Jews to be "God's chosen community" or ascribing to them a scapegoat role leads to serious misjudgments and dangerous consequences, as we have experienced aplenty. This is why I considered it necessary to at least briefly outline this important topic. Neither local nor global analyses will be accurate or purposeful if we do not consider Jewish reality.

I would like to close this theme by repeating something Karl Marx said: "If the proletariat wants to liberate itself, it must proceed in the knowledge that this is not possible without liberating the world."[38] I say that if Judaism wants to liberate itself, it must understand that to do so it must necessarily liberate the world, using its strategic ideological and material resources to this end, which above all, includes democratic modernity.

The Dimensions of Democratic Modernity

I believe that the analysis to this point has served to elucidate democratic modernity, the main elements of which we have defined and the development of which is intertwined with the history of civilization that we have addressed, as well as providing a thoroughgoing critique of civilization and modernity. Here I will try to further clarify the subject, both in terms of its key dimensions and as a whole. I will address how democratic modernity can be presented in its main dimensions from a broader point of view. The basis of our scientific work should be to shatter the monistic conception of modernity and to reveal the numerous historical-society existences it conceals. The history of civilization resembles a bottomless well that has dried. Whatever our efforts to illuminate it, new dark spots immediately arise. We may assume that under the millennia of ideological bombardment by the ruling monopolies, the social memory (conscience) will be folded in such a way that it will remind us of the twists in the brain and will give rise to a phenomenon similar to the subconscious, with thousands of winding tunnels of social memory. Yet we must not get discouraged. A human organ cannot be treated until its disease is properly diagnosed; likewise, social problems cannot be properly analyzed (diagnosed) and resolved (treated) until they are adequately explained.

It should come as no surprise that I repeatedly emphasize one thing: if the social sciences or other equally ambitious scientific disciplines had been successful, humanity would not have repeatedly experienced such terrible war, genocide, and societycide, including the huge and growing gap between the rich and the poor, unemployment, migration, cultural degeneration and immorality, monstrous monopoly forces, individuals reduced to nothing, and environmental destruction reminiscent of the apocalypse, a state of affairs it has been caught up in for the last four

centuries. It appears that over five thousand years the world civilization system exhausted all of the instruments of material and immaterial
culture that it presented as remedies. There is nowhere left to conquer or
reseize by war. Whatever the claim, the damage of a conquest would far
outweigh any potential gain. What remains of the instrument of the city
is an ultimately cancerous proliferation of urbanization without cities,
alongside an agrarian-village society doomed to perish. What endures
of the instrument called the economy is unrestrained and bloated global
monopolies that make money in a highly unethical way, for example,
making money from money, and the millions of unemployed and poor,
whose numbers continue to grow every year. All that remains of the
adored instrument of the state is completely dysfunctional monopolies
of power and nation-states, bloated from devouring domestic society,
and a completely stultified herd of citizens who have lost all connection
with moral and political society. What remains of the much vaunted ideological instruments is a religionism that has lost its moral function, a
sexism that spreads power into every pore of society, a nationalism that
has drenched us in a chauvinism a thousand times worse than any tribalism, and a scientism with no other purpose than to show the capital and
power monopolies the way to maximum profits. What remains of the
arts is a cultural industry that commodifies any sense of beauty and the
sublimity of feelings. This situation, referred to as "the end of history," is
the balance sheet of civilization. To whatever degree a society suffocated
and blinded by media monopolies in a virtual world may be deprived of its
reflexes, and no matter how thoroughly the power apparatuses monitor
and control its every nook and cranny, it is undeniable that the five-thousand-year-old world system of civilization and modernity in general, and
particularly the last four hundred years, is at the zenith of its intellectual
and structural crisis. Financial capitalism, which has become a global and
hegemonic power, is the most obvious evidence of this. A world with its
wheels turned by financial capitalism is a world of crisis writhing in the
throes of depression.

My purpose is not to develop theories about economic depression or
crisis. I do not intend to define capitalism simply as a system with cyclical
crises but as a systemic structural phase of crisis in a civilization system
prone to ongoing cyclical crises. Every phase of crisis has internal phases
that are the most severe, and we are going through just such a phase. That
being said, I must point out that I am not one of those socialists who once

hoped, and perhaps still hopes, that crises will lead to revolution. Crises not only give impetus to revolutions, they also generate counterrevolutions. Furthermore, I view such crisis-revolution-counterrevolution theories to be more rhetoric and propaganda than an expression of reality. Thus, the discourse I put forth is not based on the idea that "the conditions are rapidly becoming suitable for democratic modernity." I accept economic depressions and periods of crisis as real phenomena, but I do not see these depressions and crises as decisive factors that will produce historical developments. The universalist progressivist school of thought endeavored to derive successive forms of society that develop from worse to better from crisis theories, but concrete reality has not confirmed these theories.

So we should seek the decisive factors elsewhere, both historically and at present. Democratic modernity as an option was the result of intense efforts in just such a search. I always find it necessary to return to this option, and I am convinced that knowledge of its distinctive features will make practical efforts more productive. I am devoted to the positive, democratic legacy of history, which I highly respect. I personally also see this as a self-criticism. It is not just a matter of the lessons I've learned from history; I believe that shaping the now on the basis of history is an indispensable method. I do not have the same respect for or commitment to thoughts and actions—no matter what their value and results may be— that do not comprehend that "history must be the now, and the now must be history." I simply do not believe in such thoughts and actions. I also know that the future passes through the now, and I believe that there is no future unless you analyze and resolve your own now.

The reason I frequently emphasize this methodology is to underline that democratic civilization is not conceived as the return to some illusory past "golden age" or as an imagined future "utopia." It is the daily expression and meaning of a way of life that is constantly, even instantaneously, being realized in thought and action. It neither wallows in old memories nor consoles itself with dreams of the future. Existing realities are neither instantaneous creations nor past- or post-eternity. Perhaps we can call existence based on the flexible intelligence of social nature, with its high potential for freedom and unity in diversity, democratic modernity. However, we should never forget that modernity, having arisen as the opposite dialectical pole of the civilizations of the classical era, designates an era and must always be understood in that light.

As with *modernism*, the *hegemonic age of capitalism* is a specific term used to define the last four hundred years of classical civilization, while *democratic modernity* should be thought of as a specific term for the last four hundred years of democratic civilization.

Another important point is that democratic modernity exists as the opposite pole whenever and wherever networks of capitalist modernity are found. Whether successful or not, whether free or enslaved, whether marked by similarity or diversity, whether approaching equality or far removed from it, whether ecological and feminist or not, whether it has attained significance or not—in short, close to the characteristics of moral and political society or distant from them—democratic modernity exists at the heart of capitalist modernity always and everywhere.

The seizure of power (and therefore of the state) by the left-wing or right-wing opposition, whether by revolution or counterrevolution, to implement its brand of social engineering, i.e., its plans and programs, to create the society it longs for with methods of central planning, is not only absurd but is based on a propagandistic discourse. Moreover, I consider this approach as one that leads to thought and action that turn movements into playthings of liberalism, which will have no difficulty in absorbing them, even if it takes seventy years.

Social nature has genetic codes similar to that of biological nature. I am aware of dangers of biologism. I know that it is social Darwinism to apply this to social natures, and as vulgar materialism it provides intellectual material for social engineering.[39] What I am concerned with here is that even if they are particularly open to the option of freedom as nature with the highest level of intelligence, changing the memories and basic structural features of historical-societies have their unique sensitivities. We cannot change societies like we would plants or animals, whose genetic coding we are attempting to alter to breed new varieties. It is not for nothing that the memory of social nature has established this reality as moral and political society. It is particularly important to note that a method of changing society can only be considered legitimate if it increases moral and political social level. Any totalitarian and authoritarian method will decrease this moral and political social level and cannot be accepted as legitimate regardless of the consequences.

Democratic modernity is a system that serves the unique function of keeping the legitimate path to change open. Its high moral and political value is related to the substance of this system. The legitimate path for change, while very important, is also very simple, and every member of society, anywhere and anytime, can contribute to this change. Both a member who still carries within them remnants of Neolithic society, or even of clan society, and a member in Moscow or New York have an equal potential to contribute to change at any point. This does not require heroic deeds like those found in the grand sacred tales. The only requirement for using this ability (or virtue), which surely exists in every individual, even if only minimally, is to think and act morally and politically—the fundamental state of existence for social nature. Obviously, I'm not saying that the grand and sacred narratives that have emerged throughout historical-society and entered the memory of humanity to illuminate the legitimate path to change are unimportant. On the contrary, because the legitimate path to change is blocked by ideological and material monopolies, these narratives have a major role to play. Similarly, heroic acts have indispensable and sacred value on the path to freedom. The important thing is to understand that change in democratic modernity cannot be attained without the overall effort of historical-society. This is not to deny the role of key personalities and organizations, but their role will not mean much if it is not embedded in society's moral and political fabric and does not follow a legitimate path.

The same considerations are also true for revolutions: in terms of social development, change that is not legitimately realized and is not embedded in the moral and political fabric must not be seen as an integral part of social nature. Societies are not created but lived. No doubt there are different ways of living. There are lives that are lived more freely, equally, and democratically, but there are also those, perhaps most, that are lived in unbearable slavery, inequality, and under dictatorship. Under these conditions, democratic modernity denotes the mentality and structure that, using appropriate methods, can make life freer, more equal, and more democratic. Getting a stone out of the way is just as valuable in the context of democratic modernity as engaging in revolution as a last resort for legitimate change. On the other hand, we can regard both divine salvation and slavery-scented fatalistic Sufism within the same framework and reject both as unethical. In light of the lessons drawn from the experiences of democratic struggles for freedom and equality over the last four hundred years, it is possible to strengthen and even renew democratic modernity through far-reaching reconstruction in various places during this period of structural and systemic crisis under the hegemony of global financial capitalism. Therefore, our efforts are more likely to succeed if we reflect on and illuminate the main dimensions of democratic modernity.

The Dimension of Moral and Political Society (Democratic Society)

We have addressed capitalist modernity within the scope of its three fundamental dimensions and can do the same for democratic modernity. In contrast to the fundamental discontinuities and unique qualities of capitalist modernity—capitalist production society, the industrial society, and the nation-state society—the dimensions of democratic modernity that come to the forefront are moral and political society, eco-industrial society, and democratic confederalist society. The dimensions addressed in both systems could be formulated in greater detail, but defining these three dimensions in outline should be sufficient for our purposes. The dimensions of capitalist modernity were analyzed in detail in the previous sections. We have also tried to evaluate the historical development of democratic modernity, comparing it to classical civilization and modernity to make its main elements more visible. Defining them separately in their fundamental dimensions will strengthen our discourse and support practical approaches.

We could also have presented moral and political society as democratic society (democratic communality). Perhaps this would have been the most appropriate categoric response to counter capitalist modernity. But we did not hesitate to use the term *moral and political society*, which denotes a more fundamental category, because it includes democratic society. We've addressed this society in various parts of my defense. My intention here is to bring the various pieces together. Before describing moral and political society, I would like to say something about its substance that cannot be emphasized often enough: the essential relationship of moral and political society with happiness, righteousness, goodness, and beauty, on the one hand, and freedom, equality, and democracy, on the other hand. Goodness and happiness are, indeed, the essence of morality, while righteousness is related to truth. To pursue truth outside of moral and political society would be in vain. Anyone who is not moral and political cannot find the truth. Beauty, on the other hand, is the goal of esthetics. I do not consider beauty outside of moral and political society to be beauty. Beauty is moral and political! We have already analyzed in detail the relationship between moral and political society and the triad of freedom, equality, and democracy, qualities that no society can produce and guarantee to the extent that moral and political society can.

The first point is related to the capacity of moral and political society for change and transformation. As long as the moral and political dimension as a basis is not eliminated, we can consider moral and political society to be the society with the greatest capacity for change and transformation. Morality and politics cannot be completely eliminated in any society, but their role can be seriously restricted. For example, in the society of capitalist modernity under the rule of nation-state, morality and politics have been reduced to a bare minimum, even pushed to the edge of annihilation. We discussed the reasons and consequences at length earlier. When morality and politics are restricted, does society change? No. On the contrary, it means that they have been constricted and change and transformation have come to a halt. It could even be said that society has been forcibly homogenized and put under a very harsh legal status. There is no capacity for change; in capitalist modernity change is limited to homogenization that creates a uniform culture and citizenry and reduced to an us/others dichotomy. At the outset, a colorful picture of modern society undergoing boundless change is painted. But this is only the media's propagandistic view. The underlying reality is monochrome—almost gray or black.

In contrast, democratic society, as contemporary modern moral and political society, is the society with the broadest and most lived diversity. In a democratic society every social group can coexist in a way that includes all the diversities that are formed around its own culture and identity, without the need for a uniform culture and citizenship. Communities can develop and actively live out their potential in light of their diverse identities and politics. No community needs to worry about being homogenized. Monochromaticity is regarded as ugly, boring, and impoverished. Multicolorism, on the other hand, is associated with wealth, tolerance, and beauty. Freedom and equality are more likely to be ensured under these conditions. Only freedom and equality based on diversity are valuable. In any event, freedom and equality established by nation-states only serve the monopolies, as the world's experience proves. Capital and power monopolies do not give real freedom and equality. Freedom and equality are acquired by democratic society's democratic politics and protected by self-defense.

Perhaps one could ask the question: How can a system endure such diversity? The answer lies in the unity based on moral and political society.

The only value that no individual or group should ever compromise is the insistence on remaining a moral and political society. The only and sufficient condition for diversity, freedom, and equality is moral and political society. Democratic society, as the modern state of this historical-society, is increasingly proving itself over time.

Liberalism, the central ideology of the official system, uses numerous arguments to reverse this. It presents itself as something like the equivalent of democracy, thus creating a confusion of concepts. The identification of liberalism, an ideology, with democracy, a political system, is a typical example of such confusion. Essentially liberalism constitutes the unbridled destruction that the individual brings upon the society, and the domination of monopolies over the society proves this. Due to its undemocratic structure, all forms of individualism, from within the family to within the state, exhibit dictatorial tendencies. Democratic individuality, on the other hand, is something different. The determination of society as a common voice anticipates the individual. Individuals will only take a valuable and respected place in society if they situate themselves on the basis of this voice and this determination. Liberal individualism, for its part, as a kind of unlimited and innumerable monopoly, is anti-democratic. No liberal or neoliberal bragging and confusion of concepts can change this essential feature. Liberalism, which is synonymous with freedom, i.e., liberation, has achieved little in practice beyond the unlimited development of monopolies. The alleged freedom it offers has, in reality, been chained up in ideological and material shackles, in many respects to an unprecedented degree not even paralleled under the regime of the pharaohs. True freedom can only meaningfully exist in society if it is supported by the social dimension. Individual freedoms that are not supported by society can only exist at the mercy of the monopolies. This, however, is contrary to the true spirit of freedom. In any case, equality is not an issue for liberalism.

Under the conditions of capitalist modernity, moral society is in a more constricted, dysfunctional, and lapsed state than at any other time. Moreover, at no other time in history have moral rules been replaced by legal codes. The bourgeoisie as a class has rendered morality obsolete and imposed its class sovereignty as law on the society, codifying it down to the finest detail. Moral society is replaced by legal society. Here we face an important change. There have been other historical efforts to create law, but at no time has law been so inundated in details as in bourgeois modernity. In fact, behind the term *law* we find class monopolism and the creation of legal monopolism. It is impossible to govern a highly complex nature like that of society with laws. No doubt there is room for law in society, provided it is just; in this sense, law is indispensable. But what is being imposed on the society by the state in the name of "positive law" is not a just law but the monopoly of the ruling class and the nation, with nation-state norms embodied as law. The destruction of morality is synonymous with the destruction of society. Current events confirm this. At present, even societies like the US and Russia could not survive for even an hour without official laws and the status quo. As has been experienced in some instances of crisis, without official law society falls into savagery.

This situation actually expresses a certain reality. Previously, we defined the nation-state as a state of war that infiltrates every pore of society. This fact is quite openly evident during periods of crisis and economic depression. Official legal societies have the greatest potential for crisis, because they lack moral principle. If the environmental crisis has taken on catastrophic proportions, that is because the moral dimension is missing and environmental law is not yet sufficiently developed. Moreover, the environment is not something that can be protected by law, because it is infinite, and legal action relative to it is extremely limited. Therefore, the decline of the principles of moral society underlies the ecological problem. A society that does not give the principles of moral society the place they deserve cannot sustain its internal structures and its environment. We see this quite clearly today.

The same considerations also apply to the principle of political society. When the nation-state's gigantic bureaucratic administration replaces politics, the democratic functioning of society is destroyed. A society that the nation-state administration has infiltrated every pore of is a society that has been paralyzed. A society that has abandoned all its activities, all its common affairs, to the bureaucracy is indeed seriously paralyzed, both in thought and in will. It is not for nothing that Europe, having noticed this, embraces the principle of democratic politics. Europe is slightly more developed, because, in addition to a bureaucracy, it has allowed limited space for social politics.

In the eyes of modernity's nation-state, political society poses a threat to its existence, unity, and integrity. The nation-state administration and bureaucratization don't simply constrain the political element, the mode of society's existence, but make it virtually unusable. This doesn't simply hang over the society like the sword of Damocles, it cuts society to pieces hourly. This is not only the fundamental problem of our era's political philosophy, but, in practical terms, as fascism, this is the greatest obstacle to life. I have said elsewhere that Hitler as a person was defeated, but his system won. In terms of the elimination of political society, nation-statism is identical to Hitler's fascism (while Hitler was not the first person to succeed at this in its purest form, he was the first to officially declare and defend it).

A society that lacks the principle of politics, does not use it, or has seen it destroyed is nothing but a cadaver; at best it can be considered a colonized society. Therefore, the functionality that democratic society gives to the principle of politics is vital and is the primary proof of its superiority as a system.

The history of civilization is, in a way, the history of how political society has been constricted and rendered dysfunctional and obsolete. The division of society into classes was only made possible by the suppression of the fierce political struggle against it in favor of the state. At this point, we should be very careful. Even the Marxists, who have dealt most deeply with the question of class struggle, have been unable to correctly establish the nature of class division; they could not refrain from evaluating class division as a virtue and the driving force of civilization. The Marxists considered class division a historical materialist necessity, as if it were a stage of history or bridging relationship that had to be passed through. In my analysis of civilization, I evaluated class division as a limitation of political and moral society that rendered it dysfunctional; I emphasized that the greater the class division, the further society fell under the hegemony of power and the state. History, in this sense, is full of fierce class struggle. But the occurrence of class division itself was by no means progress or development; it was, on the contrary, social regression and decline. Morally, it was not a good but a bad development. To claim that division into classes is an inevitable stage in progress and to present this as a Marxist assertion in particular is one of the biggest mistakes made in the struggle for freedom.

Contrary to class society, the most important feature of political society is its continuous resistance to class division. The best society is the society that has the least class division. The success of a political struggle can be determined by whether or not it has allowed class division to arise. The political struggle will only prove successful if it does not allow its own society to be divided into classes and, thus, avoids being subjected to the unilateral violence of the apparatuses of power and the state. In societies that are up to their neck in the violence of power and the state, it is a serious error to speak of a successful political struggle. It is ideal for a political society to either not submit to the violence of power and the state (whether internal or external, national or foreign) or, after a hard struggle, to reach consensus on the basis of a mutual agreement with power and the state and recognize them on that basis.

Capitalist modernity is the last stage of civilization, where political society is most highly constricted and rendered dysfunctional. This we must understand clearly. If we choose to believe liberalism, which has ideological hegemony, political struggle and even democratic politics are extremely sophisticated during its rule. While this statement may seem to be correct on the face of it, in essence it expresses the opposite. Capitalist modernity is a period in which moral and political society is at its most dysfunctional as a result of the maximum expansion of individualism and monopolism. The nation-state as the maximum possible expression of power is a society that suffers the greatest loss of political character. That is the society that the nation-state creates. In reality, you cannot really speak of society at all. Society has been almost entirely absorbed by the nation-state and global corporations. This is the point at which Michel Foucault sees the defense of society as the basis of freedom.[40] He sees the loss of society (as modernity itself and through extreme individualism and monopolies) not only as the loss of freedom but also as the loss of humanity.

To the extent that it defends society and acquires freedom, democratic modernity is the only way out. By defending itself against individualism, the nation-state, and monopolies with democratic politics and making its political fabric functional a society transforms into a modern democratic society. Modern democratic society, on the other hand, proves its superiority by becoming a society where all social affairs are reflected upon and openly discussed, with the decisions arrived at being implemented, diversity created, multiculturalism embraced, and, on this basis, equality constructed. Thus, democratic modernity not only wages class struggle on the right basis but also does not suffocate its own society by creating a new power or a new state, allowing it to avoid falling into the historical trap (the tragic historical error of real socialism). It is aware that as power and the state are created, classes are formed, and the class struggle is lost.

This awareness should be regarded as one of the fundamental features of democratic modernity.

It should be clear by now that with democratic modernity we are not creating a new type of society, either capitalist or socialist. From the perspective of democratic modernity, such concepts are little more than propaganda far removed from describing actual society. No doubt there is a society coming into being, but it is a modern democratic society where moral and political principles play the greatest role and there is hardly any opportunity for classes to develop, so either power and the state apparatuses cannot exercise their power, or there is mutual recognition by consensus. In such a society, there is unity in diversity, and equality and freedom are experienced both as a feature of individuality (as opposed to individualism) and as an aspect of sociality. The achievement of greater equality, freedom, and democracy is in the nature of this society and is a consequence of the change and development that the institution of democratic politics triggers.

The Dimension of Eco-Industrial Society

The basis of the economic and industrial dimension of democratic modernity is ecological. First, it is important to correctly define the economy. In this regard, priority must be given to understanding the way that political economy is an extraordinary instrument for distraction and atrophy. The concept of *capitalist economy* in particular is nothing more than propaganda and sophistry.

In earlier volumes, I demonstrated that capitalism is not a form of economy but the archenemy of the economy. Capitalism is an organized network that makes the world uninhabitable for everyone except a handful of Nimrods and pharaohs for the sake of monopoly profit. It is essentially based not only on the plunder of surplus value but of all social value and has systematic hegemony over ideology and material culture. The difference between these networks and the forty thieves or pirates is that this network creates a multifaceted ideological legitimacy, cloaks itself in the law, and has its pillars in power, all in an attempt to hide its true face and real essence. A number of so-called scientific disciplines, in particular political economy, present capitalism as if it were the truth. Without an extraordinary armor woven of ideology and violence it would be unable to maintain its existence for even a day. With this structure, it suppresses and exploits economic activity (the main activity of moral and political society), whose meaning lies in the basic existence of society, including the environment, and prevents the further development of the economy, turning it into a source of happiness for a small minority.

Fernand Braudel defines the economy as follows: basic human needs form the ground floor, the activities of goods around the markets that do not involve monopolies and the exploitation of prices as the first floor, which is the actual economic sphere, and above these two floors, the top floor, which consists of monopoly networks and price manipulation, as the actual sphere of capitalism, which he regards as the anti-market (Immanuel Wallerstein considers this statement highly significant[41]). This is extremely instructive. In the light of this definition, it is quite clear that liberalism's insistence that capitalism is coterminous with market economy is pure nonsense. The only relationship capitalism has to the market is attaining and securing monopoly profit by manipulating prices, even triggering wars and crises when necessary. Moreover, capitalism is a savage system of games that does not abstain from preventing the entire economy from being an activity that exists to meet the basic needs of society, shifting it to the most profitable areas (the law of maximum profit). We call it a game in the sense it is an act that is extremely hostile to life and a form of attack that cuts human society off from the foundations of its existence.

Throughout history, monopolies of civilization in general and capitalist monopolies in particular (agriculture, trade, finance, power, and the nation-state apparatuses) have been the fundamental factors behind all of the economic distortions, crises, and problems, including hunger, poverty, and environmental disasters. All other evils are built on these fundamental factors: social and political class divisions, power, extreme urbanization and all the diseases that result from it, ideological distortions containing all kinds of religious, metaphysical, and scientific dogmas, and the particular ugliness that results from the distortion of the arts and moral impoverishment and decay. The last four hundred years of capitalist modernity provide numerous examples.

The economy finds its true meaning in democratic modernity. It denotes a meaningful, systematic structure that produces both use value as basic needs of the ground floor (most important characteristic: the satisfaction of basic needs) and exchange value (ratio for exchange of goods) as a real market economy. In democratic modernity, economy ceases to be an area of speculation for profit. Instead, how and with what methods basic needs can be most effectively satisfied without leading to class division or damaging the environment is clarified. The economy regains its true meaning as an area of social action. It acquires meaning as a fundamental form of activity that is both the basis for and consequence of moral and political society.

The economic understanding of modernity, including that of Marxist political economy, could not free itself from the class perspective (the hegemonic perspective of the bourgeoisie)—to associate value with the worker and the boss, it had to neglect and obscure the entire historical-society basis. Value is a product of historical-society. The boss and the concessionist worker are by no means the creators of this product; they are its main usurpers. The evidence is glaring: without free labor of women not a single boss or concessionist worker would have food to eat or even be able to manage his daily life. Indeed, this example alone clearly shows the anti-economic face of capitalism. We have also shown in detail that without historical-society, civilization in general and official modernity in particular could not have come about.

The industrial and ecological integrity of use and exchange value is fundamental to the economic dimension of democratic modernity. Industry has two determinants: the ecological and the satisfaction of basic needs and must not act outside of these parameters. This will allow for the emergence of eco-industry. An industry that is not ecological is also not economic. An industry that has lost its connection to ecology is nothing but a mechanized monster that constantly consumes and destroys its environment. In addition, an industry that has lost its connection to the economy of basic needs has no value other than making profit. As a result, eco-industry must be a fundamental principle to which all economic activities adhere. Only then can economic activity find its real meaning, making it possible to eliminate unemployment, over- and underproduction, more and less developed countries and regions, the rural-urban contrast, the gap between the classes, and the social basis for economic depressions and wars.

Unemployment is entirely a consequence of the distorted, profit-oriented economic structures. There is no room for such a distortion within the economic dimension of democratic modernity. Unemployment is the most inhumane social situation.

Over- or underproduction is also a consequence of this distorted, profit-oriented economic structure. While industry is so highly developed but basic needs are unsatisfied, neither over- or underproduction makes sense. I must emphasize that unless it is the result of natural conditions, over- or underproduction at the hands of humans is just as inhumane as unemployment.

The matter of more or less developed countries and regions is yet another expression of the same inhumane situation created by this profit-driven economy, sowing the seeds of conflict between countries and regions and leading to endless local, national, and international crises and wars. Clearly, an economy that is in the service of humanity would and must never lead to such a situation.

The village-city relationship, which throughout the history of historical-society has been based on harmony and the division of labor, has developed increasingly profound contradictions, with the equilibrium tilted to the disadvantage of agrarian-village society. This is linked, once again, to the orientation of the economy toward the pursuit of profit. Instead of a relationship where the city and the village, and agriculture, crafts, and industry nurtured one another, a relationship where they tended to eliminate each other came into being. This is yet another serious consequence of the law of maximum profit. While agrarian-village society has been brought to the brink of destruction, the city and industry began a period of cancerous growth. Not only the economy but historical-society itself is left facing destruction.

These distortions of the economy based on the law of maximum profit have resulted in class divisions and political conflict, giving rise to all types of local, national, and international wars. The narratives of civilization present all these negativities as humanity's fate. However, it is quite clear that they are based on the colonization and plunder of economy by anti-economy capitalist individualism and monopolism.

Democratic modernity is not only about rescuing the economy from these counter-tendencies, the development of its way of life would provide a system with no unemployment or poverty that would not allow for over- or underproduction, would reduce the gap between the more and less developed countries and regions, and would transform the contradiction between the city and the village into a relationship of mutual nurturing. Within its own system, social and economic differences do not expand into dimensions of class exploitation, class developments do not deepen, and sources of crises and wars, including economic exploitation and social conflicts, would be unable to flourish.

Not only would the system of democratic modernity not allow industrialism and urbanization to swallow the village and agriculture, it would also give rise to a city and industry that are viable. The mechanism for this can be found in the totality of the fundamental dimensions of democratic modernity. In their economic activities, all communities would treat the ecological and industrial elements holistically and in connection with the moral and political dimensions, which are all inseparably linked. Nothing would be left to the ripping claws of individualism and monopolism. Eco-economy and eco-industry would be taken into consideration in all social activity. Projects designed on this basis to repair the environment and revitalize agriculture, as well as to transform the village into a living area with an extremely healthy environment, would have the potential to eliminate all unemployment and poverty. Unemployment runs contrary to human nature. If people, who have the most developed intelligence, are left without work, it can only be due to human violence, and that's what it is. How could nature, where not even an ant is without work, leave its most developed existence unemployed and destitute? Why would poverty be anyone's fate in the age of technology, the great product of human activity, and the industry based on it?

Clearly, what is needed is systemic structural transformation. Both the historical and current reality of democratic modernity has the characteristic of not alienating people from their own practice or labor. The Industrial Revolution, as one of the most significant stages of this practice, was a victory for society and its economy. The problem lies in the fact that capitalist modernity put this unprecedented victory at the service of its own law of maximum profit from the outset. To do so it constructed an unprecedented level of individualism and monopolism (commercial, industrial, financial, power, and nation-state) that has brought historical-society to the brink of destruction. In a way, democratic modernity is the name of a systemic and structural revolution in this distorted understanding and application of modernity. Eco-industry is one of the most fundamental dimensions of this revolution. This argument alone proves the vitality of democratic modernity.

Although the family and professional enterprises are presented as the classic economic units of official modernity, in reality they are actually profit-oriented units with no concern beyond pursuing profit. They have spread their octopus-like arms around every sector of the economy worldwide, and the only thing they are interested in is maximizing profit.

The fact that unemployment has reached enormous dimensions, poverty has deepened, and the income gap has grown incredibly wide, with hundreds of millions of people left to die of hunger and an enormous potential for production left inactive as a result of either over- or underproduction, has paved the way for crisis, the collapse of agriculture, and the destruction of village society, all due to establishment of corporations acting on the law of maximum profit and the activities of economic—or rather non-economic—units. The main economic unit of democratic modernity will, of course, oppose both the mentality of these profit-oriented business units and their structure.

Historically, the economy has always been a delicate matter and the main concern of moral and political society. Things like famine, hunger, and death threatened society as a whole. As with accumulation, profit has never been accepted as legitimate by these societies but has always been seen as a source of evil and theft. When the opportunity arose, these accumulations were confiscated by the state. An economy cannot be built if this is the goal in itself. As previously stated, to call a quintessentially anti-economy activity the economy is a contradiction in and of itself.

The only way out of this contradiction is to build a functioning economy of eco-communities. Thousands of eco-communities could, depending on circumstances, organize themselves into an economic unit. Agricultural land, no longer unified, having been broken up into family plots, needs to be reorganized in keeping with the principle of eco-industry—this is a problem that has long been calling for a solution. The formation of eco-communities in agriculture is one of the most fundamental economic principles of democratic modernity. In this context, agricultural production in the manner of farms, a remnant of serfdom and slavery, has also come to an end. Eco-communities formed by creating agricultural units on an ecological scale are also the basis of village modernity. The village, at least the modern village, could regain its existence as an eco-community in the form of economic units on an ecologically sound scale.

Similar eco-communities could also be formed in the cities. In urban planning, an ecologically oriented economy will be part of the whole. Just as there can be no bureaucracy that devours the city, there can be no economy that devours the city. The economy will be organized according to the nature of each city in the form of not-for-profit units of an optimal size that are designed to eliminate unemployment and poverty in the city.

The city's citizens would be distributed among the units based on their structure and capabilities.

It may sound as if we are talking about a socialist planned economy, but the model we are talking about is different from and has nothing to do with centralized planning, a command economy, or the barbaric, profit-oriented, and noneconomic so-called economic enterprises. This model is a structure within which the local moral and political society makes its decisions and determines its actions. There is always, of course, a need for coordination that encompasses national, regional, and even international conditions. This necessity does not, however, remove the discretion to make decisions and take action from the local community. I must emphasize once again, the economy is not a question of the technical infrastructure; it is an activity that is of fundamental structural importance to the existence of societies that is realized by airing opinions, holding discussions, making decisions, and organizing action and work in a way that includes the whole of society. Tearing people away from the economy is the basis of all alienation. It is essential to prevent this, so all communities must take over the economy. Just as "when some eat while others look on, all hell breaks loose,"[42] if one works, while others sit idle, all hell will break loose. The economy, which must necessarily be community-oriented and organized according to both ecological principles and efficiency, is the basic condition of society's existence. No one but society and communities will have the right to this existence or the right to abolish it. All units, whether commercial, industrial, agricultural, or financial, as long as the latter plays a solely intermediary role, must comply with these basic principles. Whether a gigantic factory or an agrarian-village unit, the principles remain the same.

Property loses its importance in the economic units of democratic modernity and becomes secondary. Property will naturally belong to the communities that use it according to the established principles. Neither family nor state ownership responds adequately to the modern economy. Property that belongs exclusively to the family or the state is a remnant of the hierarchical era that cannot continue to exist in capitalist modernity. Even companies are gradually becoming the joint property of the employees as a result of economic constraints. But still we must not too sharply separate different norms of ownership. Just as two civilization systems coexist, systems of ownership shall also continue to coexist for some time to come. Just as family property continues to exist alongside common property, the state will continue to exist and have a share. The important thing is to be open to flexible property norms that can provide solutions to environmental problems, unemployment, and productivity issues. Any form of possession that serves the existence, freedom, goodness, and beauty of the individual is valuable, even if it is property. Since these values could not be created without community, it is best to solve these problems within optimal limits. Democratic modernity is in a position to restore community-based property, which throughout history has never lost its communal existence, as a basis of moral and political society under modern conditions, thereby allowing it to successfully play its historical role.

The Dimension of Democratic Confederalist Society

The third dimension of social nature concerns the level of governance, which we can call the democratic confederalist system. Despite all the drawbacks of classification, presenting it as we have, in three dimensions, may be helpful. We should keep in mind, however, that the dimensions are intertwined. It might be possible to arbitrarily replace one or more dimensions, but then the result would not be democratic modernity but something else. The three dimensions of capitalist modernity are entirely intertwined. In short, these three dimensions are interdependent.

The democratic confederalist system is democratic modernity's counterpart of the nation-state, the main state form of official modernity. We can define this as a form of non-state political governance. It is this characteristic that makes the system so specific. We must not confuse democratic steering with that of the state's administrative bodies. States administer; democracies steer. States rest on power, democracies rest on collective approval. In states, appointments are essential; in democracies, elections are central. In states obligation is essential; democracies run on voluntarism. I could go on listing such differences.

Contrary to what one might think, democratic confederalism is not a governing system that is specific to our time; it is a system that has been significantly present throughout history. History, in this sense, is not centralized and statist but confederal. The state form is widely known, because it was given a strong official status. But social life is closer to confederalism. The state always aspires to centralism, because it is dependent on the interests of the power monopolies on which it is based. Otherwise, it could not safeguard these interests; it can only guarantee this through strict centralism. In confederalism, however, the opposite is true. Since it is not based on monopoly but on society, democratic confederalism must avoid centralization as much as possible. Since societies are not homogeneous but are made up of numerous communities, institutions, and diversities, they have a duty to safeguard and ensure the harmonious totality of all of these. Therefore, an extremely centralist regime often triggers explosions in these multitudes. History provides countless examples. Democratic confederalism occurs more often, because it is more suitable for every community, institution, and diversity to express itself. It is not a widely recognized system because of the hegemonic structure and ideology of official civilization. While not officially defined as such, societies throughout history have essentially been confederal. All forms of aşiret, tribal, and peoples' leadership allow for confederalism, with its loose relationships. Anything else damages their internal autonomy, effectively causing them to disintegrate. Even empires rest on numerous different internal leaderships. Every type of aşiret, tribal, and peoples' leadership, all religious authorities and kingdoms, even republics and democracies, can be united within a single empire. In this sense, it is important to understand that even empires, which are generally seen as very highly centralized, are a kind of confederalism. It is not society but the monopoly that needs the administrative model of centralized government.

In capitalist modernity the state is maximally centralized. Modern monarchies, and then nation-states, came into being by pushing back the political and military power centers in society in favor of the strongest monopoly, called authority, thus maximally weakening society in the political and military fields and depriving it of its leadership. The consequent development of nation-states represents the type of administration that has most substantially militarily and politically weakened and disarmed society. What is meant by social peace and legal order is nothing but the consolidation of the sovereignty of the bourgeois class. The intensification of exploitation and its new forms made the existence of the nation-state necessary. The nation-state, which can be described as the organization of power as a maximally centralized state, is the main form of administration in modernity. Practices, including so-called bourgeois democracy, are the necessary foil to attain legitimacy for the power monopoly in society. The nation-state is formed on the basis of the negation of democracy, and even of the republic. Democracies and republics as forms of government are of a different nature than nation-states.

Democratic modernity's choice of democratic confederalism as its fundamental political model is not arbitrary. The choice reflects its historical basis and complex social nature, thereby determining the political framework of moral and political society. Until it is fully understood that social nature is neither homogeneous nor monolithic, it is difficult to understand democratic confederalism. The history of the last four hundred years of official modernity is the history of a kind of genocide (mostly cultural, occasionally physical) in the name of creating a homogeneous nation in opposition to multiethnic and multicultural society, with its diverse political entities and self-defense. Democratic confederalism, on the other hand, is the history of the insistence on self-defense, multiethnicity, multiculturalism, and diverse political forms that opposes this history. Postmodernism is the continuation of the conflict-laden history of modernity in new forms.

In the global financial era, the nation-state, which has been consecrated as the most divine being of the last two hundred years, has cracked. The social realities that it forcibly absorbed and suppressed are reemerging as if to take revenge. This is the product of interlinked processes. The financial era's understanding of profit necessitates a change in the nation-state. This necessary change is an essential factor in making the crisis systemic. The reconstruction of the nation-state by neoliberalism, on the other hand, has not been particularly successful. In this regard, the experience of the Middle East is instructive.

The democratic system, which must become increasingly more visible as counter-modernity, faces the challenge of successfully resolving questions of form while strengthening its existence under the current conditions. This is why we tried to show that confederalism is not something historically new, and that it is the optimal response to the increasingly complex nature of present society. We have often said that the best way for moral and political society to express itself is through democratic politics. Democratic politics is the way to build democratic confederalism. This is the source of its democratic content. The other modernity tries to maintain itself through power and the state apparatuses, which become increasingly centralized and infiltrate all of society's pores. In doing so, however, they are actually destroying the political sphere. In contrast, democratic politics offers the opportunity for all parts of and identities within society to express themselves and become a political force. While doing so, it also constitutes the political society. Politics reenters social life.

The crisis of the state cannot be solved without the intervention of politics, given that it stems from the denial of political society. Democratic politics is the only way to overcome the deepening state crisis. Otherwise, the search for more heavily centralized states will certainly lead to further severe failures.

These factors indicate, yet again, that democratic confederalism is on the agenda as a strong option. The main reason for the disintegration of real socialism was its quick replacement of confederalism, which was high on the agenda at the beginning of the Soviet Russian experiment, with a centralized state. The reason that national liberation movements were unsuccessful and were quickly corrupted is closely linked to the fact that they did not develop democratic politics and confederalism. The lack of success of revolutionary movements over the last two hundred years is also because they considered the nation-state to be more revolutionary and regarded democratic confederalism as a backward political form, and thus opposed it.

Those individuals and movements that reached for the nation-state, the very weapon of capitalist modernity, thinking it would provide a shortcut to great social transformations, understood too late that they had shot themselves in the foot.

Democratic confederalism has the potential to overcome the disadvantages stemming from the nation-state system. At the same time, it is the most appropriate means for politicizing society. It is simple and easy to implement. Each community, ethnicity, culture, religious community, intellectual movement, economic unit, etc. can structure and express itself autonomously as a political unit. The notion of federal structure or autonomy, of selfhood (*kendilik*),[43] must be evaluated within this framework and scope. Every selfhood, from local to global, has the opportunity to form a confederation. The most fundamental element of the local is the right to free discussion and decision-making. Each selfhood or federal unit is unique, because it makes the implementation of direct democracy— also known as participatory democracy—possible. They draw all their strength from the practicability of direct democracy, which is another reason it will play a fundamental role. Just as the nation-state negates direct democracy, democratic confederalism, by contrast, is the form that generates this democracy and makes it functional.

The federal units, as the mother cells of direct participatory democracy, are also unique and ideal in their flexibility to transform into confederal units according to their needs and conditions. Any type of political association is democratic if it is based on units that are themselves based on direct participatory democracy. A political functionality ranging from local unity, where direct democracy is practiced and lived, to the global structure can be called democratic politics. When all these processes take place, we can speak of a truly democratic system.

If social nature is carefully observed, then the character of the nation-state as an "iron cage" and the most appropriate character of democratic confederalism, its liberating quality, can be easily understood. While the nation-state oppresses society, imposes uniformity, and severs it from democracy, the democratic confederalist model has a liberating, pluralizing, and democratizing effect.

Further, we should make sure to think of both federal units and selfhoods in a very rich manner. It is important to understand that even a village or district will need confederal units, and every village and district can easily be a confederal unit. For example, numerous direct-democratic units, from the ecological unit (or federal unit) to the units of free women, self-defense, youth, education, folklore, health, mutual aid, and even the economic, must join together at the village level. We can simply call this new unit of units a confederal unit (the unit of federal units) or confederal union. If we take the same system to the local, regional, national, and global levels, we can easily see what a comprehensive system democratic confederalism is. The system of democratic confederalism will allow us to better understand the complementary nature of the three fundamental dimensions of democratic modernity. Each dimension having the potential to discuss, evaluate, arrange, restructure, and mobilize for action best ensures the historical-society reality and totality of social nature.

Social self-defense is best realized within the democratic confederal system. Self-defense, as an institution of democratic politics, is within the scope of confederal system. Self-defense can, in fact, be defined as the concentrated expression of democratic politics.

The nation-state is essentially a military system. All nation-states are the product of numerous very cruel and protracted wars that have been waged internally and externally in many different forms. A nation-state that is not a product of war is inconceivable. Not only during its founding phase but more so during its phases of institutionalization and disintegration, the nation-state engulfs the entire society, both from the inside and the outside, with military armor. The society is completely militarized.

The institutions of power and the state, referred to as the civil administration, are essentially a veil over this military armor. The apparatuses known as bourgeois democracies go even further in their efforts to apply a coat of democratic polish to this militarist structure and mentality and are responsible for the propaganda that a liberal democratic social system prevails. This grave contradiction of modernity must be resolved. Unless it is, it will be impossible to talk about a proper politicization and practice of democratic politics. This is what is also known as a "soldier nation,"[44] and is the reality of all nation-states formed in the last four hundred years. This reality underlies all social problems, crises, and decay. All the various fascist power practices (with or without a coup or military or civil fascism) that are frequently imposed as a solution are part of the nature of the nation-state; they are the formal expression of its purest form.

Democratic confederalism can only stop this militarization, which stems from the nation-state, with self-defense. Societies deprived of self-defense face the danger of losing their identities, political qualities, and democratization. Therefore, the dimension of self-defense for societies is not simply military defense. It is intertwined with the protection of identities, the guarantee of politicization, and the realization of democratization. Only if society is able to defend itself can we speak of protecting its identity, guaranteeing politicization, and practicing democratic politics. In this light, democratic confederalism must be simultaneously designed as a system of self-defense. We are living in the age of the global hegemony of monopolies and the militarization of the entire society in the form of the nation-state. Democratic modernity can only counter this hegemony with its own system of confederal networks based on self-defense and democratic politics that encompass the entire society always and everywhere. For every hegemonic network (commercial, financial, industrial, and ideological monopolies, as well as monopolies of power and nation-state), democratic modernity must develop the equivalent confederal networks of democratic politics and self-defense.

The final question that we must address regarding this dimension is how the relations and contradictions between the nation-state and social nature can continue. Real socialist and national liberation movements in particular have made the most tragic of historical errors due to prevailing power-centered approaches—instead of bourgeois rule, proletarian rule, or even proletarian dictatorship; instead of colonial or collaborationist rule, approaches centered around national power. This, in turn, has provided capitalism with the undeserved opportunity to sustain itself. These and other similar movements and currents can in a way be viewed as demolishing one power structure and its state only to replace them with another, making these movements the main culprits in submerging society in militarization and causing it to lose its political character, as well as making them responsible for the defeat of the democratic struggle. For around two centuries, those who pursued these approaches have single-handedly served capitalist hegemony's nation-statism victory on a silver platter. Alongside the anarchists, some postmodernist, feminist, and ecological movements that emerged later, as well as other civil society organizations and leftist currents, have adopted a more positive position on this issue.

It is inevitable that both modernity systems will coexist under the described conditions and principles for a long time with both extensive periods of peace and times of substantial conflict. This is just a fact of life. It would be incorrect to maintain this long phase of coexistence with an unprincipled and capitulationist peace or to continue to think and act in a conflict-seeking and belligerent manner regardless of the conditions. Between the nation-state system and the democratic confederalist system, there will be principled and conditional peace, but there will also be wars of self-defense in the event that these conditions and principles are violated. A political philosophy and strategic and tactical approach that take this into account is more conducive to the freedom, equality, and democracy march of historical-society.

I feel that I have sufficiently defined and attempted to analyze the dual character of modernity as the last phase of the history of civilization in this lengthy section of my defense. As with the overall dialectical development of history, modernity itself, with its even shorter history, is rife with dialectical developments. When we say "dialectical," what we mean is that it carries two poles embodying two distinct mentalities and structures that develop in relation to and in contradiction with each other. The history of the last four hundred years confirms that capitalism has left its mark on modernism, but this does not mean that modernity is completely capitalist. Moreover, capitalism is a system for the accumulation of profit and capital not a form of society. It is not an appropriate system for characterizing a comprehensive phenomenon like modernity. Although I have frequently used the term *capitalist modernity*, I have tried to emphasize that it must be understood as having left its mark on modernity. At the same time, I have tried to present an analysis that shows the accuracy of describing the other face of modernity (but do not see it as appropriate to call it modernity with a democratic mark) as democratic modernity (the name may change if a more appropriate one is found). To avoid falling into similar historical errors in distinguishing between capitalist society and socialist societies, I have tried to avoid the shallow approach of making a distinction between capitalist modernity and socialist modernity.

I used a comparative methodology for the two different moderni-ties, and compared them historically, because reality itself is forked. As with the history of civilization, we have witnessed this dichotomy in all circumstances and conflicts in the shorter period of modern times. I have tried—even if it remains only an attempt—to develop definitions and short analyses based on these observations. I have no doubt that this attempt will be understood as an initial draft of my thoughts. Undoubtedly, criti-cisms and proposals will further strengthen these analyses.

It cannot be denied that capitalism, as a system of profit and capital accumulation, has left its mark on modernism and continues to do so as the global hegemonic power ruled by financial capital. At the same time, it also cannot be denied that as a system (the global capitalist system, the world system) it contains forces that are in fierce conflict with it always and everywhere it has been established. For reasons of conceptual sim-plicity, I have called these the forces of democratic modernity. I am not only referring to real socialist and national liberation movements but also the recent emergence of anarchism in particular, and, even more recently, ecological, feminist, and radical religious systems. The system has long been riddled with holes, and internal and external forces coming from the system (more external, I must say, because the nature of society is such that external forces are more readily recognized) have always and everywhere expressed a desire for existence, freedom, and equality and acted on it. They have never stopped searching for their own system.

Just as was the case throughout the history of civilization, in modern times the efforts of systems to destroy one another and establish a monop-oly have failed—but the price for this has been very high. No doubt blindness on both sides has substantially exacerbated the consequences of these systemic wars. Systems will always try to outdo each other to survive. From the global level down to the local level, some of them will try to impose hegemony. But the resistance will continue, strengthened with the lessons learned from experience. As long as there are unresolved problems, we will always experience war and peace. But as the analyses and solutions are more successful and increasingly better reflect what is true, good, and beautiful, we can imagine and achieve a world that is more beautiful and passionate without being either in a state of war or of peace. Of course, a lot more peace and a lot less war is also a worthy goal, and efforts in that direction are noble, as long as they are principled and dignified.

We have defined the hegemony of global financial capital itself as the phase of the most profound crisis. Developments confirm this. In addition, we have argued in great detail that the crisis is systemic and structural, and news about the current crisis confirms this. Modern systems become fertile in times of crisis. Some create sound solutions, but unsound solutions are far from rare. In the liberal utopia of capitalism, there is never a lack of comprehensive and eclectic solution packages. They are constantly formulating daily, weekly, monthly, annual, ten-year, and fifty-year plans. That is their job, and they will continue to do it.

It is possible that opportunities for the forces of democratic modernity will increase even further in these times of crisis. Together, the tremendous history of resistance behind them and utopias of freedom and equality light the way forward. Furthermore, they have learned great lessons from the shortcomings and defeats already experienced. If all these are interwoven and grasped as a bouquet of intellectual, moral, and political tasks and put into practice, they undoubtedly have a great chance of success. Nevertheless, there are specific aspects that we must consider in relation to times of systemic and structural crisis. No matter the degree to which they may be on the trail of the past, they cannot ignore that the science and moral and political philosophy to be applied must include innovations. Otherwise, the shallowness experienced in the past will mean new blind spots. And the fact that liberalism is often further neoliberalized increases the danger. While everyone expected revolution in response to the world economic crisis of 1929, the outcome was quite the opposite; a fascist wave arose—it should not be forgotten—the effects of which continue to reverberate today. Society is increasingly deprived of its moral and political nature. Information technology gives the global ideological hegemonic forces far-reaching opportunities to present comprehensive virtual worlds that distort the real world. These powers have no problem packaging the decayed structures into a new system and presenting it as if it were reborn. This poses them absolutely no problem.

The present masses have long since been transformed into the fascism's herd-like masses. I say this to emphasize that we must not let our hopes fade and settle for uniting the analytical and emotional aspects of reality; we must live morally and politically always and everywhere. If we do not succeed in doing so, we could easily fail. I will address these issues in the following concluding section.

NINE

The Reconstruction Problems
of Democratic Modernity

The most tragic aspect of modern revolutions is that they are the victims of the modernism that they contribute to. These revolutions, whose common failure is the inability to analyze their relationship and contradictions with modernism, thought they could nonetheless successfully pursue their objectives. Therefore, these revolutions, with their utopian content, could not but disintegrate in the ice-cold calculations of modernity. The general conclusion to be drawn from the five thousand years of civilization, particularly the last four hundred years of modernity, is that the main factor behind the failure of all of the resistance and every revolution has been an inability to distinguish themselves from the system they opposed and establish their own system. They evaluated civilizations and modernity using a monist approach and regarded them as synonymous with the universal life that must be adhered to. Although countless resistance movements destroyed various civilizations, the success was followed by the formation of a new version of the previous civilization.

Here we encounter civilization's source of power. With very few exceptions, people—including the greatest of revolutionaries—are children of the civilization of their time. Their real parents are the era they live in. I do not mean this fatalistically; I simply want to emphasize that whether it is a question of five thousand or four hundred years, if this fundamental error is not overcome, even revolutions with the most radical of discourses and actions will be unable to avoid failure. We cannot say that social resistance and revolutions have not left a legacy. If that legacy didn't exist, our lives wouldn't make sense. However, even the crisis of highly self-assured capitalist modernity proves that we are nowhere near getting to the root of the problems and solving them. Just because it has endured for a long time does not make an error less wrong or stop a problem from being a problem. As long as this is the case, dreams of equality, freedom, and democratic life will remain utopian.

As I settle accounts with the history of civilization and modernity in my defense writings, I am also engaging in a profound self-criticism and trying to present my own alternative, no matter how insufficient. To be consistent, I must do this. Eurocentric social sciences show no such consistency. We still talk about an unprecedented era of science but are unable to overcome the savagery of war! Under such circumstances, it is illegitimate to use the weapon of scientism to criticize the ancient times. It is necessary to pursue a legitimate science, and that is the point of my efforts.

What I said about civilization and modernity should not be considered an exaggeration. There can be no doubt that when the prophets used the word of God to criticize the orders of Nimrod and the pharaoh they were being entirely sincere. But those who thought that they were walking in the footsteps of the prophets have always, in the end, built new orders of Nimrod and the pharaoh that outdid the previous ones. You can see the power of these civilizations in the way the sultans, shahs, and monarchs have fallen prisoner to the same order. Good intentions and the belief that you follow in the footsteps of the prophets will not spare you from being subjected to the system of Nimrod and the pharaohs.

Marx, Lenin, and Mao were sincere when they grappled with capitalism. In fact, they totally believed that they had built socialism. But soon enough the results showed that the structure they had built was not so different from capitalism. Here too, it was the new civilization, i.e., modernity, that was influential. Their superficial evaluations of capital were not enough to develop socialism. An analysis of modernity was missing. The positivist worldview that they were deeply submerged in presented modernity as the most holy form of reality. Not only did they not criticize it, they thought they could perfect it. The consequences are obvious. The domino effect of these historical errors means that even the noblest and most holy objectives cannot escape being instrumentalized to serve the ice-cold calculations of civilization and modernity.

Although postmodernism was one of the first serious critical movements to arise in response to capitalist modernity's unsustainability, it was far from providing an alternative. Its eclectic and obscure structure didn't even allow postmodernity to successfully distinguish itself from classical modernity. Similar efforts by the nineteenth-century Romantics effectively stopped at literature. Critiques of modernity, especially those of Friedrich Nietzsche toward the end of nineteenth century and of Michel Foucault in the second half of twentieth century, are invaluable, but they were unable to get beyond being individual efforts and give rise to a collective moral and political current. More current efforts, including the analysis of civilization and modern systems undertaken by Fernand Braudel, Immanuel Wallerstein, and Andre Gunder Frank and his close colleagues, have treated the topic more realistically and critically within the totality of historical-society but have not been as adept at offering an alternative. Civilization and modernity are regarded as closed cyclical systems that inevitably exist, and in spite of the comprehensive criticism, thoughts about possible alternatives never went beyond a few sentences. We can understand why Nietzsche went mad and Foucault's untimely death. But we don't understand how Fernand Braudel thought real social-ism was an alternative, how Immanuel Wallerstein was content with the concepts of equality, freedom, and democratization, or how Andre Gunder Frank felt an extremely general discourse about "unity in diver-sity" sufficed. These shortcomings amount to admitting that they are not completely free of the chains of the Eurocentric science that they have criticized so well.

My critical analysis of the subject and my proposals for an alterna-tive within the scope of my defense may seem like an individual adjudi-cation of the center of ancient civilization and its present representative, capitalist modernity, and that is true in a sense. However, I think that if people are unable to analyze their own convictions they will not be in a position to attempt to formulate a sound science. I am not narrowly addressing a prison sentence; I am talking about a general social convic-tion that has been imposed on free life by the civilization and modernity. The first condition for meaningful science is that the agents conducting it should analyze themselves and adopt a practical position. Otherwise, they will be unable to free themselves from the use of acquired knowl-edge—science—as intellectual capital in the market, thereby engaging in the science of the rulers.

The substance of my criticism is that the five-thousand-year-old civi-lization system (including the even older hierarchical system) stems from the accumulation of capital and the power established over the agrarian-village society and nomadic communities in the rural areas and the crafts-men and slave laborers in the cities. This reality has remained essentially unchanged until the present; these power and the state monopolies, which have taken various forms, including trade, money, and industry, have remained unchanged. The history of civilization is based on both the wars between monopolies over their respective shares and the wars they wage together against opposing forces. Beyond that are the wars of ideological hegemony and the games and contrivances for the usurpation of social value by war and through power. The period of capitalist civilization—i.e., modernity—is this system at its most advanced. The center-periphery, hegemony-competition, and ups and downs of crises characteristic of this system were there from the beginning. The period of modernity, on the other hand, in particular at a time when financial capital plays a hegemonic role, denotes the most profound structural crisis.

I suggest that the alternative solution be sought in the consciousness and movements of the social nature of all of the forces that have positioned themselves in dialectical opposition to the forces connected to the rise of hierarchy, the various periods of civilization, and the history of modernism marked by capitalism. No version of official civilization history offers any solution for these oppositional forces. If social struggles have not succeeded in putting their utopias of equality and freedom into practice, this is primarily because they have used the same weapons (power and the state) as the unraveling civilization and envisaged the future they want to build as little more than a different version of this civilization. The inability to create a distinct mentality and the structures suitable to their own social natures has caused them to dissolve into versions of their opposite pole.

The flow of history is not a system of repetitive cycles, but it also does not unfold as linear progression. It is the overall movement of consciousness and actions that have become a whole and have influence to the extent that they have formed mentalities and structural movements within themselves. It is always possible to become part of history, to become one of the rings in its flow. To do this, however, is to acquire a structural form with the necessary mental capacity. History, in this sense, has an unfailing nature. All the views and actions that were unable to develop the mental capacity and structural form necessary to have a place in history must assume full responsibility.

Civilization, Modernity, and the Problem of Crisis

Civilization systems with states produce economic depressions by their very structure. These depressions are not incidental events that arise from time to time as a result of the way internal and external factors play out over time and space. The system itself continuously produces depressions (culminating in crises when extreme). The logic of depression is very simple: power and, more formally, the state classes are established on seized social and surplus value. Due to their organized armed structures, these classes, which hover above society, tend to constantly grow. However, the people who compose the labor segment of society barely make a living and die prematurely from various diseases and in wars, with their population decreasing compared to that of the state classes. The population of all classes of the state and power increase, because they are better able to feed and protect themselves and to reproduce. Because of their dynastic character, the first rulers and states favored large extended families. Power politics entails this. This systemic state of mutual imbalance means crises. As the state classes grow and become stronger, they establish themselves over the society and usurp its social and surplus value, causing the unsustainability of the system to come into play. This is the situation that is called a period of crisis.

There are two ways out of the crisis. First, the force that destroys its rivals in the escalating hegemonic wars emerges as the new hegemon. This new hegemonic power seizes its rivals' shares, crushing them in the process and overcoming the crisis—at least relatively, and for some time—until new rivals emerge. The second option, often intertwined with the first, is efficient production and the application of commercial and industrial techniques to increase production. A hegemonic system that increases its production can secure a period of prosperity instead one of depression. The ancient civilizations, for example, experienced extended periods of depression interspersed with prolonged periods of stability. There were many crises at intervals ranging from two hundred to a thousand years. Generally, each major period of crisis resulted in a dynastic change and a shift of the center. This can be clearly seen from the Sumerian and Egyptian civilizations onward. Medieval crises shared a similar rhythm, but their duration was generally shorter. On average, these crises generally lasted for approximately 100 to 150 years.

The capitalist system's crises, although in line with the general trend outlined above, have their own peculiarities. Initially, monetary and trade monopolies play a leading role, but their relationship to production is limited. In contrast, money is widely used in the economy. The significance of money has increased greatly due to the commodification of trade becoming a dominant feature. Over time, the monopoly of money and trade concentrates in a few hands. Under these circumstances, society's purchasing power declines for lack of money. As a result, products remain unsold, setting in motion a depression that is initially experienced as a crisis of overproduction. The excess production cannot be sold and must be destroyed, while laborers who lack purchasing power because of the shortage of money fall into poverty and hunger. The reverse can also be experienced relatively rapidly. Production that fails to bring in any money declines even further, and the money at hand loses its relationship to production to an even greater degree. In the end, there is a lot of money but little production. The increased cost of living (inflation) creates a new crisis. The way out of both of these crises is to increase the state expenditure, alongside the traditional path of hegemonic wars, and to create a new wage-earning sector to address either the excess in or deficiency of production, as the case may be.

Such crises have been widespread and intertwined over the last four hundred years of capitalist hegemony. The intervals between crises have decreased to between fifty and a hundred years. Wars for hegemony have become more multifaceted, intense, and long-lasting compared to previous periods in civilization. Both national and international monopolies participated in these wars. Whereas there have always been local and regional wars, we are now seeing warfare with a genuinely global reach for the first time. Even more serious, however, is that society itself has been increasingly militarized by the nation-state and fully submerged in a kind of war. It makes sense to call present-day society a "state of war" society. This state of war is being imposed in two ways. First, power and the state apparatus control, oppress, and surveil any society they have wrapped themselves around. Second, the information technology (media monopolies) that has developed as a result of the qualitative revolution of the past fifty years has replaced real society with a virtual society. Both states of war can be called societycide. These new societycides, in addition to the now more limited practice of genocides, prepare the end of social nature by being more intense and continuous. Perhaps creatures resembling human beings will continue to exist, but they will do so as a fascist mob or a herd-like mass. The consequence of societycide is much more severe than that of genocide, manifesting itself in the loss of society's moral and political nature. That human masses feel no responsibility to act even in the face of the severest of social and ecological disasters proves this. It is beyond question that we are in a situation that is more than another depression or crisis. At the risk of repetition, it might be useful to summarize how we arrived at this point, so that the overall situation is properly grasped.

a) History, from the establishment of the first power hierarchy and state sovereignty until today, is, in a way, the history of the cumulative (snowballing) growth of power. Power struggles are the essence of the history of civilization everywhere and always. Local conflicts and world wars, tribal wars and national wars, class wars and religious wars, they have all resulted in the increase and cumulative growth of power. The proliferation of power means the development of a parasitical class that lives on social value. The administration that formed a limited hierarchy at the beginning and, with its experience and expertise, sometimes made important contributions to society. But when it transformed itself into the state, it became a caste—these caste groups, in addition to their dynastic characteristics, organized as privileged classes, gaining enough advantage to consider themselves divine. Antiquity is full of god-kings and emperors who exhibited the constant growth of power and glorified themselves with such concepts. The power and state classes that organized as the triad of priest + administrator + commander were still not numerous. In fact, they constituted a very small proportion of the population. We know from countless examples that their parasitical nature nonetheless quickly became a heavy burden on society. The pyramids, temples, and arenas fully illustrate the nature of this burden.

The growth of power in no way slowed down in the Middle Ages. History overruns with power struggles that grew as they spread to a wider area. No doubt the increased productivity of society contributed to this. A broad aristocratic class arose alongside the dynastic royals. Nonetheless, it is still not possible to speak of a cancerous ruling class. The disaster began when the middle class, the bourgeoisie, and the bureaucracy began to take their place among the ruling classes, as they took over the administration of society by undermining and transforming the monarchy and the aristocratic structures. No doubt former administrations had been also disastrous, but they were not in a position to entirely swallow up society, either quantitatively or qualitatively. The upper monopolist sections of the bourgeoisie, along with an important part of middle bourgeoisie and the bureaucracy, assumed power and became state classes, replacing a handful of former dynasties and kingdoms with thousands, even tens of thousands, of new dynastic forces. This amounted to thousands of little kings replacing the single king of earlier days. The combination of the male-dominant personality,[1] which develops in the sexist society, and the forces of this new kingdom meant that social nature as a whole was conquered and colonized by the new forces of power. All the sections of moral and political society, but in particular women, were victims of this internal colonization.

Middle-class statehood has not yet been analyzed because of the close kinship between the social sciences and this class. For the state to make any sense in the eyes of society it must function as an absolutely necessary concentration of experience and expertise. It is not difficult to understand that a very limited number of people within the administration actually have that experience and expertise. The bourgeoisie and bureaucracy, with their gigantic magnitude and presenting themselves as the state's administrative class, make the cancerous growth of power within the society inevitable.

Power and the nation-state, which denote the integration of monopolies of economic exploitation and ideological hegemony into the power apparatus, became everything, reducing society to nothing in the process. This is the essence of what we call a crisis of power. The capitalist system is the force that induces this crisis. The monstrously enlarged middle class and capital monopolies and capitalist networks that have no inhibition about using the economy for their own growth can only survive if power takes the shape of the nation-state. We call this system blockage. Thus, coming to power actually denotes the situation beyond the crisis.

b) Moral and political society, the normal state of social nature, is being stripped of its fundamental characteristics in an unprecedented way. With the onset of capitalist modernity, moral and political society, which the state developed in opposition to throughout antiquity and the Middle Ages, has been forced to cede its place to the infinitely growing number of articles of positive law and state administration. With modernity, the moral and political qualities of society have been replaced by a herd made up of inconsequential ant-like individuals, known as citizens.

Contrary to what is widely believed, the so-called modern citizen, who has no moral and political concerns, is the weakest individual of all time. This individual's link with society is limited to his "wife," over whom he exercises imperial power. This individual is, in reality, a characterless being who has been assimilated into power and state authority in a way unimaginable in the days of the pharaoh. More precisely, in response to physical and ideological hegemony and the related informatics and technical practices, the citizen has not only surrendered to the monopolistic order but has also voluntarily become an unconditional fascist. This is what I mean when I talk about a personality crisis. Social nature cannot consist of such personalities, because its main fabric is moral and political in nature, and these qualities cannot be found in such a personality. States can make progress with these personalities, but they cannot sustain a society. More precisely, this personality is the negation of society.

Since the state cannot exist without society, we yet again have a situation where the state and society are experiencing an intertwined crisis. The capitalist individualism that created the characterless personality is nothing more than a projection of the crisis of both society and the state. Obviously, neither capital or power monopolies nor the nation-state administration—the unified state form—is possible if society and the individual are not debased in this way. The social crisis denotes something more than a structural crisis. Any structure can be replaced with a new one, but the loss of the fundamental qualities of society is not something that can easily be addressed by restructuring. That would require the rebuilding of moral and political society, which is where the difficulty lies.

c) Urbanization is the other most crisis-ridden element of modernity. Urban society developed in dialectical unity with the agrarian-village society and played an important social role in the development of rationality and industry at a point when environmental conflict had not yet developed. The role of the city was distorted by the process of the state formation. Once transformed into the ruling class's base, the city took on a structure and mentality that proved detrimental to agrarian-village society and ecology as history unfolded. Once the manufacturing and merchant classes attained a central position, the city began to act against society. The negative functions of the city were limited during antiquity and the Middle Ages but increased in the extreme with modernity. The cancerous growth of cities with the onset of the Industrial Revolution made them centers for the destruction of traditional society. The industrial city is not a city at all; it is urbanization without cities and cities ceasing to be cities.[2] Never mind cities with millions of people, even cities with several hundred thousand run contrary to sound urban logic. There should be no cities with populations in the millions, but several cities with a total population reaching a million would be possible. A city with a population of five million would, in fact, constitute at least fifty distinct cities. This is the destructive feature of the cities for society. Neither normal societies nor the environment can hope to sustain such cities.

The rationale behind the explosion of such cities is based on the colonization of noncapitalist society, the proliferation of power, and the ascent of the middle class to ruling positions. All three developments took place through the elimination of moral and political society. They not only eliminated agrarian-village society and the migrant communities but also the material and immaterial culture of the traditional segments in the cities that served a positive function, including artists, craftspeople, intellectuals, and other laborers. The transition from city society to the city of the masses took place with the rural areas moving to the outskirts of cities, becoming more like tightly controlled colonies in the process. The state and capital monopoly devoured the city and the city devoured the rural areas. As for the society that is actually not a society, it has devoured the environment. As there is now no rural society, no environment, and no traditional city laborers or intellectuals to sustain the city, the situation is once again beyond crisis.

Like environmental disaster, a real societycide is closely associated with this cancerous city. Different scientific disciplines have concluded that having a large number of cities that a region, or even a country, cannot sustain deals deadly blows to the planet's ecological equilibrium. The indicators of this liquidation of society are the destruction of the moral and political fabric of society by the ruling middle class, with its cancerous growth, the proliferation of unemployed masses, and a growing multitude of irresponsible citizens.

d) The growing hegemonic power of the anti-economy monopolies has subordinated economic resources to the accumulation of profit and capital, moving society away from the objective of satisfying its basic needs. Contrary to popular belief, capitalism is not the most productive economic system but an anti-economy monopoly; the systemic economic depressions prove this. Despite all the theses developed by political economy to prove the opposite, the capitalist monopoly networks have transformed the economy from a system of production that meets basic human needs into a system that continuously procures accumulation of profit and capital incomparable to anything that preceded it in history. The developments in science and technology have the potential to meet basic human needs. The right economic administration combined with existing science and technology could meet these needs. But because this would endanger accumulation of profit and capital, the monopolies would block any and all attempts to make that possibility a reality, which necessarily makes these monopolies anti-economy bodies.

As a result, we should anticipate systemic and structural depression. To alleviate the economic depressions and crises that continuously manifest themselves (to a greater or lesser degree) through excess in or deficiency of production, reflected in unprecedentedly high levels of unemployment (seldom are unemployed slaves and serfs mentioned in historical accounts), poverty, hunger, wars, and conflicts, the traditional tools used to find solutions are augmented and extended to constitute a sort of crisis regime. The anti-economy positions adopted by the monopolies necessitate this crisis regime, as there is no other way to rule. To be perfectly clear, the nation-state administration is an extraordinary crisis regime. Preventing society from being itself and transforming it into a herd-like fascist mass is not a method unique to Hitler; it is integral to the nation-state's militaristic character. Because there is no other way to sustain the monopolist order, the nation-state, as the form of power that encapsulates society to the greatest degree possible and penetrates all its pores, must become the crisis regime. Creating a nation is a secondary objective. Nationalism, on the other hand, along with other ideological elements, is a sine qua non of this sort of administration.

Distinguishing between commercial, industrial, and financial depression is a common way of analyzing capitalist monopolies. In addition, the exaggerated phases of depression and prosperity are far from reflecting the essence of the system. Center-periphery, hegemony-competition, and the ups and downs of crises don't reflect the essence of the system. Of course, all of these factors play a role in the development of depressions. In particular, it is true that the hegemonic phase of financial monopoly is the period in which the crisis is most obvious. But unless we understand that the system is anti-economy, these facts will not seem particularly meaningful, something any analysis must take in to consideration.

e) The outbreak of ecological crisis during modernity is no coincidence. This crisis is related to the anti-economy nature of the system. It is structural. Biological equilibrium is essentially achieved through the symbiotic relationship between species. The biological element of universal intelligence has ensured this arrangement. Earlier, I defined life as the realization and development of diversity. Biological equilibrium is dependent on just such diversity. I also touched upon the link between the formation of diversity and the ability to be free and to choose. The micro-world (the smallest particles, packets of energy and matter) and the macro-world (astronomically large matter and energy islands) work in a similar system of equilibrium. The causal relationships that create diversity are not investigated here, and, for now, we shall have to be content with saying, "It is because they are." Perhaps we are incapable of grasping the truth because of our lack of knowledge and our misconceptions about science.

Human social nature is subject to this universal rule in its relationship with the environment. Humanity, with a nature that includes the most flexible intelligence, is the most advanced living species because of its ability to be free and to choose. This conflicts with the interests of capitalism's anti-economic monopolies, which transmute this symbiotic relationship into a relationship of maximum sovereignty, power, and domination within society, while transforming ecological ties into the domination and colonization of nature. Just as with killer algae or any other similar species, it dominates the whole environment and all of society, ultimately outgrowing them. It becomes a giant entity (a Leviathan). A system based solely on the accumulation of profit and capital cannot act otherwise. If it acts contrary to this and bases itself on a symbiotic relationship, then the law of profit breaks down, which would force a transformation of the system.

Contrary to popular belief, nature/the environment is in an equilibrium within its own system of logic. The idea of being at the mercy of blind forces is wrong. What has broken down this sensitivity is the civilization system, or, more specifically, today's domineering monopolist modernity. The cancerous growth of the middle class, which has become the ruling power, and the similar cancerous growth of its main living quarters—the cities—as well as a world under the sway of a chain of nation-states, are the real social causes of environmental destruction. This destruction is the result of fighting against the structures of social nature, which are laden with flexible intelligence, and transforming the symbiotic relationship with nature into one of domination and colonialism. This is why there is a very close link between social crises (better referred to as society-cides) and ecological crises. The crises experienced in both areas constantly feed one another. Monopoly profit inevitably leads to an increase in population, unemployment, hunger, and poverty, and to overcome this unemployment, hunger, and poverty, the growing population turns to the environment, destroying it in the process. The forest and the flora and fauna have never faced a greater threat.

Clearly this translates into more profit for the monopolies. As this cycle continues (e.g., the population reaches ten billion and continues to grow) the ability for the world to sustain itself will dissolve completely. This is how we will arrive at the much anticipated doomsday. Just as healthy growth and cancerous growth coexisting at the level of a cell in our bodies creates chaos that leads to cancer and death, in a similar way, the growth of monopoly profit inhibits a healthy growth at all levels of social nature, triggering cancerous social and environmental developments. Furthermore, medical evidence shows that the cancers suffered by humans are the result of these social cancers. The ability of the human species, the species with the highest level of flexible intelligence, to be free and make choices is probably no less than that of an ant. Have you ever seen an ant without a job? Why does unemployment plague humans, in spite of their current level of intelligence? If the law of profit were not observed, ecological adjustments alone would create sufficient job opportunities to eliminate all unemployment. Ecologically based employment would help rescue the environment and could end unemployment once and for all. There are hundreds of similar fields of employment, but because they are not suitable to the law of maximum profit, they are not considered options. The relationship between the system and ecological soundness is problematic and completely unsustainable.

f) Liberalism, the system's hegemonic ideology, cannot produce solutions, either in its classical or its neo-forms. *Liberalism*, a word related to *freedom*, is a concept that is strictly relative. What is freedom to one person or group is slavery for those who are at the opposite pole. The god-kings of antiquity, who had virtually unlimited freedom, created their opposite as the slave class. Freedom for the medieval aristocracy was made possible by the enslavement of broad masses of peasants and serfs. The bourgeoisie liberalism of the new age is closely intertwined with the minimum-wage slavery of the proletarian, semi-proletarian, and other laborers, who are the new slaves. While liberalism officially means freedom for all nation-state classes, for the citizens who are the modern slaves it actually means unemployment, unpaid labor, poverty, hunger, inequality, a lack of freedom, and the deprivation of democracy. We must understand that liberalism is not libertarianism in its true sense. Hegel regarded the state as the best means of achieving freedom. But, in the end, this freedom was reserved for the classes that controlled the state and the bureaucracy. Put another way, the maximum freedom for economic and power monopolies (the elites) means every type of slavery for the rest of us.

It is quite important to acknowledge liberalism as an ideology. To define it as individualism or libertarianism is inadequate. Liberalism, as a concept, came to the fore together with the famous *liberté, égalité, fraternité*: the concepts of *liberty, equality,* and *fraternity* of the French Revolution. As a central concept this has conservatism on its right, and first democrats and later socialists on its left. It took on a mild appearance arguing for change to the system (capitalist monopolism) through evolution rather than revolution. The conservatives were totally against progress either through evolution or revolution. They fanatically defended the monarchy, the family, and the church. Socialists and democrats thought that revolutions were necessary to expedite change. But they all shared modernity as a common denominator. They all may have had one objection or another, but at the end of the day they all thought they had ideas about modernization. You only needed to experience a transformation in the most general terms to become a modernist. The modern life, which was European-based, its foundations laid with urbanization and accelerated by the Renaissance, Reformation, and Enlightenment, represented the common horizon of the three main ideologies. The remaining issue was to determine which ideology and parties, which methodology and practices, which actions and wars, would best capture that horizon.

Liberalism understood the situation accurately. It grasped that modernity was developing with the stamp of capitalism and would continue to do so, and as a result it quickly and skillfully manipulated the ideologies and structures on both its right and its left, dividing itself into left- and right-wing liberalism. While right-wing liberalism neutralized the conservatives and turned them into one of its wings, left-wing liberalism partially positioned the democrats and socialists as its backup, this is how liberalism seized the central position. In each intensifying crisis it was able to position one or the other as backup for consolidating its position. The bourgeoisification of the aristocrats and the social democratization of a number of concessionist workers developed throughout crisis regime. Setting aside a modest share of monopoly profit was more than enough to achieve this. In this manner, not only were the opponents of the system in the nineteenth and twentieth centuries neutralized, but they were reduced to a permanent backup power for the management of the crisis-ridden system. This is how the ideological hegemony of liberalism was established.

Liberalism made use of four important ideological variants to maintain its ideological hegemony:

1) It used nationalism effectively. Nationalism was liberalism's number one ally, both in legitimizing internal and external wars and facilitating the state's nation building. It is effectively the first ring in an eclectic chain. Liberalism has gained much experience at overcoming the worst of crises by firing up nationalist sentiment. Nationalism was turned into a holy ideology akin to a religion. The cover that nationalism provided not only served to easily overcome crises, but it also provided monopolies with a way to cloak their most exploitative and corrupt systems.

2) The traditional religious ideology was rendered nationalistic. Under its hegemony, liberalism nationalized traditional religions draining them of their moral and political features. Or, more precisely, it turned them into national religions. Religious sentiments, deeply rooted and easily assuming a nationalist flavor, have played a similar, or maybe even more important, role in creating cohesion within society. Sometimes both ideologies have been intertwined in the attempt to build a nation on an ethnic-religious basis. Jewish and Islamic ideologies in particular easily identified themselves with nationalism. Other religions (Christianity, Far East religions, ancient religious traditions in Africa) would not waste much time catching up. Liberalism used religion to channel and integrate the immaterial cultural legacy into capitalist civilization, which had already inherited civilization's material culture.

The role of religious nationalist ideologies cannot be ignored in overcoming the unsustainable levels of systemic crisis.

3) The ideology of positivist scientism in particular made a strong contribution to liberalism as a philosophical variant. Positivist ideology benefited from the favorable reputation of the natural sciences and played a leading role in influencing both left-wing and right-wing ideologies. It is easily integrated into different ideologies as scientific label, leading to massive distortions. It particularly left its mark on the emerging left-wing ideologies, with real socialism leading the way. It was through positivist scientism that they all fell into the trap of capitalist modernism. Fascism, which drew all its power from positivist scientism, was the prominent current on the right. In this manner, positivism offered a range of ideological options to liberalism from the extreme left to the extreme right. Liberalism draws upon left-wing and right-wing options as required, always and everywhere making maximum use of them to overcome the structural crises of the system.

4) It is during the age of liberalism that sexism has been ideologically developed to the highest degree and been most frequently used. Liberalism, which took over a sexist society, did not just settle for transforming women into an unpaid labor force. It got more out of turning them into commodities as sex objects and putting them on the market. While, with men, it was only their labor that was commodified, with women, their bodies and souls were entirely commodified. In fact, the most dangerous form of slavery was being constructed. Being disparaged as nothing more than "a wife to a husband" subjects a woman to limited exploitation, but having her whole personality commodified makes her a slave living in conditions worse than those of the pharaoh's slaves. Being opened up to being everyone's slave is much more dangerous than becoming the slave of a state or a particular individual. This is the trap that modernity set for women. It is made to appear that women have been opened up for freedom, when, in fact, they have been degraded into the most disreputable tools of exploitation. As a vehicle for advertising, sex, and pornography, women are the basic tool of exploitation. I can easily say that women carry the heaviest possible load for sustaining capitalism.

For the system, women play a strategic role in the reproduction of power and exploitation. Men, as the representatives of the state in the family, feel they have the responsibility and the authority to both exploit and control women. By expanding upon the traditional suppression of women, men are transformed into a component of the power apparatus. The society, in this way, embraces the syndrome of thinking it has become maximal power. Women's status gives male-dominant society an unlimited sense and thought of power. On the other hand, it is the women laborers, women themselves, who are made to pay the price for all of the negative developments—from the formation of concessionist workers to the unemployed, from unpaid laborers to minimum-wage workers. Liberalism's eclectic sexist ideology not only distorts the situation and reflects it differently, it also generates a number of elaborately developed ideological varieties for women. It is as if women are made to espouse their slavery voluntarily. It can be said that by exploiting women the system not only overcomes its most serious crisis, it also procures and secures its existence. Women are both the oldest and the most recent colonized nation in the overall history of civilization, and in capitalist modernity in particular. If there is an unsustainable crisis in all respects, the key reason is the colonization of women.

The current world capitalist system under the hegemony of global financial monopolies experiences not only general systemic depression but also crises that are specific to finance. The general systemic depression (because it is anti-economy) is intertwined with crises specific to the area of finance (money detached from gold, even from the dollar itself, represented by various virtual arguments, such as bonds and shares), which is at its weakest point in history. The system has generally overcome its depressions in one of two ways: by continuously reproducing its power and expanding the nation-state's repressive apparatus—all sorts of wars, prisons, mental hospitals, hospitals, torture chambers, and ghettos—accompanied by the most dangerous genocide and societycide or by the apparatuses of the liberal ideological hegemony, which continuously develop by integrating new factors. Liberalism is the ideological core that integrates nationalism, religiosity, scientism, and sexism. Its tools are schools, barracks, place of worships, the media, universities, and, most recently, internet platforms. We could also add the arts, which have been turned into a cultural industry.

Even the most ordinary of scientists would agree that both of these approaches are the development of a crisis regime not of a way to find solutions. Depressions and crises cannot be overcome as they were in the past. On the contrary, the depressions and crises that were once exceptional have become generalized and stable, while "normal" periods have become the exception. Although elements of crisis lie at the base of civilization systems, human society had never witnessed such severe crisis. Societies, if they are to survive, cannot endure this sort of crisis regime for very long. They will either go into decline and disintegrate or resist and develop new systems, thereby overcoming the crisis. We are in just such a period.

The State of Anti-System Forces

The concept of being anti-system is quite problematic. First of all, does this opposition also mean being anti-civilization? Which aspects does it include or exclude? How does it view the system's relationship with modernity? Is it possible to construct a new system outside of the existing system without opposing the system's modernity? How does this opposition see modernity? Has it been able to identify its dual character? Does it have an understanding of alternative modernity? Failing to answer such questions leaves the concept of anti-system forces up in the air. It is difficult to develop a meaningful opposition to the system without both projects for the future and a correct analysis of the past. To overcome these difficulties and arrive at potential answers to these questions, I based my analysis on the concepts of democratic civilization and democratic modernity. I think this is the correct method in the quest for an alternative that will not fall into the previous vicious circles.

Despite their problematic structure, anti-system forces are a reality. They have affected our age as much as the system has. They have been unable to realize their systems theoretically or practically, but it is indisputable that they have accumulated a great deal of experience. While there are important differences across the spectrum of anti-system forces, they also clearly share many common values.

They mean capitalism when they speak of the system, not necessarily modernity as a whole. They particularly differ when it comes to industrialism and the nation-state, the other two dimensions of modernity. They are unclear when it comes to civilization. With their convoluted views, they often take their place at opposite poles. It is not often that their future utopias go beyond modernity. In short, they are not attempting to go beyond modernity but to improve it. For most of them, modernity without capitalism would suffice, and they fail to understand that this is entirely utopic.

They usually agree about the system and that it is in a crisis, but when it comes to how to move beyond the crisis, the differences between them grow. Many methods from evolutionary to revolutionary, from peaceful to bellicose, are proposed. There are those who think that changing the state and rulers is a revolution and those who propose a society with no state or power structure. They all essentially have their roots in the French Revolution. Their mindset offers a broad perspective, from nationalism to communism, from religiosity to positivism, and from feminism to ecology. Although they are heavily intertwined with these ideologies they do not seem to realize it. If a generalization were to be made, it could be said that in terms of their social status they are based on the main part of the middle class that is outside the capital and power monopolies. These movements, which include intellectuals who have received a certain modern education and who face increasing difficulties opposing capitalism, do not embody the majority of society. If roughly 10 percent of the population has an active interest in the continuation of capitalism, approximately the same percent oppose it. The remaining 80 percent of society, the non-capitalist society, is an object not a subject in the analyses of both sides and in the solutions they offer. While capitalism calculates the profit to be made when considering society, the opposition considers society to be a mass that can be externally driven, which is why they are unable to overcome modernity.

When we say that capitalist modernity as a system is under an unsustainable crisis regime, we are not talking about a new "revolutionary situation." The evaluation of similar situations as the objective conditions necessary for revolution has been misused in past discussions, with no conclusions that led to any meaningful success. The crisis regime is not the only result of the crisis, there may also be even harsher counterrevolutions. Perhaps the revolution has the worst chance. Moreover, the role of revolutions in transformation is generally exaggerated and usually wrongly analyzed. Fundamental transformations are not achieved by revolutions but from differences within the system. Revolutions can only lead to meaningful change within the system that they are part of. No doubt anti-system forces are severely affected by economic depressions and crises, but it would be an error to vest all hope in the outcome of these crises. In the past, this was a common mistake that resulted in profound disappointment.

The fact that within a century real socialism, social democracy, and national liberation movements were incorporated into capitalism had a profound negative effect on opponents of the system. Movements incurred a loss of power. This was the result of their structural inadequacies and a faulty ideological and programmatic perspective. When their mentalities and structures are examined, it is clear that they failed to genuinely overcome liberalism and modernity. Whether they are at the far left or far right of the liberal spectrum, liberalism eventually integrates them. Whether or not they are incorporated into capitalist monopolies depends on their understanding of modernity. Postmodern, radical religious, feminist, and ecological movements are new movements that have emerged in response to these developments. Their current ideological and practical positions make it doubtful that they will be as effective as the system's former opponents, which is why neoliberalism and radical religionism are able to be somewhat influential. Therefore, what we need is a radical intellectual, moral, and political renewal of opposition to the system. In this context, it is important, necessary, and useful to familiarize ourselves with the history of anti-system forces.

The Legacy of Real Socialism

Communism was one of the first movements to consciously react against the capitalist system. Its founders Karl Marx and Frederick Engels acknowledged trying to develop their counter-system on the basis of three primary sources: German philosophy, English political economy, and French utopian socialism. It would seem that they took their dialectical materialism from German philosophy, their value theory from English political economy, and the concept of class struggle from French utopian socialism. They developed a novel interpretation by synthesizing these three sources. Their very first foray into opposition occurred in the years 1840–1850, a period of serious capitalist crisis that had quite an effect on them, giving rise to the hope that the system could be immediately destroyed. At the time, Germany was struggling to maintain its national unity, while in France the republic had its own problems. England, for its part, was at its peak as the system's hegemonic power. The 1848 popular revolutions in Europe were seen as a sign that this hope would be fulfilled. Karl Marx and Frederick Engels's *Communist Manifesto* was intended as a general program for these revolutions.[3] Meanwhile, the Communist League was established as the first internationalist party or organization.

These two endeavors clearly indicate that they expected success and victory out of the crisis of capitalism and from the popular revolutionary movements.

When the revolutions were suppressed, Marx and Engels felt the need to examine capitalism in more depth. Karl Marx went into exile in London, settling in the *kaaba* of capitalism,[4] where he had regular contact with Frederick Engels. The First International of 1864 was the product of this period. An equally important development at the time was a realization that the revolution might well be delayed, making more protracted evolutionary work necessary, for which unions and parliamentary work might be suitable. Although the 1871 Paris Commune renewed their hopes, the rapid suppression of the uprising led them to increasingly focus on issues like dictatorship, power, and the state. Taking a pro-centralized nation-state position led to opposition from the anarchists, giving rise to the first discussions about revisionism.

The Second International was established in 1889 under a shadow of national chauvinism. Vladimir Lenin, in his work *The Proletarian Revolution and the Renegade Kautsky,*[5] would call what was experienced during that period "revisionism" and blame the Sozialdemokratische Partei Deutschlands (SPD: Social Democratic Party of Germany—the original party under Eduard Bernstein) for leading this revisionism. The Russian October Revolution again strengthened hopes that communist utopia could be realized (achieving what the Paris Commune could not). This revolution resulted in worldwide developments. Supporting the Anatolian Turkish-Kurdish national liberation movement was an initial contribution to the successful development of the age of national liberation. The early death of Lenin, the period of "the struggle against liquidationism," the socialist construction, the anti-fascist struggle during World War II, the Warsaw Pact established in opposition to NATO during the Cold War, the work done on space travel, the economic competition with capitalism, and the widespread support for national liberation movements were all key developments.

The Third International was formed in 1919, but like the Second International it experienced internal liquidation because of an impasse around the issue of the nation-state. Soviet Russia would, however, effectively play a role as the new candidate for hegemony, influencing one-third of the planet. Soviet Russia would ultimately leave the socialist movements within various nation-states to their own fates and take the same revisionist path as the German SPD, setting the Communist Party of the Soviet Union on the road to capitalism. On the other hand, the short-lived Chinese (period under Mao from 1960 to 1976) and Albanian resistances failed to produce any results. The speedy integration of the national liberation movements and the syndicalist workers' movements into the capitalist system, followed by China's official renunciation of real socialism in the 1980s, with Russia and its allies following suit in the 1990s, brought the era to a close.

The two hundred years of experience (if we take the French Revolution as the starting point) that led to these movements called real socialist allows us to evaluate them:

1) They seemed to primarily oppose private monopolies without criticizing state capitalism, either in terms of power or capital monopoly, leading to a shallow analysis of power and the state. These movements had a profound faith in their capacity to build socialism if they could take over the state and become the ruling power. Nothing else occurred to them. They even interpreted democracy as the dictatorship of one of two classes (the bourgeoisie or the proletariat). They developed a very narrow analysis of capitalism as a result of their reliance on English political economy.

2) They seemed to be unaware of the class basis of modernity or, at least, see no reason to analyze it. And when they did the result was an entirely right-wing deviation. They were not able to extend capitalism, the first pillar of modernity, beyond boss-laborer, profit-wages, and value-surplus value dichotomies to see that capitalism was a mode of accumulation that has existed since the Sumerians. They did not regard the three hundred years of capitalism of the Italian cities as the beginning of the system but treated the emergence of capitalism in sixteenth-century England and Netherlands as a sort of beginning of history. Industrialism, the second pillar of modernity, was praised. Its qualitative link with capitalism and later related drawbacks were not criticized. On the contrary, it was treated as a savior. By regarding the nation-state, the third pillar, to be a step forward, they left the door ajar for subsequent national and social chauvinism. Instead of confederalism, they preferred the centralized nation-state. Just like the

traditional historians of civilization, they couldn't help but evaluate the flip side of modernity as "backward, dormant, barbaric, reactionary movements reversing the wheels of history."

3) By ideologically accepting the most vulgar materialist form of positivism as scientific, they made a historical mistake in this field too. They treated the socialism they built as scientific in the same way as the revolutions of Darwin and Newton in the areas of biology and physics. Their sociological approach never got beyond a vulgar Darwinism. They did not feel the need to determine the qualitative differences of social nature, instead they believed that they were subject to the same laws of nature as first nature, opening the door to rigid determinism. During the subsequent development phase, their followers took advantage of this opening to equate even the most vulgar of interpretations with rigid scientific facts.

4) They did not analyze power in general or the nation-state in particular, and they regarded the nation-state as composed of commissions that manage the affairs of the bourgeoisie. The most important shortcoming of their theory was the inability to figure out that power, in particular the nation-state, was the most concentrated form of monopolistic capitalism. Their analysis amounted to nothing but an affirmation of the nation-state. They were sure that socialism could be best built by a nation-state. Not only were they unable to surpass Hegel's analysis of the state, they were certain that if they were able to seize the state they could use it to make all kinds of adjustments and establish freedom and equality. The relationship between socialism and democracy is one of the major issues that they addressed most superficially and incorrectly. The Russian and Chinese Revolutions developed using this approach. Other national liberation and social democratic applications of power failed to produce anything different. The only thing that distinguished them from private capitalism was their preference for state capitalism, as their use of power clearly shows.

5) Their critique of civilization is even shallower and more insignificant. They did not acknowledge that the capitalist civilization phase is part of historical civilization, the last link in the main chain. They did not feel the need to determine the character of

power that had the nature of historical cumulative accumulation. They did not think that their system could easily become a similar kind of power and civilization. Instead of grasping that power is accumulated capital, filth, war, lies, ugliness, and torture, they tried to develop theories about how it could be used to achieve historical progress. History has proven that they were unwarranted and wrong in their views.

6) They did not feel the need to analyze the anti-civilizational forces that are the second pole of the historical dialectic they appear to be attached to. Their comments in relation to these forces are generally negative. In contrast, they have not failed to praise the progressive nature of capitalist colonialism in America, Asia, and Africa, accusing their opponents of defending the former societies. The fact that they were not able to see that the opposite pole of civilization had great significance, democratic tradition, resistance, and freedom, and that it had pursued equality and justice, and experienced communality is closely related to their bourgeois and petite bourgeois class realities. They cannot see this, because those coming from such classes do not have the eyes to see these realities.

7) A positivist universalist, linear-progressive methodological approach to social nature led to a conception of socialism as inevitable and just a matter of time. The eschatology of the holy books was in a way reflected as socialism. Societies were depicted as models that developed linearly, from primitive society to slave-owning through feudalism to capitalism, finally arriving at socialism. Here, a sort of fatalism is at play. At the root of these dogmatic conceptions, which have profoundly affected all of us, was a religious fatalism and the belief in the apocalypse. An understanding of this came too late. They were unable to see that social nature essentially has a moral and political character, and that civilization systems eroded these features, replacing them with vulgar rules of law and state administration. That capitalist modernity developed this process to an unlimited depth and breadth, resulting in an economic and social crisis, as well as a crisis of power and the state. They did not foresee that what is right, good, and beautiful is a democratic confederal system that completely

ensures the moral and political character of society and, to this
end, moves forward on the basis of democratic politics. No such
analysis or solution developed. They were unable to understand
that a free, equal, and democratic society could not be established
by power and state apparatuses, and that, on the contrary, they
were in contradiction with such apparatuses. Thus, they were
unable to develop a theory and practice for coexisting alongside
capitalist modernity on the basis of a principled peace and the
acceptance of one another's existence. When revolution-power-
socialism is accepted as the fundamental paradigm it should come
as no surprise that nothing but state capitalism is possible.

Another reason that the real socialist movement ended in
state capitalism relates to its class base. I must reemphasize that
the bourgeoisie and petite bourgeoisie, as well as the bureaucracy that largely comes from these classes, failed to find what
they hoped for in private monopolies, were unable to accumulate
capital, and, in fact, depleted what they had. Thus, the only option
was to use the state to become a collective capitalist. The national
bourgeoisie and national capitalism are nothing but this. They
thus acquire a very strong position as a collective monopoly based
on state capitalism, or, otherwise stated, a nation-state. This is
why the nation-statism of real socialism is so much more powerful than in other nation-states. This material basis also explains
why they could easily reconcile with and integrate into modernity.

8) Feminist, ecological, and cultural movements have been seen as
an obstacle to the class struggle. The extreme colonization that
women have experienced not only in terms of labor but also all
of their bodies and souls has not been seriously analyzed. In
trying to resolve these questions real socialism failed to surpass
the equality standards of bourgeois law. These laborers, who are
both the oldest and the newest, as well as the most often unpaid or,
at best, minimally paid laborers, in keeping with male-dominant
history, are nothing but objects. It is clear that the class that is
being analyzed is the male. Ecology was approached similarly.
Not only were such problems not foreseen, they were thought to
have a negative effect on the totality of the class struggle. Cultural
movements, for their part, were seen as the revival of something

old and, therefore, as something else that disrupted the class struggle. The end result was an abstract class ideology detached from all possible allies and suffocated by economism.

9) Class division was not seen as a negative development in moral and political terms; instead it was evaluated as good, progressive, a necessity for freedom, and an inevitable stage. That to accept class divisions is to objectively be in the service of power and the state classes was not grasped. Slavery, serfdom, and being a proletarian were interpreted as the price to be paid for historical progress and freedom from nature. However, we can assert that, to the contrary, all three class divisions are essentially the same and have nothing to do with progress or freedom. Moral and political society cannot coexist with these class divisions, and we must wage a moral, political, and intellectual struggle against them.

We cannot say that the current successors to the two hundred years of the real socialist movement have undergone a radical transformation, although there has been limited self-criticism. They are, however, going through a major crisis of confidence and have been weakened. Still, it is a movement with its place in history. Although it was unable to surpass the capitalist system, it deeply troubled it. It played a role that was both positive and negative in getting us to where we are now. Its crisis is part of the system's structural crisis. Nonetheless, it is important to acknowledge real socialism as the phase that most influenced all opponents of the system and, with the lessons of its legacy taken into consideration, it would be the right approach to see it as part of building democratic modernity and to relate to it thusly and form alliances with it in that light.

Reevaluating Anarchism
Anarchist movements that have their roots in the French Revolution and appeared at the same time as real socialism deserve to be reevaluated in the wake of the dissolution of real socialism, or, rather, its integration into the system. It is better understood today that the criticism made by anarchism's famous representatives, including Pierre-Joseph Proudhon, Mikhail Bakunin, and Pyotr Kropotkin, against both the system and real socialism were not entirely unjustified. As a movement that criticizes capitalism not only as a private and state monopoly but also as modernity, they stand out by taking their place at the opposite end of the system. The

anarchist critique of power, both from moral and political perspectives, was accurate to a significant degree, but the effects of social structures they came from are evident in their movement. The class reactions of the aristocratic sections that had been removed from power by capitalism and city artisans, who found themselves far worse off than they had been, projected this reality. The fact that anarchists have been unable to develop a strong base, have remained individuals, and were unable to develop an opposing system is closely linked to their social structures. They understand very well what capitalism is doing, but they do not have a very clear idea of what they need to do. To summarize their views:

a) They criticize the capitalist system from the extreme left. They understand better that this system dismantles moral and political society, and, unlike Marxists, they do not attribute a progressive role to capitalism. Their approach to the societies that have been dismantled by capitalism is more positive. They do not see such societies as reactionary and doomed to decay but instead consider their survival moral and political.

b) Anarchism's approach to power and the state is much more comprehensive and realistic than that of the Marxists. Bakunin, for example, argues that power is absolute evil. But the demand that power and the state be abolished immediately and at all costs is utopian and does not have much of a chance of being realized. Anarchists were, however, able to foresee that you can't use power and the state to build socialism, and that if you did you would perhaps end up with an even more dangerous bureaucratic capitalism.

c) The prediction that building a centralized nation-state would be a disaster for all of the working-class and popular movements and a major blow to their hopes proved realistic. The anarchists were also quite right in their criticism of the Marxists in relation to German and Italian unity. They have also asserted that the development of history in favor of the nation-state was a huge loss for any utopian vision of equality and freedom, and they strongly criticized the Marxists' pro-nation-state stance, accusing them of treason. The anarchists, for their part, argued for confederalism.

d) Anarchist views and criticisms of bureaucratization, industrialism, and urbanization have also been largely confirmed and played an important role in the anarchist movement developing an anti-fascist and ecological attitude early on.

e) The anarchist critique of real socialism has been confirmed by the dissolution of the real socialist system. Anarchists were best at identifying the fact that what had been established was not social-ism but bureaucratic state capitalism.

Despite these important and confirmed views and criticisms, the fact that the anarchist movement has failed to become a mass movement like real socialism and has never had the chance to implement its idea is worthy of reflection. I believe that this is due to a serious deficiency and flaw in anarchist theory related to the weakness of its analysis of civili-zation and an inability to develop an implementable system. They have neither developed a suitable analysis of historical-society nor proposed any solutions. Moreover, they too have been influenced by positivist phi-losophy, and it would be wrong to suggest that they have overcome the Eurocentric social sciences. Their most important flaw, however, is that they lack systematic thought about democratic politics and modernity and the related structures. The rigor they showed in developing correct views and criticisms was, unfortunately, not replicated in systematizing and implementing their ideas. It was perhaps their class backgrounds that hampered this. Another important obstacle was their opposition to any type of authority, both theoretically and in their day to day lives. They dis-placed their rightful reaction to power and state authority onto all forms of authority and order. This affected their ability to develop democratic modernity theoretically and in practice. I believe that the most important point for anarchist self-criticism would be the inability to see the legiti-macy of democratic authority and the need for democratic modernity. In addition, the fact that they have been unable to develop the option of democratic nation in place of nation-state is an important deficiency that also deserves some self-critical reflection.

The dissolution of real socialism, the development of ecological and feminist movements, and a general surge in civil society sentiment have no doubt had a positive impact on anarchists. But sitting around talking about having been right is pointless. The question they need to answer is why they were unable to develop or build an ambitious system that reflected their goals, a question that draws attention to the chasm between their theory and their lives. Have they really overcome the modern life they criticize so much? More precisely, how consistent are they in this regard? Can they leave behind a Eurocentric way of life and truly step into global democratic modernity?

It is possible to multiply similar questions and criticisms. What is important, however, is that this movement, which has made huge sacrifices, has important thinkers, whose views and criticisms are respected within the intellectual community, and a legacy that can be brought together in a consistent system that is open to development and opposed to the existing system. Anarchists are more likely to engage in practice informed by self-criticism than are real socialists. Taking their rightful place within economic, social, political, intellectual, and ethical struggles could prove significant. It is possible for anarchists to both renew themselves and make a strong contribution to the struggles that have hastened in the Middle East and whose dimensions of culture and civilization have become more prominent. They are an important ally in the rebuilding of democratic modernity.

Feminism: Rebellion of the Oldest Colony

The term *feminism* translated as *movement for women* by no means fully address the women's question and could potentially lead to an even greater impasse, because it makes it possible to conceive "masculinism" as its opposite. It suggests the meaning that she is merely the oppressed woman of the dominant man. Yet women's reality is more comprehensive than that and includes other meanings beyond gender with far-reaching economic, social, and political dimensions. If we do not limit our understanding of colonialism to countries and nations but include all human groups, we can easily define women as the oldest colony. No other social phenomenon has experienced colonization of the body and the soul to the degree that women have. We must understand that women are kept in a colonial state, the boundaries of which cannot be easily determined.

The masculine discourse has left its mark on the social sciences, like it has on all the sciences. The lines that refer to women are laden with nothing but propaganda that fails to come close to reality. This discourse repeatedly conceals the real status of women, just as the historiographies of civilization conceal class, exploitation, oppression, and torture. Instead of feminism, perhaps the concept of jineolojî (science of women) might better meet the purpose.[6] I am certain that the facts that jineolojî reveals will be no less true than those of theology, eschatology, politology, pedagogy, sociology, and all the other *ogies* that deal with many areas of the social sciences. It is beyond dispute that women represent the greatest part of social nature, both physically and in terms of meaning. That being the case, why is this very important part of social nature not the subject of science? That sociology, which has been divided into multiple branches, including, for example, pedagogy for the education and upbringing of children, has not developed jineolojî is best explained by the male-dominated discourse underlying it.

So long as the nature of women remains in the dark, it will be impossible to illuminate social nature as a whole. A genuine and comprehensive illumination of social nature is only possible through a realistic and far-reaching elucidation of the nature of women. Revealing the status of women that includes the history of their colonization and encompasses the economic, social, political, and intellectual aspects of this colonization would greatly contribute to the enlightenment of other historical issues and all aspects of contemporary society.

No doubt revealing the status of women is one dimension of the issue, but the more important dimension is related to the question of liberation. Put another way, the solution of the problem is of greater importance. It is often said that the general level of freedom in a society is directly proportional to the level of the freedom of women.[7] How we go about adding content to this fundamentally correct statement is extremely important. Women's freedom and equality are not merely measures of social freedom and equality. They also require a corresponding theory, program, and organization, as well as mechanisms of action. More importantly, this also shows that there can be no democratic politics without women, that even class politics would be inadequate, and that peace cannot be developed and the environment cannot be protected.

We need to remove the status of "the holy mother," of "fundamental honor," and of "indispensable partner" from women and explore the reality of women as the subject-object sum. Of course, such research should first be cleared of the buffoonery of love. In fact, the most important dimension of this research should be to expose the huge villainy (in particular rape, murder, beatings, and endless insults) disguised by the term *love*. Herodotus's saying that all wars between the East and the West were fought because of women can only mean one thing: women have gained value as a colony and thus becomes the object of major wars.[8] While this is the case in the history of civilization, capitalist modernity represents a colonization of women that is a thousand times worse and more complex; inscribing colonialism into the identity of women. Their colonization takes many forms, and the list is long; they are the mothers of all labor, unpaid laborers, minimally paid workers, the most frequently unemployed, the target of men's boundless appetite and oppression, the system's birthing machines and nannies, a means of advertising, and a means of sex and pornography. Capitalism has developed a mechanism of exploitation in relation to women that surpasses all other mechanisms of exploitation. We wish it were otherwise, and we could avoid returning to the status of women, because it causes us pain, but the facts have a language of their own, and they cannot be otherwise for the exploited.

In this light, the feminist movement undoubtedly must be the most radical anti-system movement. The women's movement, whose contemporary form can be traced back to the French Revolution, has developed through various phases into what it is today. In the first phase, the movement pursued equality under the law. This equality, which does not mean much, seems to have been widely attained today, but we must be aware that it is hollow inside. There were formal developments in terms of rights, including human rights and economic, social, and political rights. Women appear to be free and equal to men. But the most significant fraud is hidden in this sort of equality and freedom. It is not only official modernity but the entire hierarchical and statist civilization system that has infiltrated the social fabric and imprisoned women both physically and mentally, condemning them to the most profound slavery, essentially reducing them to slave labor. Therefore, the freedom, equality, and democracy of women require extensive theoretical efforts, ideological struggles, programmatic and organizational activities, and, most importantly, strong action. Without this, feminism and women's studies can have no meaning beyond the liberal women's activities that are only intended to relieve the pressure on the system.

I hope to show with an example how the problems could be better solved were a science of woman to be developed. Sexual instinct is one of the earliest forms of learning in life. This instinct is an answer to life's need to continue. The fact that an individual cannot live infinitely forced the development of the potential to reproduce the *one* as a solution. What is called the sexual instinct is the continuation of life by using this potential for reproduction when favorable conditions occur. This, in a way, is a remedy to a certain extent to the danger of death and extinction of the species. The first cell division, the cell—the one—makes itself immortal through reproduction. If we generalize even further, it is the tendency of the universe to become eternal by constant variation and reproduction to confront the void and nothingness that wants to devour it and the continuation of this tendency in the living.

Within the human species, the one or the individual where this universal process takes place is more likely to be a woman. Reproduction takes place in women's bodies. Men's role is entirely secondary in this process. It is therefore scientifically understandable that the entire responsibility for the continuation of the family rests with the woman. Moreover, women not only carry the fetus, nurture its growth, and give birth to the child, but they are, of course, also responsible for caring for the child, a responsibility that lasts most of their lives. Therefore, the first conclusion we should draw is that women must have absolute decision-making power about all sexual acts, because for the woman all sexual intercourse involves potential problems that are very difficult to overcome. We must understand that a woman who gives birth to ten children will find herself in physical and emotional situations that are worse than death.

Men's view of sexuality is more distorted and irresponsible, largely because of ignorance and the blindness that comes with power. In addition, during the hierarchical period and the dynastic state having many children meant indispensable strength for a man. It not only meant the continuation of the lineage but also guaranteed that he would continue to exist as power and the state. In a way, not losing the state, which is a kind of a monopoly over property, depends on the size of the dynasty. Women, in this manner, are transformed into instruments for giving birth to many children for both biological existence and the existence of power and the state. This is how the ground is prepared for the terrible colonization of women in connection with both first and second nature. Accordingly, it is of utmost importance to analyze the decline of women in connection with both of these natures. There is no need to further explain that under this status of both natures it is not possible for women to maintain herself both physically or psychologically for very long or to escape unscathed. Physical and psychological decline develop in an intertwined way early on, causing to have a shortened life full of pain and grief in return for sustaining and securing the lives of others. It is very important to analyze and understand the history of civilization and modernity on this basis.

Let's leave aside the severity of the problem from a woman's point of view. Another dimension of the problem is the excessive growth of the population. The policy of having many children has severe impact on social nature and the ecological environment as a whole as a result of this population increase. One of the fundamental lessons that both the science of women and all social sciences must learn from this is that the human population cannot be maintained, reproduced, or, in rare cases, decreased by an "instinctive learning" method. The main reason for the extreme population growth is that instinct, a very primitive method of maintaining the lineage, is supported by scientific methods developed throughout the history of civilization and modernity. To maintain the human species as a social nature only by instinct, particularly sexual instinct, is extremely backward. Intelligence and our cultural level offer a potential for learning that would be able to sustain social existences in a more advanced manner. Individuals and communities could potentially use their intelligence and cultures, as well as their philosophical and political institutions, to stay alive for a very long time. Therefore, continuation and reproduction of the lineage by way of sexual instinct no longer makes sense. Human culture and intelligence has long since overcome this method. Therefore, it is the profit principle of civilization and modernity that is primarily responsible for this primitiveness. No doubt extreme population growth means extreme monopoly and extreme power, which in turn means maximum profit. The extreme growth of the human species throughout history has not only brought society but also the environment and nature to the brink of destruction. This is most definitely a consequence of the cumulative accumulation of capital and power and, therefore, the law of maximum profit. All other factors are secondary and incidental.

Therefore, the responsibility for solving the demographic problem, which is essential to resolving the women's question in its gigantic dimensions and preventing ecological destruction, should in principle lie with women. The first condition for this is complete freedom and equality for women, their complete right to engage in democratic politics, and the right to have a complete say and absolute free will concerning all matters relating to gender relations, otherwise, the complete liberation, freedom, and equality for women, society, and the environment will not be possible, nor would democratic and confederative forms of politics.

As a fundamental component of moral and political society, women play a crucial role in the formation of an ethics and esthetics of life that reflect freedom, equality, and democratization. The science of ethics and esthetics is an integral part of the science of woman. Due to their heavy responsibilities in life, women will undoubtedly be both the driving intellectual and implementing force behind breakthroughs and progress in all ethical and esthetic matters. Because of their advanced level of emotional intelligence, women's bond with life is a lot more comprehensive than men's. Therefore, esthetics in the sense of beautifying life is an existential matter for women. Women bear a more encompassing responsibility when it comes to ethics (ethics = the theory of morality, esthetics = the theory of beauty). It is in women's nature to behave more realistically and responsibly in the sense of moral and political society when evaluating, determining, and deciding upon the good and bad aspects of human education, norms of fairness and justice, the importance of life and peace, and the evil and horrors of war. Of course, I am not referring to the women who are men's puppets or shadows. The women in question are the ones who are free and equal and who have absorbed democratization.

It would also be more useful to develop the science of economics as a component of the science of women. From the very beginning, the economy has been a form of social activity in which women played an essential role. The economy is of crucial importance to women, since the question of children's nutrition rests on women's shoulders. In fact, *economy* in Greek means *law of the house and the rules for the maintenance of the house*. Obviously, this is woman's main occupation. Taking the economy out of women's hands and putting it into the hands of usurers, merchants, capitalists, power, the state and its agents who act like lords (agas) was the greatest blow to economic life. The economy that has been handed over to anti-economy forces has rapidly been turned into the main target of power and militarism and, thus, has been transformed into the main factor behind an unlimited number of wars, conflicts, and struggles throughout the history of civilization and modernity. Today, the economy has been turned into the playground of people who have nothing to do with the economy and who by playing games with their scraps of paper, using methods that are worse than gambling, usurp innumerable social value. The economy, the sacred occupation of women, has been turned into an area they have been completely pushed out of, that has been handed over to factories where war machines, vehicles that make environment inhabitable, and unnecessary products that bring profit but have little to do with meeting essential human needs are produced and where prices and interest rates are manipulated on stock exchanges.

The women's movement for democratic freedom and equality, including feminism, based on the science of women, will clearly play a leading role in solving social problems. The women's movement should not be content with the criticism of the women's movements of the recent past alone but must rather focus on the history of civilization and modernity, which have rendered women a lost identity. If the women's question and the women's movements go almost unaddressed in the social sciences, it is the hegemonic mentality of civilization and modernity, as well as the structures of their material culture, that bear the greatest responsibility. We might contribute to liberalism with limited legal and political approaches to equality, but with such approaches we will not even be able to analyze the women's question as a phenomenon, let alone solve the problem. To claim that the existing feminist movements have detached themselves from liberalism and become anti-state forces would be self-deception. If, as it is said, one of the main problems of feminism is around radicalism, then it must first break with deep-seated liberal habits, ways of thinking and feeling, as well as the corresponding life, and rethink the misogynous civilization and modernity underlying all this, and on this basis set out on meaningful paths to finding solutions.

Democratic modernity must regard the nature of women and their freedom movement as one of its fundamental forces and prioritize both developing it, allying with it, and involving it in the work of reconstruction.

Ecology: The Rebellion of the Environment

One of the main problems caused by the civilization system is the destruction of the critical equilibrium of society and the environment. Social nature has always lived in harmony with the environment and has maintained this critical equilibrium during the long period of its existence and development. The fact that we do not see deviations in spontaneous development that could profoundly change this equilibrium is part of natural development. Essentially, systems tend to develop by mutual nurturing rather than by destroying one another. When deviations do occur, they must be overcome according to the logic of the system. In this sense, civilization is a deviation in the system of social nature. The very expression, civilization system, is nothing more than propaganda, this term was invented to replace the real system of social nature. While those who actually are the system have been called barbarians, nomads, and marginal groups, the networks parasitically feeding on social value came to be labeled the "civilization system." No matter how you view it: wars, pillage, destruction, massacres, monopolies, tributes, and taxes are the main features of the development of civilization and deserve to be regarded as the real barbarism. The constant destruction and burning down of villages and towns, the murder of millions of people, and the subjugation of the vast majority of the society under a system of exploitation cannot be described as the natural necessity of the system of social nature and can only be regarded as an anomaly.

The five-thousand-year history of civilization is also the history of the development and growth of this anomaly. The eruption of ecological disasters during the age of capitalism—seen as the most advanced age of civilization—is irrefutable proof of this anomaly. Social nature did not cause similar disasters over the course of its approximately three million years of existence. Society and the environmental system nurtured one another. The ecological crises that erupted during the short history of civilization are the result of its destructive profit-oriented essence. Not only capitalist profit but all of the extreme accumulation of value has gone hand in hand with the destruction of both natures in all civilization phases. The pyramids are an example of this accumulation. The price paid in social destruction for this can to some degree be imagined. An abundance of similar forms of accumulation constantly placed additional burden on the environment. Social collapse brought with it environmental collapse. The structures of capitalist modernity based on unlimited monopolist profit took on such proportions that the equilibrium between society and the environment could not endure. As a result, we have entered "the age of ecological crisis." The strategic role of industrialism, with fossil-fuel based industrialization and modernism as the main factors, were thus decisive. In addition, the use of fossil fuels in automobiles, indirectly leading to disasters through traffic accidents, along with other issues, result in a further chain reaction of destruction. Environmental disasters turn into social disasters and social disasters then exacerbate the environmental disasters in a reciprocating chain reaction. That is why it is wrong to call the capitalist age the age of reason. The accumulation is blind. We see before us the consequences of a blind accumulation that never corresponded to the rationality of environment and society. Analytically, this may be rational. In terms of emotional intelligence, which is the only intelligence relevant to the environment, it is sufficiently clear that ana-lytical intelligence is an intelligence of total blindness and destruction.

Based on previous analysis, we can say that extreme population growth and urban sprawl accelerated as the city and the middle class became the center of power, creating a situation that was more than the environment could endure, nor could social nature endure these develop-ments. Power and the state, which have grown intertwined in the process of capital accumulation, have reached a level of significance that prevents any society or environment from maintaining its equilibrium. The fact that environmental and social crises converge and become permanent is related to the monopolistic growth in both areas, both becoming crisis systems that reciprocally foster one another. All scientific data indicates that if this spiral continues for another fifty years the collapse will reach unsustainable dimensions. But because of their blind and destructive nature, capital and power monopolies cannot see or hear this; such is their nature.

The relatively new history of environmental science and environ-mental movements further develops with each passing day. What applies to women also applies to the environment: with the development of envi-ronmental science consciousness develops, and as consciousness develops so does the movement. It is the area where the civil society movement is broadest. It also attracts both real socialists and anarchists. It is the move-ment where the opposition to the system is most felt. Because it affects the whole community, participation has attained a transnational and cross-class character. Here too the impact of liberal ideological hegemony on the movement can be clearly seen. As with all social issues, liberalism ignores the structural core of the problem in the ecological area and tries to shift the responsibility onto technology, fossil fuels, and consumer society. But all these are side effects that are the product of the system (or lack thereof) of modernity. Therefore, the ecological movement, like the feminist move-ment, urgently needs ideological clarity. It needs to shift its organization and activism out of narrow city alleys and into the whole of society, in par-ticular into the agrarian-village communities in the rural areas. Ecology is the fundamental guide to action for the rural areas, agrarian-village communities, all nomads, the unemployed, and women.

These factors constitute the basis of democratic modernity and show perfectly clearly the important role ecology will play in the work of reconstruction.

Cultural Movements: Tradition's Revenge on the Nation-State

Throughout the entire period of civilization, there has never been a lack of cultural movements. The reason they are often mentioned during the post-modern period is related to the dissolution of nation-state borders. It would also be appropriate to call these cultural movements the rebellion of tradition. During the process in which the nation-state—the nation based on a dominant ethnicity, religion, denomination, or some other group phenomenon—tried to homogenize the society, many traditions and cultures were eliminated by genocide or assimilation. Thousands of tribes, aşirets, and peoples, along with their languages, dialects, and cultures were brought to the brink of extinction. Many religions, beliefs, and sects were banned, folklore and traditions were assimilated, and those that could not be assimilated were forced to emigrate, resulting in marginalization and the fragmentation of their cohesion. All historical entities, cultures, and traditions were sacrificed to a meaningless nationalism in the context of historical-society, based on "one language, one flag, one nation, one fatherland, one state, one anthem, and one culture," ultimately serving to conceal the concentration of modernity's commercial, industrial, financial, and power monopolies as nation-states. This process continued for two hundred years at full speed and was perhaps the longest and most violent period of warfare in history. It caused the massive destruction of cultures and traditions that were thousands of years old. The highly organized monopolies driven by the greed for profit did not feel any pain at the loss of any sacred tradition or culture.

When some unsystematic movements, also called postmodern, pierced through modernity's "nation-state armor" or broke out of its "iron cage," these cultures and traditions, which were at the brink of extinction and mostly confined to a marginal existence, began to flourish and multiply once more, like flowers blossoming after rain in the dessert. While the collapse of real socialism had an important impact, the 1968 youth movement was the spark that ignited this development. In addition, all the currents and stages of all national liberation movements that resisted capitalist colonialism, which had not yet become a nation-state, also had an impact. In any case, traditions and cultures are resistance in and of themselves. They will either be destroyed or will survive, because their character is such that they do not know how to capitulate. At the next opportunity, their very nature requires that they resist even more vigorously. Nation-state fascism failed to take this reality into account. Suppressing them, even assimilating them, does not necessarily mean that they will cease to exist. The resistance of cultures is reminiscent of the flowers that blossom, piercing rocks to prove their existence, and this is evidenced by the fact that they continue to reach daylight by smashing through the concrete of modernity poured over them. Let's briefly break these movements down into several groups.

Ethnicity and Movements of the Democratic Nation

One of the main cultural movements that cannot be completely suppressed by the nation-state is the micronationalism of ethnic phenomena. They are different from nation-state nationalism, in that the democratic content predominates within them. Instead of pursuing a new state, their most important goal is to become a democratic political formation based on their own culture. The formation they strive for differs from regional or local autonomy. It is not limited to a specific space and denotes the unity and solidarity of those who share the same cultural identity, even if they do not live within the same borders. Protecting their existence in the face of a dominant ethnicity is another important goal.

Calling the movement, which is a step beyond the various oppressed ethnic groups or peoples, the Movement of the Democratic Nation is meaningful from a sociological point of view and is perfectly accurate. It is really difficult for an oppressed ethnic group to survive and maintain its existence. The movement of those whose cultures have similar languages and dialects, and who share the same geography and political borders must be characterized as the Movement of the Democratic Nation for several reasons. First, they do not aspire to a separate state but to a democratic political formation and governance. Living as democratic political formations under the umbrella of a single state has been a very common political form of existence throughout history. History has, in fact, seen an overwhelming number of political formations representing different cultural groups. The normal form of government allowed for the existence of different political formations within the borders of each state or empire. What was abnormal was either ignoring or suppressing these political formations. Assimilation, for its part, was a method that was hardly ever employed. The Roman, Byzantine, Ottoman, Persian-Sasanian, and Arab-Abbasid Empires considered the existence of hundreds of different political-administrative units as their raison d'étre—as long as these entities recognized the legitimacy of the emperor or the sultan, of course. A way of life that preserved their language, religion, folklore, and self-governance was the norm. But the nation-state monster (Leviathan) destroyed this order, also providing the basis for fascism. The outcome was a multitude of cultural and physical genocides.

Interpreting the right of oppressed ethnic groups or peoples to be a nation solely as the right to establish a nation-state was a major distortion and disaster on the part of both liberalism and real socialism. This situation was a consequence of fascist nationalism and totalitarianism. Not limiting a normal nation to borders but building it on the basis of culture and principles of democratic governance would have been the right and humane way to proceed and would have been in accordance with social nature. Historical facts also tend to indicate this. Monopolist capital's ambition to rapidly accumulate capital in pursuit of maximum profit was the most important factor blocking this path. The abnormal nation-state approach to being a nation became the norm, while the normal democratic approach of becoming a nation was increasingly seen as abnormal—or simply totally ignored. This is the great distortion.

As the various dead ends of the nation-state (world and regional wars, bloody national conflicts, obstruction of capital by national walls) became apparent, the normal way of becoming democratic nations became increasingly prominent. After World War II, what all of Europe essentially went through was the transformation from the nation-statism to democratic nationhood. The US has always managed to maintain itself as a nation of democratic nations. In spite of monopolism's many nation-statist distortions, in the USSR, nation-statism and democratic nationhood were intertwined. In India, there are strong tendencies toward democratic nationhood. In Africa and South America, these tendencies have always been predominant. The very few rigid nation-states were limited to specific geographic areas, in particular the Middle East, where they are now also rapidly disintegrating.

Second, if power-centered and statist nation-building was not to be the basis, then the option was either using some leftover institutions from the Middle Ages (agas, sheiks, sects, the heads of aşirets) and the generally collaborationist henchman administrations based mainly on family interests or developing democratic governance. The first path was the modernized version of the classic collaborator system well known in history. The second path, however, was the path that represented democratic modernity's real goal. The leadership of the resistance to the nation-state and its collaborators can only be democratic. And this is the soundest liberationist and egalitarian approach to democratic nationhood.

Third, the plural structure of cultures, languages, and dialects also called for a democratic nation. It contradicted the very essence of democratic nation to base itself on the dominance of the predominant ethnic group's language, dialect, or culture. The only option was to become a nation with many languages, cultures, and political formations. It is clear that this means a democratic nation. Of course, forming a single democratic nation out of several democratic nations is also an option. Developments of this sort are taking place in Spain, India, and the Republic of South Africa, which some people might not like, and even in Indonesia and a number of African countries. Even the US and the EU could in some way be defined as a nation of democratic nations. The Russian Federation is yet another similar important example.

Fourth, if the economic, social, political, intellectual, linguistic, religious, and cultural differences are to be more strongly protected, it is immediately obvious that this would be easiest in a democratic nation. If every difference is turned into separation, this will be to everyone's loss. "Unity in diversity" is ideal for all, and a democratic nation is its most suitable form. Such solution potential alone is sufficient to explain the enormous solution power of the democratic nation movement and the structural alternative it provides to the nation-state.

The nation-state, which is at an impasse, finds itself squeezed between the global movements of capital above and the grassroots urban, local, and regional autonomy movements, as well as democratic-nation and religious movements, below. The resulting chaos offers the opportunity for the emergence of new systems, of which we have already seen numerous examples.

While, on the one hand, liberalism tries to surpass and reconstruct the classical nation-state ideology, on the other hand, it takes pains to present this as taking place under the cloak of promoting democracy. The rigid proponents of nation-state fight with such a conservatism and backwardness that they leave the former conservatives far behind. These forces have, so to speak, become the true conservatives of our day. The representatives of religious ideologies, on the other hand, are in search of the traditional ummah.[9] It is highly probable that they will realize modernism in religious garb and establish a religion-based nation-state. Iran is an instructive example in this regard.

The option of democratic nationhood promises a future because of its high potential for solving the complicated ideological and structural problems that we currently face. In this respect, the path EU has taken is particularly impressive. It is quite important that democratic modernity, both ideologically and structurally, treats the option of the democratic nation as one of its fundamental dimensions. This approach would both contribute to civilization and offer an opportunity for liberation. The efforts to rebuild democratic modernity through the democratic nation offer the most promising projects for solving the fundamental problems of society and the environment.

Religious Cultural Movements: Revival of Religious Tradition
As in the case of ethnicity, we observe a revival of religious tradition, which modernity, and in particular the nation-state, tried to colonize with the concept of laicisim. Undoubtedly this is not a revival that brings it close to the function that religious tradition once had for society. Rather, this comeback is under the influence of official modernity, both in terms of its radical elements and its moderate wings. This comeback is one where many aspects of modernity have been absorbed. In fact, the issue is a little more complicated. Although laicism is defined as religion completely relinquishing worldly affairs, state affairs in particular, it actually remains an ambiguous concept. Laicism, as claimed, is neither worldly nor can the state be completely isolated from religion. More importantly, religions are never about organizing the afterlife. What they actually organize is the functioning of the worldly and the social and, in particular, power and the state.

Laicism is a kind of (masonic) denomination that was developed to break the hegemony of the Catholic world. Masonic lodges were first founded in the Middle Ages by stonemasons, including some Jews. Although laicism developed in connection with the positive sciences, it is highly probable that it was a derivation from the rabbinical elements of Jewish ideology. Without understanding this we cannot understand laicism or the problems it has caused. Laicism carries rabbinical elements at least as much as other religious traditions (divine; *rabb* means *master* in Hebrew), but this fact had to be constructed in secret and with a special packaging, as a result of the relentless oppression at the hands of medieval Catholicism. The laicists who made their move with the Dutch and the English Revolutions benefited more from them than from the French Revolution. With the construction of the nation-state they organized themselves in a way that made them the most difficult part of the state's core to reach, recognize, and topple from power. They have continued this dominance ever since. This is one aspect of the phenomenon known as the "deep state." The more than two hundred nation-states around the world are as Masonic as they are secular. Masons are the fundamental force behind the ideological hegemony of capitalist modernity. Their influence is global and they continue to consolidate it. Other areas of influence include a number of civil society institutions that play a key role in the strategic direction of the world, such as media monopolies and university teaching staff. They are the masterminds and controllers of modernity, which they call the "secular world." Their function, which they call earthly or secular, takes place within this framework.

As particularly Catholicism but also Sunni Islam and other rigid religious traditions erode under the influence of modernity, laicism loses its importance as an ideology and a political program. The revival of traditional religions, especially in societies where the Islamic tradition still has a strong influence, has rekindled the discussion about the relationship between laicism and religion. These developments are related to the ideological and political power struggles between the nation-state and the concept of the ummah. Therefore, it would be wrong to present it as if it were only about the modern way of life. A struggle similar to that between Christianity and Judaism is now unfolding between the Islamic world and Judaism. This is what underlies the great conflicts in the Middle East. The goal is to arrange some kind of reconciliation between Judaism and Islam, like that found in Europe and the US. Radical elements oppose reconciliation and are confrontational, while moderate elements appear to be much more open to reconciliation.

Still, it is important not to see the revival of traditional religious cultures exclusively as reactionism rising from the grave. They carry democratic content to the extent that they revolt against modernity and nation-state ideology. Nor should we overlook the fact that they represent a strong moral vein. It is important for democratic modernity to pay close attention to the developments occurring within these religious traditions, because they are among the many cultures that modernity has thoroughly tampered with and colonized. A similar revival can be seen in all suppressed cultures and religious traditions. The issue is global, so it is more than just a dispute between Islam and Judaism but concerns processes that are taking place on a global scale.

Just as it is possible to have different ethnic cultures in a democratic nation, the same is true of the democratic content of religious culture as a free, egalitarian, and democratic element of the democratic nation and making it part of a solution is important. The conciliatory alliance approach of democratic modernity to the anti-system movements should also be applied to religious cultures with democratic content. This is another important task that is vital to the work of reconstruction.

Urban, Local, and Regional Movements for Autonomy

Autonomous governance, which has always played an important part in history at urban, local, and regional levels, is among the other very important cultural traditions that fell victim to nation-statism. In all the forms of social and state governance implemented to date, there has always been governments of the city, locality, and region, each with its own specific characteristics. In fact, it would otherwise be impossible to govern large states and empires. Rigid centralism, essentially a monopolistic character of modernity, is a nation-state disease. Imposed as a necessity of maximum profit, it was organized in such a way that the bureaucrats of the tumultuously proliferating middle-class bourgeoisie came to power, and developed as a model that establishes not one but thousands of kingdoms that can only function through fascism.

The rural, local, and regional autonomous movements shouldered the biggest responsibility for the development of cultural movements— mostly liberal postmodernist and some representing a radical rupture— that accelerated the disintegration of classical modernity. In fact, it is a return to and revival of cultures that include the political, economic, and social dimensions that have been central to them throughout the ages. They are among the movements that have and must have great importance in terms of historical-society. Without the liberation of the city, the local, and region, liberation from the disease of the nation-state is impossible. This is best understood and implemented by the EU member states. The four hundred years of barbarism that they experienced in the name of modernity and the severe devastation of the two world wars have sufficiently taught European culture a lesson. It is no coincidence that, having understood what the genocide the nation-state implies for all national and cultural entities, one of the first measures the EU implemented were urban, local, and regional autonomy laws.

The efforts being made in the European Union in the context of urban, local, and regional cultures are among the most important contributions to solving all global problems. Although not particularly radical, they are important and necessary cultural movements. In any case, many urban, local and regional autonomies have maintained their vitality because central governments have not been able to impose and enforce complete homogeneity on any continent. The most active and current issues related to autonomy and autonomous work are found in areas stretching from the Russian Federation to China to India through the entire American continent (the US is a federal state, Canada has a high degree of internal autonomy, and South America has significant regional autonomy) to Africa (in the absence of traditional aşirets and regional governance, states can neither be formed nor govern). Rigid centralism, a disease of the nation-statism, is implemented only in a limited number of states in the Middle East and some dictatorships around the world.

There is an effort to replace the rigid centralized nation-state structures of classical modernity, which is being squeezed between global capital above and the cultural movements below and gradually disintegrating, with autonomous governance at the urban, local, and regional levels. This tendency is growing increasingly strong at present and will inevitably develop in step with the movement of the democratic nation. In terms of its form of governance, the democratic nation is quite close to confederalism. Confederalism, in a way, is the democratic nation's form of political governance. A strong city can only secure its existence through autonomous local and regional governance. As such, the form of governance of both movements is identical and overlaps. Democratic nationhood and the democratic nation cannot attain the capacity of governance without urban, local, and regional autonomy. They either fall into chaos and disintegrate or are overtaken by a new nation-state model. To avoid both possible outcomes, the movement of the democratic nation must develop urban, local, and regional democratic autonomy. On the other hand, autonomous urban, local, and regional governance needs to complement the movement of the democratic nation toward a democratic nation to avoid being totally swallowed up and to use their economic, social, and political power to the full. These movements can only completely overcome the nation-state's extremely centralist monopolistic forces, which nation-states constantly holds and tries to impose on them, by forming strong alliances. Otherwise, neither movement (even as a phenomenon) will be able to avoid being liquidated and absorbed under the threat of renewed homogenization, as has happened so often before. Just as the historical conditions in the nineteenth century generally favored nation-statism, current conditions—the realities of the twenty-first century—favor democratic nations and strengthened urban, local, and regional autonomous governance at all levels.

Of course, we must be very careful that liberalism does not corrupt and absorb these positive tendencies for democratization under its ideological and material hegemony, as it has done so often in its history. The most important strategic task of democratic modernity, as with all opponents of the system, is to bring together in a new ideological and political structure the current of historical-society's urban, local, and regional political formations in a complementary way. In this sense, it must engage in comprehensive theoretical efforts while developing the necessary program, organizational structures, and actions intertwined with one another. The conditions for ensuring that the fate of the confederal structures destroyed by nation-statism in the mid-nineteenth century is not repeated in the twenty-first century are present, instead the conditions to turn it into a victory for democratic confederalism are quite promising. If we are to emerge from the long and continuous depression in the financial-capitalist phase of modernity, which can only be kept alive and continued by a crisis regime, with a victory for democratic modernity, it is vital that the intellectual, political, and moral tasks in the reconstruction work are successfully realized.

TEN

The Tasks in Rebuilding Democratic Modernity

I'm not talking about reviving some past "golden age" memories or imagining a new future "utopia." I wouldn't consider a proposal in either sense meaningful. Even though the mentality of societies is laden with such thoughts, these recollections and utopias are not explanations or narratives that add much of value to the reality of the moral and political society that I'm trying to interpret here. Even if we don't deny the contributions of such recollections and utopias, it is necessary to deliberate about them and address them in certain narratives, knowing that they bring with them possible drawbacks.

In these respects, the concept of democratic modernity neither heralds the return to a "golden age" nor a future "utopian paradise." It is also not a historical era or the social form that positivist science asserts it is. I have to point out, at least in relation to my own approach, that in terms of method I would never espouse such narratives of history or society, whether they are approached with metaphysical or a positivist method, both of which, in fact, produce similar results, and, contrary to what they claim, their interpretations of truth and reality are incoherent. I consider the material and its experiences available in history absolutely necessary for thinking. It is not just a matter of what historical material has to offer, the material in nature and its experiences are also essential. I do not adopt a typical empirical approach, but I also do not share the perspective of the idealists, who claim that they can produce ideas independent of natural and historical material and experience. I know that over the course of the history of civilization a huge corpus was created using these methods. While I believe it is necessary to be aware of this body of work, I am convinced that it is hardly indispensable for interpreting the truth. What I am trying to say is that it is entirely possible to interpret the truth without recourse to this body of work. In particular, I consider the positivist school of research buried in the plethora of historical material to be pitiful and miserable. Similarly, I do not think that those who, without the need for any material, foretell the future like a sheikh bearing a self-proclaimed prophecy are in any way in touch with the truth. They are equally pitiful and miserable.

It would not be sufficient to restrict our criticism to the empirical and idealist approaches. It is also important to criticize the different forms of these two methods; universalist linear progression and relativism. In general, the truth cannot be built or explored using either linear progressive or relativist methods. The flexible high intelligence level of social nature undoubtedly presents a broad freedom option when building social reality. But this does not mean, as proponents of the relativist method argue, that "everyone can build their own truth as they like." It also does not mean, as the idealists assert, that "everything happens when its time comes," as is written in the levh-i mahfuz. To build social realities with new ideas (social natures from clan to nations, class, the state, etc.), the social material within a given time and space, as new realities seems to be the way of the mentality and its most realistic method and can be accepted as such.

The point I am repeatedly attempting to make is that the method must necessarily be based on social nature, in particular on the fundamental state of existence of this nature, which I am certain is moral and political society. In short, any school of thought, any movement of science, philosophy, or the arts, that is not connected to moral and political society will be born crippled and sooner or later cause problems. I designate as my very first condition that all methods adhered to and the products of knowledge, ethics, and esthetics must be based on moral and political society. I would like to draw attention to the fact that all methods, knowledge, ethics, and esthetics not based on this first condition will be unreliable and crippled, loaded down with errors, ugly, and rife with evil. I insist that this is not merely my personal opinion and perception, but has, in fact, the merit of being a fundamental norm on the path to truth.

I have presented my approach to democratic modernity. In my analysis up to this point, it can be seen I have tried to develop a two-way approach.

My first specific analytical point is that the civilization system develops by continuously eroding and exploiting the society with a moral and political nature, the given state of social nature, and by constructing monopolies of exploitation and power over it. This matter is very important and must be understood and properly analyzed. That's what I have done. I have tried to analyze the civilization system, using the limited material at hand due to the conditions I am being held in, and essentially, I interpreted life in general, which is the sine qua non of truth, and my life in particular in an intertwined way with this limited material. I did not think that providing an excess of material was necessary, as this would have risked suffocating the analysis in detail. But, with the data I have presented, I have tried to show that it is necessary to have access to sufficient material.

Here is the result: dialectically speaking, against whom were the gigantic civilizations of the historical ages developed? Where, how, and with whom did they build their relationships and develop their contradictions? Despite having minimal material and a minimal capacity to interpret it, I did not hesitate to designate the sum of the antagonistic forces civilization was in contact with as the *demos*, adding to this an already well-known word, *kratia*, to arrive at *demoskratia*—self-governance—a concept known and widely used in the intellectual world. Of course, demoskratia does not encompass all units of moral and political society, it corresponds to the "confederation of tribes" that existed for a time in Ionia. Therefore, it may not, and, in fact, does not, include some of the lower, upper, or other distinct moral and political units. Nonetheless, it seems to me to be the most suitable term available to us. If a more appropriate term were developed, I would not have a second thought about using it. The important thing is the substance of the term and what we mean by that substance.

There is not much of a need to explain what is meant by the second word *modernity*. As generally understood, it denotes periods, eras, and durations of time that have occurred with certain norms. Along with the numerous eras of civilization, there have also been just as many, in fact, even substantially more, demoskratia, or democratic modernities. There are numerous moral and political society units that I would interpret as democratic modernity that the civilization systems were unable to completely encompass and subject to their exploitation and power monopoly. History offers much material in this regard, and I have touched upon but a few examples in my analysis.

The second important point is that democratic modernity did not or could not organize itself in terms of its ideological and material culture as well as civilization systems. There is ample easily available historical material for anyone interested that shows that because civilizations have to operate the apparatuses of monopolistic exploitation and power on a daily basis, they are highly ideologically equipped and organized and in terms of their material structures they must maintain unity and be in action. But this is not the case for units of democratic modernity. Rather, since they constantly shift between resistance and colonization, and their independent units, which can be found in some isolated corner, on mountain peaks or in the middle of deserts, are not fully developed, they cannot have the same systematic ideological and material structure. I don't mean that they can never develop any system, ideology, or structure. History is undoubtedly replete with examples of democratic modernity providing richer ideologically and materially structured cultures. Just because the ideological hegemony of civilization obscures these examples does not mean that history does not provide very rich data.

I have attempted to outline both sides (statist and democratic) of civilization up to the present. Although I only provide a rough outline, I believe I was able to uncover the main tendencies, even if insufficiently. In particular, it should be evident I tried to extensively analyze the modernity that is called capitalist. On the other hand, it should also be apparent that I have assessed the opposite poles of the same period of modernity more extensively and with certain criticisms. The conclusion to be drawn from these criticisms is that democratic modernity clearly faces the task of rebuilding itself. Whether renewed or not, we know that the forces of the official capitalist modernity led by liberalism are highly skilled and experienced in presenting themselves in whatever guise necessary. The same cannot be said about the forces of democratic modernity. Whether we look at their historical experience or their recent past in terms of their attitude toward liberalism, it is possible to see how they were ideologically dissolved and have lost their clarity. To avoid as much as possible once again falling into this situation, or to at least avoid the painful and tragic positions of the recent past, it is necessary to clarify the tasks the units of democratic modernity face in rebuilding.

By *unit*, I mean any individuals, communities, or movements that live in a more or less self-consciously anti-system way. These existences, which constitute the overwhelming majority of social nature, unfortunately subsist as qualitative forces far weaker than their numbers. Therefore, above all, rebuilding must pursue the objective of the quantitative multitudes gaining a qualitative capacity that equals their quantity. If we always keep in mind how extensive and intertwined the commercial, industrial, financial, ideological, power-centered, and nation-statist monopoly networks are at a global level and how they treat their targets destructively and unpredictably, we will understand that rebuilding the units of democratic modernity and ensuring that they gain a capacity that is proportional to their multitudes are clear tasks that cannot be postponed—if we are to at least eliminate the enormous imbalance between them. These tasks, which can be sorted into three main categories, are all strongly connected and have intellectual, moral, and political dimensions. But the strong and reciprocal connection between them does not eliminate the need for them to be institutionally independent of one another. On the contrary, there was, is, and will be a need for each of these areas to preserve its independence as an institution, or they will be unable to function properly. Clarifying the required institutionalization and the tasks related to these areas, which have become quite intertwined in history, and organizing them for maximal cooperation are issues that must be resolved.

It may be elucidating to provide some examples that explain the historical process in this respect. In tribal units, intellectual, moral, and political tasks were usually carried out in an intertwined way. Separation and specialization had not yet really developed. *Aşiret* confederations were predominantly associated with political tasks. Moral tradition was represented by the experiences of the elders, while enlightenment and reflection were represented primarily by the institutions of shamanism, sheikhdom, and the priesthood. During the longue durée of history when the Abrahamic religions also gained moral and political dimensions, these three tasks were institutionalized to some degree. In Islam, for example, madrassas tend to be intellectual institutions, while mosques function as moral institutions, and the sultanate as a political institution. However, the overly intertwined nature of the three has prevented their creative development. The fact that they have not developed to at least the same degree as the corresponding institutions in Christianity and Judaism is linked to this reality. The dominant form of relationship among them is ecumenicism, or ummah, which, in a way, represents their internationalism.

During Greco-Roman civilization, intellectualism attained greater independence. Philosophical schools were essentially intellectual institutions and were highly independent. Morality was institutionalized in the temple. Politics, which had once been institutionalized in the assembly (ecclesia) and the republican senate, suffered a major blow with the development of the empire. The empire is in a way the negation of political institutionalization at the central level, a major factor behind the assassination of Julius Caesar.

In contemporary modernity, intellectualism is trapped in the university, while morality has suffered a major blow and faces elimination. The substitution of morality with positive law is an attempt to liquidate the role that morality plays in society. Politics, whose area has been increasingly narrowed down and forced into the sheath of parliamentarianism, has almost been brought to a standstill under the administration of nation-state bureaucracy. Like morality, it can no longer play its true role. However, in the units of democratic modernity there have been various and complex institutional developments. In a certain sense, fraternal organizations combine these three tasks, as do utopians. Intellectual, moral, and political tasks attain functionality and are fulfilled under the guidance of a single person, much like in a sect. Especially during the period of real socialism, all three areas were institutionalized in the Communist League and the First, Second, and Third Internationals. The *Communist Manifesto* was effectively their program. These institutions shared the assimilationist inclinations of capitalist modernity regarding these three tasks. While politics is sacrificed as an institution to the administrative mechanisms of nation-state god, morality is sacrificed to the same mechanism's positive law, which regulates the captivity of the citizen. The area of intellectual tasks, on the other hand, is sacrificed or negated by being left to the intellectual capitalists and load donkeys (like a donkey carrying knowledge) of the universities, which play the role of the nation-state's new temple. This short historical overview clearly indicates how important it is for the units of democratic modernity to take responsibility for these three tasks by forming counter-networks, if they want to avoid complete disintegration as a society.

Before discussing the tasks, it might be useful to briefly touch upon the issue of units and networks. A unit is any type of community that is anti-monopoly. Any community, from the democratic nation to a village association, from an international confederation to a neighborhood branch, can be a unit. Each governing body from the tribal level to the city, whether local or national, is a unit. A unit might represent two people—even one person—or billions of people. Viewed from this rich perspective the concept will prove extremely instructive. But what is important here is that each unit should be evaluated as a moral and political society. Therefore, the collaboration of all units in intellectual, moral, and political tasks is of principle value. Just as it is necessary to be a moral and political society to be considered a unit, being a moral and political society requires a commitment to the intellectual, moral, and political tasks. The fact that the opposite side is organized as a network is related to its organizational structure and administration. In addition, internal unities can best be organized into networks. Rigid centralism and a hierarchical chain of command in organization and administration are inimical to the organizational and governance principles of units of democratic modernity.

Intellectual Tasks

Let me say in advance that I will not be casting intellectual tasks as the constitution of unitary consciousness and its transmission to the units. First, we must evaluate what intellectualism is. It is often said that the Age of Enlightenment (eighteenth-century Europe) determined how modernity was shaped. Numerous systematic physical and cultural genocides by the nation-state, in particular the Holocaust, dealt a fatal blow to modernity's idea of enlightenment. It was at that point that the intellectual Theodor Adorno demanded that all divinities fall silent.[1] This, at the same time, is the ultimate stage of civilization to date. This is an important moment; without an analysis of it you cannot hope to move forward. We are talking about a moment of historical failure, lies, and genocide. As an act of enlightenment, awareness, and the growth of knowledge, intellectualism cannot isolate itself from this moment. It must be judged to be one of the main culprits. Placing responsibility for the crime on a few dictators like Hitler is among liberalism's most disgusting acts of propaganda. The truth cannot be discovered if the system that nurtured Hitler from cradle to the grave is not elucidated; this would be nothing but a betrayal of truth. When the main task of intellectualism, "the pursuit of truth," has been betrayed and this betrayal is largely the work of intellectual capitalists and load donkeys, there are issues that need to be carefully scrutinized. Without evaluating and resolving these issues nothing but the creation of new intellectual capitalists and load donkeys can be expected from the newly assumed position.

If the system, which is in a global crisis, can only be sustained through an extraordinary crisis regime, then the fact that we are not talking about the intellectual crisis can only be because we are totally blind or are the system's incorrigible intellectual capitalists and load donkeys. An ordinary intellectual with a sense of dignity should have no difficulty understanding that the crisis is effectively the result of an occlusion in the field of mentality. Furthermore, there is a link between system structures and their mentalities like that between the body and the soul. The crisis of the body—the structurality—not only necessitates the crisis of the soul—the mentality—it makes it the precursor of that crisis. The priority is not the crisis of the body—but of the soul. Just as brain death is conclusive evidence of bodily death, the mentality crisis is certainly evidence of a structural crisis. It is quite clear that we are currently faced with a profound intellectual crisis. Because in certain areas the crisis cannot be addressed by innovations; a profound response to the crisis is required, and it must be related to the transformation of the system. The solution to the system's intellectual crisis inevitably lies with an "intellectual revolution." Before discussing intellectual revolution in our current context, it might be useful to look at some historical examples.

As far as can be determined, the first great intellectual revolution took place in Mesopotamia c. 6000–4000 BCE. This was a period when the power of society and the natural forces was observed extensively for the first time with enormous practical results, which Gordon Childe found comparable to the developments in post-sixteenth-century Europe. Most of the social achievements made to date, both in terms of tools and intellect, have their roots in that period. The second great revolution occurred with the foundation of the Sumerian and Egyptian civilizations. In the first period, the ability to transform the achievements of the Neolithic Revolution to the civilization system was demonstrated, both in terms of tools and intellectual achievements. Many of the inventions and discoveries in different areas, including writing, mathematics, literature, medicine, astronomy, theology, and biology in particular, are the result of the revolutionary intellectual developments of this period. Until the Greek-Ionian revolution, history continued to learn from and duplicate these developments.

The Greek-Ionian intellectual revolution constituted the third major step. The period 600–300 BCE was another period that was very rich in terms of both philosophical mindset and scientific development. No doubt the transition from mythology blended religions to philosophy was a major intellectual revolution. There were also revolutionary developments in areas such as writing, literature, physics, biology, logic, mathematics, history, the arts, and politics. Until the sixteenth century, the products of these revolutions were transmitted and duplicated. While there were certainly many other intellectual developments at other times and in other places, they cannot be regarded as having constituted major revolutions. It is possible to interpret the emergence of monotheistic religions as important revolutions in mindset. Furthermore, the Zoroastrian moral revolution was a major intellectual revolution. Confucius in China and the Buddha in India developed important intellectual values. The intellectual sparks seen in Islam from the eighth to twelfth century were also important. It is a great loss that they did not lead to a revolution.

The European intellectual revolution is undoubtedly deep-rooted and extensive. However, it is indisputable that its source is the revolutions and intellectual sparks that we have been discussing. I must clearly point out that none of these intellectual revolutions had any link to the exploitation and power monopolies. On the contrary, it was these monopolies that distorted these revolutions and prevented them from adequately developing, causing them to atrophy and be tied to the monopolies and turned into capital. This reality is even more strikingly clear in the great intellectual revolution of Europe. Absolutism and the nation-state systems, as capitalist monopolies and state monopolies, have gone to great lengths to prevent and distort the intellectual revolution and to bind it to their own rule, considering this their foremost duty. Many great struggles have been waged in this regard. Giordano Bruno, Erasmus, Galileo Galilei, Thomas More, and other thinkers and scientists resisted the relentless tyranny of the rulers to protect their intellectual independence and retain their dignity, whether at the hands of the Inquisition or the French revolutionary courts, where some even ran the risk of being burned at the stake.

During the nineteenth and twentieth centuries, as in all areas and units of society, the hegemony of monopolist capital and the nation-state was strongly reflected in the intellectual area and the intellectual units. Science, philosophy, the arts, and even religion were all heavily integrated into the structures of power, particularly the nation-state. Monopolism in both these areas dealt a major blow to intellectual independence. In this situation of dependence, the intellectual either became an intellectual capitalist or, more often, a knowledge load donkey within the universities and other school systems. The schools, particularly the universities, became the new temples of the nation-state, where each successive generation's mind and soul are washed to render them servant-citizens who worship the nation-state god in an unparalleled way. Naturally, the community of teachers at every level have become the new priestly class. No doubt there are a handful of intellectuals who preserve their intellectual dignity, but they are the exceptions that prove the rule.

Of greater importance are the contextual developments of the intellectual revolution in Europe. We should point out that the pioneers of this revolution thoroughly absorbed the religion, science, philosophy, and arts of the previous eras, and it is clear that this was the basis of their contributions. It must be acknowledged that European intellectuals made huge progress toward the truth. They were certainly successful in terms of method and application. While this is particularly true in the area of first nature (physics, chemistry, biology, astronomy), it is not so much the case with their scientific, philosophical, artistic, and moral approach to society as second nature. European intellectuals wrote meaningful manifestos and developed scientific disciplines, philosophical schools, artistic tendencies, and ethical teachings. However, they were not successful enough to preserve the moral and political character of society. On the contrary, the more their dependency on the capital and power monopolies grew, the more they became complicit, targeting moral and political society to the point of destruction, which cannot be explained away with talk of inadequacies, failures, and errors. This is precisely how the intellectual crisis began.

Undoubtedly, the responsibility for not only society becoming the target of destruction but also the environment is on the intellectuals. The fact that they are held jointly responsible for the global crisis is because they are part of the crisis. The most important issue to be elucidated is the way the intellectual defeat, corruption, and distortion developed, both strategically and tactically. Who should we hold responsible for the development of the great turmoil, defeat, and betrayal in the field of social sciences in particular? (Here, I must first express my belief that sciences that address first nature have or, at least, should have a social quality.) Are we only talking about a disease of the scientific paradigm? Should we primarily look for the problem in particular disciplines? Is the disease structural or incidental? Is treatment possible? How can we develop the means and method of treatment? What would be the main indicators of a new scientific revolution or a new scientific paradigm? Strategically, what is our starting point? Only if we have clear and concise answers to these and similar questions can we overcome the intellectual crisis and determine what our new paradigmatic and scientific tasks are.

The crisis of the European civilization–centered science is structural, and this is related to developments experienced at the beginning of civilization. The centralization of science in the temple means its integration with power. There are many examples indicating that in the Egyptian and Sumerian civilizations science became an integral part of power. The institution of priesthood that pieced together science was already the most important partner of power. The structure of science in the Neolithic period was, however, different. Women's knowledge of plants likely laid the foundation of both biology and medicine. In addition, observing seasonal cycles and monitoring the moon gave rise to the need for calculations. It can easily be construed that the life practices of the agrarian-village communities that existed for thousands of years provided a wealth of knowledge. This knowledge was pieced together and turned into a component of power during the period of civilization. What we have here is a negative qualitative transformation.

In pre-civilization societies and later in societies that opposed civilization, knowledge and science were a component of moral and political society. Unless the vital interests of the society necessitated it, it was not possible to use science in any other way. The sole purpose of knowledge and science was to ensure society's continued existence and provide it with protection and nourishment. Anything else was unthinkable. Civilization radically changed this situation. It established its monopoly over knowledge and science and severed their ties to society. With society deprived of knowledge and science, the rulers and the state forces used knowledge and science to maximize their power. They consolidated their monopolies by binding those who produced and carried knowledge to their dynasties and palaces. The profound severing of science from society, and from women in particular, also meant its detachment from life and the environment. This developed alongside a profound severing of analytical intelligence from emotional intelligence and the continuous growth of the distance between the two.

In social nature science was understood as divine. Society deified the level of knowledge and consciousness related to its own nature as an expression of its own identity and equated it with divinity. Civilization changed this too. When science fell under the control of the dynasties and their partners, this divine status was also modified. While the society was assigned the rank of servitude and the non-divine, the dynasty and its immediate surroundings were reassigned in mythology and religion as god's nobility. God-kings and god's nobility were the product of this process. The severing of the producers and carriers of science and knowledge from society in this way continued throughout the ages of civilization. There were of course those who resisted this, but they were easily liquidated. Those who dealt with knowledge and science became a sort of caste. As for European civilization, the producers of knowledge and science experienced a period of limited independence, particularly because of the confrontation between the Church and the kingdoms, as well as the quasi-autonomous atmosphere in the monasteries. The intense power struggles gave them the opportunity to easily find protection and to carry on without their research suffering. The Renaissance, Reformation, and Enlightenment are closely linked to the autonomous environment that resulted from these power struggles. The absence of a Chinese- or Ottoman-style autocracy also contributed to this autonomy. The result was a philosophical and scientific revolution. However, the hegemonic rise of capitalism, on the one hand, and the formation of the nation-state, on the other hand, resulted in the establishment of a monopoly of capital and power over science during the nineteenth and twentieth centuries. Science became an integral part of capital and power. This situation, which had already developed during the history of civilization to the detriment of moral and political society, peaked with European modernity.

Eurocentric scientific paradigms had long been detached from society. Those dealing with knowledge and science had predominantly adopted the perspective of capital and power. Moral and political society had already been discredited. This process only escalated with the defeat of the Church. Science, whose main concern was no longer moral and political society, had no other area of engagement aside from being locked into the objectives of capital and the state. At the same time as science began to produce capital and power, capital and power were appropriating science. The severing of all ties between science and morality and politics threw the door wide open for war, conflicts, battles, and all types of exploitation. Indeed, the history of Europe became the history of the most intense wars. The role cast to science was now to focus on inventing the perfect instruments of war to ensure victory. The rapid increase in the production of instruments of war resulted in a nuclear arms race. In a society where the rules of moral and political society were still intact, never mind nuclear weapons, there would be no reason to even invent a popgun, and if one were invented it would never be used against society.

The collapse of morality is the most important factor for the onset of war. The severing of the ties between science and morality provided the foundation for the invention of all sorts of destructive instruments. It is unthinkable that this relationship between science and power and society would not be echoed in the fundamental paradigm and method. Removing society from this relationship also meant its objectification, much like the objectification of women and slaves that preceded it. Then the subject-object distinction that began with Francis Bacon and René Descartes was transferred to all sciences. Being objective in scientific studies is highly praised, but the fact is that the door to the greatest of catastrophes was opened by this sharp subject-object distinction, which was later deepened by the self-other distinction, with both eventually transforming into destructive dialectical poles. These contradictions are certainly a reflection of the separation and contradiction between moral and political society and capital and power. The reduction of nature to an object, followed by a similar objectification of women and slaves, and finally of the entire society, emerged as the much revered "objectivity rule" that is still widely applied in science. The former god-servant relationship was transformed into the subject-object relationship. The earlier understanding of "a living nature" was replaced by "nature as a dead object," with the "human as the divine subject."

These paradigmatic approaches had a devastating impact on science, the social sciences in particular. For example, physicists who base themselves on physical nature, which is entirely objective, believe that they have the freedom to conduct unlimited experiments and dispose of nature as they wish. They feel they are free to do anything from nuclear tests to setting in motion all types of technological development. They feel no moral qualms about any of this. This objectifying approach to nature creates the conditions for the unlimited use of and disposal of any material, leading in the extreme to developments like the atomic bomb. When divine science becomes instrumental science it ceases to have any connection to society; in the hands of power and capital it becomes a tool dependent on the law of maximum profit. At the outset, physics appears completely neutral and deals with objective nature. However, in its essence, it is clearly one of the main sources of strength for power and capital. Were this not the case, the science of physics would not be able to maintain its current status. The fact that it has turned into an anti-society force tells us that it is not the neutral and objective science it claims to be. The power relations called the laws of physics are in the final analysis nothing more than a reflection of human power. We know, on the other hand, that the human being is a social being in the absolute sense.

When we make sense of positivist philosophy, which has left its mark on the entire scientific structure of modernity, we can better expose the penetralia of the relationship between civilization, power, and science. We know that positivist philosophy acts on the basis of absolute objective facts, not allowing for any other scientific approach. If we take a closer look it becomes clear that science, as the study of the relationship between objects, is a lot more idolatrous and metaphysical than all of the ancient idol worship practices and the various metaphysical forces. Briefly touching on historical dialectics will make the issue clearer. Just as the monotheistic religions emerged and shaped themselves on the basis of a criticism of paganism (in a way, idolatry is the religion of the deification of facts), positivism also emerged as a counterattack and, in a way, as a new idolatry. Will to truth, based on the critique of religion and metaphysics, has been shaped as neo-metaphysics, the new idolatry (will to truth based on facts is definitely neo-paganism).[2] Friedrich Nietzsche was one of the first philosophers to identify this reality, and his analysis made significant contributions to the study of truth. It is of great importance to identify the concept of so-called objective fact as far removed from truth. Facts on their own do not provide us with any meaningful information about the truth, and when they do they bring with it the most erroneous of outcomes.

Earlier we said that if facts do not find meaning in the context of their complex connections, they either provide no information or lead to the most erroneous of outcomes. Let's put the facts of physics, chemistry, and biology to one side, focus on one social fact, and take a close-up look at the actual outcomes. From the point of view of positivism, the nation-state is a fact. Each of the elements that constitute it is also a fact. Each of the thousands of institutions and of the millions of people is also a fact. When we include the relationships between them, we complete the picture. According to positivism, we have thus formed a scientific concept. We now face an absolute truth: the truth of the nation-state! Positivism does not view this definition as an interpretation but as a fact of absolute truth. It takes the same approach to all other sociological facts. Just as with the facts of physics, chemistry, and biology, each of these is also a fact. This is positivism's definition of truth. We witnessed with dismay that while this approach was seemingly innocent and appeared to pose no danger, we have now seen its role in ethnic cleansing and genocide and know this is not the case. All leaders of nation-states, from Hitler to the most moderate, would say that their actions are perfectly correct from a (positivist) scientific point of view, that they are purifying the realities of their nation and creating a more homogeneous nation is not only their right but also in line with the laws of evolution. They are telling the truth based on the science they use. This power is given to them by positivist philosophy and sciences. As a matter of fact, it was during the period of capitalist modernity that, in keeping with this positivist approach, there were countless wars in the name of the homeland, the nation, the state, ethnicity, ideology, and the system. Because all these concepts were sacred, it was necessary to fight to the end. This way of seeing things made history a bloodbath. This was the grin on the bloody face of a seemingly innocent positivism.

Let's dig a little deeper into this. At present there are about two hundred nation-states in the world. If all of the abovementioned institutions and their citizen masses and relationships and these states confront one another, inevitably, a new kind of order or chaos of at least two hundred or more gods with thousands of temples and an unlimited number of sects will rise, because the facts that each of them represent are seen as sacred and worth dying for. It is important to note that there is absolutely no mention of the moral and political society that reflects the real social nature, even in name. If there is a reality worth dying for in the event of attack, it is the reality of moral and political society. In the nation-state, on the other hand, everyone fights in the name of the fact idols that they themselves created or that others created and placed before them. We face a period of wars for idols a thousandfold more horrifying than anything previous. The result is the operation of the law of maximum profit of the capital and nation-state monopolies, providing a happy minority with benefits more opulent than anything the pharaohs ever had. What is called modern life is, in fact, nothing but the consequences of the reality of positivism, or, put another way, positivism's murdering of reality. We have now reached the age of the virtual society; no other reality can explain positivism better than virtual society. A positivist society is a virtual society. Virtual society is the real face of positivist society. Moreover, it is truth itself. The meaninglessness of facts (here, meaninglessness should be understood in the sense of the bloodbaths, imaginary society, and consumer society) peaks with virtual society. Media-oriented societies, societies of the spectacle, magazine-driven societies are the unveiled truth of objective understanding, i.e., of positivism. This is, in fact, the negation of truth.

We could extend this list, with similar results, without the need for further investigation. Terms like *Islamic, Christian, Mosaic, Buddhist, capitalist, socialist, feudal,* and *slave-owning society* are realities that are the product of this approach, and here the metaphysical face of positivism is also clearly present. And, yes, the labeling as *Islamic society* and *capitalist society* are the result of the same approach. These are factual terms; in other words, they are terms related to ascription, the image. The same can be said about the sense of belonging to a nation. Terms like *German, French, Arab, Turkish,* and *Kurdish nations* are truths with a positivist character. However, in essence, they are only the faint images of truth. We might ask: "What is the reality—the truth?" I think the answer is simple. There is the truth of moral and political society, which is a natural part of the reality of society, and there is the truth of civilization, which constantly seeks to erode society. I am not saying that nothing outside of this represents reality. What I am saying is that this represents the image and its simple and frequently changing form not the essence.

For example, let's look at the reality of the Arab nation. Being an Arab means very little beyond the reality of a society that has a moral and political character—even though it is considerably weakened—in a place called Arabia, where the power that became an authority over society for thousands of years has today brought it to the brink of collapse. There are thousands of different types of Arab people, some in contradiction with one another, some even enemies. This means thousands of contradictory truths! According to positivism, this is how it should be. But we know very well that this is not the essence of Arab reality.

A better example might be the trees. A tree, as a fact, has thousands of branches and innumerable leaves. A tree is, however, only valued if it produces a known and desired product, not on the basis of its branches and leaves. Positivism is the blindness of giving everything equal weight. Of course, the branches and the leaves are realities too, but they are not the meaningful reality. A bunch of grapes, say a kilo, has a value, a meaning, but a leaf has only an image, something that does not reflect its essence—a positivistic reality that only gives it a visual form.

The main reason for the scientific crisis is the drowning of the sciences in facts and the emergence of a new scientific discipline every day, with each regarding itself as a truth of the same magnitude as all others. Earlier we identified the connection of this crisis to the system. Truth is being fragmented into ever deeper opposing pairs, including subject-object, self-other, body-spirit, religion-science, mythology-philosophy, god-servant, oppressed-oppressor, and ruler-ruled. This is essentially the result of the erosion and colonization of moral and political society by the civilizational monopoly networks established upon it. Capitalist modernity has infinitely replicated and deepened this dichotomy of civilization, bringing society to our present point of disintegration and decay. The collaborationist science of the system plays a great role in all of this. The crisis becomes apparent when the contradiction between ideological essence and instrumental structuring reaches an agonizing juncture; through unemployment, war, hunger and poverty, oppression and genocide, inequality and lack of freedom, it transforms itself into screams in the flesh and souls of the overwhelming multitudes.

I feel the need to say a little more to ensure that my criticism of positivism is not misunderstood. First, I am not saying that facts have no value, or that they do not have any connection to reality. What I am saying is that their value is limited and so is their connection to reality. When this is taken to the philosophical level, I am saying that positivism will result in major shortcomings, as the European system of thought makes quite clear. A second misunderstanding could lead to the criticism that I have slipped into a kind of Platonism. This might be the response to the previous example of a tree, where I said that essence is decisive. My point was not the idea of a *tree*. I was trying to describe the reality that a tree embodies for society. I am also not presenting a utilitarian approach. All I am saying is that a tree's reality must be determined by moral and political society. A tree may be very useful to an individual or a group, but if moral and political society does not construe it as such, then it does not have any true beneficial value.

Liberalism wants us to adopt a philosophy that says, "Individuals as philosophers, scientists, soldiers, politicians, capitalists, etc. will find whatever is true and live according to that," but I criticize this as most definitely immoral and apolitical society. I think this is the greatest ideology of demoralization and depoliticization to arise during the history of civilization, one that the capitalist system is trying to sell to the whole of society, or, more precisely, it is the contemporary mythological narrative sheathed within modernism that society is made to adopt through propaganda.

In that case, the question or problem that will prove more important is: Where and how can we find the truth? I would like to answer by recalling a very simple rule: you can find something only by looking for it where you lost it. You will not find it anywhere else, even if you look the world over, because the method is wrong. The method of looking anywhere other than where it was lost is just a waste of time and energy. I see our era's search for the truth in this light. Despite the daunting research laboratories and funding, the facts uncovered are laden with crisis and pain. It is clear that this cannot be the truth humanity is pursuing. My response is to emphasize what I have already said: the truth can only be social. When moral and political society is eroded and subjected to the strict domination of the exploitation and power monopoly during the process of civilization, social truth is lost. Whatever has been lost was lost along with moral and political values. If you want to recover them you have to look for them where you lost them. You must look for and find moral and political society and its reality, as opposed to civilization and modernity. However, you cannot be content with this alone, you must also rebuild its existence, which has been transformed beyond recognition. Once you have done this, you will find that bit by bit you can recover the golden valued truth that you lost throughout history. You will thus be much happier, and you will understand that the only way this can be done is through a moral and political society.

As we reorganize the intellectual area, based on criticism and at the level of principles, I would like to present some of my suggestions regarding the tasks:

a) Intellectual efforts—studies of knowledge and science—should be developed within the scope of moral and political society, social nature's fundamental form of existence. The reality of moral and political society, which we have increasingly been severed from, has been gradually eroded throughout the history of civilization and has been completely fragmented, left to decay, and brought to the brink of extinction during the modern age shaped by capitalism.

b) Therefore, intellectual efforts, studies of knowledge, and science must first and foremost aim to stop this course. Because there can be no science of something that has been destroyed. There may be memories of it, but memory is not science. Science is about things that exist and are alive. If under such conditions a society does not wish to be completely annihilated, then it and all of its constituents must resist capitalistic modernity. Resistance is now on the same plane as existence and identical with it. If intellectuals want to live with the dignity of genuine researchers—not viewing intellectualism as intellectual capital or as doing donkey work—then they must inevitably resist in all their endeavors, and the elements of their research should have the dimensions of resistance. In this sense both the intellectuals and their science must adopt an attitude of resistance. Anything else would be self-deception or disguising an essentially capital or load donkey identity.

c) The science to be developed must foremost be organized as a "social science." Social science must be accepted as the mother goddess of all sciences. Neither the sciences related to first nature (physics, astronomy, chemistry, biology) nor human knowledge sciences related to second nature (literature, philosophy, the arts, economy, etc.) can play that leading role; they cannot establish a meaningful bond with truth. Only if these two areas can successfully establish a bond with the social sciences can they gain a share of the truth.

d) Social science should base its studies on moral and political society, which is its main topic, not as an object or duality deeply entrenched in human perception and widely separated, such as subject-object, us-other, body-spirit, god-servant, or dead-alive, but using a method that overcomes these dualities. Differentiation, a way of life for the universe, is also valid in social nature and is an attribute that can be found to be more flexible, freer, and more concentrated. But to carry this differentiation to the level of the subject-object distinction, which has been made the foundation of all the ideological structures of civilization and modernity, would most definitely come to mean fragmentation and the loss of both universal and social truth.

e) We cannot develop a meaningful social science paradigm (a radical anti-civilizational philosophy of science) unless we throw positivism—which is the general philosophy of this objectivity that science in general and social science in particular emerged from, and which reached its peak in European modernity—into the dustbin of history on the basis of a thoroughgoing criticism. Even though it is highly fragmented, and there is a danger of loss of truth, it is essential to understand and absorb the constructive achievements and parts of truth revealed by Eurocentric science in general and the social sciences in particular. While it is imperative that positivism be criticized and overcome, it is also important that any truth it has exposed be adopted. In the exploration of truth, wholesale anti-Europeanism can lead to outcomes that are just as negative as those resulting from the wholesale adoption of Europeanism.

f) Although the exploration of truth called postmodernism criticizes positivism and rejects Eurocentric social sciences, this approach is easily liberally twisted and can be readily shaped into an anti-Europeanism that is more significantly anti-truth. Postmodern quests that take advantage of the crisis of the social sciences shouldn't be totally rejected but should be approached very critically. Just as the universalist progressive linear method and perspective of modernist positivism leads astray, the excessively relativist cyclical method of many postmodernists is open to similar deviations. To not drift to these extremes, it is necessary to absorb and adhere to the fundamental principles that we are attempting to outline here. The crisis-ridden atmosphere creates a situation that would allow almost anyone to seek their own path to the truth, which in itself can distort the exploration of truth in many ways.

g) Our main method of researching truth can neither be positivist objectivism nor relativist subjectivism. They are essentially two faces of liberalism, and, by combining them, it produces an abundance of methods, which it in turn uses to create intellectual capital and load donkeys. The most effective way to preclude truth is with this abundance of methods. This in turn means that by combining the objective and subjective methods you produce as many methods as there are individuals. It is important not to be deceived by this abundance of methods, which act to depreciate truth. There is no doubt that there are both subjective and objective aspects to reality. Consciousness, truth, in the final analysis, denotes the convergence of the observer and the observed (I am not talking about them becoming one and the same; it would be better to understand them as becoming identical). The greater the depth and focus attained in relation to this issue, the more parts of the truth will be revealed. In this case, the observer is not a subject and the observed is not an object. Rather, the two, approaching each other, do not become one but undergo a process of identification. The process in which truth is maximized is the process that engenders the opportunity of identification. For now, I will define the question of method as I have without giving it a name. Of course, we should never, anywhere or anytime, ignore the fact that the main unit observing and being observed is moral and political society.

h) The primary research centers cannot be the official institutions of civilization and modernity, foremost the universities. Whether in the past or in the present, tying science to power and producing it in official state institutions means the loss of its bond with truth. Severing the bond of science with moral and political society and not allowing it to be of use to society helps the development of oppressive and exploitative monopolies ruling atop society. Just as a woman who is confined to a private home or a brothel loses her free reality and truth, the intellectuals and sciences confined to official institutions lose their freedom and genuine identity. This does not mean that no intellectuals can arise in these institutions, or that science cannot be developed. The thing we need to understand is that when the intellectual and science become power-centered they detach from their purpose, research and invention in the service of social reality. The existence of exceptions—encountering a genuine intellectual or the discovery of a work with scientific value—does not change the overall reality.

i) An institutional revolution, i.e., restructuring, is essential for the social sciences. Just as during the Greek-Ionian Enlightenment, independent philosophical and scientific academies were formed, and during the medieval period, *khanqahs, dargahs,*[3] and monasteries played a similar role within Islamic and Christian traditions, just as the European Renaissance, Reformation, and Enlightenment movements were all intellectual and scientific revolutions, we now need similar revolutions to exit the present crisis. The four-hundred-year-old ideological hegemony of modernity is as profound and continuous as its hegemony over material culture and cannot overcome the crisis. Without the intervention of democratic modernity in content and form, it is inevitable that the crisis will play an increasingly corrosive and degenerative role. There is a rich intellectual and scientific legacy that extends from the utopian socialists to the scientific socialists, from the anarchists to the Frankfurt School, from the French philosophy of the second half of the twentieth century to 1968 youth culture revolution, and finally to the postmodernist, feminist, and ecological movements that emerged in the 1990s. Democratic modernity has to make its own intellectual and scientific revolution by absorbing the positive aspects of the intellectual sparks and revolutions of the civilization period, as well as of the anti-modernity intellectual breakthroughs.

Institutionalization is one of the conditions of this revolution. For success on a global scale, the intellectual revolution needs a new institutional center based on the lessons learned from the historical experiences we have raised. To address this need, a World Confederation of Culture and Academies could be built. Such a confederation should be built at a free geographical location and should not be attached to any nation-state or ruling power but should be formed on the basis of opposition to capital monopolies. Furthermore, it is essential that the confederation be independent and autonomous. Every local, regional, and national academy would be free to participate on a voluntary basis and in accordance with the principles of its program, organization, and action. This confederation could establish institutions with tasks at the local, regional, national, and continental levels.

j) Democratic politics and culture academies may be the appropriate institutions for this task. These academies could provide the intellectual and scientific support that is necessary for moral and political society units to restructure themselves. Rather than imitating the official and private monopoly institutions, they should construct themselves in original ways. Imitating the institutions of modernity could well lead to failure. These academies should be autonomous and democratic, form their own program and cadres, and base themselves on the principle of their members being both voluntary students and voluntary teachers. It is quite easy to imagine that to begin with the positions of teacher and student will be readily interchangeable. From a shepherd in the mountains to a professor in the city, anyone who has an idea and a purpose should be able to contribute. Academies primarily for women might also prove appropriate, to allow for the scientific treatment of the unique aspects of women's reality, while still having content similar to that of other academies. To avoid remaining purely theoretical, the participation of women in every aspect of the implementation would be a sought-after quality. Academies would be established and run in response to practical needs, whenever and wherever they might arise. As seen in numerous historical examples (the fire temples of Zarathustra on mountaintops,[4] Plato and Aristotle's gardens, the pavements of Socrates and the Stoics, medieval monasteries and khanqahs), these would be simple and voluntary establishments. From a mountaintop to a neighborhood corner, any place can be chosen as the site for such an establishment—we do not seek buildings that prove the grandeur of their rulers. As is the case in monasteries and civilian madrassas, the duration of education would be determined by the level and the number of the participants. There is no need to determine the exact duration for education, as official institutions do, but, of course, it cannot be completely without form or rules. It must have its own ethical and esthetic rules.

When rebuilding the units of democratic modernity, intellectual and scientific contributions will be necessary. It is clear that this requirement cannot be met by the intellectual capital available on the market. Such a need can only be met by the cadres and science that come from these new academies.

This short assessment and my proposed principles regarding the scope of intellectual tasks necessary for a solution are nothing more than recommendations requiring further debate. The crisis conditions can only be positively overcome on the basis of new intellectual and scientific breakthroughs. Since the crisis in question is global, systematic, and structural, finding the way out also requires global, systematic, and structural interventions. Numerous revolutionary experiences teach us that we cannot get anywhere by imitating former patterns, institutions, and science or by using an eclectic approach.

One of the foremost lessons to be learned from the past is that rebuilding democratic modernity must be accompanied by a revolution of radical enlightenment. At the same time, I must emphasize that the past is the present. In particular, we should not ignore the fact that Neolithic society, agrarian-village communities, nomadism, tribes, and aşirets, as well as religious communities, still persist. We have not spoken much about the overall history of moral and political society, social nature's main form of existence. However, to regain the values that have been lost by five thousand years of capital accumulation and power monopolies and rebuild democratic modernity, revolutionary intellectual and scientific production shall constitute the much-needed support. To meet these absolutely essential needs, it is more important than ever to focus on our intellectual tasks and intensify our analytical efforts and find solutions.

Moral Tasks
Despite much discussion, morality is one of the social institutions that cannot really be analyzed. Regardless of the efforts to theorize it as ethics, developments in practice have been quite disappointing. That social existence is becoming increasingly devoid of morality is a common scientific finding. However, the causes and the consequences have not been sufficiently addressed. Morality has become an increasingly discredited institution and subject. But morality, both as an institution and as a subject, is more important than has been recognized. Both the crises experienced throughout history and the present-day global crisis are largely the result of a lack of morality. In history, when social conscience explained that Sodom (a city near the Dead Sea in antiquity) and Pompeii disappeared under the lava of volcanic eruptions because of moral corruption, it was perhaps trying to relay a certain truth! Moral corruption does cause societies to collapse. Indeed, what is called the curse of the gods is in essence nothing other than the way that social conscience (morality) punishes immorality projected into the heavenly realm. If we interpret the concept of God as society's most supreme and sacred identity, then these curses are the typical act of punishment unique to society.

It is simple to conceptually define morality. Knowing how to live in accordance with social customs, habits, and rules would be a suitable definition. But that does not explain its essence. The analyses of ethics attempted by philosophers, both in antiquity and in modern times (Plato, Aristotle, Kant, and others), have generally been contributions to an introduction to state theory. More precisely, these analyses resemble preliminary preparations for severing individuals from society and making them members of the state. They clearly approach the issue as if the task of morality is to groom individuals to best serve their state. In short, their interpretation of morality is pro-civilization.

As with all social issues, it would be more instructive to refer to history in relation to morality. We know that for 98 percent of the longue durée of social ages, it was not laws but moral rules that were valid. That's why we say moral society. If we do not understand the need this longue durée morality met, our interpretation of morality will remain incomplete. Defining social nature as the nature most charged with flexible intelligence may shed some light on the subject. What we mean by flexible intelligence is the ability to do while thinking. The relationship between thinking and doing will necessarily require rules, because determining how something is to be done is itself a rule. This initial act in relation to something that needs to be done can be considered the initial moral rule. When we talk about doing something, we include all social activity, including eating and sleeping, walking and finding food, being friends with animals or fighting with them, taking care of plants and fishing—each of these acts is work, and this work cannot be successful if there are no rules. Failure, on the other hand, would mean the death of society.

At this point, concepts like economic base and moral superstructure that divide the society seem ridiculous. Morality can be defined as the best way to address the economy, or, more precisely, to meet the basic needs of life. Morality, in terms of customs and procedures, determines the economy, or how the products required to meet basic needs are procured. Therefore, base-superstructure distinctions are far from being concepts that explain what is going on. Morality refers to carrying out all social activity, especially economic efforts, in a good way. Thus, everything that is social is moral, and everything that is moral is social. For example, just as the economy is moral, so too is religion. Politics as direct democracy is effectively morality itself.

Therefore, ever since the beginning, the first rule, the morality, has been a vital issue for the society. The best way to do a job settles in the mind as the best moral rule. Furthermore, it will be perfected over time, taking its place within social memory as a sound tradition. With this, morality takes shape. This is what is called tradition and customs. What we most need to understand here is that morality is related to the affairs of society as much as it is an intellectual act. It requires both an intellectual effort and community activism. Personally, I prefer to call this the original state of democracy. In this situation, original democracy and morality become identical. As society is always chasing after its vital affairs, it is inevitable that society as a whole will think about and discuss work, and it will not be content with this alone. It is an indispensable necessity of life that society will focus a good deal of energy on how to best manage its affairs and how to succeed. Clearly, thinking and discussing, decision-making, and coordinating the implementation of decisions so that the work is successful is direct, participatory democracy, the most face-to-face form of democracy. It is, at the same time, society's moral governance and way of life. Thus, the source of morality and democracy is one and the same: the collective mind of social practice and its capacity for work. It is not only 98 percent of historical society's life span that has unfolded in a state of morality and original democracy, both morality and democracy have made their way into the present, even if in social units that are very fragmented and that have been left to themselves, it is overwhelmingly morality not law that is applied. Although morality has greatly deteriorated, we must still understand that without morality there can be no life at any level, ranging from the family to the ethnic group, or even in relation to the work done in many institutional areas, where even the smallest details are determined by law. Law is just a cover. I am quite certain that the force that actually makes things run remains morality.

When we look at the civilization process, the very first thing we note is the consistent attempt to replace morality with state norms. That the first code of law, the Code of Hammurabi, was engraved on a stele clarifies the situation perfectly. It may be said that morality is no longer sufficient, making law necessary, but that is simply wrong. The problem is not the insufficiency of morality but the erosion of moral society. We identified how the erosion of morality took place. This was how the manifold capital and power monopolies first established themselves over society and how social values began to be usurped. Under these conditions, we cannot talk about the insufficiency of morality but about dominating society and subjecting it to oppression and exploitation by the application of the rule of law, the application of the so-called rules of state administration.

Therefore, the reach of morality and, in connection with it, direct democracy is increasingly shrinking. In contrast, the reach of state governance and law is expanding. One side's loss is the other side's gain. Explicitly stated, morality loses in the face of the force applied by the state. This is achieved by shrinking morality's reach and making its implementation more difficult. In all the later civilized societies, the reach of morality (as well as of direct democracy) continued to shrink, and the reach of law constantly increased. Indeed, Roman civilization, the end point and the sum of ancient civilizations, was the state administration that applied law most vigorously, confirming what we have been saying. Roman law remains a cornerstone of modern law. Over the course of European civilization, in other words, during modernism, society experienced the invasion of law, so to speak. Indeed, there has been a kind of legal colonialism. While the reach of morality was restricted to the remotest corners, law has been offered a seat of honor at every table.

What does this reality reflect? It shows the increased weight of capital monopoly and power in society. When we look at the modernity of the last four hundred years, what we see is the maximum possible capital accumulation and the proliferation of power, or, more correctly put, the intertwined cumulative accumulation of the two. We cannot say that morality has become dysfunctional, but, rather, that it has been stripped away from society. The society where morality was applied has been torn down and carted away. The claim that there is a need for law because society has become too complicated to be governed by morality is a great lie and, therefore, an immoral conclusion. It truly is not a matter of failure, insufficiency, or an inability to function due to the complexity of society. This is nothing more than a very simple rule of liberal ideological hegemony: the rule that propaganda and attrition easily eliminates opponents. During the era of capitalist modernity, the role of liberalism's ideological hegemony in shaping a negative approach to morality is completely obvious. Who could fail to see that the law substituted for morality is fraught with the most irrational and unconscionable rules? It is not for nothing that there is a local saying, stating that what happens to you at court is worse than what happens to a boiling hen. The more legal codes in any given place or institution, the more effective the monopoly of oppression and exploitation. The practical reality of even setting foot in any institution confirms this.

Another important related question is: Does morality or law govern better? Although our narrative answers that question, the very fact that law is an enforced governance should be enough to clarify reality. As we all know, law is defined as "the execution and enforcement of rules and regulations by the state." With morality, there is no forced execution of rules. In fact, a rule that has not been internalized cannot be called a moral rule. If governance based on the enforcement of law and moral governance are compared, it is clear that the good will prevail and the scales will surely tip to morality.

Another important issue that requires analysis is the relationship between morality and religion. Just as it is possible to establish a similitude between morality and direct democracy, for the communities that are outside of civilization or anti-civilization, we can also establish a similitude between religion and morality. In circumstances in which religion had not yet been shaped by civilization, morality, religion, and direct democracy were intertwined. Morality is an institution that predates religion and primarily addresses the aspect of morality that deals with emotions and thoughts around taboos, sacredness, enchantment, things that elude easy definition, and the inability to control the forces of nature. When a society acknowledges and understands how to accept a nature different from its own it creates both fear and a sense of compassion. The idea of avoiding the negative elements of nature and its forces and benefiting from their positive aspects, knowing that human life is very much bound to them, seems to be the source of the original primitive institution and tradition of religion.

It is undisputed that religion is a precivilization institution. It encompasses the elements of morality that are more prohibitive and addresses what needs to be avoided, as well as the need for compassion and forgiveness. With time, it became a much more rigid tradition. In this sense, morality's most stringent and holy commands and rules of order constitute religion. Despite emerging from morality, of which it was initially a part, religion has been strengthened by changes in time and place, making its institution and rules into laws that are more stringent and compulsory (e.g., Moses's typical Ten Commandments order), thereby declaring its independence and dominance. It can be compared to law, which emerged in a similar way. As the state arose, rules of law that were initially aspects of morality were transformed into forcibly imposed laws, becoming what we call the law today. Religion went through a further change with the development of the civilization process; it was turned into a divine force that could severely punish society, with its nature being transformed to benefit the forces of exploitation and power. Where law executed monopoly interests through state administration, religion—with the stamp of the new civilization—tried to administer it through god.

Both of these transformations were important. They represent the two most important moments of rupture in history. The fundamental rule of ideological hegemony is that the rising authority of power and the kingdom would strengthen its position by attributing divine terms to itself. When you dig into the concept of *god*, you find the tyranny and plunder of oppressive and exploitative monopolies and state and power apparatuses, as well as their use of power to impose slavish work on the people. What is most important is to determine that the elements of those parts of religion with democratic social dimension that are identical with morality are gradually turned into units of nature and society. Thus, it is possible to make sense of how, throughout the history of civilization, religion developed an identity, tradition, and culture with two distinct characteristics. While the religion and the god identified with civilization forces is fraught with fear, punishment, the threat of being cast into hell, starvation, destruction, mercilessness, war, domination, dominion, ownership, and worship (concepts primarily related to characteristics of the representatives and forces of civilization), the religion and the god identified with moral and political society is rife with courage, forgiveness, mercifulness, hope, constant nurturing, creation and sustainment of life, compassion, love, peace, dissolution within the self, and rejoining.

Therefore, it is extremely instructive to define religion throughout the history of civilization in terms of these two identities. Abrahamic religions typically carry within them these two tendencies. The more the high-level religious representatives (priests, rabbis, shaykhs al-islam, ayatollahs, etc.) reflect the civilization tendency, the more people of the ummah at the lower levels tend to reflect the democratic civilization tendency. These tendencies may exist in equilibrium, or one of them might be dominant, depending on the time and place. Abrahamic religions, which reflect this equilibrium, remind us of modernity's social democrats. Just as social democrats represent the reconciliation of differences between the bourgeoisie and the working class (under the hegemony of capital and power monopolies, of course), the Abrahamic religions represent the reconciliation of differences between the forces of capital and power, on one hand, and forces of democratic civilization, on the other hand (once again under the hegemony of ruling powers).

Historically, we find Zoroastrianism to be an exceptional teaching and Zarathustra an exceptional personality in terms of the relationship between religion and morality. Studies define Zarathustra's teachings as a great moral revolution. Located in the foothills of Zagros Mountains, in a social and cultural setting based on agriculture and animal husbandry (a culture that arose in the wake of the Neolithic Revolution that accompanied the end of the fourth ice age, or perhaps even before that, having potentially existed for as long as twenty thousand years), this moral revolution developed as a tendency that advocated secular and worldly morality rather than holiness and that opposed the mythological and religious hegemony of Sumerian civilization (3000 BCE onward). Although it is called Zoroastrianism in reference to Zarathustra, its roots are much older. It is clear that Zarathustra, with his famous dictum, "Tell me, who are you?" passes judgment on the mythological and religious divinity of Sumerian civilization. This first moral critique of religion and the gods of civilization is of great importance. It wasn't just happenstance that the philosopher Friedrich Nietzsche named his famous work, which arrives at judgments similar to those of Zoroastrian morality, *Thus Spoke Zarathustra*.[5] In this regard, he is known as the most powerful interpreter of civilization. It is thought-provoking that he uses the epithets of "disciple of Zarathustra" and "disciple of Dionysus."

In Zoroastrianism, elements of democratic civilization predominate and relationships between women and men in families are closer to equal. No pain is inflicted on animals; while it is essential to benefit from their produce, they are not generally used for meat. Agriculture is greatly valued. Concepts of good and evil that are free from divinity come to the fore. The dualistic way of thinking (forces of light and darkness) evocative of the very first seeds of dialectical thinking is quite apparent, and there is an attempt to understand the universe dialectically. The use of strong moral principles to govern society is essential. All of this reflects a strong moral revolution against the Sumerians and civilizations with Sumerian roots. It could be argued that the most important result of this revolution, although distorted, was the Median Confederation and the Persian Empire that inherited it (sadly, with numerous contortions). Mani (c. 250 CE) attempted to carry out a second revolution in this moral teaching, but the extremely corrupt Sasanian emperors prevented this, severely punishing him. There was a clash between these two religious and moral identities.

There are still traces (Mazdean, Yazidi) of the Zarathustra-Mani moral tradition present in places ranging from the Middle East to India and into Europe. The word *zendik* is Zoroastrian.[6] I suspect it is also the root for the word *science*. It is worth noting that the Jewish prophets of the Babylonian exile (600–546 BCE) and Greek-Ionian philosophers during the time of the Median-Persian Empire, as well as European Orientalists, were all directly influenced by the Zoroastrian tradition. Confucius, Socrates, and the Buddha, who are believed to have lived in the same period as Zarathustra (sixth and fifth centuries BCE), based their fundamental teachings on moral society and represented a very strong defense of morality against civilization's threat to morality. In the Middle Ages, the moral element held a very important place in Islamic and Christian teachings. There has been a great erosion of morality during the period of European civilization, the reasons for which we discussed in detail earlier.

Even these brief historical reminders indicate the great resilience of moral society. As long as morality remained true to itself, it did not capitulate to the forces of civilization. There was never a lack of moral insistence on the part of the demos in the face of civilization's imposed religion and law. The main questions about and the tasks of morality today are around how it should be positioned. Obviously, the study of ethics (the theory of morality) as a branch of social sciences is a task to be taken up in the intellectual area. The key issue, however, is to determine how ethics will become a united whole with society and how the eroded moral society will more strongly reequip itself with morality. The task of rebuilding morality is not only a question of the sustainability of the century or the current modernity but of society itself. It has become quite clear that the global crisis will not be overcome by the force of law. The return to religiosity is also a lost cause. It is necessary to understand that if the strong moral fabric of social nature is not made to function again, there is no way out of this global crisis for modernity. The crisis we are experiencing was created by all the anti-society forces of five thousand years of civilization to the disadvantage of moral society. Therefore, to find a way out, it is a dialectical necessity to look to both moral society and political society— because morality and direct democracy are identical. If we fail to agree in principal on this assessment, no moral task can be correctly determined. Since morality is democratic modernity's major weapon for finding a way out of the global crisis of modernity, let us try, in the form of principles, to identify the moral tasks that await in any effort to rebuild morality:

a) The global crisis of modernity (the present-day systemic structural crisis) is the result of the destruction of moral society by the forces of five thousand years of civilization. Dialectically, seeking the way out of the crisis by rebuilding moral society is correct, and, as such, is our main option.

b) Moral and political society, the fundamental unit of democratic modernity, continues to predominantly exist as social nature, despite all of the erosion and deterioration it has suffered at the hands of the forces of civilization and modernity and the attempts to eliminate it altogether. Civilization forces are a limited elite network (perhaps never more than 10 percent the size of moral and political society); the oppressed and exploited nations, peoples, and ethnicities, women, agrarian-village societies, the unemployed, nomads, youth, marginalized groups, etc. still constitute the vast majority.

c) What primarily sustains and maintains society is not the state's legal system but the moral element, albeit weak and despite efforts to completely cut it off from society. If society is not totally destroyed, morality also cannot be totally destroyed. The depth of a society's crisis is linked to the degradation of morality in that society. Eventually morality must play its role as the most fundamental social fabric and institution, not only for us to get out of the crisis but so that societies can happily continue to exist.

d) While ethical studies are tasks within the intellectual area, and democratic politics relate to the political area, neither can play its role if it does not become a united whole with moral society. Morality denotes the reality of a society where the tasks related to both of these areas have been implemented. Within its democratic scope, there is an identity between religion and morality. Thus, places of worship must be the institutions where social morality is most thoroughly instilled. Houses of worship, in particular churches and mosques, should be regarded as practical moral institutions, and therefore it would be good to utilize them in building moral society. It is especially important for mosques to regain their role as moral centers, as they widely were during Mohammad's time, when mosques were more than just sites for extremely simple rituals like prayer but were primarily centers for rebuilding moral and political society. Prayer was conceived as ritual approval of this work. Later, the rituals became essential, and the more fundamental building of moral and political society was forgotten and cast into oblivion.

The program, organization, and mode of operation of democratic modernity, as moral institutions in which moral and political society is rebuilt, should, if necessary, be reformed and restructured. Alevi *cemevi*,[7] which for the most part play the role of moral and political society institutions, also need to be restructured to assume a leading role in the efforts to rebuild. Moral and political society units have the right to engage in sacred and moral resistance to the impositions of power and the state, a right they should exercise, if necessary. Freedom of religion and conscience (morality) also necessitates this.

e) Contrary to popular opinion, laicism with a modern cover and the radical or moderate new religionism that claims to be acting on the basis of tradition are not two opposing tendencies but two eclectic ideological versions of liberalism and, thus, cannot play a moral and political role. To avoid falling into these traps, it is important to develop an approach that integrates the democratic content of religion and the partially free and secular elements of laicism. Both elements can only play a role in rebuilding democratic modernity in this way. We should not be party to centuries-old games and fights between them; instead, we should do what we can to frustrate their efforts to corrupt religion and morality and to reintegrate religion and morality into modernity in a way that serves their interests.

f) We should not be fooled by the terror that law inflicts on society via state violence. Morality is essential; law is secondary. So long as it is just, law is respected. If not, it is essential to insist to the end upon the principles of moral and political society. It should not be forgotten even for a minute that to defend and sustain society we must take a moral stance.

g) Vatican-style Catholic ecumenicalism and institutions of the former caliphate representing the Islamic ummah, along with Judaism, Buddhism, and similar moral and religious traditions, should reinstitutionalize themselves under a common roof to constitute an institution for the global representation of moral-ity. If they were to focus on ethical practices rather than theology, they might well play a major role in rebuilding moral and political society on behalf of humanity. In a way, just as the nation-states are united under the umbrella of UN, to be successful it is neces-sary that all fundamental moral teachings unite and establish an institution that opposes the attacks of modernity. In keeping with this necessity, the Global Confederation of Sacredness and Moral Studies must be established in opposition to the monstrosities of civilization and modernity that are attempting to engulf all sacredness and all moral teachings.

h) The forces of democratic modernity must understand that if they do not embrace and implement their tasks in the moral area, they cannot successfully defend and sustain democratic society units from the attacks carried out by the forces of civilization and modernity using extensive weapons of ideological and material culture.

These brief assessments in relation to the definition of morality as a subject and an institution are intended as proposals for a solution and will require extensive discussion. Neither moral society nor social nature fit into schemes of superstructure/base. Every social unit, and even each individual, should know full well that living without morality is impos-sible. The important thing is that society and the individual are equipped with good morality. Whatever the degree of the attack waged by the mon-strosities of civilization and modernity, we have no choice but to defend moral society to the same degree. Those who cannot defend their society lose the right to a dignified life. Yet without morality society cannot be defended. In the rebuilding efforts of democratic modernity, the success attained by all the social units in their moral tasks will be the fundamental criterion for victoriously exiting the system's global crisis.

Political Tasks

Politics, like *morality*, is a word surrounded by a swirl of conceptual confu-sion and chaos. The word's meaning is simple: it has roots in Ancient Greek, and *the art of city governance* is what it should be understood to mean. But the search for truth in words is a fairly limited method that will prove dis-appointing. Terms regarding social nature are in general quite ambiguous.

They may point to reality, but they cannot constitute it. We should look a bit beyond the terms to find reality. Unfortunately, this can only be possible with terms, in which case, what becomes important is our capacity to interpret. Thus, the intention might be better expressed if we specify the core meaning of politics to be *the art of freedom*. Freedom evokes a proximity to truth. Of course, when we use terms like *politics, freedom*, and *truth*, our fundamental research unit is yet again moral and political society. Frankly, I steer clear of assessments based on individuals or other basic research units that distance themselves from the social. My uneasiness increases when I think of terms like *war, conflict*, and *exploitation*, which have become almost identical with the term *politics*. It further increases my pessimism if politics and polis (the state) are considered identical.

It is not as easy as it looks to make a successful breakthrough with something as challenging as the political task. Rather than not try at all, it is important to engage in a modest attempt to at least encourage discussion and, as a result, research. Above all, I think it is necessary to determine what is not politics. First, it is important to understand that state affairs are not political but administrative affairs. Based on the state, one cannot engage in politics, but can only administer. Second, affairs that do not concern the vital interests of the society do not constitute essential politics. They are at the same level as the routine work that is performed by other social institutions. Third, things that are not related to freedom, equality, and democracy are fundamentally of no concern to politics. The opposite of all these affairs fundamentally concerns politics; the vital interests of society are its well-being, security, nourishment, along with the freedom, equality, and democracy, which power and the state prevent. As we can see, political affairs and state affairs are not one and the same; to the contrary, they are in open contradiction. This means that the more the state expands and concentrates, the narrower and more stagnant politics become. The state means rules, whereas politics means creativity. The state administers what is readily there, whereas politics governs as it constitutes. The state is a craft, whereas politics is an art.

The relationship between power and politics is a lot more ambiguous. It may be that, even more than the state, power is the negation of politics. Power is a lot more entrenched in society than the state. This indicates how difficult it is to engage in politics in society and how restricted the options to do so are. Ultimately, the relationship between politics and power is always tense, with lots of action.

We have no choice but to approach the subject more concretely, because politics without a practice is meaningless. We have tried to analyze many related areas of moral and political society. The reader will forgive some necessary repetition here. Society is not only a moral but also a political fact or nature. Society is political, not in terms of official state work as believed but in terms of social nature. If the function of morality is to conduct matters pertaining to life in the best possible way, the function of politics is to find what these good matters are. It should be noted that politics has a moral dimension but entails more than that. It is not that easy to find what these good matters are. It requires a reasonable overview of the matters that need to be addressed, knowledge and science, and research. When the concept *good* is added, it also requires moral knowledge. As can be seen, politics is a very difficult art. It is a major misconception to think of politics as intertwined with bulky terms like the *state, empire, dynasty, nation, corporation, class*, and so on. It might diminish the significance of politics if it is thought of as intertwined with these and similar facts and terms. Genuine politics is hidden in its definition: the only terms that can explain the vital interests of society are *freedom, equality*, and *democracy*, which means that politics is essentially the acts of freedom, equality, and democratization needed for moral and political society to sustain its nature or existence under any and all circumstances.

When we talk about moral and political society, we are not talking about prehistoric times. We are talking about the natural state of social nature that is constantly lived and will continue to exist so long as the society's existence does not end. No matter how much moral and political society is corroded, decayed, and fragmented, it will always exist. So long as social nature exists so will moral and political society. The role of politics is to make this existence free, equal, and democratic, in order to further develop it without further erosion, decay, and fragmentation. Any moral and political society that lives such a situation is the best possible society; it is the realization of the society we aim for.

For a better understanding of the essence of this term, we must yet again turn to history, with *civilization* once again being the prevailing term, not only because it embodies *power* and the *state*, but also in terms of its relationship to class division and urbanism. The role of politics shrinks as the ideological and material networks of civilization continuously expand and concentrate, encapsulating moral and political society and resulting in the decline or negation of social freedom, equality, and democratization. The history of civilization is full of such developments. The further enslavement, serfdom, and proletarianization of those societies already under civilization's domination will continue by becoming a process of oppression and colonization of outside societies that are freer, more equal, and more democratic. The law of maximum profit of the capital and power monopolies necessitates this. In this situation, politics becomes meaningful as the resistance of democratic civilization units. In the absence of resistance, none of the steps taken for freedom, equality, and democratization can succeed nor can the erosion, decay, fragmentation, and colonization of the existing level of morality and politics be prevented or the exploitation of the monopolies be stopped. Politics is defined as the art of freedom, because it has played this role throughout history. Every class, city, community, tribe, religious community, and people-nation that has been unable to or has been prevented from engaging in politics has had a huge blow delivered to its voice and willpower. When a society has no collective voice or willpower, there is only deadly silence.

In ancient times, Athens and Rome gained a reputation as a result of their political power. If Rome's republic and Athens's democracy are still remembered with awe, despite their limited implementation, it is primarily because they were proficient at urban politics. While Athens effectively used its urban politics to ward off the gigantic Persian Empire, it simultaneously laid the groundwork for its own defeat. On the other hand, Rome, with its republican politics, would become the center of the world. Be that as it may, at the end of the day, the politics of these two cities played a decisive role in the development of Greco-Roman culture.

The Babylonian example is even more striking. We could perhaps present Babylonia as the first major example of the independence or autonomy of a city. To avoid falling under the yoke of the greater powers and state forces surrounding them, Babylonia pursued a politics of independence and autonomy with great skill and mastery. Facing all the famous empires of history, from the Assyrians to the Hittites, from the Kassites to the Mitannis, from the Persians to Alexander's Macedonian Empire, this city was able to stand on its two feet as a result of its masterful policies. With the science, arts, and industry it developed, it became a civilization that proved to be a long-lasting center of attraction (until around 2000 BCE). The urban policy it pursued played an evident role in this. Clearly, this is one of the most striking examples proving that politics is freedom and creativity.

We could possibly point to Carthage and Palmyra as similar examples. With its resistance politics, Carthage held out against Roman hegemony for a long time and continued its creative development. It was only when Carthage fell into the trap of wanting to become an empire like Rome that it could no longer escape defeat. Becoming an empire runs contrary to resistance politics; it is, in fact, the negation of politics. The result was a tragic loss. The process in Palmyra was similar. The famous Palmyra, perhaps the most developed city after Babylonia that was able to stay autonomous and independent for a very long time (300 BCE–270 CE), created a paradise in the desert, but when it deserted its politics of equilibrium and autonomy with the Roman and Persian-Sasanian Empires and tried to become an empire in its own right (during the time of its famous Queen Zenobia, 270 CE), it could not escape its tragic end. The tragedy of Palmyra presents another striking example that illustrates resistance for freedom leads to victory, whereas the struggle for power leads to disaster.

During the Middle Ages, similar autonomous urban politics were more widely practiced. Cities resisting the large empires were like a constellation of stars. In the name of autonomy, thousands of cities, from the Pacific Ocean to the Atlantic Ocean, and even to the American continent, from the Great Sahara to Siberia, resisted the Islamic empires (Umayyad, Abbasid, Seljuk, Timurid, Babur, Ottoman), Genghis Khan's Mongol empire, the Christian empires (Byzantium, Spain, Austria, Tsarist Russia, Britain), and the Chinese empires, even at the cost of being wiped out and disappearing from history. Like Carthage, the city of Otrar (Farab) resisted Genghis Khan and was totally destroyed. There were hundreds of examples of European cities resisting both the imperial forces and nation-state centralism for centuries. Until mid-nineteenth century, Italian and German cities in particular exhibited substantial resistance to protect their autonomous structures. Venice and Amsterdam are the two most famous examples.

The victory of nation-states everywhere in the nineteenth century was a major blow to the autonomy of cities that had existed for thousands of years. But with postmodernity, the autonomy of cities is again becoming widespread, with urban politics coming to the forefront.

Historically, there were numerous examples of autonomous political forces resisting civilization forces in order to remain autonomous. This resistance came not only from politicized cities but perhaps even more so from the tribes, aşirets, religious communities, philosophical schools, and certain social groups. Perhaps the story of the 3,500-year-old

(1600 BCE to the present) Hebrew tribe's autonomy is the most famous example. The politics of autonomy implemented by the Hebrew tribe have been the decisive factor in Jewish people being rich and creative, not only historically but even more so today. Many great denominations that displayed great resistance emerged against the conversion of Islam into an instrument of power and empire. Denominations like the Alevi and the Kharijite reflect the policy of autonomous living adhered to by the tribes and aşirets. The widespread oppositional denominations resisting Sunni sovereignty and the sultanate tradition found within the fabric of every people are in essence the result of the resistance and libertarian policies of tribal and aşiret peoples. In a way, these are the first people's liberation and independence movements against Sunni Islamic colonialism. There are many similar resistance denominations in Christianity and Judaism. The Middle Ages were overrun with local, urban, tribal, and religious communities struggling for freedom and autonomy. The three hundred years of semisecret insurgent monastery life of the first Christian communities played a leading role in laying the groundwork for contemporary civilization. The autonomous policies of the ancient Greek philosophical schools were the fundamental force that laid the base for science. Peoples and nations that have survived to date owe this to their tribal and aşiret ancestors, who resisted for hundreds and thousands of years on mountaintops and in deserts.

The national liberation struggles of the modern era are the continuation of this tradition. Their pursuit, even though it may have been distorted to seeking an independent state, was political independence. Although liberalism transformed political independence into nation-state independence and, thus, deflected politics from its true function, national liberation struggles are, nonetheless, the continuation of a very important tradition of political resistance.

Local and regional autonomy policies have always existed in history and played an important role in the survival of moral and political society. In a very widespread geography in our world, especially in the mountainous, desert, and forested areas, peoples and nations living in tribal, aşiret, village, and urban societies have continuously resisted civilization forces with the politics of autonomy and independence. This is why we emphasize that the democratic confederal tradition is a predominant tradition in history. Throughout the history of civilization, the dominant tendency has been resistance not submission. If that were not the case, the whole world would be like the Egypt of the pharaohs. We cannot adequately interpret history if we are not aware that there was not a single locality or region without resistance and politics. If peoples in South America, Africa, and Asia, in all their colors and with all their diverse cultures, continue to resist, it is because their history is one of resistance, and because history is "now."

Humanity has not only developed political resistance at the social or regional level to protect its existence and dignity, history offers numerous examples of insurgent individuals who have played a significant role akin to that of a nation. From Adam and Noah to Job (Ayyub), from Abraham to Moses, from Jesus to Mohammad, it is said that there are 124,000 prophets in the Holy Scripture, as well as many individuals and countless sages, ranging from the goddess Inanna to Aisha, from Zenobia to Hypatia, from Cybele to Mary, from the Buddha to Socrates, from Zarathustra to Confucius, from witches to Zeynep[8] to Rosa, from Bruno to Erasmus, all of whom resisted to the death to maintain their freedom and dignity. If society remains moral and political, it owes much to these individuals. Without their contributions, we would not be able to distinguish societies from herds of slaves.

Undoubtedly, it is currently even more important that we are able to interpret politics. But we cannot do so without stating that history overwhelmingly carries on today. Regarding the shrinking area of politics, we continue to emphasize that "capitalist modernity is a thousand times worse than civilization in general." Recalling our analysis of the nation-state, we indicated that society was not only subjected to state domination from above, but that it was opened up to influence, invasion, and colonization by the power apparatus in all of its most hidden nooks and crannies. Grasping how this reality has besieged, conquered, and colonized society on a global scale is important. Let me just remind you how the networks of ideological and material culture spread. This is a new situation. It does not matter what we call it, a global super hegemony, an empire, or the UN order, because its essence remains the same. In addition, we emphasized that while financial capital has left its mark on the global hegemony, there is also a global, systemic, and structural crisis that has become permanent.

Under these circumstances, as we try to determine what is left of moral and political society, we must also question whether politics is still capable of playing a role. Looking at the present picture, we see many falling into pessimism and hopelessness. It is precisely at this point that we can deduce from a profound political examination of the situation that this pessimism and hopelessness is not only unfounded but is meaningless. Every trend has a maximum and a minimum (that's a universal truth). All indications are that at present the rule of civilization and modernity has begun its descent. Power, which has been dispersed throughout society, is losing its strength, much in the way a wave weakens. Just like a big stone that falls from a peak breaks into smaller, lighter pieces when it hits the ground, power that penetrates all of society's pores breaks into smaller pieces in much the same way.

It is possible to determine the sociological significance of this reality. The more power spreads to all of society's units and individuals, the greater the resistance against it by the individual and the units. Power creates resistance to itself in every individual and unit it extends into. It would be against the universal flow of nature if power did not run into resistance, as it encounters every individual and unit laden with oppression, exploitation, and torture. The modern reality of power differs quite a bit from the reality of power in any other historical age. Capitalism, in the form of capital monopolies that wrap a web around the world's economy, has completed its expansion in search of maximum profit, and now there is nowhere else for it to go. Moreover, if we consider the crisis in the area of ecology, there isn't a single family or clan that has not been touched in profound ways. The consequences of industrialism's capitalistic laws have taken the destruction it has caused in the internal structures of the society and in the environment to catastrophic levels. The nation-state, as the most powerful divinity in history, has penetrated every citizen and established its hegemony. At no previous point in history has there been a period like this. The "discontinuities" mentioned by Anthony Giddens apply precisely to these matters.

Faced with this reality of power (capitalism, industrialism, and the nation-state), politics, as its opposite pole, must also undergo an unprecedented change. Since we are not in a period that can be characterized as either pre- or post-civilization, the structure of politics that is specific to modernity must necessarily be different. Briefly formulated: since the web of power is everywhere, politics must also be everywhere, and since power rests on every individual and social unit, politics must also rest on every individual and social unit.

It is obvious why we need to develop and extend the webs of politics to meet and oppose the webs of power wrapped around society, and it is clear that this cannot be achieved using former organizational models. The former organizational models were state-centered. First and foremost, politics must begin as a form of resistance to power. Since power tries to conquer and colonize every individual and social unit, politics must try to win over and liberate every individual and social unit that it rests upon. Since every relationship, whether that of an individual or a unit, is related to power, it is also political in the opposite sense. Since power breeds liberal ideology, industrialism, capitalism, and the nation-state, politics must produce and build an ideology of freedom, eco-industry, communal society, and democratic confederalism. Since power is organized in every individual and unit, every city and village, at local, regional, national, continental, and global levels, politics must respond in kind. Since power enforces numerous forms of action at all these levels, including propaganda and war, politics must counter at every level with the appropriate propaganda and different forms of action.

If we fail to grasp the reality of power in modernity, which we have attempted to outline here, we will be unable to correctly approach any political task. Let's keep in mind the Soviet experience, as well as the earlier stages of real socialism: capitalism versus workers' syndicalism (wage beggary), industrialism versus even more developed industry, and centralized nation-statism versus an even more centralized nation-statism. In short, there was an internal collapse under the unendurable weight of the gigantic power apparatus that can be described as power versus power, fire versus fire, dictatorship versus dictatorship, and state capitalism versus private capitalism. In this way, the real socialist denomination (left-wing capitalism) not only engaged in politics against power but also exercised power against politics. Reading the history of real socialist parties is enough to make this perfectly obvious. The social democratic denomination (centrist capitalism) made power more permanent by reforming it, as the history of these parties in Europe makes entirely clear. The national liberation movement denomination (right-wing capitalism), on the other hand, became the leading force in the spread of capitalism around the world by immediately becoming nation-states when successful. I addressed other opponents of the system, outside of these three denominations, earlier. Their most serious shortcomings and failures were that even in opposition to power they either tried to hang on to a part of that power (through the nation-state) or, like the anarchists, created a total power vacuum or fiddled around with civil society organizations. None of them had a systematic understanding of power or the ability to generate politics as an alternative nor did they feel the need to do so. While they left politics in the hands of all sorts of power subcontractors, they were not even aware that they were hoping for the impossible. What remains, as a result, is to be the middleman who announces the crisis of capitalism— i.e., globalism—which has not and never can remedy any of our problems.

The language of democratic modernity is political. It envisages and builds its systematic structure using the art of politics. The moral and political society aspect of the fundamental sciences evokes politics not power. Moral and political society's primary problem today is beyond that of freedom, equality, and democracy, it is existential; its very existence is in danger. The multidimensional attacks of modernity make moral and political society's priority defending its very existence. The response of democratic modernity to these attacks is resistance in the form of self-defense. If society is not defended, there can be no politics. Let me be perfectly clear, there is only one society, and that is moral and political society. The problem is to rebuild society under the more developed conditions of modernity, which has been highly eroded by civilization and, has been subjected to invasion and colonization by power and the state. Along with self-defense, democratic politics is the essence of politics in the present period. While democratic politics develop moral and political society, self-defense protects it from the attacks of power on its very existence, its freedom, and its egalitarian and democratic structure. We are not talking about a new kind of national liberation struggle or a social war. We are talking about defending our identity, freedom, equality in diversity, and democratization. If there are no attacks, there will be no need for self-defense.

The political way of life—which is the main tendency in history—of the anti-civilization forces is confederal. All social units accept loose interdependence on the condition that respect is shown for their autonomy. They consent to the existence of civilization's ruling and statist forces only on that condition. When there is no consent, there is a state of permanent war. When there is consent, the result is peace. The principle of social governance that can counter the phenomena of power and the nation-state structures, which have encapsulated all of society in the modern era, is politics and democratic confederalism. When politics is exercised as democratic politics, all social units participate in the confederal process as federate forces. This system is a new political world. While civilization and modernity always administer through a command structure, democratic civilization and democratic modernity govern through discussion and consensus, i.e., through genuine politics. No matter how badly the historical and present facts have been distorted and obscured, the essential social developments have been achieved under the leadership of the art of politics. As capitalism struggles to protect its power in conditions of global crisis and on the basis of the reconstruction of its nation-state, the fundamental task of all forces of democratic modernity is to build a democratic confederal system that aims to defend and develop moral and political society, thereby responding to the crisis.

In the light of these comments, it is possible to summarize the general principles related to the political tasks facing the forces of democratic modernity:

a) Social nature is essentially a moral and political formation, a way of existence. As long as societies continue to exist, their moral and political qualities will also continue. Societies that lose their moral and political quality are doomed to erode, decay, and perish.

b) Envisaging societies as forms that continuously progress in a linear way—e.g., from primitive to slave-owning to feudal to capitalist to socialist—only serves to distort and obscure their truths rather than contributing to understanding them. Such explanations are primarily laden with propaganda. The moral and political quality is the main characteristic of society, and thus it is best to characterize societies by its degree of existence. Both the qualities of class and the state and the level of industrial and agricultural development are transient phenomena that do not constitute the essential character of society.

c) The social problem arises in connection with the domination and exploitation exercised by power. As power and exploitation develop, so do social problems. Class-based states imposed as instruments for a solution may generate some limited solutions, but they essentially transform into a source of new problems.

d) Politics is not only a fundamental tool for the solution of social problems but also for determining, protecting, and sustaining all the vital interests of society. Self-defense, for its part, is necessary to protect society and is merely the continuation of politics by military means.

e) Throughout history, as civilizations tried to rule society with a state administration, the role of politics in the society has continuously shrunk. As long as they exist, societies respond with resistance to the shrinking role of politics. The interaction of these two factors means that history has neither seen a complete administration of civilization nor complete democratic political governance. Historical conflicts stem from the contradictory characteristics of these two main factors.

f) Times of peace in history have occurred when civilization forces and democratic forces reciprocally recognized each other and respected one another's identities and interests. Neither conflicts nor cease-fires as maneuvers to attain power have anything to do with peace.

g) During capitalist modernity, power besieges society both internally and externally and turns it into a kind of internal colony. The nation-state, as power and the fundamental state form, are in constant war with the society. This reality is the source of resistance politics.

h) Capitalist modernity's all-out war makes the democratic modernity alternative more urgent and necessary. Democratic modernity, as the present actuality of the forces of democratic civilization, is neither the memory of a past golden age nor a future utopia. It is the existence of and stance adopted by all individuals and social units whose interests and existence contradict the capitalist system.

i) The struggle of the anti-system forces over the last two hundred years has failed and is at an impasse due to their perspective to come to power or the error of leaving the political area empty. Although these forces bring with them a precious legacy, they cannot offer an alternative to either modernity or the systemic crises because of the old mentality and structures.

j) Becoming an alternative requires developing a system against the three pillars of modernity: capitalism, industrialism, and the nation-state. The opposing system can be called democratic modernity, with democratic society, eco-industry, and democratic confederalism as its three pillars. The legacy of democratic civilization and the system's opponents convening within the new system increase the likelihood of success.

k) Democratic confederalism is the fundamental political form of democratic modernity and will play a vital role in the work of rebuilding. Against the nation-state, the fundamental state form that continuously breeds problems, democratic confederalism, the fundamental political option of democratic modernity, is the most appropriate means for democratic politics to arrive at solutions to problems.

l) In moral and political societies, where democratic politics are in effect, freedom, equality in diversity, and democratic development are achieved in the healthiest possible way. Freedom, equality, and democracy are only possible through the discussion, decision-making, and action of a society with its own conscience and intellectual power and cannot be achieved through any form of social engineering.

m) Democratic confederalism offers the option of the democratic nation as the fundamental means for solving the ethnic, religious, urban, local, regional, and national problems that arise from modernity's monolithic, homogeneous, and monochrome fascist society model implemented by the nation-state. All ethnicities, religious views, urban, local, regional, and national realities have the right to take part in the democratic nation with their own identity and democratic federate structure.

n) The global union of democratic nations, the World Confederation of Democratic Nations, would be an alternative to the United Nations. Continental areas and broad cultural spaces could form their own Confederation of Democratic Nations at the local level. Were the EU not to act hegemonically, its initiatives could be considered a first step in this direction. Objections to global and regional hegemonic power should be understood in this context.

o) Capitalist modernity forces and democratic modernity forces can coexist peacefully by acknowledging each other's existence and identity and recognizing each other's autonomous democratic governance, as has often occurred between civilization forces and democratic forces throughout history. Within this scope and under these conditions, democratic confederal political formations and nation-state formations can coexist peacefully, both within and outside of nation-state borders.

The principles established above in relation to the tasks in democratic modernity's political area could either be reduced or added to. The important thing is to determine the necessary scope and the principles of implementation. I think the principles outlined above serve that purpose. Discussion and the reality of freedom in life will determine the outcome.

The same is true for the principles I attempted to identify in relation to the three main areas of democratic modernity. I cannot too strongly emphasize that the democratic modernity that will be rebuilt will neither be a new republican project like that discussed during the French Revolution nor a Soviet-style state like that of the Russian Revolution, either in its principles or its implementation. Nor will it be like Mohammad's Medina social project. The only thing I am concerned about and that I wish to make crystal clear is that my analysis of the truth of social nature and the methods and principles to be applied to solve the problem of social freedom must not lead to profound misconceptions, as has been experienced many times in history, or to mistakes and results that serve to obscure it.

The goal of our rebuilding efforts, while neither denying the historical legacy of forces that do or, given their interests, should oppose the system nor falling into the trap of liberalism, is to approach all individuals and social units with a systematic understanding (a paradigm) and practice and to organize them and launch them into action. In these rebuilding efforts there can be both those who choose a revolutionary approach and those who pursue reform. It is all valuable work. Capitalist modernity represents the civilized system's most crisis-ridden period. It is also the age when financial capital has furthest extended its global hegemony and its structural systemic period, during which the crisis has become permanent. The capitalist system searches daily for theoretical and practical ways to exit this crisis without suffering any systemic losses. It acts in the context of a comprehensive and eclectic liberal ideology with a well-established historical legacy. Moreover, the well-developed and sprawling electronic organizational networks allow it to immediately implement its chosen tactics. It has even grown critical of the nation-state, its strategic administrative tool, and is attempting to restructure it in a number of areas. Corporate power exceeds the power of nation-states at this point and manipulates the increasingly fashionable civil society organizations at will.

Under these circumstances, those opposing the system have no other choice but to develop their own system of understanding and practice.

The French and Russian Revolutions (and numerous other revolutions and movements that followed them) were not entirely within the scope and objectives of capitalist modernity. In fact, they had substantial contradictions with capitalist modernity and claimed to represent a new system. They experienced many different periods—including some extraordinary ones—of implementation of these aspirations, but in the end, capitalism, whether in the short- or long-term, was able to dissolve these revolutions into its modern intellectual framework and course of action. Undoubtedly, as with all historical legacies, especially these great revolutions, it is our primary task to defend the freedom, equality, and democratic legacy of contemporary revolutions. However, it is also clear that we must learn the lessons of the errors made. In this study, I've been at pains to emphasize that. Learning the lessons of these experiences is an essential task for individuals and organizations that share the same ideals.

Whether the crisis continues or not, our main tasks will remain the same. Intellectual, moral, and political tasks will always need to be carried out. Of course, different periods will require different strategies and tactics, but the essential nature of the tasks will remain unchanged. I believe that the explanations I've offered and principles I've developed regarding the tasks in all three areas are important. That said, they are also an expression of both criticism and self-criticism of every event, relationship, personality, and institution that I have been responsible for. As I am aware that an individual criticism and self-criticism is of little value without a comprehensive analysis and critique of our age, and even of civilization, I have tried to approach things accordingly.

At the risk of repetition, I must stress that the work that needs to be done regarding the intellectual, moral, and political tasks is essentially intertwined. No matter how independently the three areas work within themselves, they must complement each other's services with the products they produce. Without intellectual enlightenment, not only can morality not improve the good, it cannot avoid causing evil. Whenever and wherever there is a lack of good morality, there will be bad morality. The political area refers to the application of the present enlightenment and morality. In this sense, politics is where social enlightenment and moral activity play out on a daily basis—in short, politics is enlightenment and morality itself. In addition, without politics and morality we cannot seriously talk of enlightenment, and without enlightenment no real intellectual work is possible. Intellectual knowledge that has lost its connection to politics and morality can only become intellectual capital or something of the sort, and, lacking a moral and political foundation, cannot be considered an intellectual task.

When and only when intellectual, moral, and political tasks are fulfilled in the intertwined way that moral and political society requires can we hope to attain maximal freedom, equality, and democracy. Therefore, the measure of success of anti-system individuals and organizations is related to their ability to cohesively and effectively address the tasks they face in these three areas.

ELEVEN

Conclusion

Consciousness is related to universal existence. An explanation of the existing universal order is only possible with the help of the concept of consciousness. What is interesting is how consciousness expresses itself. It seems that the entire diversity of the universe is a consequence of the passionate need consciousness has to express itself. We know nothing at all about the multi-consciousness of consciousness. The quest of consciousness for almost endless diversity raises the question of cause, and the question of purpose remains even more unclear. Famous philosophers, even some of the holy books, relate these questions to the universe's desire to remember itself or God's desire to be recognized by its servants. To me, the term "becoming aware" seems a lot more enchanting and enlightening. From the smallest particle to cosmic existence, becoming aware of oneself may be the answer to the questions of cause and purpose. The meaning we give to awareness cannot be described as anything other than life. The definition of *life* that comes closest to truth can be defined as *becoming aware*. Even more importantly: Why is becoming aware of such importance? We know that life without awareness is possible, but if we try to understand this intuitively we begin to feel that this is perhaps impossible. When there is an extended period of low awareness, the value of life gradually declines and even begins to dissipate altogether. Even death, which makes us aware of life, appears to be a game or an act of mastery on the part of nature that seeks to make life possible. For example: What would be the difference between being punished with eternal life and the tragedy of Sisyphus (a mythological hero who is sentenced to repeatedly roll a stone up the hill, because each time the stone rolls back down)?[1] Grief about death is a reminder that increases the value of life.

Knowing means nothing other than the awareness of life. Something that you know is something that you have become aware of. Although we cannot say much about physical beings, with biological beings it is impossible not to feel a kind of love for recognition. As we move closer to the human species, it is as if this love has been realized. The advanced state of knowing can best be described with the word *love*. But the human is a strange being, because with the human we may also encounter qualities that are easily capable of betraying and destroying knowledge in profound ways. It seems to me this reality of human beings is best explained by processes in social nature, which we also call second nature.

Social science, as a concept, developed with Eurocentric civilization. There is no doubt that as long as social nature has existed there has always been some kind of discipline that we can call social science. For example, we can safely call animism a prehistoric social science. Is animism, the concept itself a development of the Eurocentric social sciences, merely the primitive consciousness of primitive people, as is claimed? Who issued the fatwa saying that today's social sciences based on the subject-object distinction are superior to animism? The very the same social scientists! It is increasingly clear that the animist school actually offers a more valuable paradigm than one that leads to the sharp separation of subject and object that inevitably views the object as lifeless. It is clear that animism more accurately describes the universe than can a concept of lifelessness. Scientific developments confirm this. Can the fact that without the enigmatic movements of subatomic particles, which remain a mystery, no diversity can arise be explained by anything but animism? Although its adherents claim otherwise, positivism (the scientism of phenomena), a highly dangerous form of metaphysics, has also inflicted serious damage on the social sciences.

The civilization process that we refer to as historical periods brought with it a change in the nature of science from animism to mythology. In many ways, although not completely, mythology was shaped by civilization. The first distortion of consciousness and the first seepage of betrayal into the social sciences are related to civilization's ideological hegemony. The power and capital monopoly established over social nature would not have been possible without lies, distortions, and people betraying their word. Mythology is largely imbued with animism and is, therefore, precious. But as soon as the hierarchical system and order formed by the triad of priest + ruler + commander came into play, mythological reflection took the form of the tales of heroes (semideification) and deification, making distortions and corruption inevitable. As long as this dual nature is taken into consideration, mythology can be a very instructive social science, and I believe it will become increasingly important. There is certainly much to be learned about history from it.

The solidification of mythology into religion led to a second kind of social science. Of course, the legacy of religion is not merely mythology. Religion has its own dogmas. Although it was predominantly shaped by the forces of civilization, the religious interpretation of truth by anti-civilization forces is a lot simpler and, because of their naturalness, a lot more realistic. This is what paved the way for contemporary science. These two opposing forces are reflected within monotheistic religions. While the dictatorial, punitive, and subjugating dimension of theology reflects the forces of civilization, its participatory, rewarding, and liberating dimension reflects the faith and thought of the anti-civilization forces. The Middle Ages overflowed with conflicts between religions and denominations around these two different views. Without these religious and denominational conflicts, European social sciences would certainly not have emerged. Taking the influence of Islam into consideration helps make this fact even clearer. And, of course, there have also been moments of wisdom and philosophy through the ages. These are no doubt valuable sources for the social sciences.

While the social sciences of the age of European civilization were the product of this historical legacy, they also emerged as a requirement of the great social struggles taking place. Basically, they were conceived of as disciplines, instruments for resolving problems. From the outset, the boundless exploitation and oppression caused by capitalism meant that modernity inevitably emerged weighed down with crises. While all sciences, in particular the social sciences, were put at the service of an exploitative and oppressive system, they were also given the task of explaining the system in a positive light and legitimizing it. The rhetoric of the new power and capital monopolies also shaped the social sciences.

Positivist sociology crippled the social sciences from the beginning. The main concern of positivist sociologists was to establish a republic based on the French Revolution that protected the interests of the bourgeoisie. British political economists, for their part, pursued the rationalization and legitimization of capital. The German ideologues in all fields were focused on the formation of the gigantic German nation-state. The leading opponents of the system, the founders of scientific socialism, Karl Marx and Frederick Engels, wanted to turn these three rhetorical devices of capital into a science with a proletarian stamp. Their anti-capitalism and the related analysis in Marx's *Capital*,[2] could have contributed to the social sciences. However, by limiting the sources of their departure and system of opposition to anti-capitalism, they left all the structures of the system without defense against capitalist modernity. Anarchists, who have a more meaningful analysis of power, have, however, left the political sphere virtually empty. European social scientists of both political wings struggled with systemic problems rather than exploring social nature, in a sense, taking on the role of crisis regime experts. The world and history became secondary. We should not be surprised that social science is Eurocentric. It was not realistic to think that European social scientists could rapidly overcome hundreds of years of accumulated knowledge and science. Liberal ideology proved to be the smartest, finding a way to integrate them all into the system, thereby neutralizing not only the French Revolution but all the revolutions of that era, including the Russian Revolution, and all opponents of the system. It successfully transformed science into the science of power and capital.

But it would have been unthinkable that European modernity, the most abusive and power-centered system in the civilization process, could totally eliminate and silence its opponents. As this modernity developed it encountered strong resistance, not only on the ideological front but also on the political and moral front. The opponents of the system renewed themselves at least as much as the system did. As the system became global, the counter-system also became global. The civilization system's hegemony over science was gradually broken. Slowly everyone began to understand that history can only be world history, and that the brief period of European hegemony is nothing more than a small part of this history.

In the wake of World War II, French philosophy, the 1968 youth culture revolt, the dissolution of the Soviet system from within, the collapse of the welfare state, postmodernist quests, and the liquidation of classical colonialism prepared the ground for the beginning of a new phase in social science. Freed of the obstacle of positivism and Eurocentrism, the exploration of truth is now on a more favorable path. A social science that makes social nature as a whole in all places and at all times the topic of research cannot be content with merely solving problems and addressing crises. On the one hand, it must provide a direction for physics, chemistry, biology, and cosmology, all of which are basically connected to society, and, on the other hand, it must orient the humanities, including philosophy, literature, and the arts, thereby playing the role of the queen of sciences. The family tree of science can only be drawn with the social sciences at its root. This would eliminate both excessive fragmentation and the danger of being too abstract. As with the general crisis, overcoming the crisis in the social sciences is a priority. Social sciences that interpret awareness of life as freedom and truth as the exploration of freedom provide indispensable guidance for moral and political society's enlightenment and development.

The fact that I evaluate the social sciences in particular in this text relates to the scope of the text. The rhetoric of scientific socialism, which I have used for so long, has now become too narrow. I have always completely rejected liberal rhetoric. Becoming more familiar with anarchism had a positive impact on me, but anarchism falls far short of solving the problems before me. As I mentioned at the beginning, the views of some sociologists I hold in high esteem made important contributions to my analysis, but I still had to find my own way. Without establishing my understanding of the social sciences, I would have been in no position to proceed to other challenging topics. As I said it would be at the outset, this is an attempt that can only further unfold through criticism. I am certainly not one of those metaphysical and positivist dogmatists who believes that the social sciences can address everything. My multidimensional definition of the social sciences should serve both to avoid this danger and to allow me to be vigilant and honest with those who are interested. Once this was in place, my main focus was democratic civilization and modernity. The reason I prioritized the social problem was to better understand the civilization system and correctly lay a foundation for its opponents. I believe I did a thorough job of this. My criticism of other opponents of the system helped me arrive at an overall assessment. Although I do not completely reject the scientific socialist method, which bases its opposition to the system on the conflict between two classes, I recognize that this is a very limited part of history and is far from providing an analysis of society. I have tried to overcome this with the concept of a five-thousand-year-old civilization system whose development resembles the flow of a main stream.

If we are looking for a dialectical contradiction—and I am convinced this is necessary—it is essential to develop it at the level of the civilization system. I am aware that civilizations have been researched by many esteemed philosophers and sociologists. I didn't want to add new research to the existing research but to open up to systematic and comprehensive discussion aspects that have not been touched upon or that have been treated incoherently and fragmentarily. In particular, I must emphasize that I applied the dialectical methodology Karl Marx used in *Capital* to civilization. I have often wished that Marx had done this himself; it would have been of great service to all of us. Nonetheless, perhaps the best support you can get from a master is to understand his methodology. The critique formulated by those who are interested and the social praxis that develops will determine to what extent I have succeeded. In fact, as explained in *Capital*, civilization polarizes and creates groups and opposition. Even the bourgeoisie-proletariat contradiction is only one of many contradictions that civilization created. In this sense, it would be more accurate to interpret my work not as in opposition to Marx but as an attempt to complement and develop Karl Marx's views and evaluations on the basis of serious criticisms. It should not be interpreted as antagonistic when I point to mistakes and shortcomings in numerous areas (monopoly, capital, the state, ideology, positivism, history, civilization, market, economy, democracy, revolution, the social sciences, and especially power, the nation-state, hegemony, system analysis, etc.). I think it would be more appropriate to see this as according him and the other currents fighting against the system the appreciation they deserve, and thereby making my own contribution.

In the previous volumes of my defense, I tried to provide a broad analysis of the dominating and abusive (exploitative and colonial) branches of civilization. In these sections, I have tried to go into this as little as possible, instead focusing on the demos, the forces of democratic civilization, as the antithesis. I did my utmost to clarify this historical pole. I think that history, especially on this subject, is fraught with errors and shortcomings. It was important and necessary to highlight this with a thick red line, to say the least. The main conflict throughout history has not been among the dominant groups in civilization, as is so often claimed (the latest example is the evaluation of Samuel P. Huntington) but between the two opposing poles of civilization.[3] There are, of course, plenty of contradictions and conflicts among the dominant groups. Monopolies are always in conflict among themselves over carving up the cake. The crux of the matter, however, is who was this cake stolen from and how. According to dialectics, the real contradiction and conflict is between those who produce the cake and those that want to steal it. On this subject, which needs to be thoroughly historically researched, the only thing I could do was to, once again, highlight it with a thick red line. This is exactly what I did, and I believe that the results will not disappoint.

I have also tried to give comprehensive space to the opponents of modernity. In doing so, I wanted them to participate in the work of building a new system in the right way. There was a need to categorize the increasing turmoil that followed the dissolution of the Soviet Union in a meaningful way, but despair was unnecessary. Real socialists and anarchists have to understand the need for renewal, while feminists and ecologists should know that they will not get far without building a system. They have no other choice if they do not want to end up being a continuous source of water for the mills of liberalism. Nothing can be achieved without engaging in politics and ensuring the development of a system or, at best, the fate of the real socialist and anarchist movements awaits them. I am convinced that I have sufficiently analyzed the cultural movements. The democratic content of these movements, which are trying to free themselves from the claws of the nation-state monster, is important. They can play a historical role within the framework of democratic modernity.

I have taken care to theoretically and practically approach the problems and tasks of rebuilding democratic modernity in both an analytical and a solution-oriented way, and I think I have succeeded in presenting my conclusions as striking principles. Democratic modernity has nothing to do with the search for a past golden age or a future utopian project. There has been plenty of material in opposition to the system, but we have lacked our own system. I believe there is an urgent need for meaningful narratives on this topic. What is important is not the term *democratic modernity*, but its content, which needs to be systematized. Otherwise, we will get stuck between "the poverty of philosophy" and the "philosophy of poverty" and make no progress.[4] My analysis is intended to clarify and correct this situation. The intellectual, moral, and political tasks were identified in pursuit of practical solutions. There was a lot of turmoil in this area too. I think it has become sufficiently clear how the practical implementation should be approached. In particular, I believe that the principles I have outlined will lead to new and creative practical action.

Another important topic of this work concerns the qualities of the fundamental unit of research. Positivist social science contented itself with objectifying society like the other objects in nature, and giving a general answer. Scientific socialism emerged as a left-wing reflection of that understanding of science and was even more rigid and fixed on phenomena. Its contribution has been to classify societies according to modes of production, perceiving and applying universalist linear progressive positivism as absolute truth. This led to the division of society into primitive, slave-owning, feudal, capitalist, and socialist/communist phases. There is a certain fatalism in this; sooner or later socialism will inevitably come. This is obviously a dogmatic approach. The consequences of approaching all social activities in this way have been even more problematic than has generally been assumed. The result was not socialism but global capitalism, which scientific socialism unwittingly served in spite of its criticisms. The fact that Russian state capitalism provided the system with at least a hundred years of life probably confirms this.

Throughout my work I chose moral and political society, which I consider to be the very state of existence of social nature, and which I tried to identify and define, as my fundamental unit of research. My argument was that although phenomena such as the mode of production, class, the state, ideology, and technology have formed differently in each society and have constantly changed, and although they are significant, none of them carry enough weight to constitute the fundamental topic of research.

In contrast, I criticized the world-system and civilization analyses as one-sided interpretations that rest on closed and circular development. I tried to analyze and show that social nature, the qualities human beings will and must experience as long as they exist, is inevitably moral and political society, which humans cannot do without, and when they do it indicates the disintegration and fragmentation of society. With a long list of examples, I tried to show that even if, in the course of civilization's history and under siege from capital and power networks, moral and political society has been seriously eroded and left to decay, societies have always found a way to protect their moral and political qualities, to respond to these forces, and to live in resistance to them. I analyzed in detail how capitalist modernity and capital and power networks have wrapped themselves around society, leaving no pore unpenetrated (the nation-state, industrialism, the media in particular, eclectic ideologies, security services, internal colonization, the extreme burden borne by women, and other factors). I tried to present a comprehensive analysis that showed how these developments inevitably create a correspondingly strong counterreaction, giving rise to opportunities for resistance and alternative ways of life for every individual and every social unit. I have also shown that moral and political society is by no means static but has been constantly evolving since prehistoric times.

Clans, tribes, families, and aşiret confederations, being subjected to hierarchy, division into states, and the transition from village agricultural society to urban society, and then to national industrial society, experienced a series of continuous developments accompanied by greater or lesser polarization. I also tend to agree that the civilization process has a continuous character, which is a back and forth of center-periphery, hegemony-competition, and the ups and downs of crises. I tried to analyze in theory and to demonstrate in practice that, despite all of this, moral and political society cannot be destroyed; that it will always maintain its tendency toward freedom, equality, and democracy; that through a shared understanding and the fulfillment of intellectual, moral, and political tasks these characteristics will unfold with maximum vitality.

I also tried to show in detail that while capitalist modernity bases its existence on capitalism, industrialism, and nation-statism, democratic modernity can exist as democratic communality, eco-industrial society, and the democratic nation. I did not define democratic communality as the egalitarianism of a homogeneous society but as any kind of community ranging from one person to millions of people (from women's to men's communities, from sports and arts to industry, from intellectuals to shepherds, from tribes to corporations, from families to nations, from villages to towns, from local to global, any society from the clan society to the global society) that carries the characteristics of moral and political society. I argued that an eco-industrial society would be a society where agrarian-village society and urban industrial society nourish one another and consist of ecologically adapted eco-industrial communities. I have defined and presented the democratic nation as a new kind of nation, or rather as a nation with multiple identities, multiple cultures, and multiple political formations, that is opposed to the nation-statist monsters, and whose basic political form will be a democratic confederalist practice and autonomous political formations—all kinds of cultural existence, from ethnicities to religions, and including urban, local, regional, and national communities.

Time and again, I have tried to present democratic modernity in detail as an option that, based on these structures, is highly solution-oriented and combines the historical legacy and the experience of the system's opponents in the modern era and will allow it to continue to grow and eventually develop into a predominant option.

Another part of my analysis focused on the polarization of state civilization and democratic modernity, not only in terms of conflict and abuse (exploitation and colonialism) but also in terms of the likelihood of freedom from conflict and peace.[5] Assessing the probability of and necessary conditions for sustainable peace is a very delicate but important issue. The civilization process has a rich legacy in this regard. There have been times when practice accorded peace more holiness and sublimity than war. Even during modernity, war and peace have been intertwined as everyday practices. In particular, an understanding that a mutually nurturing dialectic could very well replace the destructive dialectic, and, at a minimum, that dialectical processes are neither solely destructive nor purely mutually nurturing, could contribute to this process. But it is equally true that a broad and complicated spectrum of options could exist between these two perspectives and the related realities. Thanks to the evolution of science, we can better and more accurately understand that natural reality does not function according to a Darwinian philosophy of the survival of the fittest dating back to savage capitalism or according to the old metaphysical templates of a life free of contradictions but, rather, offers a highly rich, intense, and creative nature.

Just as it is wrong to interpret peace processes entirely as evolutionary, it is equally wrong to interpret phases of war as the midwife of the old system about to give birth to a new system.[6] The wars between capital and power monopolies revolve around grabbing a bigger or a smaller piece of the cake. They don't have much to do with peace. A real peace rests on two opposing forces of civilization accepting each other's existence, identities, and right to autonomous governance. This begins between two classes and expands to embrace a spectrum that includes various tribes, aşirets, peoples, nations, strata, religious communities, cultural currents, and even economic groups. Once it is accepted that conflict does more harm to the parties involved, the possibility of peace emerges and is pursued in a process of dialogue and reconciliation. Whether at a local or global level, both within nations and between nations, numerous conflicts have ended in peace in just this way. What is crucial is reaching an agreement that makes it possible for the parties to preserve their identities and their dignity. As long as this is the case, peace is possible at every level and between societies of any size, within any group, and even between individuals.

An analysis of the five-thousand-year history of civilization makes it clear that for some time to come both poles will continue to coexist, because it seems highly unlikely that one pole could rapidly destroy the other. Even dialectically, this does not seem realistic. Real socialism's premature attempt to build a system without analyzing civilization and modernity ended in its dissolution. It is important to make both poles clear in any theoretical and practical effort, not to let oneself be absorbed by the dominant, exploitative pole, while at the same time constantly finding new and constructive ways to develop democratic civilization and modernity as an authentic system in its own right. The more we develop our system, using both revolutionary and evolutionary methods, the more likely we will be able to positively resolve the questions of "duration" and "space" and stabilize the system.

Democratic modernity is a system that is suitable for real peace because of its fundamental elements. The idea of the democratic nation offers solutions from the level of very small national communities to a world encompassing nation. At the same time, it is an extremely valuable option for peace. With its eco-industrial element and its productive use of industry within society, it lays the groundwork for solutions to serious social problems, including unemployment, poverty, and hunger, which are, so to speak, the result of modernity's war on society, and for ending industrialism's war on the environment and establishing peace between society and the environment. Democratic communality offers each unit and individual in society the option of being a moral and political society, thus representing the most radical peaceful approach. What is clear is that the more democratic modernity develops as a system, the greater the likelihood that we will arrive at a dignified peace.

At this point, I have to issue a warning and at the same time beg for forgiveness: I use the terms of *moral and political society*, *democratic communality*, and *democratic society* synonymously. When necessary I did not hesitate to use all three terms to express a wealth of meaning. Clearly, moral and political society and democratic communality are reminiscent of democratic socialism and social equality—equality in diversity. Equality in diversity differs from the real socialist understanding of equality, with equality denoting homogeneity. To emphasize this, I felt the need to refer to real socialism as *pharaoh socialism*. When using the concept of *democratic society*, I am emphasizing the aspect of moral and political society that encompasses both freedom and equality. We must not make these identical concepts uniform. This is what I mean by richness of meaning. Making them uniform would impoverish them. I warn against getting entangled in contradictions because of the very frequent use of these concepts, and ask for indulgence for being unable to develop a different terminology.

I have not limited myself to describing democratic modernity as a counterpart to the three fundamental elements of capitalist modernity (capitalism, industrialism, and the nation-state). These elements are moral and political society (or democratic communality, democratic socialism, democratic society), as well as eco-industrial society and democratic confederal society. As I have tried to illustrate in the relevant section, I wanted to define democratic modernity with an even richer bouquet of characteristics. The twelve fundamental issues that I enumerated in relation to the social problem simultaneously explain the twelve solution-oriented characteristics of democratic modernity.

I have often emphasized that this work could be published under the title *The Sociology of Freedom*. In attempting to define the social sciences I stressed that the ultimate goal must be to develop the option of freedom. In any event, if we add that, in a way, to solve problems is to ensure freedom, then I see no difficulty in calling the social sciences the "sociology of freedom" within this framework. At least a significant part of the sociological work dealing with problem-solving and the promotion of an awareness of life should appropriately be published under that title. No doubt, sociology is not exclusively about freedom. Sociology should, in fact, deal with a broad and complicated social spectrum (prehistoric society, hierarchy, class, the state, the city, civilization, capital, the economy, power, democracy, the arts, religion, philosophy, science, politics, war, strategy, organization, institutionalization, ideology, ecology, jineolojî, theology, eschatology, and so on). Throughout this work, I have particularly emphasized that breaking moral and political society into many parts and treating them separately has major disadvantages and can lead to negative rather than positive results. As I have already said, I strongly agree that the best methodology is to examine social nature in its historicity and wholeness.

As I end another part of my defense writings, I would like to conclude with two interpretations: one from Socrates, the other from Zarathustra. Socrates often said, "Know thyself." I imagine he wished to emphasize that those who do not know themselves cannot learn or know much. I believe that the human being is the sum of the reality, as far as science explains it, that stretches from the assumed big bang, at least fifteen billion years ago, to today and spatially across the entire universe. I both feel and know that. In this sense, knowing thyself is synonymous with knowledge of all time and the entire universe. Moreover, in his famous defense, Socrates speaks not of the gods of Athens, whom he allegedly disavowed, but of his inspirational spirit beings, the daemons, who visited him from time to time. This is knowing thyself through intuition and inner focus. This is in a way prophetic learning and prediction. It is clear that this is a more advanced way of learning than was idolatry. After receiving a reminder from my intuition, or my daemons, "Whatever you seek, find it in thyself," I had no choice but to write in this way.

Zarathustra's account was even more impressive. It is said that Zarathustra heard a voice when the sun rose in full glory over his much beloved Zagros Mountains. He shouts at this voice, "Tell me, who are you?"[7] This account tells us that Zarathustra encounters God and settles accounts with him. I, on the other hand, am convinced that it is a matter of his reckoning with the presence of the Sumeric god-kings, who for thousands of years had threatened the freedom of the people of Zagros. In a way, he questions the sacredness of these god-kings, who are, in a sense, civilization itself, and accomplishes the Zoroastrian moral revolution. This revolution is about the dichotomy of light and darkness, good and evil.

I absolutely hate the exaggerations about me that are circulating. My passionate desire is to be understood in all my simplicity and to be a friend. With time I have come to better understand that my personality, which receives life in its simplicity, full of passion, as a celebration of friendship, has stood up against all those who have attacked me. When they attacked me, my question was a little like that of Zarathustra: "Who are you?" The lines that I have written reflect what I have learned from knowing myself and from my reflections based on the accumulation of consciousness that arose when I asked my attackers: "Who are you?"

Analyzing both myself and the sanctities of civilization, which appear in thousands of disguises, also means resolving the difficult conditions. When civilization divinities crossed all boundaries of morality and politics and tried to trample me, I questioned them with these lines. In a passionate atmosphere of celebration, this in turn made me familiar with my personality, my traditions, my people, my region, my humanity, and my universe. Getting to know means becoming aware, which, in turn, means living life fearlessly in all its richness and strongly defending it!

Notes

Foreword

1   Very many thanks to all who have commented on an earlier versión of this Preface: Azize Azlan, Edith González, Panagiotis Doulos, Lars Stubbe, Vittorio Sergi, Sagrario Anta Martínez, Havin Guneser, Andrej Grubaćić.

2   Murray Bookchin, *The Ecology of Freedom* (Andover, MA: Cheshire Books, 1982), accessed February 9, 2020, https://theanarchistlibrary.org/library/murray-bookchin-the-ecology-of-freedom#toc11.

3   David Graeber, *Debt: The First 5,000 Years* (Brooklyn, NY: Melville House, 2011).

4   Herbert Marcuse, *One-Dimensional Man* (Boston: Beacon Press, 1964).

5   Radha D'Souza, "Reading Öcalan as a South Asian Woman," in *Building Free Life: Dialogues with Öcalan* (Oakland: PM Press, 2020), 103–18.

Preface

1   In its 2005 judgment, the ECtHR ordered Turkey to reopen the Öcalan case on the grounds that the original trial did not comply with the principles of a fair trial, i.e., that it violated Article 6 of the European Convention on Human Rights. Turkey avoided implementing this judgment by creating an unprecedented procedure that did not actually lead to any renegotiation. Öcalan's renewed complaint was directed against this procedure. The entire five-volume *Manifesto of the Democratic Civilization* represents his submission to this procedure; see Öcalan v. Turkey, Application no. 46221/99, European Court of Human Rights, Strasbourg, May 12, 2005, accessed August 15, 2019, https://hudoc.echr.coe.int/eng#{%22tabview%22:[%22document%22],%22itemid%22:[%22001-69022%22].

2   Abdullah Öcalan, *Manifesto for a Democratic Civilization, Volume I: The Age of Masked Gods and Disguised Kings* (Porsgrunn, NO: New Compass Press, 2015), a new revised edition will be published by PM Press in 2021; Abdullah Öcalan, *Manifesto for a Democratic Civilization, Volume II: Capitalism: The Age of Unmasked Gods and Naked Kings* (Porsgrunn, NO: New Compass Press,

2017), a new revised edition will be published by PM Press in 2020; see www. ocalanbooks.com, accessed November 1, 2019.

3 See "CM Documents," *Council of Europe*, March 23, 2007, accessed March 22, 2019, https://wcd.coe.int/ViewDoc.jsp?id=1110095&Site=CM.

4 See "World: Öcalan Presumed Hiding in Russia," *BBC News*, February 3, 1999, accessed March 22, 2019, http://news.bbc.co.uk/2/hi/europe/269533. stm; "World Europe: Öcalan 'Turned Away by Belgian Jets," February 5, 1999, accessed March 22, 2019, http://news.bbc.co.uk/2/hi/europe/273570.stm.

5 Possibly a reference to Anthony Blinken, who served on the National Security Council during the Clinton administration, and who confirmed on January 31, 2002, on Turkish television, that the order to deport Öcalan was given by Bill Clinton. Blinken coordinated the operation for the National Security Council.

6 In previous volumes the author used the term *main civilization* instead of *central civilization*, coined by David Wilkinson.

7 In fact, the fifth and final volume, the author's most comprehensive book to date, could only be completed one and a half years after this third volume. As the authorities had long refused to forward the manuscript to the ECtHR, the 576-page book was only published three years after the third volume, in the summer of 2012.

8 According to one interpretation of the legend, an oracle declared that any man who could unravel the elaborated Gordian knot was destined to become ruler of all of Asia. When Alexander arrived in Phrygia, he struggled unsuccessfully to untie the knot. He then reasoned that it would make no difference how the knot was loosed, so he drew his sword and sliced it in half with a single stroke.

Introduction

1 The author often follows Frank and Gills's preferred spelling of the term *world system* and not Wallerstein's term *world-system*. Wallerstein assumes that there are several world systems, each forming its own world. Wallerstein's reasoning: "My 'world-system' is not a system 'in the world' or 'of the world.' It is a system 'that is a world.' Hence the hyphen, since 'world' is not an attribute of the system. Rather the two words together constitute a single concept. Frank and Gills's system is a world system in an attributive sense, in that it has been tending over time to cover the whole world. They cannot conceive of multiple 'world-systems' coexisting on the planet. Yet until the nineteenth century, or so I contend, this has always been the case."; Andre Gunder Frank and Barry K. Gills, *The World System: Five Hundred Years or Five Thousand* (New York: Routledge, 1999), 294.

2 For instance, the German theoretical physicist Werner Heisenberg, winner of the Nobel prize for his work in quantum mechanics, distanced himself from positivism; see Werner Heisenberg, "Positivism, Metaphysics, and Religion," in *Physics and Beyond: Encounters and Conversations* (New York: Harper & Row, 1971); see Max Weber, "The Nature of Social Action," in W.G. Runciman, *Weber: Selections in Translation*, (Cambridge: Cambridge University Press, 1991) and the works of the Frankfurt School theoreticians, Theodor Adorno and Erich Fromm, in particular.

3   Here the author is referring to Immanuel Wallerstein; see, for example, Immanuel Wallerstein, *Open the Social Sciences* (Palo Alto, CA: Stanford University Press, 1996); Immanuel Wallerstein, *Unthinking Social Sciences: Limits of Nineteenth-Century Paradigms* (Cambridge, UK: Polity Press, 1991).

4   Abdullah Öcalan, *Prison Writings: The Roots of Civilization* (London: Pluto Press, 2007).

5   Andre Gunder Frank and Barry K. Gills, eds., *The World System: Five Hundred or Five Thousand?* (London: Routledge, 1993); other authors include Immanuel Wallerstein, Samir Amin, David Wilkinson, and Janet Abu-Lughod.

6   V. Gordon Childe, *What Happened in History* (London: Aaker Books, 2016).

7   Abdullah Öcalan understands historical time as divided into the short-term, medium-term, and long-term and, thus, uses the formulation "historical terms" to reflect this.

8   The market hostility of capitalism is discussed in detail in Fernand Braudel, *Civilization and Capitalism 15th to 18th Century, Volume II: The Wheels of Commerce*, trans. Siân Reynolds (Berkeley: University of California Press, 1992 [1979]).

9   Original quote: "Imperialism and colonialism are as old as the world, and any reinforced form of domination secretes capitalism, as I have often repeated to convince the reader and to convince myself"; Fernand Braudel, *Civilization and Capitalism, Volume III: The Perspective of the World* (New York: Harper & Row, 1984), 295.

10   Original quote: "Power is accumulated like money"; ibid., 50.

11   Abdullah Öcalan, *Beyond State, Power, and Violence* (Oakland, PM Press, forthcoming 2020).

12   In recent research, very large Neolithic settlements such as Çatalhöyük have also been referred to as "mega-villages." These were organized, egalitarian, and larger than the original Sumerian cities, with their hierarchical structures.

Some Problems of Methodology

1   This so-called "basic biogenetic rule" was first formulated by Ernst Haeckel, in 1866: "The development of germs is a repressed and shortened repetition of the development of tribes."

The Question of Freedom

1   As usual the author quotes from memory; the actual quote is: "But it cannot emancipate itself without abolishing the conditions of its own life. It cannot abolish the conditions of its own life without abolishing all the inhuman conditions of life of society today which are summed up in its own situation." Karl Marx & and Frederick Engels, *The Holy Family or Critique of Critical Critique*, 1845, accessed September 8, 2019, https://www.marxists.org/archive/marx/works/download/Marx_The_Holy_Family.pdf.

2   A detailed description can be found in Abdullah Öcalan, *Prison Writings I: The Roots of Civilization* (London: Pluto Press, 20017); a shorter version can be found in Abdullah Öcalan, *Manifesto of the Democratic Civilization, Volume*

I: The Age of Masked Gods and Disguised Kings (Oakland: PM Press, rev. ed., forthcoming 2021).

3 See Georg Wilhelm Friedrich Hegel, *Philosophy of Right* (London, G. Bell, 1896), §57, 65: "the Idea of freedom is genuinely actual only as the state," and §260, 237: "The state is the actuality of concrete freedom," accessed November 2, 2019, https://www.marxists.org/reference/archive/hegel/works/pr/philosophy-of-right.pdf.

The Power of Social Reason

1 The author uses the terms *reason* (*akıl*) and *intelligence* (*zekâ*) in this section alternately and often synonymously, at least not sharply delineated from each other. The reader should take this into account when reading.

2 Max Weber has used the term *stahlhartes Gehäuse* (hardened steel casing), translated as "iron cage," to describe the increased rationalization inherent in social life; Max Weber, *The Protestant Ethic and the Spirit of Capitalism* (Mineola, NY: Dover Publications, 2003).

3 This is a Turkish play on words. In Turkish *genelev* euphemistically means a *brothel* and literally means a *public house* whereas *özelev* means a *private home* and refers to the family household.

4 See, for example, Karl Marx, *Capital*, vol. 1, (London: Pelican Books, 1976), 187: "The riddle of the money fetish, is therefore the riddle of the commodity fetish, now become visible and dazzling to our eyes."

The Emergence of the Social Problem

1 Jacques Mallet du Pan (1749–1800) coined the adage: "The revolution like Saturn devours its own children." The saying became popular and was used by many people, most famously Georges Danton (1759–1794), a leading figure in the French Revolution.

2 Andre Gunder Frank and Barry K. Gills, eds., *The World System: Five Hundred Years or Five Thousand?* (London: Routledge, 1993).

3 They are the ones who possess the quality of ʿ*ilm*, or *"learning."* Speaking broadly, they are the guardians, transmitters, and interpreters of religious knowledge, i.e., Islamic doctrine and law.

4 This is a Turkish play on words. In Turkish *genelev* euphemistically means a *brothel* and literally means a *public house* whereas *özelev* means a *private home* and refers to the family household.

5 Hittites established an empire centred on Hattusa in north-central Anatolia around 1600 BCE, and Mittanis in northern Syria and southeast Anatolia, from 1500 to 1300 BCE.

6 *Karums* were Assyrian trading posts from the twentieth to the eighteenth centuries BCE; *kârhaneler* is a play on words: the word itself means places of profit and is similar to *kerhane*, a word meaning *brothels*.

7 The Hittite Empire and the Egyptians fought for over two centuries to gain mastery over the lands of the eastern Mediterranean. The conflict culminated with an attempted Egyptian invasion in 1274 BCE that was stopped by the Hittites at the city of Kadesh (in what is now Syria). The conflict continued

inconclusively for about fifteen more years before the treaty was signed. Both sides had common interests in making peace; Egypt faced a growing threat from the "Sea Peoples," while the Hittites were concerned about the rising power of Assyria to the east. The treaty continued in force until the Hittite Empire collapsed eighty years later.

8   Carthage fell in 146 BCE at the Battle of Carthage. The end of a series of wars marked the end of Carthaginian power and the complete destruction of the city. The Romans pulled the Phoenician warships out into the harbor and burned them, then went from house to house, capturing and enslaving the people. Fifty thousand Carthaginians were sold into slavery. The city was set ablaze and razed to the ground, leaving only ruins and rubble.

9   Maimonides's history (Laws of Idolatry 1:3) tells us that Abraham was educating people about monotheism. Terach informed on Abraham to Nimrod. According to the Midrash, Abraham was then cast into a furnace but was miraculously saved.

10   The Ummayad dynasty, which ruled in Damascus in 661–750 CE, claimed descent from Umayya, the cousin of the Prophet Mohammad's grandfather.

11   Here the author is referring to a play on words: Amr ibn Hishām was a pagan Quraysh leader whose epithet was Abu al-Ḥakam, meaning Father of Wisdom. He showed relentless animosity to Islam and rejected Mohammad's message. Therefore, Mohammad referred him as *Abu Jahl*, meaning *Father of Ignorance*.

12   In volume 2, at the end of section I and continuing into section 2, Öcalan addresses historical-society, civilizations, and capitalism. While there Öcalan often uses the term that Anthony Giddens popularized—"discontinuity"—in this case he prefers "unprecedented."

13   Klaus Schmidt, "Göbekli Tepe, Southeastern Turkey: A Preliminary Report on the 1995–1999 Excavations," *Paléorient* 26, no. 1 (2000), accessed November 17, 2019, https://www.persee.fr/doc/paleo_0153-9345_2000_num_26_1_4697.

14   Charles V (1500–1558), also known as Charles I of Spain, was the Duke of Burgundy and ruler of Netherlands beginning in 1506, the ruler of the Spanish Empire beginning in 1516, and Holy Roman Emperor from 1519 until he voluntarily stepped down from all positions between 1554 and 1556. He ruled extensive territories in Central, Western, and Southern Europe, and the Spanish colonies in the Americas and Asia. His domain spanned nearly four million square kilometers and was the first to be described as "the empire on which the sun never sets." Philippe II (1527–1598) was King of Spain beginning in 1556 and of Portugal beginning in 1581. Beginning in 1554, he was King of Naples and Sicily, as well as Duke of Milan. During his marriage to Queen Mary I (1554–1558), he was also King of England and Ireland. Beginning in 1555, he was lord of the Seventeen Provinces of Netherlands. During his reign, Spain reached the height of its influence and power.

15   Fernand Braudel specifically says: "Imperialism and colonialism are as old as the world and any reinforced form of domination secretes capitalism"; *Civilization and Capitalism, 15th–18th Century, Volume 3: The Perspective of the World* (London: Collins, 1984), 295.

16 Öcalan defines the *aşiret* as a kind of federation of tribal communities, see page 182 in this book.

17 *Sharia*, an Arabic word meaning *the right path*, refers to traditional Islamic law. As well as being Koranic, sharia stems from Prophet Mohammad's teachings and interpretations of those teachings by certain Muslim legal scholars.

18 *Zillullah* means *shadow of God*; the title given to sultans.

19 Dr. Hikmet Kıvılcımlı (1902–1971) was among the first generation leaders of the communist movement of Turkey. In total he was in prison for twenty-two years, and he was only able to publish his theoretical work after the mid-1960s. Most of his work written in prison was published only after his death. Kıvılcımlı developed a Marxist interpretation of history that was not economic reductionist and one that emphasized the importance of cultural traditions. His monumental work called "Tarih, Devrim, Sosyalizm" (History, Revolution, Socialism) has examined the five-thousand-year-long historical period not only through the lenses of Marxist literature but also from the perspective of social and political theory of İbn-i Haldun (whom he called Marx of Islam). He has numerous books, and was also the first Turkish Marxist to define Kurdistan as Turkey's colony, which he did while in a prison located in a Kurdish town. His works can be found at the website of Institute of Social History, accessed February 7, 2020, https://iisg.amsterdam/en/search?search=Hikmet%20K%C4%B1v%C4%B1lc%C4%B1ml%C4%B1.

20 This is a reference to the Latin proverb "Homo homini lupus est," which translates as "a man is a wolf to another man," or more tersely, "man is wolf to man," which was also used in Thomas Hobbes, *On the Citizen* (Cambridge, UK: Cambridge University Press, 1998 [1642]), 3.

21 Rosa Luxemburg, *The Accumulation of Capital* (London: Routledge & Kegan Paul, 2003 [1913]), chapter 26, accessed February 7, 2020, https://libcom.org/files/luxemburg%20the%20accumulation%20of%20capital.pdf.

22 This is a play on words; the original Turkish word used is "*şebeke*," which can mean either *gangs*, *systems*, or *networks*.

23 These are Turkish idioms and sayings.

24 In Turkish, *millet* means an *ethnic nation*, which is how the author is using it; in Arabic it means a *community that shares similar ideals*.

25 Hozan Serdarî was born in Şarkışla, Sivas. The date of his birth is uncertain, but his poems suggest 1834. He died either in 1918 or 1921. The quote is from a poem titled "Nesini Söyleyim Canim Efendim," accessed July 25, 2019, https://siirlerlesarkilarla.wordpress.com/2012/12/07/serdari-nesini-soyleyim-canim-efendim-sadik-gurbuz.

26 This refers to a 1963 play by Sadik Sendil, the story of Hürmüz, who married seven different men who were unaware of one another. Will she survive?

27 *Hemşehriler* means *fellow townspeople* in Turkish; *bajariler* means *city dwellers* in Kurdish.

28 The Hanseatic League was a mercantile league of medieval German towns. It was amorphous in character; its origin cannot be dated exactly. Originally a Hansa was a company of merchants trading with foreign lands. After the German push eastward and the settlement of German towns in the Slavic lands

of the Baltic in the thirteenth century, the merchant guilds and town associations became leagues; see "Hanseatic League," Encyclopedia.com, accessed July 26, 2019, http://www.encyclopedia.com/doc/1E1-Hanseati.html.

29 This is the use of "term" as Fernand Braudel used it.

30 Eschatology, from the Greek word *eschaton* (the last), is the theological study of the last things, the final state of each individual, of the community, of all individuals, and of reality itself. Thus, traditionally eschatology has dealt with the themes of death, judgment, heaven, hell, purgatory, the resurrection of the dead, the end of the world, and "the new heavens and the new Earth"; William R. Stoeger, "Eschatology," Encyclopedia.com, accessed November 16, 2019, https://www.encyclopedia.com/philosophy-and-religion/bible/bible-general/eschatology.

31 In 64 CE, most of Rome was destroyed in the Great Fire of Rome, which many Romans believed Nero had purposely set to clear land for his planned palatial complex, the Domus Aurea. Nero's rule is often associated with tyranny and extravagance. He is known for many executions, including that of his mother, and the probable murder by poison of his stepbrother.

32 One important example of this practice from the Ottoman Empire was the selection and training of children for the military or the civil service, also known as the blood tax or tribute in blood.

33 There were four institutions within the Ottoman Empire state structure. The function of the *ilmiye* was to propagate the Muslim religion, while the *kalemiye* was administrative.

34 Max Weber has used the term *stahlhartes Gehäuse* (hardened steel casing), translated as "iron cage," to describe the increased rationalization inherent in social life; Max Weber, *The Protestant Ethic and the Spirit of Capitalism* (Mineola, NY: Dover Publications, 2003).

Envisaging the System of Democratic Civilization

1 The 114 chapters of the Koran are referred to as suras.

2 Henri de Saint-Simon (1760–1825) was a French political and economic theorist and businessperson whose thinking influenced politics, economics, sociology, and the philosophy of science. His economic ideology, known as industrialism, recognized an obligation to meet the needs of the working class for the smooth functioning of the economy and society.

Charles Fourier (1772–1837) was a French philosopher and "utopian socialist." Fourier is credited with having coined the word *feminism*.

Pierre-Joseph Proudhon (1809–1865) was the founder of mutualism and the first person to self-define as an anarchist.

Auguste Comte (1798–1857) was the founder of sociology and positivism, which called for a new scientific doctrine to respond to the problems that arose with the French Revolution.

Émile Durkheim (1858–1917) was a French sociologist, social psychologist, and philosopher whose work addressed the maintenance of social integrity and coherence in the face of the breakdown of social and religious ties in modernist period.

3 "The march of God in the world, that is what the state is"; see Thom Brooks, ed., *Hegel's Philosophy of Right* (Oxford: Wiley-Blackwell, 2012 [1820]), part 3, section 3.

4 *Shāhanshāh* is a Persian honorific meaning *king of kings*.

5 The Levh-i Mahfûz, Arabic for the *protected tablet*, is, in the Islamic tradition, the divine book where all that has happened and will happen is written. See also Öcalan: *Beyond State, Power, and Violence*, (Oakland: PM Press, forthcoming).

6 Here is the statement referenced: "Whatever the theoretical aspects, the accumulation of capital as an historical process, depends in every respect upon non-capitalist social strata and forms of social organisation." Rosa Luxemburg, *The Accumulation of Capital*, section three, chapter 26, Marxists .org, accessed December 4, 2019, https://www.marxists.org/archive/luxemburg/1913/accumulation-capital/ch26.htm.

7 The author uses the word *şebeke*, which can mean either *gangs* or *networks*; in this case, both meanings are intended.

8 Michel Foucault, *The Order of Things: An Archeology of Human Sciences* (London: Tavistock Publications, 1970 [1966]).

9 *Zillullah* is an Arabic word meaning *shadow of God*.

10 For example, the archeological remains at Tepe Gawra.

11 *Rabb* means *Lord, Sustainer, Cherisher, Master, Nourisher*. In Islam, Ar-Rabb is often used to address Allah, although Ar-Rabb is not one of the 99 names (or attributes) of Allah.

12 The Sabians were grouped by early writers with the ancient Jewish Christian group the Elcesaites and with gnostic groups like the Hermeticists and the Mandaeans. Today, the Mandaeans are still widely identified as Sabians.

13 Mohammad's adoption of facing north toward Jerusalem, Islam's first qiblah, or direction of prayer, later changed to facing toward the Kabah in Mecca, when performing the daily prayers.

14 *Ahl al-Bayt* means *People of the House* or *Family of the House*. Within the Islamic tradition, the term refers to the Mohammad's family. *Khawarij* means *those who went out* and refers to a sect in early Islam that revolted against the authority of Caliph Ali ibn Abu Talib after he agreed to arbitration with his rival Muawiyah to decide the succession to the caliphate following the Battle of Siffin.

15 The Mughal Empire, based in the Indian subcontinent, was established and ruled by the Muslim Persianate dynasty of Chagatai Turco-Mongol origin that extended over large parts of the Indian subcontinent and Afghanistan.

16 *Asabiyyah* is a concept of social solidarity with an emphasis on unity, group consciousness and a sense of shared purpose, and social cohesion, originally in a context of "tribalism" and "clanism." It was familiar in the pre-Islamic era, but was popularized in Ibn Khaldun's *Muqaddimah*, where it is described as the fundamental bond of human society and the basic motive force of history, pure only in its nomadic form.

17 Öcalan uses *mülkiyetçilik*, derived from the Turkish word for *ownership*, to describe it as an ideology, similar to nationalism.

18 The saying is thought to have originated with Saint Bernard of Clairvaux, who, in 1150, wrote *"L'enfer est plein de bonnes volontés ou désirs"* [Hell is full of good wishes or desires]. Many people have used some form of the phrase, including Karl Marx.

19 *Maqam* and *tekke* are buildings for the gatherings of a Sufi brotherhood.

20 Every wise old religious man or woman is said to belong to an *ocak*, which is seen as sacred.

Democratic Modernity versus Capitalist Modernity

1 *Elah* is the Aramaic word for *God*. The word *Elah* is also an Arabic word which means *God*. *Elah* is etymologically related to *Allah*.

2 See Anthony Giddens, *The Consequences of Modernity* (Cambridge, UK: Polity Press, 1990); see also Abdullah Öcalan, *Manifesto of the Democratic Civilization Volume II: Capitalism: The Age of Unmasked Gods and Naked Kings*, 2nd rev. ed. (Oakland, PM Press, forthcoming 2020).

3 Michel Foucault, *The Order of Things* (London: Routledge, 1989), 373, accessed July 31, 2019, https://is.muni.cz/el/1423/jaro2013/SOC911/um/Michel_Foucault_The_Order_of_Things.pdf.

4 In Andre Gunder Frank and Barry K. Gills, eds., *The World System: Five Hundred Years or Five Thousand?* (London: Routledge, 1993); several authors argue for an extension of world system analysis beyond the last five hundred years. The concept of central civilization is also developed in this book.

5 Croesus was the king of Lydia from 560 BCE until his defeat by the Persian King Cyrus the Great in 546 BCE.

6 *Karum*, meaning *port*, or *commercial district*, the word used for ancient Assyrian trade posts in Anatolia (present-day Turkey) from the twentieth to eighteenth centuries BCE.

7 An expression used in Turkish to refer to the "three 'F's" (Fado, Fátima, Futebol—music, religion, sports), the three pillars of the Salazar dictatorship in Portugal.

8 Theodor Adorno, *Minima Moralia: Reflections from the Damaged Life* (London: Verso, 2006 [1951]).

9 Immanuel Wallerstein, *Historical Capitalism and Capitalist Civilization* (London: Verso, 1995), 98; the complete quote correctly reads: "Even as I write this, I feel the tremor that accompanies the sense of blasphemy. I fear the wrath of the gods, for I have been molded in the same ideological forge as all my compeers and worshiped at the same shrines."

10 In sociology, *demos* from Greek δῆμος, describes a political and legal concept of people, in contrast to *ethnos* as an ethnic concept of people.

11 Lenin completed his work "The State and Revolution," which the author alludes to here, in September 1917, just before the October Revolution; see V.I. Lenin, "The State and Revolution," in *Collected Works*, vol. 25 (Moscow: Progress Publishers, 1964), 381–492, accessed December 23, 2019, https://www.marxists.org/archive/lenin/works/1917/staterev.

12 The original quote is: "Power is accumulated like money"; Fernand Braudel, *Civilisation and Capitalism 15th to 18th Century: Volume 3: The Perspective of*

the World (Berkeley: University of California Press, 1992), 50. Elsewhere he also says that capitalism is an accumulation of power; see Fernand Braudel, *The Perspective of the World: Civilisation and Capitalism 15th to 18th Century, Volume 2: The Wheels of Commerce* (Berkeley: University of California Press, 1992).

13 Ewen MacAskil, "George Bush: 'God told me to end the tyranny in Iraq'" *Guardian*, October 7, 2005, accessed August 1, 2019, http://www.theguardian.com/world/2005/oct/07/iraq.usa.

14 G.W.F. Hegel, *Elements of the Philosophy of Right* (Cambridge: Cambridge University Press, 1991), 219.

15 David Shasha, "Understanding the Sephardi-Ashkenanzi Split," Huffington Post," May 25, 2011, accessed September 9, 2019, http://www.huffingtonpost.com/david-shasha/understanding-the-sephard_b_541033.html.

16 The decisions of the Fourth Lateran Council in 1215 were even more radical. For example, it became mandatory for Jews and Muslims to dress differently from Christians and to wear badges.

17 The term *dönme* (*convert*) is generally used in Turkish to describe converted Jews, especially those who continue to practice Judaism in secret, so-called crypto-Jews. Among them were the followers of the self-declared Messiah Shabbtai Zevi in the seventeenth century, the Sabbatians, many of whom, like him, later converted to Islam.

18 Membership in Masonic lodges requires a belief in a single God, but the Lodges are neutral with regard to the individual religions. That is why Jews and Muslims were accepted relatively early. The discussion of religious matters in the lodges is forbidden.

19 This refers to Cyrus II, also known as Cyrus the Great, c. 585–530 BCE.

20 *Taqiyya*, which literally means *fear* or *caution*, describes the Islamic practice of Muslims denying their faith to the outside world in the event of danger, while in reality continuing to practice their faith.

21 His sons were called Mikâ'îl (Michael), Arslan Isrâ'îl (Israel), Mûsâ (Moses), and Yûnus (Jonah).

22 In 1391, extensive pogroms against Jews took place in Spain, with tens of thousands of them murdered.

23 In 1492, after the Reconquista ended, the Alhambra Decree was issued. As a result, tens of thousands of Sephardic Jews who did not want to be baptized were expelled from Spain.

24 *Sabbatians* (sometimes rendered *Sabbateans*) is a complex general term that refers to a variety of followers of and, disciples and believers in Sabbatai Zevi (1626–1676), a Jewish rabbi who was proclaimed to be the Jewish Messiah in 1665 by Nathan of Gaza.

25 *Müsadere* refers to the ruler's right to confiscate unfairly acquired property, which is common in many Muslim states.

26 In reference to Max Weber, who saw capitalism favored by certain forms of Protestantism, Werner Sommbart postulates this applies even more to Judaism; Werner Sombart, *Die Juden und das Wirtschaftsleben* (Leipzig: Duncker und Humblot, 1911).

27 In 1938–1939, R.G. Collingwood wrote: "Modern Germany thus stands officially committed to the same error which infected ancient Jewish thought, and which Paul exploded—the error of regarding a given community's historical function as bound up with its biological character, i.e. with the common pedigree of its members—and thus persecutes the Jews *because it agrees with them*. Intellectually, the Jew is the victor in the present-day conflict (if you can call it that) in Germany. He has succeeded in imposing his idea of a chosen people (in the biological sense of the word people) on modern Germany: and this may explain why the victims of this persecution take it so calmly." R. G. Collingwood, *The Principles of History and Other Writings in Philosophy of History*. (Oxford: Oxford University Press, 1999), 7S.7.

28 These three pillars are capitalism, industrialism, and the nation-state.

29 *Rabb* translates approximately as *the Lord* or, *the Great*. The term is a common name of God in the Islamic world, the Hebrew form is *rav*. It corresponds in meaning to the Hebrew *adonai*; perhaps this is what is meant here.

30 Immanuel Wallerstein, *The Modern World-System: Capitalist Agriculture and the Origins of the European World-Economy in the Sixteenth Century* (New York: Academic Press, 1976).

31 This is another name used for the people previously known as the Assyrians.

32 The Committee of Union and Progress (CUP: İttihat ve Terakki Cemiyeti), later the Party of Union and Progress (İttihat ve Terakki Fırkası), began as a secret society established as the "Committee of Ottoman Union" (İttihad-ı Osmanî Cemiyeti) in Istanbul, on February 6, 1889, by medical students İbrahim Temo, Çerkez Mehmed Reşid, Abdullah Cevdet, İshak Sükuti, Ali Hüsyinzade, Kerim Sebatî, Mekkeli Sabri Bey, Selanikli Nazım Bey, Şerafettin Mağmumi, Cevdet Osman, and Giritli Şefik. This was the political party of the so-called Young Turks, and the ruling party in the final years of the Ottoman Empire.

33 From 1897 onward, Geneva was CUP's headquarters, while the first Zionist congresses were held in Basel.

34 Moiz Cohen was a Turkish writer and philosopher of Jewish origin active in pan-Turkism movement. Born to a Jewish family, he later changed his name to Munis Tekinalp. He was a proponent of the assimilation of minorities within the Turkish Republic into Turkish culture, and in 1928 issued a pamphlet on the subject titled *Türkleştirme*. Hungarian Ármin Vámbéry, also known as Arminus Vámbéry, was a prominent Turkologist.

35 Öcalan's thesis of the Democratic Republic is detailed in Abdullah Öcalan: *Declaration on the Democratic Solution of the Kurdish Question* (Neuss: Mesopotamian Publishers, 1999).

36 The question is addressed in Abdullah Öcalan, *Manifesto of Democratic Civilization, Volume IV: Civilizational Crisis in the Middle East and the Democratic Civilization Solution* (Oakland: PM Press, forthcoming).

37 In Turkish Miryam and Maria are both rendered as Meryem.

38 The Marx and Engels passage referenced here, reads "When, in the course of development, class distinctions have disappeared, and all production has been concentrated in the hands of a vast association of the whole nation, the public power will lose its political character. Political power, properly so called, is

merely the organised power of one class for oppressing another. If the proletariat during its contest with the bourgeoisie is compelled, by the force of circumstances, to organise itself as a class, if, by means of a revolution, it makes itself the ruling class, and, as such, sweeps away by force the old conditions of production, then it will, along with these conditions, have swept away the conditions for the existence of class antagonisms and of classes generally, and will thereby have abolished its own supremacy as a class. In place of the old bourgeois society, with its classes and class antagonisms, we shall have an association, in which the free development of each is the condition for the free development of all"; Karl Marx and Frederick Engels, *The Communist Manifesto*, Chapter 2, accessed February 8, 2020, https://www.marxists.org/archive/marx/works/1848/communist-manifesto/cho2.htm.

39 Biologism is the use or emphasis of biological principles or methods to explain human, especially social, behavior; "Biologism," ScienceDirect, accessed September 5, 2019, https://www.sciencedirect.com/topics/social-sciences/biologism.

40 Michel Foucault, *Society Must Be Defended: Lectures at the Collège de France, 1975–76* (New York: Picador, 1997).

41 "Braudel's influence was crucial in two regards. First, in his later work on capitalism and civilization, Braudel would insist on a sharp distinction between the sphere of the free market and the sphere of monopolies. He called only the latter capitalism and, far from being the same thing as the free market, he said that capitalism was the "anti-market." This concept marked a direct assault, both substantively and terminologically, on the conflation by classical economists (including Marx) of the market and capitalism. And secondly, Braudel's insistence on the multiplicity of social times and his emphasis on structural time-what he called the *longue durée* became central to world-systems analysis." Immanuel Wallerstein, *World-Systems Analysis: An Introduction* (Durham, NC: Duke University Press, 2004), 19.

42 A Turkish idiom: "biri yer biri bakar kıyamet ondan kopar." It literally means "some sections of society live in hardship, others live in luxury, this creates a contradiction that will lead to doomsday."

43 The author uses here his own term for an autonomous unit, which subsequently became popular, especially in its Kurdish language form, *xwebûn*.

44 One of several militaristic terms commonly used in Turkey to describe the Turkish nation. It is also formulated as "every Turk is born a soldier."

The Reconstruction Problems of Democratic Modernity

1 The author specifically uses the term *"male-dominant"* rather than the equivalent for *patriarchal* in Turkish. There is no distinction in meaning; the author sometimes prefers to use terms that are more descriptive and reveal the content, I maintained the use of *"erkek egemen"* (*male-dominant*) rather than using *"ataerkil"* (*patriarchy*) [translator's note].

2 Murray Bookchin, *Urbanization without Cities: The Rise of Urbanization and the Decline of Citizenship* (Montréal: Black Rose Books, 1992).

3 Karl Marx and Frederick Engels "Manifesto of the Communist Party," in *Selected Works*, vol. 1 (Moscow: Progress Publishers, 1969), 98–137, accessed August 9, 2019, https://www.marxists.org/archive/marx/works/1848/communist-manifesto.

4 A small, cubical building in the courtyard of the Great Mosque at Mecca containing a sacred black stone: regarded by Muslims as the House of God and the objective of their pilgrimages.

5 Vladimir Lenin, "The Proletarian Revolution and the Renegade Kautsky," in *Lenin's Collected Works*, vol. 28 (Moscow: Progress Publishers, 1974), 227–325, accessed August 9, 2019, https://www.marxists.org/archive/lenin/works/1918/prrk/index.htm.

6 The word *jin* means *woman* in Kurdish, and *-lojî* is *-logy*.

7 This formulation, often attributed to Marx, comes from the French utopian socialist Charles Fourier, whom Marx quoteds. Murray Bookchin refers to this in his major work *The Ecology of Freedom* (Andover, MA: Cheshire Books, 1982), accessed February 9, 2020, https://theanarchistlibrary.org/library/murray-bookchin-the-ecology-of-freedom#toc11. The title of this volume references Bookchin's work.

8 Herodotus begins his history with an explanation of the causes of the wars between the Greeks and the "barbarians." It deals with several women being "carried off," by Phoenicians and Greeks, including Io, Europa, Medeia, and Helena, as the prehistory of the wars between the Greeks and the Persians. Reference is also made to the view if the women had not wanted to be "carried off," they would not have been.

9 *Ummah* is commonly used to mean the *collective community of Islamic peoples*.

The Tasks in Rebuilding Democratic Modernity

1 This is likely a reference to the following statement: "After Auschwitz there is no word tinged from on high, not even a theological one, that has any right unless it underwent a transformation." Theodor Adorno, *Negative Dialectics*, (London: Routledge, 1973), 367.

2 For a detailed discussion of the will to truth, see Friedrich Nietzsche, *Genealogy of Morality* (New York: Cambridge University Press, 1994 [1887]); "However, the *compulsion* towards it, that unconditional will to truth, is *faith in the ascetic ideal itself*, even if, as an unconscious imperative, make no mistake about it, – it is the faith in a *metaphysical* value, a *value as such of truth* as vouched for and confirmed by that ideal alone (it stands and falls by that ideal). Strictly speaking, there is no 'presuppositionless' knowledge, the thought of such a thing is unthinkable, paralogical: a philosophy, a 'faith' always has to be there first, for knowledge to win from it a direction, a meaning, a limit, a method, a *right* to exist. (Whoever understands it the other way round and, for example, tries to place philosophy 'on a strictly scientific foundation,' must first *stand on its head* not just philosophy, but also truth itself.)"

3 *Tekke*, *khanqah*, and *maqam* are the Turkish, Farsi, and Arabic names of buildings used for the gatherings of a Sufi brotherhood, or *tariqa*. *Dargah* are the shrines of Sufi saints.

4 *Zoroaster* is the Grecized version of the name *Zarathustra*.
5 Friedrich Nietzsche, *Thus Spoke Zarathustra* (Mineola, NY: Dover Publications, 1999 [1883]).
6 In fact, *zendik* is related to words like *gnosis*, *know*, and *narrate* via the proto-Indo-European root **gno*, meaning *to know*.
7 *Cemevi* is *house of gathering* in Turkish.
8 This probably refers to Zeynep Kınacı (Zîlan) whose political accurate analysis and courageous action made her a role model for the Kurdish women's movement.

Conclusion

1 Sisyphus was king of Ephyra, and punished for his self-aggrandizing craftiness and deceitfulness by being forced to roll an immense boulder up a hill, only to watch it roll back down, repeating this action for eternity.
2 Karl Marx, *Capital*, vols. 1–3 (Moscow: Progress Publishers, 1965–1967), accessed February 10, 2020, vol. 1, https://www.marxists.org/archive/marx/works/download/pdf/Capital-Volume-I.pdf; vol. 2, https://libcom.org/files/Capital-Volume-II.pdf; vol. 3, https://www.marxists.org/archive/marx/works/download/pdf/Capital-Volume-III.pdf.
3 Samuel P. Huntington is the father of the "clash of civilizations" theory, an important talking point in the neoconservative movement that arose in the US after the collapse of the Soviet Union; *The Clash of Civilizations and the Remaking of World Order* (New York: Simon & Schuster, 1996).
4 Pierre-Joseph Proudhon, *The Philosophy of Poverty* (1847), accessed December 24, 2019, https://www.marxists.org/reference/subject/economics/proudhon/philosophy/; Karl Marx, *The Poverty of Philosophy: Answer to the* Philosophy of Poverty *by M. Proudhon* (1847), accessed December 24, 2019, https://www.marxists.org/archive/marx/works/1847/poverty-philosophy.
5 Abdullah Öcalan wrote all five volumes of the *Manifesto of Democratic Civilization* and the *Roadmap for Negotiations* in 2008–2010, when secret talks involving the Turkish state and the PKK and him were already taking place. In this respect, this incipient "peace process" is referred to here when a 'process' is mentioned, even if it is not openly addressed. At the end of 2012, these talks became public knowledge, which triggered the hope for peace and a democratization of Turkey and also formed the background for the Gezi protests. In the spring of 2015, President Erdoğan unilaterally ended the dialogue and opted for an escalation of violence.
6 "Force is the midwife of every old society pregnant with a new one"; Karl Marx: *Capital*, Chapter Thirty-One, accessed December 24, 2019, https://www.marxists.org/archive/marx/works/1867-c1/ch31.htm.
7 See, e.g., John T. Lysaker, *Philosophy, Writing and the Character of Thought* (Chicago: University of Chicago Press, 2018), 71.

Index

"Passim" (literally "scattered") indicates intermittent discussion of a topic over a cluster of pages.

About the Authors

Abdullah Öcalan is the founder of the Partiya Karkerên Kurdistanê (PKK; Kurdistan Workers' Party). Since his abduction in 1999, he has been imprisoned on the island of İmralı under aggravated isolation conditions. In prison, he wrote more than ten books that revolutionized Kurdish politics. He writes extensively about history, philosophy and politics and is considered a key figure for the political solution of the Kurdish question. Öcalan makes contributions to the discussion about the search for freedom and developed democratic confederalism as a non-state political system. His main work is the five-volume manifesto of the democratic civilization. His writings have been translated into more than twenty languages.

John Holloway is a professor of sociology at the Instituto de Ciencias Sociales y Humanidades in the Benemerita Universidad Autonoma de Puebla, Mexico, and honorary visiting professor at the University of Rhodes, South Africa. He has published widely on Marxist theory, the Zapatista movement, and new forms of anti-capitalist struggle. His books *Change the World without Taking Power* (London: Pluto Press, 2010 [2002]) and *Crack Capitalism* (London: Pluto Press, 2010) have stirred international debate and have been translated into eleven languages.

Publications by Abdullah
Öcalan in English

Books

Declaration on the Democratic Solution of the Kurdish Question (Neuss: Mesopotamia Publishers, 1999).

Prison Writings I: The Roots of Civilization (London: Pluto Press, 2007).

Prison Writings II: The PKK and the Kurdish Question in the 21st Century (London: Pluto Press, 2011).

Prison Writings III: The Road Map to Negotiations (Neuss: Mesopotamia Publishers, 2012).

Beyond State, Power, and Violence (Oakland: PM Press, 2020).

Building Free Life: Dialogues with Öcalan (Oakland: PM Press, 2020).

Manifesto of the Democratic Civilization newly edited and published by PM Press

Volume I: Civilization: The Age of Masked Gods and Disguised Kings (2nd revised edition, 2021).

Volume II: Capitalism: The Age of Unmasked Gods and Naked Kings (2nd revised edition, 2020).

Volume III: The Sociology of Freedom (2020).

Volume IV: The Civilizational Crisis in the Middle East and the Democratic Civilization Solution (2022).

Volume V: The Manifesto of the Kurdistan Revolution (2022).

Pamphlets Compiled from the Prison Writings

War and Peace in Kurdistan (Cologne: International Initiative Edition, revised edition, 2017).

Democratic Confederalism (Cologne: International Initiative Edition, revised edition, 2017).

Liberating Life: Woman's Revolution (Cologne: International Initiative Edition, 2013).

Democratic Nation (Cologne: International Initiative Edition, 2016).

ABOUT PM PRESS

PM Press is an independent, radical publisher of books and media to educate, entertain, and inspire. Founded in 2007 by a small group of people with decades of publishing, media, and organizing experience, PM Press amplifies the voices of radical authors, artists, and activists. Our aim is to deliver bold political ideas and vital stories to all walks of life and arm the dreamers to demand the impossible. We have sold millions of copies of our books, most often one at a time, face to face. We're old enough to know what we're doing and young enough to know what's at stake. Join us to create a better world.

PM Press
PO Box 23912
Oakland, CA 94623
www.pmpress.org

PM Press in Europe
europe@pmpress.org
www.pmpress.org.uk

FRIENDS OF PM PRESS

These are indisputably momentous times—the financial system is melting down globally and the Empire is stumbling. Now more than ever there is a vital need for radical ideas.

In the years since its founding—and on a mere shoestring— PM Press has risen to the formidable challenge of publishing and distributing knowledge and entertainment for the struggles ahead. With over 450 releases to date, we have published an impressive and stimulating array of literature, art, music, politics, and culture. Using every available medium, we've succeeded in connecting those hungry for ideas and information to those putting them into practice.

Friends of PM allows you to directly help impact, amplify, and revitalize the discourse and actions of radical writers, filmmakers, and artists. It provides us with a stable foundation from which we can build upon our early successes and provides a much-needed subsidy for the materials that can't necessarily pay their own way. You can help make that happen—and receive every new title automatically delivered to your door once a month—by joining as a Friend of PM Press. And, we'll throw in a free T-shirt when you sign up.

Here are your options:

- **$30 a month** Get all books and pamphlets plus 50% discount on all webstore purchases

- **$40 a month** Get all PM Press releases (including CDs and DVDs) plus 50% discount on all webstore purchases

- **$100 a month** Superstar—Everything plus PM merchandise, free downloads, and 50% discount on all webstore purchases

For those who can't afford $30 or more a month, we have **Sustainer Rates** at $15, $10 and $5. Sustainers get a free PM Press T-shirt and a 50% discount on all purchases from our website.

Your Visa or Mastercard will be billed once a month, until you tell us to stop. Or until our efforts succeed in bringing the revolution around. Or the financial meltdown of Capital makes plastic redundant. Whichever comes first.

DEPARTMENT OF ANTHROPOLOGY & SOCIAL CHANGE

Anthropology and Social Change, housed within the California Institute of Integral Studies, is a small innovative graduate department with a particular focus on activist scholarship, militant research, and social change. We offer both masters and doctoral degree programs.

Our unique approach to collaborative research methodology dissolves traditional barriers between research and political activism, between insiders and outsiders, and between researchers and protagonists. Activist research is a tool for "creating the conditions we describe." We engage in the process of co-research to explore existing alternatives and possibilities for social change.

Anthropology and Social Change
anth@ciis.edu
1453 Mission Street
94103
San Francisco, California
www.ciis.edu/academics/graduate-programs/anthropology-and-social-change

Beyond State, Power, and Violence

Abdullah Öcalan
with a Foreword by Andrej Grubačić
Edited by International Initiative

ISBN: 978-1-62963-715-0
$29.95   800 pages

After the dissolution of the PKK (Kurdistan Workers' Party) in 2002, internal discussions ran high, and fear and uncertainty about the future of the Kurdish freedom movement threatened to unravel the gains of decades of organizing and armed struggle. From his prison cell, Abdullah Öcalan intervened by penning his most influential work to date: *Beyond State, Power, and Violence*. With a stunning vision of a freedom movement centered on women's liberation, democracy, and ecology, Öcalan helped reinvigorate the Kurdish freedom movement by providing a revolutionary path forward with what is undoubtedly the furthest-reaching definition of democracy the world has ever seen. Here, for the first time, is the highly anticipated English translation of this monumental work.

Beyond State, Power, and Violence is a breathtaking reconnaissance into life without the state, an essential portrait of the PKK and the Kurdish freedom movement, and an open blueprint for leftist organizing in the twenty-first century, written by one of the most vitally important political luminaries of today.

By carefully analyzing the past and present of the Middle East, Öcalan evaluates concrete prospects for the Kurdish people and arrives with his central proposal: recreate the Kurdish freedom movement along the lines of a new paradigm based on the principles of democratic confederalism and democratic autonomy. In the vast scope of this book, Öcalan examines the emergence of hierarchies and eventually classes in human societies and sketches his alternative, the democratic-ecological society. This vision, with a theoretical foundation of a nonviolent means of taking power, has ushered in a new era for the Kurdish freedom movement while also offering a fresh and indispensible perspective on the global debate about a new socialism. Öcalan's calls for nonhierarchical forms of democratic social organization deserve the careful attention of anyone interested in constructive social thought or rebuilding society along feminist and ecological lines.

"Öcalan's works make many intellectuals uncomfortable because they represent a form of thought which is not only inextricable from action, but which directly grapples with the knowledge that it is."
—David Graeber author of *Debt: The First 500 Years*

Capitalism: The Age of Unmasked Gods and Naked Kings (Manifesto of the Democratic Civilization, Volume II), Second Edition

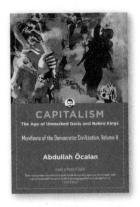

Abdullah Öcalan
with a Preface by Radha D'Souza

ISBN: 978-1-62963-787-7
$26.95   384 pages

Capitalism: The Age of Unmasked Gods and Naked Kings is the second volume of Abdullah Öcalan's definitive five-volume work *The Manifesto of the Democratic Civilization*. For years he has unraveled the sources of hierarchical relations, power, and the formation of nation-states that has led to capitalism's emergence and global domination. He makes the convincing argument that capitalism is not a product of the last four hundred years but a continuation of classical civilization.

Unlike Marx, Öcalan sides with Braudel by giving less importance to the mode of production than to the accumulation of surplus value and power, thus centering his criticisms on the capitalist nation-state as the most powerful monopoly of economic, military, and ideological power. He argues that the fundamental strength of capitalist hegemony, however, is the competition in voluntary servitude that a market economy has given rise to—not a single worker would reject higher wages—resulting in an unprecedented ability to convince people to surrender their individual power and autonomy. Öcalan further contends that the capitalist phase of city-class-state-based civilization is not the last phase of human intelligence; rather, the traditional morals upon which it is based are being exhausted and the intelligence of freedom is rising in all its richness. That is why he prefers to interpret capitalist modernity as the era of hope—but only insofar as we are able to develop a sustainable defense against it.

"Öcalan builds upon the past insights to provide what is, in my opinion, the most succinct and most elaborate definition of democracy."
—Andrej Grubačić, coauthor of *Wobblies and Zapatistas: Conversations on Anarchism, Marxism and Radical History*

"Öcalan presents himself as an outstanding expert on European intellectual history as well as the history and culture of the Near and Middle East. Against this background he reflects on the state of the international system and the conflict region of the Middle East after the collapse of real socialism as well as—very self-critically—the history of the PKK and his own political actions."
—Werner Ruf, political scientist and peace researcher

Building Free Life: Dialogues with Öcalan

Edited by International Initiative

ISBN: 978-1-62963-704-4
$20.00   256 pages

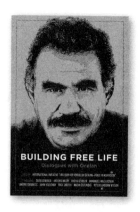

From Socrates to Antonio Gramsci, imprisoned philosophers have marked the history of thought and changed how we view power and politics. From his solitary jail cell, Abdullah Öcalan has penned daringly innovative works that give profuse evidence of his position as one of the most significant thinkers of our day. His prison writings have mobilized tens of thousands of people and inspired a revolution in the making in Rojava, northern Syria, while also penetrating the insular walls of academia and triggering debate and reflection among countless scholars.

So how do you engage in a meaningful dialogue with Abdullah Öcalan when he has been held in total isolation since April 2015? You compile a book of essays written by a globally diverse cast of the most imaginative luminaries of our time, send it to Öcalan's jailers, and hope that they deliver it to him.

Featured in this extraordinary volume are over a dozen writers, activists, dreamers, and scholars whose ideas have been investigated in Öcalan's own writings. Now these same people have the unique opportunity to enter into a dialogue with his ideas. *Building Free Life* is a rich and wholly original exploration of the most critical issues facing humanity today. In the broad sweep of this one-of-a-kind dialogue, the contributors explore topics ranging from democratic confederalism to women's revolution, from the philosophy of history to the crisis of the capitalist system, from religion to Marxism and anarchism, all in an effort to better understand the liberatory social forms that are boldly confronting capitalism and the state.

There can be no boundaries or restrictions for the development of thought. Thus, in the midst of different realities—from closed prisons to open-air prisons— the human mind will find a way to seek the truth. *Building Free Life* stands as a monument of radical thought, a testament of resilience, and a searchlight illuminating the impulse for freedom.

Contributors include: Shannon Brincat, Radha D'Souza, Mechthild Exo, Damian Gerber, Barry K. Gills, Muriel González Athenas, David Graeber, Andrej Grubačić, John Holloway, Patrick Huff, Donald H. Matthews, Thomas Jeffrey Miley, Antonio Negri, Norman Paech, Ekkehard Sauermann, Fabian Scheidler, Nazan Üstündağ, Immanuel Wallerstein, Peter Lamborn Wilson, and Raúl Zibechi.

"*Öcalan's works make many intellectuals uncomfortable because they represent a form of thought that is not only inextricable from action, but also directly grapples with the knowledge that it is.*"
—David Graeber, author of *Debt: The First 5,000 Years*

The Battle for the Mountain of the Kurds: Self-Determination and Ethnic Cleansing in the Afrin Region of Rojava

Author: Thomas Schmidinger with a Preface by Andrej Grubačić

ISBN: 978-1-62963-651-1
$19.95   192 pages

In early 2018, Turkey invaded the autonomous Kurdish region of Afrin in Syria and is currently threatening to ethnically cleanse the region. Between 2012 and 2018, the "Mountain of the Kurds" (Kurd Dagh) as the area has been called for centuries, had been one of the quietest regions in a country otherwise torn by civil war.

After the outbreak of the Syrian civil war in 2011, the Syrian army withdrew from the region in 2012, enabling the Party of Democratic Union (PYD), the Syrian sister party of Abdullah Öcalan's outlawed Turkish Kurdistan Workers' Party (PKK) to first introduce a Kurdish self-administration and then, in 2014, to establish the Canton Afrin as one of the three parts of the heavily Kurdish Democratic Federation of Northern Syria, which is better known under the name Rojava.

This self-administration—which had seen multiparty municipal and regionwide elections in the summer and autumn of 2017, which included a far-reaching autonomy for a number of ethnic and religious groups, and which had provided a safe haven for up to 300,000 refugees from other parts of Syria—is now at risk of being annihilated by the Turkish invasion and occupation.

Thomas Schmidinger is one of the very few Europeans to have visited the Canton of Afrin. In this book, he gives an account of the history and the present situation of the region. In a number of interviews, he also gives inhabitants of the region from a variety of ethnicities, religions, political orientations, and walks of life the opportunity to speak for themselves. As things stand now, the book might seem to be in danger of becoming an epitaph for the "Mountain of the Kurds," but as the author writes, "the battle for the Mountain of the Kurds is far from over yet."

"Preferable to most journalistic accounts that reduce the Rojava revolution to a single narrative. It will remain an informative resource even when the realities have further changed."
—Martin van Bruinessen, Kurdish Studies on *Rojava: Revolution, War and the Future of Syria's Kurds*

The Art of Freedom: A Brief History of the Kurdish Liberation Struggle

Havin Guneser with an Introduction by Andrej Grubačić and Interview by Sasha Lilley

ISBN: 978-1-62963-781-5
$15.95   192 pages

The Revolution in Rojava captured the imagination of the Left sparking a worldwide interest in the Kurdish Freedom Movement. *The Art of Freedom* demonstrates that this explosive movement is firmly rooted in several decades of organized struggle.

In 2018, one of the most important spokespersons for the struggle of Kurdish Freedom, Havin Guneser, held three groundbreaking seminars on the historical background and guiding ideology of the movement. Much to the chagrin of career academics, the theoretical foundation of the Kurdish Freedom Movement is far too fluid and dynamic to be neatly stuffed into an ivory-tower filing cabinet. A vital introduction to the Kurdish struggle, *The Art of Freedom* is the first English-language book to deliver a distillation of the ideas and sensibilities that gave rise to the most important political event of the twenty-first century.

The book is broken into three sections: "Critique and Self-Critique: The rise of the Kurdish freedom movement from the rubbles of two world wars" provides an accessible explanation of the origins and theoretical foundation of the movement. "The Rebellion of the Oldest Colony: Jineology—the Science of Women" describes the undercurrents and nuance of the Kurdish women's movement and how they have managed to create the most vibrant and successful feminist movement in the Middle East. "Democratic Confederalism and Democratic Nation: Defense of Society Against Societycide" deals with the attacks on the fabric of society and new concepts beyond national liberation to counter it. Centering on notions of "a shared homeland" and "a nation made up of nations," these rousing ideas find deep international resonation.

Havin Guneser has provided an expansive definition of freedom and democracy and a road map to help usher in a new era of struggle against capitalism, imperialism, and the State.

"Havin Guneser is not just the world's leading authority on the thought of Abdullah Öcalan; she is a profound, sensitive, and challenging revolutionary thinker with a message the world desperately needs to hear."
—David Graeber author of *Debt: The First 500 Years* and *Bullshit Jobs: A Theory*

We Are the Crisis of Capital: A John Holloway Reader

John Holloway

ISBN: 978-1-62963-225-4
$22.95   320 pages

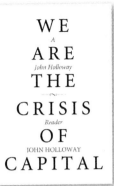

We Are the Crisis of Capital collects articles and excerpts written by radical academic, theorist, and activist John Holloway over a period of forty years.

Different times, different places, and the same anguish persists throughout our societies. This collection asks, "Is there a way out?" How do we break capital, a form of social organisation that dehumanises us and threatens to annihilate us completely? How do we create a world based on the mutual recognition of human dignity?

Holloway's work answers loudly, "By screaming NO!" By thinking from our own anger and from our own creativity. By trying to recover the "We" who are buried under the categories of capitalist thought. By opening the categories and discovering the antagonism they conceal, by discovering that behind the concepts of money, state, capital, crisis, and so on, there moves our resistance and rebellion.

An approach sometimes referred to as Open Marxism, it is an attempt to rethink Marxism as daily struggle. The articles move forward, influenced by the German state derivation debates of the seventies, by the CSE debates in Britain, and the group around the Edinburgh journal *Common Sense*, and then moving on to Mexico and the wonderful stimulus of the Zapatista uprising, and now the continuing whirl of discussion with colleagues and students in the Posgrado de Sociología of the Benemérita Universidad Autónoma de Puebla.

"Holloway's work is infectiously optimistic."
—Steven Poole, the *Guardian* (UK)

"Holloway's thesis is indeed important and worthy of notice."
—Richard J.F. Day, *Canadian Journal of Cultural Studies*

In, Against, and Beyond Capitalism: The San Francisco Lectures

John Holloway
with a Preface by Andrej Grubačić

ISBN: 978-1-62963-109-7
$14.95   112 pages

In, Against, and Beyond Capitalism is based on three recent lectures delivered by John Holloway at the California Institute of Integral Studies in San Francisco. The lectures focus on what anticapitalist revolution can mean today—after the historic failure of the idea that the conquest of state power was the key to radical change—and offer a brilliant and engaging introduction to the central themes of Holloway's work.

The lectures take as their central challenge the idea that "We Are the Crisis of Capital and Proud of It." This runs counter to many leftist assumptions that the capitalists are to blame for the crisis, or that crisis is simply the expression of the bankruptcy of the system. The only way to see crisis as the possible threshold to a better world is to understand the failure of capitalism as the face of the push of our creative force. This poses a theoretical challenge. The first lecture focuses on the meaning of "We," the second on the understanding of capital as a system of social cohesion that systematically frustrates our creative force, and the third on the proposal that we are the crisis of this system of cohesion.

"*His Marxism is premised on another form of logic, one that affirms movement, instability, and struggle. This is a movement of thought that affirms the richness of life, particularity (non-identity) and 'walking in the opposite direction'; walking, that is, away from exploitation, domination, and classification. Without contradictory thinking in, against, and beyond the capitalist society, capital once again becomes a reified object, a thing, and not a social relation that signifies transformation of a useful and creative activity (doing) into (abstract) labor. Only open dialectics, a right kind of thinking for the wrong kind of world, non-unitary thinking without guarantees, is able to assist us in our contradictory struggle for a world free of contradiction.*"
—Andrej Grubačić, from his Preface

"*Holloway's work is infectiously optimistic.*"
—Steven Poole, the *Guardian* (UK)

"*Holloway's thesis is indeed important and worthy of notice*"
—Richard J.F. Day, *Canadian Journal of Cultural Studies*

Beyond Crisis: After the Collapse of Institutional Hope in Greece, What?

Edited by John Holloway, Katerina Nasioka, and Panagiotis Doulos

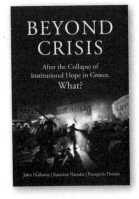

ISBN: 978-1-62963-515-6
$21.95   256 pages

The government led by Syriza in Greece, elected in January of 2015, seemed, at least in its initial months, to be the most radical European government in recent history. It proclaimed itself as the "government of hope" and became a symbol of hope throughout the world. It represented for many the proof that radical change could be achieved through institutional politics. Then came the referendum of July 2015, the vote to reject the austerity imposed by the banks and the European Union, followed by the complete reversal of the government's position and its acceptance of that austerity.

The dramatic collapse of the Syriza government's radical discourse showed the limits of institutional politics, a lesson that is apparently completely overlooked by the enthusiastic followers of Jeremy Corbyn and Bernie Sanders. But it also poses profound questions for those who reject state-centered politics. The anarchist or autonomist movement in Greece has been one of the strongest in the world yet it has failed to have a significant impact in opening up alternative perspectives in this situation.

Is there then no way out? Is there nothing beyond the world of capitalist destruction or can we still see some possibility for radical hope? The essays in this collection reflect on the experience of the crisis in Greece and its political implications for the whole world. They do not point a way forward but seek to open windows in the darkening sky of apparent impossibility.

"Beyond Crisis *does not look on the bright side. It looks straight into the eye of the storm and unfolds the hopelessness of conventional left politics in Greece and how it became part of the unfolding cycle of state violence and austerity. And it unfolds the community of hope, its courage of resistance and negativity, that has come to fore in Greece, and elsewhere too, as the direct democracy of a society of the free and equal."*
—Werner Bonefeld, professor of politics, University of York, England

"*With Jeremy Corbyn calling for a 'new way of doing politics' and offering hope to millions, the publication of this book about Greece's erstwhile 'Government of Hope' is timely. The questions it asks are essential. How does rage, hope and optimism turn into to despair and depression? Why can't the institutional Left break through the 'Wall of Reality'? And, if not Syriza, Podemos or Corbyn's Labour, then what?*"
—David Harvie, The Free Association

Re-enchanting the World: Feminism and the Politics of the Commons

Silvia Federici
with a Foreword by Peter Linebaugh

ISBN: 978-1-62963-569-9
$19.95   240 pages

Silvia Federici is one of the most important
contemporary theorists of capitalism and feminist
movements. In this collection of her work spanning over twenty years, she provides
a detailed history and critique of the politics of the commons from a feminist
perspective. In her clear and combative voice, Federici provides readers with an
analysis of some of the key issues and debates in contemporary thinking on this
subject.

Drawing on rich historical research, she maps the connections between the
previous forms of enclosure that occurred with the birth of capitalism and the
destruction of the commons and the "new enclosures" at the heart of the present
phase of global capitalist accumulation. Considering the commons from a feminist
perspective, this collection centers on women and reproductive work as crucial
to both our economic survival and the construction of a world free from the
hierarchies and divisions capital has planted in the body of the world proletariat.
Federici is clear that the commons should not be understood as happy islands
in a sea of exploitative relations but rather autonomous spaces from which to
challenge the existing capitalist organization of life and labor.

"Silvia Federici's theoretical capacity to articulate the plurality that fuels the
contemporary movement of women in struggle provides a true toolbox for building
bridges between different features and different people."
—Massimo De Angelis, professor of political economy, University of East London

"Silvia Federici's work embodies an energy that urges us to rejuvenate struggles against
all types of exploitation and, precisely for that reason, her work produces a common: a
common sense of the dissidence that creates a community in struggle."
—Maria Mies, coauthor of Ecofeminism